LAW AND POLICY IN CHINA'S FOREIGN RELATIONS

LAW AND POLICY IN CHINA'S FOREIGN RELATIONS

A STUDY OF ATTITUDES AND PRACTICE

James Chieh Hsiung

1972
COLUMBIA UNIVERSITY PRESS
NEW YORK AND LONDON

JX
1570
.H68

James Chieh Hsiung is Associate Professor of Politics
at New York University, New York City.

Copyright © 1972 Columbia University Press
ISBN: 0-231-03552-7
Library of Congress Catalog Card Number: 75-180045
Printed in the United States of America

DEDICATED TO THOSE IN EAST AND WEST
WHO BELIEVE THAT THE TWAIN SHALL MEET, AND WHO
ASPIRE TO WORLD PEACE THROUGH LAW AND JUSTICE

42514

Preface

THIS BOOK is an outgrowth of a study which began with my Ph.D. dissertation at Columbia University,[1] and it is more than a revision of the original manuscript. In the first place, the scope of inquiry has been expanded beyond international law to the broader question of interaction between law and policy, as will be explained in the Introduction. Secondly, the original work has been completely rewritten, not a single page remaining intact. The present volume also incorporates results from my more extensive research in wider areas of interest, in part made possible by the stimulating atmosphere afforded by the Politics Department, New York University. Moreover, the volume has been enriched by my participation in the work of the Panel on Communist China and International Order, American Society of International Law, chaired by Professor Jerome Alan Cohen of Harvard Law School. The panel's monographic studies and exchange of views have been an extremely rewarding experience.

Much of the volume was completed before the Ping Pong Diplomacy and the "thaw" that has since been unfolding. I am glad to see that what I wrote still stands good in the light of the latest developments. The subject will only gain in importance as the "thaw" gathers momentum. When Washington and Peking finally come to deal with each other in businesslike fashion, many businesses—old and new—will have to be taken care of within some sort of a legal framework, as well as follow some formal procedures yet to be instituted. The exchange of diplomatic envoys and consular officers, settlement of old claims by Americans whose properties were expropriated in mainland China, conduct of trade, exchange of visitors, and so on will have to be guided by both established norms under general international law and those to be established between the parties *inter se*. In any event, it will become increasingly necessary for Americans to understand the Chinese Communist attitudes and practice in these and other areas, in order to react adequately and efficaciously. The gaps of our knowledge in this respect, however, are just beginning to be felt. In a communication to this author, Andrew T. McGuire, general counsel of the Foreign Claims Settlement Commission of the United States, best summed up the deplorable state of our current understanding of how to deal with Peking, among other things, on the question of international claims:

> The source material used by the Commission concerning Communist China's attitude toward international law insofar as international claims are concerned, was obtained, in the most part, from the Library of Congress. This material, however, has never been catalogued or consolidated by the Commission. Some of this material does appear in the Commission's decisions.
>
> Unlike other Communist nations, however, the Commission found, generally, a lack of published laws and decrees by Communist China pertaining to the nationalization or other taking of property by that Government. Whether this was the result of the lack of material in the Library of Congress or the failure of Communist China to publish such laws and decrees the Commission cannot estimate despite extensive research regarding the matter.[2]

This book is a modest attempt to bridge the kind of gaps alluded to in Mr. McGuire's letter. I have made use of most of the materials known to exist in the West which may shed some light on the subject. Drawing upon wider background information, I have offered my evaluation and analyses on a wide range of vital issues concerning law and policy in Peking's foreign relations, including those which will have a significant bearing on future normal relations with the United States. I hope that the work will be of some use to professionals and laymen alike and that it will at least have laid the first building blocks for more inquiries to come when more information becomes available.

For my sustained interest in this subject I remain indebted to Professors A. Doak Barnett (now at Brookings Institution) and Oliver J. Lissitzyn, of Columbia University, whose collective wisdom, encouragement, and counsel not only sustained me through the rigors of dissertation writing (and the subsequent expansion and revision), but, more important, introduced me to rigorous standards of scholarship.

The present volume would not have been possible if not for a generous grant from the East Asian Institute of Columbia University, which eased much of my teaching responsibility at New York University during 1968–1969, when the bulk of the revision was undertaken. I am deeply indebted to the late Dr. John M. H. Lindbeck—the Institute's eminent director until his untimely death on January 9, 1971—who, next to Professor Barnett, was most responsible for persuading and enabling me to revise the original work for publication. A research grant from the Arts and Science Fund, New York University, has helped in defraying the typing and other research expenses, which, along with the Institute's grant, I gratefully acknowledge.

Professors Jerome A. Cohen and Hungdah Ch'iu, of Harvard Law School, have read the entire manuscript; John N. Hazard, Oliver J. Lisstzyn, and Victor H. Li, of Columbia University Law School, Shao-ch'üan Leng, of the University of Virginia, and Thomas M. Franck and I. William Zartman, of New York University, have read portions thereof; and all have offered valuable suggestions. Needless to say, I alone bear the responsibility for the final product.

Mrs. Barbara Mutstsos typed the entire manuscript with admirable skills. My editor, Miss Paula Schonwald, of Columbia University Press, executed her job with superb efficiency and lent greater readability and clarity to the manuscript. To both I owe my sincerest thanks. Last but not least, my indebtedness to my family, whose understanding, support, and loving concern has taken the sweat out of the labor of research and writing.

J.C.H.

New York
August, 1971

Contents

LAW AND POLICY IN CHINA'S FOREIGN RELATIONS

Introduction

AGAINST THE background of the debate concerning whether the universality of international law can be maintained in the face of the current ideological and cultural disunity of mankind, the name of Communist China is often cited with a question mark. *To what extent can Communist China, armed with a militant ideology, be expected to accept the existing rules of the game in international relations?* The answer is of no small interest to those concerned with the maintenance of world peace and order. As one scholar has pertinently put it, in the years since 1949, the People's Republic of China (hereinafter referred to as the CPR) has "emerged as one of the most dynamic, disrupting, and disturbing influences on the world scene." [1]

One can attempt to approach a question of this nature from at least three different perspectives. First, one can examine the implications of a state's ideology or cultural heritage, to identify its overall world view and ascertain if it is hostile or amenable to the prevailing framework of world order. Such an approach has been adopted by, for example, H. A. Smith and K. Wilk in their studies of the cases of Nazi Germany and, more extensively, the Soviet Union.[2] Their anxiety about a "crisis" in international law has since found new expression in the writings of Julius Stone, who views the emergence of a growing multitude of non-Western states in recent years as proceeding at the price of "continuing dilution of [the] contents" of international law.[3]

In the case of the CPR, some Western scholars have found a similar threat to international peace and order, basing their fears on her pronounced ideological position.[4] The CPR's foreign policy is seen by them as a projection on the world scene of planned, class-oriented, ideology-determined domestic policies—that is, a class struggle writ large.[5] One writer has gone so far as to suggest:

> Communist China is motivated by a revolutionary ethic thoroughly incompatible with the existing structure of international law and relations. It struggles to attain unbridled freedom of action. . . . If it accepts restraint, it does so from political and tactical considerations alone and not from any sense of legal obligation under international law. *International law does not even receive its lip service.*[6] (Emphasis added)

Elsewhere, the same writer has labored to show that the CPR's foreign policy is but an extension of her domestic policy, and that the "bonds" are provided by Marxism-Leninism:

> [For the CPR] Marxism-Leninism provides the closest bonds between domestic and foreign policy because its teachings . . . are seen as universal in their application, finding the cause of international war as for domestic revolution (class struggle). . . . So complete is the linkage between the two that the People's Republic of China does not have a foreign policy distinguishable from domestic policy. . . .[7]

Alternatively, viewing the problem from another perspective, one can examine a state's actual conduct of foreign relations, its ideological stance notwithstanding. From the results of such empirical study one can infer an evaluation of its concept of world public order. On the basis of empirical studies of this nature, some more pragmatic jurists have found that the Soviet Union and a number of the major "new" states with non-Western backgrounds are, like the Western states themselves, confronted with the same recurrent dilemma between compliance with international standards and promotion of national political interests.[8] Quite contrary to common assumptions, they have found that (a) it is national interests which "inspire both the formulation of ideologies and the pursuit of power," [9] and (b) rather than cultural tradition, it is the "present [national] interest, rightly or wrongly understood . . . [which is] the immediately decisive factor" in shaping a state's international behavior.[10]

A similar view has been advanced with respect to the CPR by R. Randle Edwards. Although not as fully documented with empirical evidence, he has proposed a thesis that the attitude of the CPR toward international law is not one of total rejection, but is "selective and pragmatic, not unlike that of Western nations." He predicts that "so long as the world power balance is unfavorable to Red China, her position in regard to international law will remain relatively constant." [11]

Still another approach is to direct attention to a broad spectrum of factors that include: (a) the influence of traditional Chinese cultural perspectives upon the present Communist elites; (b) the ideological impact of Marxism–Leninism–Maoism; (c) propaganda-oriented rhetoric in defense of international law; and (d) the actual pragmatic use of international law for the resolution of outstanding issues and for the fulfillment of basic foreign policy needs.

In the present study we shall attempt to keep all these factors in view, although we realize that it is all but impossible to explore each of them to the fullest extent that one might wish. Our emphasis will be on the latter two levels of analysis, but we shall keep in view the interrelations between these and the first two criteria. An analysis focused on the cultural and ideological roots alone tends to overstress the militancy in Peking's world outlook, while an empirically oriented study can help give a more balanced view by gauging doctrinal (verbal) militancy against practical sobriety. On the other hand, an empirical evaluation without regard to the cultural-ideological background is likely to view things out of context. The title of the present volume suggests a consciousness of the insufficiency of any singularistic approach. We have used the terms "law and policy" broadly, and the underlying theme is twofold: (a) that *law* is inseparable from policy, in the present as in other cases as a whole; and (b) that *policy* has within its purview broad considerations that encompass national interests, historical experience, expediency, reciprocity, and even prestige and "vanity," as well as cultural-ideological factors.

With this contextual framework in mind, we propose to inquire into certain essential, identifiable patterns and instrumentalities by which the CPR executes her foreign relations, asserts claims, and finds solutions to pragmatic problems. We fully realize the difficulty of maintaining a balanced view, given the current division of opinions and the confused state of the science of international law. Before we proceed any further, we shall outline some general assumptions which underscore and support our research in the present study.

First of all, we believe that international law grows from a "family of nations" which share (a) a common desire for a modicum of security and public order, (b) a need for some measure of stability and predictability in relations between its members, and (c) a need for standards of official conduct that are recognized and normally followed to prevent unnecessary friction and irrational destruction of values and resources.[12] However, as members of the international "family" are often in dispute with one another, their governments do not always agree on precisely what those "standards of official conduct" are or ought to be, though in principle they are agreed on a common need for them and on their utility. It is further assumed that differences of opinion on the specific norms may reflect different perspectives from which states of differing ideologies and cultures perceive and attempt to order the world. This view, of course, presupposes that states as actors are purposive, though they may or may not be fully conscious of the purposes of their behavior.[13]

It is our belief that by studying a state's actual espousal, interpretation, and application of norms of international conduct one will be able to infer much about the implicit position of that state regarding world order as a whole, which may or may not conform to the official doctrine or ideological stance which the state professes.

The current cultural-ideological disunity of mankind has not only manifested itself in the changing structure of international society and the nature of international relations but also in the nature of international law. Years ago it was possible to maintain, as L. Oppenheim did, that international law was a set "body of rules" governing the relations between "civilized states." [14] The concept reflected both the existence of a relative consensus on shared values in a Europocentric international society from 1815 to World War I and also the slow pace at which interstate relations were conducted. The static situation of the nineteenth century has long departed. The expansion of the international society to non-Western peoples and the fluidity accompanying modern technological advances call for the reinterpretation of existing norms and the creation of new ones at a far faster pace than ever before. The phenomenon has led an increasing number of modern jurists to consider international law as a process of decision-making, far more dynamic than a set body of rules. The new view conceives of international law, like all living law, as being continuously reinterpreted and reshaped in the process of its application by authoritative decision-makers.[15] While there is an identifiable "hard core" of norms which most decision-makers agree are applicable in certain situations,[16] the process of actual application in a given situation usually requires the making of a value judgment. Old norms gain new meaning and new norms are created through a process of reciprocal claims and mutual tolerances. The uniformity of conduct which emerges from this process often creates expectations of continuation of the same kind of conduct. Decision-makers have a common interest in the fulfillment of these expectations and in the stability of conduct. Thus the "general consensus and expectations of states" are the ultimate basis of international law in a rapidly changing world.[17]

Expectations may rest not only on actual conduct but also on other forms of communication, including acquiescence, and even verbal commitments or disclaimers. The "practice" of states is important only as substantive evidence of a general consensus or expectation accepted or acceptable as law. Dissent or shift in consensus is an indicator that a given norm is not universally supported, although it is impossible to measure precisely how strong a dissent must be (i.e., how many states give dissent) before an existing norm is changed, or precisely when a rejected norm ceases to exist. A related intricate question—which cannot be answered with precision—is: How does dissent, if supported by a growing number of states, bring about a new norm or a revision without violating the existing law before the change becomes definitive? Nevertheless, what is important is that the discovery of dissent or erosion of consensus at least indicates a possible change in the offing.

Accepting this to be true, our study here ought not to be conditioned by a mentality that seeks to gauge the CPR's international behavior by any set of rules presumed to be immutable. On the contrary, we should be concerned with such basic questions as: (a) In what specific ways and for what reasons does the CPR give (or withhold) her share of consensus to certain "hard-core" norms? (b) Does the CPR manifest "expectations" in dealing with other states over concrete issues which may be taken as evidence of her reliance on international law? (c) To what extent does her actual conduct, or other forms of communication, including the verbal, create "expectations" of continuity and stability on which other states may rely as the basis of their action or nonaction? (d) What can be inferred about the CPR's world view, i.e., concept of world order, from her practice and attitude concerning the role and nature of international law?

Put more directly, the immediate attention of the present study will be focused on: first, evidence of the CPR's invocation of international law for support of her claims and positions or for the sake of "moral rectitude" (*cum* ideologically motivated assertions); and, secondly, examples of the CPR's pragmatic use, observance, and application of international law for the settlement of outstanding problems and gratification of some basic needs in foreign relations. To the extent possible, we shall trace these to the policy roots of the CPR's decision-making process in an evaluation of the interaction of law and policy.

It may be suggested that in international law it is often not the intention of a state in accepting certain norms of behavior that is most important, but the objective reality of its conceding the existence of certain limitations upon the methods it may employ for the achievement of its goals. States may observe the law for different reasons—and this is part of the value judgment alluded to above—but the law will have served its purpose and function, to a certain extent at least, so long as it is observed. This does not suggest that the study of intention is not relevant; in fact, we believe it is.

But, one must not discredit actual compliance with international law by a given state simply because it has verbally dissented. There is vast ground between the offering of dissent by one or more states and the final overthrow of a disputed norm by general consensus. Compliance with a given norm under challenge may be a transitional phenomenon pending the final change anticipated. Besides, a dissent singularly offered or unsupported may not result in substantive change of existing law at all. In that case, a state which started to comply with existing law as an *interim* measure may soon become accustomed and reconciled to it when the anticipated change does not materialize.

Contrary to general assumptions, states are not necessarily more disposed to paying lip service to international law than they are ready to apply it in practice. That may be the case in most instances. But sometimes, however strange it may seem, it is the opposite. Many new states have declared themselves not bound by norms in whose making they have taken no part. Yet, in actual conduct they have shown restraint in their conscious effort to avoid any direct breach of the norms in question. A most recent example is North Vietnam, which for a time had declared that it would treat captured American fighting men as "war criminals" but which in actual practice was found by the Western press to have committed no systematic mistreatment of the Americans actually held in its hands.[18] It is our concern in the present study to examine whether this reverse gap between deeds and words may also be true of the CPR in certain instances.

An empirical investigation can serve to enhance substantially our understanding of the subject matter, precisely because ideological stance is not the most reliable criterion by which to judge the predictability of a state's international behavior. We do not mean to slight the importance of ideology. In fact, this author has devoted an entire book to the study of the function of ideology as a process of cultural, social, and political transformation in Communist China.[19] But, we do wish to stress that, in international relations especially, ideology is not and cannot be the sole determinant of a state's patterns of action and conduct.

Although it is generally understood to be "action program . . .

derived from certain doctrinal assumptions," [20] ideology cannot operate in a vacuum. The application of ideology to current situations leaves room for a "wide range of interpretations whose determination is inevitably contingent on geography, history, national traditions, past experiences and present requirements of a country." [21] There is another complication at a higher level of abstraction. Some essential aspects of China's traditional (i.e., pre-Communist) cosmological outlook gives the appearance of sharing a somewhat similar orientation with those of Marxism–Leninism as interpreted by Mao Tse-tung and the Maoists. For example, in the ancient Chinese "philosophy of organism," [22] the teleological (though secular) outlook of a *ta-t'ung* (great harmony) utopia could be said to have anticipated Hegelian historical redemption and the Marxist apocalyptic image of the future. The antinomy of *yin* and *yang* (negative versus positive), or *shan* and *o* (good versus evil),[23] might even be made a theoretical justification for a world view of "two mutually hostile camps," [24] independent of the Marxist–Leninist doctrine of class struggle (derived from Hegelian dialectics).[25]

Saying this is not denying the fact that the Communists have introduced changes in the traditional Chinese world view. The most significant example is the Communist substitution of a "progressive" for the traditional "cyclical" notion of historical development.[26] This substitution perhaps represents the most important theoretical "improvement" upon traditional Chinese dialectics. But, this and other vital differences have not prevented scholars like C. P. Fitzgerald from viewing Chinese Communism as a "re-appearance of the fundamental concepts of Chinese society in a form fitted to the changing world." [27]

It is self-apparent that it would be hardly rewarding to attempt to find answers to all questions regarding the CPR exclusively in her Communist ideology, any more than in her cultural tradition. One has to admit that practical national interests often compete with, and sometimes even override, ideological considerations. On matters concerning the status of Tibet and Taiwan, for example, there seems hardly any distinction between the position of the Communists and that of the Nationalist government.[28]

Equally unrewarding would be to base one's speculation solely on an imagined "historical momentum," like the momentum of mass in motion. Those who attempt to place the CPR within the historical framework of *pax sinica* find it difficult to shed the stereotyped impression that the CPR today, allegedly seized with a "sino-centrism," still considers herself the "center of the world." [29] Andrew L. March has commented on the fallacy of applying a "historical momentum" view to interpreting current relations between the CPR and Southeast Asia. History, he points out, "has continuity as well as change. . . . But it is no good to think about people, ideas, and institutions in such crude physical models [as historical momentum, etc.]. It is at once clear, when one thinks of them explicitly, how vague and harmful they are, and how little light they shed. . . ." [30]

No matter whether imperial China looked upon herself as the "center of the world," or whether the CPR's self-image today is "one of victimization at the hands of a great historical and evil force invading China from the West," [31] we must not let any conviction blind us to facts. If, as Professor John K. Fairbank has correctly pointed out, "no Chinese Alexander ever set out from the Middle Kingdom to conquer the farther reaches of the world," [32] we must also examine whether the CPR has ever really crossed her borders without provocation but specifically to "liberate" the world and whether her concrete actions appear to have been based on specific, limited goals or broad, expansive objectives. Any conclusions reached before such empirical scrutiny would only be ill-founded, just as empirical studies without reference to historical and cultural-ideological backgrounds would be out of context.

We make no pretensions that the conclusions from the present study are final and definitive. Given the prevailing uncertainty, we doubt whether any conclusions thus far can be more than tentative. But we do believe that an attempt at a more balanced evaluation, drawing upon the various considerations suggested above, should be made. The study will have served a purpose if it should help in clarifying anything or even in pointing up the difficulty of arriving at a balanced judgment concerning an important subject of our time: Will international law have a role to play in the face of challenges from revolutionary nations like Communist China?

Partly because of the tentative nature of available data and partly because of the magnitude of the research involved, the present study tends to be more illustrative than exhaustive, just as it seeks to strike a balance between description and analysis. In order to make the discussions flow more smoothly and to keep the focus on Communist China, much of the background information, especially that which concerns the general practice of other states and the status of international law in general, is relegated to the footnotes. The footnote section also contains a rather exhaustive bibliography on the subject. Most of the original sources cited are available in the Chinese collections of Columbia University, New York City, and Harvard University, Cambridge, Massachusetts. All Chinese personal names are spelled according to the Wade-Giles system of Romanization and arranged in the Chinese order, family name preceding the given name. Unless spelled otherwise in general usage, all place names are also Romanized the same way. When there is no indication that a translation is taken from an official source or other sources, it is the author's own.

I

General Attitudes Toward International Law

IT IS OFTEN assumed that all states attempt to utilize international law to cloak their foreign policies with the mantle of legality, and that the intensity and extent of a particular state's effort vary with its position in the international society.[1] A state which enjoys the reputation of being law-abiding will usually strain for a legal rationale to support actions not clearly sanctified under generally accepted norms of conduct. The United States espousal of the concept of "quarantine" during the 1962 Cuban missile crisis and those of "aggressive defense" and "hot pursuit" in the Vietnam War have been offered as examples. On the other hand, the theory continues, a state with a reputation for "lawlessness" and only partially accepted by the international society, such as the CPR, has a lesser need to advance a legal rationale for its actions.[2]

While this theory is generally true, it tends to gloss over some crucial points which require clarification. In the first place, the degree of a state's concern for the "mantle of legality" is inseparable from a prior sense of identity with the international community in which it exists and a conviction that there is a generally accepted body of law whose sanctity must be consciously defended for the good of the community at large.[3] Few would deny that the current ideological-cultural diversity, resulting from the massive emergence of

Communist and less developed states in Asia and Africa, has severely strained the very sense of community and the consensus about the higher good which informed the traditional norms of international conduct.

Furthermore, traditional international law was exclusive to states of European background. Its exclusive nature can be seen in the classic example of the Treaty of Paris (1856), which declared the Porte (Turkey) "admitted to the benefits of the public law and the Concert of Europe." [4] The reason for this Europocentric character is that traditional international law arose and grew in response to the needs of the international society that was developing in the West following the breakup of medieval politico-religious institutions. As a number of relatively small, secular nation-states rose in Europe, the Continent witnessed a marked increase in trade activities, overseas conquests, and growing diplomatic and consular relations. The movement of persons, goods, and capital beyond national boundaries required the establishment and mutual observance of certain common standards of conduct, in both official and private domains, to assure a modicum of order and security, as well as predictability. Although similar norms were likewise known to exist in other cultures and ages,[5] it seems that only those developed in modern Europe have been widely disseminated and have come down to us as susceptible of interpretation and application by legal methods. Most possibly, this legal form is the result of a "law tradition" or "law habit" in the Western civilization; it reflects in part the influence of the Roman legal tradition. The pragmatism born of modern science, no doubt, has reinforced that tradition.[6] In this light, whether a state shares the same craving for the "mantle of legality" is in a large measure determined by its relative distance to this Western heritage.

Whether a state is to be considered as "lawless" because of its rejection of certain norms presumed to be of universal applicability involves a rather subjective value judgment. The question could be posed in drastically different ways: Does the present divided and fast-changing world have a "universal" international law, one that is accepted by most states representing the main forms of existing civilizations and ideologies? If not, then by whose law is a given state to be held "lawless?" The more sensible question to ask, therefore, is: How universal is existing international law, and how can that law be made more universal? In the past, international law survived the addition of non-Western states partly because Western countries wielded pre-eminent power to enforce it, and partly because the law possessed a high degree of practical utility and adaptability.[7] As many Western jurists agree, never before has international law faced so great a challenge from so many new states hailing from so different cultural-ideological backgrounds.[8] The future of international law rests all the more with the law's utility and its adaptability to the changing demands and aspirations of the vastly changing international society.

In our study of the CPR, we shall examine the extent to which she accepts the utility of existing international law, at least parts thereof, and what new principles and norms she advocates for a modern international law in the making.

Utility of International Law

Whether the CPR takes international law seriously can be studied at least at two different levels. First, one can probe into the extent to which the regime makes practical use of international law in its foreign relations and the place of international law in its foreign policy thinking. Secondly, one can reasonably deduce the regime's attitudes from the opinions of mainland Chinese commentators. In the present section we shall focus on the second concern, leaving the first to the various chapters that follow. From available CPR literature we find explicit acknowledgement of the utility of existing international law. Ying T'ao, a frequent critic of "bourgeois international law," has made the following candid admission:

> Owing to its technical rules and institutions, bourgeois international law has its *utility* as a means for facilitating international intercourse. It may and should be given necessary introduction [in China's domestic legal training].[9]

Ying T'ao further pointed out that "technical rules and institutions constitute a very great proportion of the entire body of bourgeois international law." Among the examples he gave were norms governing diplomatic intercourse (e.g., ranks and appointment of envoys, presentation of credentials, establishment of diplomatic missions, etc.); the laws of disputes, war, and neutrality.[10]

Many mainland Chinese commentators have challenged the "purely legalistic viewpoint" regarding international law and characterized the law, like any other legal system, as a "political instrument." [11] In a blunt and naked comment, Chu Li-ju put forth what may be presumed to be a semiofficial view:

> International law is an *instrument* for settling international problems. If this instrument is useful to our country, to the socialist cause, or to the cause of peace of peoples of the world, we will use it. But if it is disadvantageous [to them] . . . , we will not use it, and we should create a new instrument to replace it.[12]

Calling international law an instrument of foreign policy, Chu is challenging the juridical underpinnings of traditional international law and echoing the Soviet view that law is a process for the promotion of policies.[13] However, this view is not really exclusive to Communist jurists. In the West, for example, adherents to the Myres S. McDougal school have shown an equal concern for reformulating international law in terms of policies and public interests, calling law a "policy science" and "decision-making process." [14] Just as McDougal is so centrally concerned with the use of law as an instrument for the realization of the "values of human dignity," so is Chu with the realization of the "cause of socialism." Their main difference, and a crucial one at that, is over the specific political master which law should serve. Needless to say, a long-standing controversy remains to be settled among Western jurists over the definition and content of the "values of human dignity." [15] Likewise, one has reasons to suspect that there is no final agreement among CPR writers on the precise form which the law serving the "cause of socialism" should take.

"Universality" of International Law

Serious discussions and debates began in mainland China after 1957 on whether traditional international law is bourgeois in nature, whether there is a separate socialist international law, or whether there is only one international law equally applicable to states of different political and socio-economic systems. These could have been influenced by a rearoused Soviet interest in international law after the Twentieth Congress of the Communist Party of the Soviet Union in 1956. That year was a historic landmark in the development of a new Soviet theory of international law; more works on international law appeared after the Twentieth Congress than in the preceding forty years of Soviet existence.[16] On the other hand, throughout mainland China during this time, there was a belated interest in law as a whole, including international law. Between 1949 and 1954 the regime's existence was marked by a lack of interest in law. To varying degrees after 1957, legal studies were reintroduced, many law schools being reopened and expanded. The revived interest came in the wake of the 1957 antirightist campaign. Although much of the blast of that campaign was aimed at jurists who had spoken out, the rediscovered interest may be an indication that their criticisms were after all taken to heart by the regime.[17] The trend continued to about 1965; like all other intellectual pursuits, it was disrupted during the Cultural Revolution.

Scanning through published CPR literature on the question of the "universality" of international law, one is impressed with the rather abundant amount of writing that has been produced.[18] To generalize in the broadest fashion, there are three schools of thought in this respect. One school, represented mainly by Lin Hsin, is inclined to the view that there are two systems of international relations, the bourgeois and the socialist, necessitating two systems of law.[19] The second school, disagreeing with the first, postulates one single system of international law, binding both upon bourgeois and socialist countries. It resembles largely the view in the West, although the precise meaning may not be the same. The proponents of this school sought to skirt (or compromise?) the Marxist-Leninist doctrinal dilemma over the state superstructure by distinguishing international law from municipal law. As Chou Fu-lun puts it:

> The major unique characteristic of international law is that its norms are formulated not by a super-legislature but through agreement reached by the process of struggle, cooperation, compromise, and consultation.[20]

Other principal adherents to this school include Chu Ch'i-wu and Chou Tzu-ya.[21]

The third and apparently the strongest school holds, in effect, that there is a general international law over and above, as well as distinct from, the bourgeois legal system. K'ung Meng calls it the "generally recognized" international law, which serves as a yardstick for measuring the validity of the components of bourgeois international law, such as the latter's law regarding the recognition of new states.[22] Ying T'ao, an important advocate of this school, posits, as an antithesis to bourgeois international law, a "modern international law," which "reflects the aspirations of the great majority of peoples in the world." A clear example of the differences between the two systems of international law, he claims, is that general international law prescribes strict respect by states of each other's sovereignty, whereas bourgeois international law has been employed by "imperialists" for aggression and exploitation "in blatant violation of the inviolability of sovereignty" of other states.[23]

The view is shared by Yi Hsin, Ch'ien Szu, and Hsin Wu.[24] Also belonging to this third school is Chou Keng-sheng, who may be considered as the dean of mainland Chinese scholars of international law and whose importance can be seen from his position as a key member of the Legislative Committee of the National People's Congress. *In his Hsien-tai ying-mei kuo-chi-fa te szu-hsiang tung-hsiang* (Trends in Contemporary Anglo-American Thinking on International Law), Professor Chou critically reviews the contemporary bourgeois juridical thinking against the standards of what he simply calls "international law." [25]

Despite the extensive debates the question of the universality of international law is not officially resolved in the CPR. A special symposium held in Shanghai in February, 1958, failed to come to any conclusion but merely voiced a near unanimous opposition to the bourgeois-socialist dichotomous theory held by the first school above. There were strong indications, however, that the third school had the widest support, paralleling similar experiences in the Soviet debates on the same subject.[26] (While both CPR and Soviet jurists have since the 1950s advocated a new law of peaceful coexistence as a single body of international law, they have arrived at the conclusion by separate paths, and they have also interpreted and applied peaceful coexistence differently. Chapters II and III below will discuss this divergency in detail.)

The Nature of International Law

Although mainland Chinese jurists are agreed on the utility of international law, some of them argue that modern international law cannot be understood if divorced from its "class nature." In a series of articles dealing with specific topics on bourgeois international law published in the once important *Kuo-chi wen-t'i yen-chiu* (Studies of International Problems) in 1959 and 1960, the point received repeated emphasis. Ying T'ao set the general tone in a broad critique. In the first place, the capitalist states manipulated the badge of "civilized nations" to secure and protect their class interests against other nations beyond the pale of Western civilization. Secondly, norms sanctifying conquest, prescription, and other forms of territorial acquisition were designed to offer the capitalist states a legal justification for their territorial encroachments upon non-Western peoples. Thirdly, capitalist states used "unequal" treaties to extort concessions from the "oppressed" nations. Fourthly, the purpose of the so-called law of disputes, including the means of pacific settlement (such as negotiation, mediation, arbitration, etc.) and compulsory settlement (e.g., reprisal, blockade, intervention, etc.), was to help capitalist states pursue their class interests. Lastly, the laws of war and neutrality, according to Ying T'ao, were used by capitalist states to whitewash and cushion the brutal nature of "imperialist" wars of aggression.[27]

Even among some adherents to the second school, which sees existing international law as universally applicable to states of different ideologies, the same view was echoed with a familiar dogmatic tone. Chou Tzu-ya, a prominent scholar, suggested that from studies of the origin and development of international law one could find the inherent class character in each stage. After quoting from A. Y. Vyshinsky that international law orders the relations between nations in the course of their conflict and collaboration,[28] Chou Tzu-ya evaluated the development of law in the relations between ancient Egypt and Hittites (c. 1750–1200 B.C.), the interstate relations in ancient China during the Spring and Autumn Period (722–481 B.C.), down to the age of capitalist domination in world relations and to the present era. The writer reached the conclusion that in every international society there were laws which represented the wills of the ruling classes of two or more countries of different socio-economic systems (e.g., Soviet Union, as a socialist state; the United States, as a bourgeois-*qua*-imperialist state; and Afghanistan, as a feudalist state).

Chou Tzu-ya realized the dilemma facing the simultaneous claims about the "universality" and the "class nature" of international law, the two being contradictory to each other. He therefore insisted that there was continuity in international law though the class structure of the international society changed with time.[29] According to him, the principle of nonintervention in internal affairs and the declaratory theory of diplomatic recognition had a historic place during the "bourgeois democratic revolution" that overthrew feudal domination. These principles, he claimed, served to foil the attempts by the Holy Alliance to suppress the emergent nation-states and revolutionary regimes in Europe. As the capitalist era advanced to the imperialist stage, he continued, new doctrines were advanced as tools for intervention by the imperialist states, such as the Monroe Doctrine, to justify or disguise United States intervention in Latin America.[30] The writer implied that during the present era "proletarian" values would replace the old bourgeois norms and that from this process of purification international law would emerge truly "universal."

To some CPR writers the "class nature" is not only limited to customary international law but is found also in treaties. Commenting on the capitalist theory that the Covenant of the League of Nations was a source of international law, Ying T'ao attributed to the Covenant a class character. The document, he claimed, was signed by the victor powers of World War I to maintain their acquired interests over the vanquished and to prescribe a postwar international order most amenable to their tight grip on their colonies.[31] Wei Liang, in an extensive study of nearly all major international treaties that appeared since the end of World War II, had the same conclusion, suggesting that the great powers sought to protect their vested class interests by imposing treaties favorable to them on the weaker states.[32]

A similar charge was raised by Wang Yao-t'ien that capitalist states had made use of treaties to further the following ends: (a) acquiring of special privileges through nominal "equality of opportunity" clauses, which actually favored the capitalist powers because of their financial superiority; (b) the use of bilateral "economic cooperation" agreements concluded under the Marshall Plan as a ruse for intervention in the internal affairs of the "Marshallized" countries; (c) acquiring of raw materials from less developed areas, at costs far below world-market quotations, under bilateral trade agreements (e.g., between the United States and Chile for the supply of copper; between Britain and Argentina for mutton; between Britain and Canada for wheat, etc.); (d) embargo against the CPR and freezing of Chinese assets in United States' banks, etc.[33] Conceivably, from the Marxist point of view, all these provisions are manifestations of exploitation by the ruling class in the capitalist states of the peoples in the less developed countries.

However, references to "class nature" appeared only in mainland Chinese critiques of bourgeois international law or its residual forms. They probably represent a delayed outburst of Chinese grievances against Western powers (Czarist Russia included) in whose hands international law was employed as a tool for exploitation of a prostrate China between 1840 and 1943. As we shall see, no references to "class nature" are made in regard to the "modern" international law of peaceful coexistence or, for that matter, to the single body of general international law which most CPR jurists believe is becoming universal over the dying body of "imperialism."

Sources of International Law

The traditional sources of international law as enumerated in Article 38 of the Statute of the International Court of Justice (ICJ) are: treaties, international custom, general principles of law, and (as a "subsidiary" source) judicial decisions and opinions of publicists. Although the CPR is not a party to the ICJ, circumstantial evidence suggests that she does not reject the enumeration in Article 38. The entire text of the article is reproduced under the section on "sources of international law" in the *Kuo-chi kung-fa ts'an-k'ao wen-chien hsüan-chi* (A Selection of Reference Materials on Public International Law), a supplementary textbook. Two other documents are included in the same section: (a) U.N. General Assembly Resolution (December 11, 1946) on the Progressive Development and Codification of International Law, and (b) General Assembly Resolution (same date) on Affirmation of the Principles of International Law Recognized in the Charter of the Nuremberg Tribunal.[34]

The book was compiled and published by the Department of International Law, Institute of Diplomacy, in Peking. Although the book's official status is impeccable, the materials selected are, as its title suggests, mainly for "reference" and are obviously not limited to those acceptable to the regime. However, whereas certain materials considered to be unacceptable, such as the Tobar Doctrine on recognition, are explicitly labeled "bourgeois," the rather unqualified inclusion of Article 38 of the ICJ Statute, along with other documents that are obviously acceptable, may indicate a Chinese readiness to endorse its contents. This speculation is substantiated indirectly.

In an article summarizing the first chapter of a textbook on international law which he had written, Chou Tzu-ya, professor of international law at the East China Institute of Political Science and Law (Shanghai), enumerated the sources of international law as follows: (a) treaties, (b) international custom, (c) norms from domestic legislation, as an auxiliary source, (d) resolutions of international organizations, and (e) "others." [35] He did not specify what the "others" were. But the two other sources given in Article 38 of the ICJ Statute not included in Chou's listing are: "general principles of law recognized by civilized nations," and "judicial decisions and the teachings of the most highly qualified publicists of the various nations, as subsidiary means for the determination of rules of law." We shall reserve these last two for later discussion.

First of all, it is interesting that Chou Tzu-ya has explicitly included resolutions or decisions of international organizations as a source of international law. This perhaps indirectly explains why the two General Assembly resolutions, especially the one affirming the Nuremberg Charter, are included in the *Reference Materials* under the heading "sources of international law." On occasion, U.N. General Assembly resolutions have been cited by CPR writers as evidence of the existence or absence of a norm in international law. For example, in an article by Li Hao-p'ei, Research Fellow at the Institute of International Relations, Chinese Academy of Sciences, in Peking, General Assembly Resolution 626 (VII) of December 16, 1952, dealing with permanent sovereignty over natural resources, was cited as evidence that a state enjoys the right under international law to nationalize its natural resources without the obligation to pay compensations to foreign investors engaged in their exploitation.[36] The text of the G.A. resolution is included in the *Reference Materials*.[37]

There seems to be some confusion over whether the CPR accepts the primarily Western view, currently supported by the Soviet Union, that decisions of international organizations may be a source of international law. In view of Peking's exclusion from the United Nations,* one might presume that it is hostile to decisions made by U.N. organs, especially those unfavorable to the CPR's interests and international position. The issue is far from clear. A very informative article published in the *American Journal of International Law* (AJIL) in 1966 speculated that Peking's attitude in this connection would be negative, citing a statement by Professor Chou Keng-sheng to that effect.[38] Actually, in the original writing Professor Chou was not discussing sources of international law. He was offering a general criticism of alleged "imperialist" attempts to convert the United Nations into a "world government," using its resolutions as a tool of legitimation.[39] In other words, Chou was warning of the danger, as he perceived it, of substituting "world law" (i.e., the dictate of a "world government") for international law. His argument rang a faint echo of a similar warning by Josef Kunz in an editorial comment in *AJIL,* which Chou quoted.[40]

* By a vote of the General Assembly on October 25, 1971, the CPR was given the right of representation, to replace the Republic of (Nationalist) China. It is still too early to judge what effect this changed situation will have on Peking's views on international law. I believe, however, that there will be a relatively long period of readjustment, in which much of my analysis in this volume will hold good.

From the views of Chou Keng-sheng and Chou Tzu-ya and from what can be inferred from the position reflected in the *Reference Materials,* we may attempt to piece together a general picture. It appears that to the extent that a given resolution of the General Assembly or, for that matter, a decision of an international organization, embodies a construed *opinio juris*—representing the consensus of a majority of the "nonimperialist" states and subscribed to by the CPR itself—it may be taken as a source of international law so far as Peking is concerned. In the past, the CPR singled out specific resolutions of the U.N. General Assembly as "illegal" on the ground that they violated the Charter of the United Nations. The *Reference Materials* lists the following as "illegal" resolutions: (a) the three G.A. resolutions which established or reinstituted the Interim Committee of the General Assembly (November 13, 1947; December 3, 1948; and November 21, 1949); (b) the "Uniting for Peace" resolution (November 3, 1950); (c) the resolution on voting in the Security Council (April 14, 1949); and (d) the resolution which extended the term of office of Secretary-General Trygve Lie (November 1, 1950).

Undoubtedly, these are not the only General Assembly resolutions considered to be objectionable by the CPR. For example, the particular 1950 G.A. resolution condemning Communist China as an "aggressor" for its participation in the Korean War is not included. Nevertheless, it is significant that the six "illegal" resolutions appear in an "appendix" to the section dealing with "International Organizations of a Worldwide Nature" in the book. Among other things, the section contains full texts, in Chinese translation, of the Covenant of the League of Nations, the Charter of the United Nations, Rules of Procedure of the General Assembly, Provisional Rules of Procedure of the Security Council, G.A. Resolution on the Organization of the United Nations Secretariat (February 13, 1946, in excerpts), and the G.A. Resolution on the Terms of Appointment and Compensation for the Secretary-General of the United Nations (January 24, 1946).[41]

The separation of this main text from the "appendix" provides some food for thought. In the first place, it serves to illustrate that the CPR adopts a rather selective attitude toward decisions of international organizations. Not all of them are objectionable. Secondly, the six resolutions in the appendix are earmarked "in violation of the Charter of the United Nations," hence, illegal. This could be indirect evidence that the U.N. Charter is in some way considered by the CPR as embodying a higher law against which the legality of the decisions of the U.N. organs is to be tested. Thirdly, when found not to conflict with the provisions of the U.N. Charter and general international law, certain decisions of international organizations may be acceptable as a source of international law; of course, each case would have to be judged on its own merits.

Let us now return to the proposition made by Chou Tzu-ya that norms from "domestic legislation" could be an auxiliary source of international law. The one example he gave was the Soviet institution of commercial representatives abroad, which, he said, had originated from Soviet municipal law.[42]

Because of the need for trade between capitalist and socialist states, he added, the institution came to be commonly accepted and regulated by international law. It is obvious that Chou followed the Soviet view.[43] In its foreign relations the CPR follows the Soviet practice of legalizing the status of "commercial representatives" by special bilateral agreements. By the terms incorporated in the CPR-Mongolian Treaty of Commerce (April 26, 1961), the commercial representative's office is considered to be part of the embassy of the sending state. The commercial representative and his deputy are also accorded all "rights and privileges of diplomatic personnel." [44] Thus, by virtue of this special devolution, those norms of general international law governing diplomatic privileges and immunities are extended to the commercial representatives. Whether this example really substantiates the assertion that domestic legislation can be a source of international law is uncertain. Nevertheless, what it shows is that the institution of commercial representatives, born of municipal laws, is elevated through bilateral agreement to a status coequal with diplomatic personnel and thus enters the province of general international law.

In published CPR literature, allusions to judicial decisions as a source of international law are relatively few, but not totally lacking. One example is found in an article by Kuo Chi, which supported the CPR Government's Declaration of September 4, 1958, claiming a twelve-mile territorial sea measured from straight base lines. The author cited the decision of the ICJ in the Anglo-Norwegian Fisheries case (1951) to prove that China's adoption of the base-line position and the twelve-mile breadth of territorial waters was in conformity with international law.[45] The same case was also cited in a booklet by Fu Chu defending the CPR Government's decision regarding the territorial sea.[46]

In the first 55 pages of a 135-page treatise entitled *Kuo-chi-fa chung te szu-fa kuan-hsia wen-t'i* (Judicial Jurisdiction in International Law), Ni Cheng-ao made references to twenty-seven cases decided by either international tribunals (e.g., the *Lotus* case) or national courts (e.g., *Wildenhus*).[47] Although no Chinese case was cited, Ni made a number of references to CPR laws that a domestic court would be expected to follow in a given case, such as one involving maritime collision.[48] The omission of any case decided by Chinese courts is most probably due to the fact that Chinese courts (including those in Nationalist China), following the Continental legal tradition, do not make use of *stare decisis* in deciding upon cases.[49]

But, as Ni himself indirectly suggested, studies of judicial decisions (which he dubbed "legal practice"), as well as domestic legislation and treaties and agreements, would help a court in determining the law to be applied, especially in cases involving nationals of a state whose courts in their practice accept judicial decisions.[50] CPR municipal law sometimes accepts principles formulated by foreign or international tribunals that have become part of general international law. For example, the CPR accepts the principles of "passive personality," "territoriality," and "nationality" in determining whether a Chinese court has competence to exercise jurisdiction in a given case involving foreign nationals.[51]

In addition to judicial decisions, opinions or teachings of "qualified publicists" on international law are sometimes quoted in CPR literature to prove or illustrate a rule *de lege lata* or *de lege ferenda*. Writing in 1959 on the nascent law of outer space, Liu Tse-jung cited freely the views of C. Wilfred Jenks,[52] Myres S. McDougal and Leon Lipson,[53] etc., in addition to Soviet bloc writers, to prove his points.[54]

Although CPR theory is silent on the "general principles of law" as a source of international law, there is a limited number of instances of their being actually used in legal treatises and arguments. In an article defending China's rights concerning Taiwan, Mei Ju-ao, a former judge on the International Military Tribunal for the Far East, which tried Japanese war criminals in Tokyo after World War II, drew upon the principle in domestic law governing "lost properties." The true owner of a lost property, he noted, had the right to reclaim it from a thief or robber, or from someone who had obtained it from the latter.[55] In a similar defense of China's right of sovereignty over Taiwan, Ch'en T'i-ch'iang, writing in the *Review of Contemporary Law* (Brussels), invoked from municipal law the dictum *ex injuria jus non oritur* (a person cannot acquire a right through an illegal act).[56]

Between custom and treaties, the two indisputable sources of international law accepted by all CPR writers, treaties are usually given priority as a "major" (*chu-yao*) source of international law.[57] However, CPR jurists do not seem to emphasize treaties as much as their Soviet counterparts do, for the obvious reason that the CPR has thus far been excluded from much of international life and many of the existing multilateral treaties that have a quasi-legislative effect. In the circumstances, CPR jurists tend to look for certain peremptory norms as the source of specific derivatives which either have been crystallized in international conventions to which the CPR is not a party or are in need of future codification in multilateral treaties pending the improvement of the international climate. One can think of the U.N. Charter and the Five Principles of Peaceful Coexistence as two handy examples. Before we get into the subject of *jus cogens,* we might mention in passing that, where it accepts treaties and international agreements as a "major" source of international law, Peking tends to focus on the consensual quality or the willingness to be bound at the time an agreement is reached as the ultimate source of its binding force upon the parties, and to minimize any differences that might accrue from the modality in which an agreement is contracted. A joint "declaration" between two governments may be considered to have the binding effect of a formally concluded treaty if at the time of its signing both parties' commitment is firm and both intend to be bound by it. Admittedly, this attitude may be related to Peking's desire to see the Cairo Declaration of 1943 (in which the wartime allies pledged the return of Taiwan to China at the end of the war) respected by its original signatories (United States and Britain, besides China under the Nationalist Government) and by others concerned. It is nevertheless true that many of the joint "declarations" Peking has signed with other governments are included in the official Chinese *Treaty Series,* presumably with the binding force of duly prosecuted international agreements.[58]

Jus Cogens (?)

The term *"jus cogens"* as used in the current science of international law in the West gained currency with the work of the International Law Commission on the codification of the law of treaties. Sir Hirsch Lauterpacht, as the ILC's first Rapporteur, enunciated the idea in his first Report on the Law of Treaties of 1953. Without using the term *"jus cogens,"* or peremptory norm from which no derogation is permitted, he suggested a provision (Article 15 of his draft) that "a treaty, or any of its provisions, is void if its performance involves an act which is illegal under international law and if it is declared so to be by the International Court of Justice." In his "Comment" Lauterpacht explained that "the test was not inconsistency with customary international law pure and simple, but inconsistency with such overriding principles of international public policy." [59] Sir Gerald Fitzmaurice and Sir Humphrey Waldock, his successors, introduced the concept of consistency with a general rule or principle of international law having the character of *jus cogens.*[60]

As Egon Schwelb adequately points out, aside from the ILC's efforts to codify *jus cogens,* the concept of an international *ordre public* has been in existence for a very long time in the literature of international law in the West.[61]

Although CPR writers do not use the term *"jus cogens,"* their endorsement of the concept can be deduced from the way they justify their acceptance or advocacy of certain overriding principles which they consider to be fundamental to all states. As we shall see in Chapter II below, the Five Principles of Peaceful Coexistence have been characterized both as having derived their legal basis from pre-existing fundamental principles (e.g., sovereignty, nonintervention, etc.), to which the U.N. Charter has only given new expression, and as forming a body of peremptory norms necessary for the international *ordre public*.[62]

The concept of *jus cogens* as we find it in CPR literature is not limited to the law of treaties but has a wide application. CPR jurists are concerned with more than "consistency" or prohibition of "derogation" as suggested by Lauterpacht. They seem to postulate a body of *a priori* principles from which "new" norms can be derived and which encompass both customary and treaty law. Given the current tension surrounding Peking's international relations, this postulation seems to be a convenient way to bypass the restrictions imposed by the ideological conflict, capable of transcending the gaps between capitalist and socialist states and between traditional (under bourgeois influence) and "modern" (under socialist influence) international law. Peking's exclusion from many multilateral treaties and agreements of an international legislative character has made it practically impossible to deprecate custom in favor of "agreement" as the ultimate source of international law to the same extent as Soviet jurists do.[63] G. I. Tunkin, the current Soviet spokesman, has gone so far as to suggest that:

> the concept that customary norms of international law recognized as such by a large number of states are binding upon all states not only has no foundation in modern international law but is fraught with great danger.[64]

To the best of my knowledge, no such extreme deprecation of custom is found in CPR literature as yet. The assumption about a *jus cogens* broadly interpreted seems to have resolved the dilemma arising from the fact that international custom could have originated from practices of the capitalist states. In practice, Peking has on occasion consciously sought aid from "international custom" or "international practice," such as in attempts to protect the immunities and privileges of its diplomatic, consular, and other official personnel abroad.[65] Although assertions in these cases are politically motivated, the point is that when the CPR cannot invoke, for example, the 1961 Vienna Convention on Diplomatic Relations or its 1963 counterpart on consular relations or any similar conventions, being not a party to any of them, the only logical alternative is to invoke international custom and practice.

Provisions of the 1961 CPR-Indonesian Treaty of Friendship had the following stipulation: "The Contracting Parties agree to continuously consolidate the diplomatic and consular relations between the two countries in accordance with the principle of reciprocity and *international practice*." [66] The clause seems to suggest that provisions of the treaty were not meant to derogate from certain peremptory norms established under "international practice." From the fact that in the preamble of the treaty mention was made of the Ten Principles of the 1955 Bandung Conference and the Five Principles of Peaceful Coexistence, it may be further speculated that these principles were supposed to be part of the peremptory norms which the drafters of the treaty had in mind.

II

The International Law of Peaceful Coexistence

AMIDST THE inconclusive debate in mainland China over the universality of international law, what can be said is that CPR literature tends to blur the distinction between "general" and "modern" international law. Presumably, the two convey some different nuances. The term "general" (*yi-pan*) or "generally recognized" (*yi-pan kung-jen*) seems to predicate a body of peremptory norms (*jus cogens*) which transcend the rigidity of positivism as well as ideological and temporal gaps. On the other hand, "modern" (*hsien-tai*) appears to anticipate reformulation of existing norms that are not responsive to current needs and conditions and to suggest the development of new "progressive" norms or even *de lege ferenda.*[1]

The frequent interchangeable use of the two terms by the writers we examined in the previous chapter reflects an ambivalence: Neither can the CPR, bound by its Marxist ideology, blindly and indiscriminately accept existing international law without questioning whether its norms were formulated by capitalist states to further their interests. Nor can she, on the other hand, ignore international law completely in view of the foreign policy needs it can serve.

Peking's rather limited participation in international affairs is understood to have made it highly critical and selective in regard to norms already in existence. It follows that the regime is anxious to see the development of a law that is, in its view, more responsive and amenable to the aspirations of the "oppressed" nations. Nevertheless, the present state of the CPR's science of international law appears to acquiesce in the practical coexistence of norms and principles of differing origins, that is: (a) those of bourgeois origin which have thus far survived the onslaught of the new era, partly because of their utility and partly because they have been made more "progressive" under the impact of socialist countries; and (b) new "progressive" elements introduced by the forces of socialism and the third bloc states.[2] The law pertaining to diplomatic and consular relations, for example, falls under the first category. Included in the second group are the principles of absolute sovereignty, true (as opposed to nominal) equality, self-determination, and peaceful coexistence.[3] Because of its alleged importance, the last mentioned will be discussed first, both here and in the next chapter. We must add that in CPR thinking the interaction between socialist and bourgeois states is conceived as having an inevitable impact upon the evolution of old norms and the formulation of new ones. One example is the socialist claims regarding the absolute character of state sovereignty and the response by bourgeois states attempting to place curbs on certain acts of states that are not within the public domain (*jure gestionis*).[4] Unquestionably, this interaction underscores the fluidity of contemporary international law in a divided world.

Origins of the Five Principles

In Communist writings the term "peaceful coexistence" has been ascribed to Lenin. Western scholars have, on the other hand, recalled that it was Chicerin, the People's Commissar for Foreign Affairs, who referred to the 1920 Soviet peace treaty with Estonia as the first experiment in peaceful coexistence with bourgeois states.[5] However, the Five Principles (*wu-hsiang yüan-tse,* also known by its Indian name *panch shila*) of Peaceful Coexistence, as they are known today, were first enunciated in the Sino-Indian Trade Agreement in Tibet, April 29, 1954.[6] They were more ceremoniously reaffirmed in a joint declaration which Premier Chou En-lai signed with Prime Minister Jawaharlal Nehru of India on June 28, 1954, and in Chou's joint declaration the next day with U Nu, Prime Minister of Burma.[7] The Five Principles are:

a) Mutual respect for each other's territorial integrity and sovereignty;
b) Nonaggression;
c) Noninterference in each other's internal affairs;
d) Equality and mutual benefit;
e) Peaceful coexistence.

The Five Principles represent an expansion of the three cardinal principles which the CPR, on October 1, 1949, declared to be the cornerstone of all its relations with foreign countries willing to reciprocate. The 1949 triad included: "equality, mutual benefit, and mutual respect for territorial sovereignty." [8] The Common Program, which until 1954 served as quasi-Constitution, further elaborated upon the three principles. Article 54 of the Common Program stipulated:

> The foreign policy of the People's Republic of China is based on the principle of protection of the independence, freedom, integrity of territory, and sovereignty of the country, upholding lasting international peace and friendly cooperation between the peoples of all countries, and opposing the imperialist policy of aggression and war.[9]

When the CPR Constitution was adopted in 1954, the triad was further affirmed but slightly rephrased to read: "equality, mutual benefit, and mutual respect for each other's sovereignty and territorial integrity." The Constitution further claimed that the CPR's foreign policy was devoted to "the noble cause of world peace and the progress of humanity." [10]

Thus the third principle in the 1949 triad, as rephrased in 1954, became the first of the Five Principles of Peaceful Coexistence. The original first and second principles—i.e., "equality" and "mutual benefit"—were joined together to become the fourth. The idea of "opposing the imperialist policy of aggression and war," which appeared in Article 54 of the Common Program, was probably the precursor of the principle of nonaggression, now the second of the Five Principles. "Noninterference," which ranks third, is a clear addition. The pledge made in the 1954 Constitution to work for the "noble cause of world peace and the progress of humanity" found expression in the catch-all phrase "peaceful coexistence," the last in the Five Principles.

Of course, one should not overlook Nehru's contribution in the formulation of the Five Principles. Nor should one ignore the historical events that underscored their formulation and announcement. When Chou En-lai visited India and Burma in 1954, he was between sessions of the Geneva Conference, which was seeking a "peaceful" settlement for both the Korean and the Indochina conflicts. Peking was seriously planning an all-out invasion of Taiwan, and Chinese Communist artillery was to commence shelling across the Taiwan strait on September 3. The only immediate obstacle for Peking's plan to take Taiwan was the presence of United States' armed might. Secretary of State Dulles was already looking beyond Geneva toward a collective defense system in Southeast Asia (SEATO). Chou was consciously promoting friendship with neighboring Asian states, not only to stabilize regional peace on China's southern flank (Tibet included) but also to offset the impact of the SEATO design. The call for nonaggression and noninterference, and, for that matter, for peaceful coexistence in general answered the needs of Peking's strategy of securing peace along its southern borders in anticipation of action in the Taiwan strait.[11]

Not surprisingly, CPR literature claimed credit for China's contribution to the formulation of the international law of peaceful coexistence.[12] After his return from the 1954 Geneva Conference, Chou En-lai made a formal report to the Central People's Government Administrative Council (GAC) on August 11. Chou reaffirmed that the policy of peaceful coexistence would apply to China's relations with all Asian nations and to "international relations in general." [13] The GAC adopted a resolution approving Chou's report and explicitly declared that the Five Principles "should apply to China's relations with Asian states and other countries in the world." [14] In so doing, the GAC formally "ratified" the Five Principles as outlined in Chou's report, leaving the extent of their application as vague and broad as their content.

The Heyday of Peaceful Coexistence

Since June, 1954, peaceful coexistence became an important addition to Peking's ideological arsenal and the asserted hard core of its foreign policy; but its specific meaning never remained the same. At the time of its birth, this "soft line" was intended to protect China's southern flanks as Peking was contemplating an offensive in the Taiwan strait. But after the latter campaign collapsed in the face of United States' threats of nuclear retaliation and the unenthusiastic Soviet response, peaceful coexistence soon turned into the vehicle of a full-fledged "peace offensive." [15] The conclusion of the SEATO treaty (September 8, 1954) and the United States-Nationalist Chinese Mutual Defense Treaty (December 2, 1954) forced Peking to reverse the original order of priorities between invasion of Taiwan and peaceful coexistence in Southeast Asia.

During the abortive 1954 Taiwan strait campaign Peking realized that Soviet intervention could not be counted upon to help expel the United States' influence from the area. A shift in CPR strategy followed. Mao Tse-tung saw that the struggle in the immediate future between the socialist and the "imperialist" camps was to take place in the intermediate zone, which included some capitalist and many neutral countries, as well as many Asian and African territories still under colonial powers. The new scenario, a projection of Mao's domestic strategy of "encircling the developed areas from the underdeveloped areas," called for friendship with the neutral and nonaligned states but anticipated continued hostility with the "imperialists." "Liberation" of Taiwan would depend upon Peking's own resources. Growing distrust of Moscow further enhanced Peking's desire to assert greater autonomy; we shall see in the next chapter that Peking probably attempted in 1954–1956 to make the Five Principles replace the more authoritarian norm of proletarian internationalism within the socialist bloc. In the world at large, peaceful coexistence became Peking's weapon for forming a united front in its struggle with the United States.[16]

At the Bandung Conference of Afro-Asian States, April 18 through April 24, 1955, Chou En-lai crowned Peking's peace offensive with a stunning announcement that his government was ready to "sit down and enter into [bilateral] negotiations with the United States government . . . [over] the question of relaxing tension in the Far East and especially . . . in the Taiwan area."[17] This "sensational initiative," as one writer calls it, led to the opening of the marathon CPR-United States Ambassadorial Talks some ninety days later.[18] Chou acted as though his country was willing to extend peaceful coexistence to the United States in a settlement of the Taiwan question. At the conference Chou promoted *ho-ping kung-ch'u* (peaceful coexistence) with all his charm and affability. Although with some difficulty, Chou was able to ease doubts about Peking's sincerity, eschewing any thorough discussion of its Marxist ideology.[19] The concept as expressed in the original could be construed from "mutual tolerance of each other's existence" to "mutual accommodation and cooperation in peace." Chou focused on the latter connotation, to maximize the impact of peaceful coexistence. In his speech Chou stretched the original Five Principles to seven points:

a) Respect for each other's sovereignty and territorial integrity;
b) Abstention from aggression and threats against each other;
c) Abstinence from interference or intervention in the internal affairs of one another;
d) Recognition of equality of races;
e) Recognition of equality of all nations;
f) Respect for the rights of the people of all countries to choose freely a way of life, as well as political and economic systems;
g) Abstention from doing damage to other nations, and peaceful cooperation.[20]

The twenty-four Afro-Asian nations at Bandung reached agreement on ten principles for the "promotion of world peace and cooperation." The first three of Chou's seven points became the second, seventh, and fourth of the Ten Principles, respectively. Chou's fourth and fifth points were incorporated into the third principle. The sixth of Chou's suggestions, dealing with the rights of each nation to choose its own ideology and social system, was bypassed. Chou's last point became the backbone of the ninth of the Ten

Principles, which called for the "promotion of mutual interests and cooperation." The remaining five of the Ten Principles were obviously added on the initiative of the other Afro-Asian countries, especially those which were members of the United Nations. They called for:

1) Respect for fundamental human rights and for the purposes and principles of the Charter of the United Nations (Principle One);
2) Respect for the right of each nation to defend itself, singly or collectively, in conformity with the Charter of the United Nations (Principle Five);
3) Abstention from the use of arrangements of collective defense to serve the particular interests of any of the big powers. Abstention by any country from exerting pressures on other countries (Principle Six);
4) Settlement of all international disputes by peaceful means, such as negotiation, conciliation, arbitration or judicial settlement as well as other peaceful means of the parties' own choice, in conformity with the Charter of the United Nations (Principle Eight);
5) Respect for justice and international obligations (Principle Ten).[21]

These additional principles paraphrased the provisions of Articles 2, 33, and 51 of the U.N. Charter, with the sole exception of Principle Six, which was an obvious allusion to the newly instituted SEATO alliance. While the CPR can be counted on to support wholeheartedly the denunciation of security pacts like the SEATO,[22] it is not clear to what extent she truly accepted the other additions in the Ten Principles, although Chou En-lai signed the Final Communiqué of April 24, 1955. Certainly, the exhortation that states settle their disputes by arbitration or judicial means would mean a departure from an established Communist practice of not submitting disputes to any international tribunal like the International Court of Justice in the present conditions. Peking's 1963 Boundary Agreement with Pakistan explicitly declared that its terms were reached "on the basis of the *ten principles* as enunciated in the Bandung Conference." This specific reference notwithstanding, Article 5 of the Boundary Agreement stipulated that boundary disputes between the CPR and Pakistan "shall be settled peacefully by the two parties through *friendly consultations*." [23] It is plain that "friendly consultation" took the place of arbitration or judicial settlement.

CPR literature and official documents continued the use of the lexicon of *wu-hsiang yuan-tse* (Five Principles). In the CPR-Nepalese Agreement on the normalization of diplomatic relations, reached on August 1, 1955, it was stated that the Five Principles "are the basic principles governing the relations between the two countries." [24] The same assurance was repeated in a joint statement issued by Chou En-lai and Prince Norodom Sihanouk of Cambodia on February 28, 1956.[25] When the CPR-Burmese Treaty of Friendship and Mutual Non-Aggression was signed in 1960, it was hailed in Peking as "a further step forward" in the progressive development of the Five Principles.[26]

In retrospect, it appears that an immediate effect of the Bandung Conference was Chou En-lai's realization that the doctrine of peaceful coexistence represented the aspirations of most Afro-Asian nations, who preferred to remain neutral and nonaligned between the two camps.[27] This evaluation reinforced the emerging Chinese views after 1954 that the world was divided between three, rather than two, camps, and helped to make peaceful coexistence the cornerstone of Peking's policy toward the nonaligned countries.

Although by the end of 1955 it had already become apparent to Peking that the direct Ambassadorial Talks with Washington would not resolve the Taiwan impasse, it was not until the second Taiwan crisis of 1958 that the CPR abandoned its peace offensive launched at Bandung. During the interim Chou En-lai maintained optimism that Taiwan could be "peacefully liberated." [28] Conciliatory overtures were extended to Nationalist Chinese leaders with the aim of a direct negotiated settlement, though to no avail.[29] The years between 1954 and 1958, in any event, saw the heyday of peaceful coexistence in Peking's foreign policy vocabulary. In an important report on January 30, 1956, Premier Chou stressed that the policy of peaceful coexistence applied to "countries of different social systems," that "revolutions cannot be exported," and that "peaceful competition" was permissible between the two contending camps.[30] The last statement showed Khrushchev's short-lived influence in Peking. In an attack on the "economic aggression" of the "imperialists," Chou advocated genuine assistance to the less developed countries so that they could attain "economic independence." The basic Chinese Communist tenet of forming a united front with the emerging nations in a common struggle against the "imperialists" was muffled and could be detected only between the lines.[31]

Outwardly, Chou maintained that peaceful coexistence was to be universally applied, regardless of ideological barriers. At a Calcutta news conference on December 9, 1956, Chou claimed that the CPR-United States' deadlock was not caused by ideological differences. If ideological differences were truly insurmountable, Chou asked, why did the United States maintain contacts with socialist countries in the first place? "We believe," he continued, "that countries of different ideologies [including the CPR and the United States] can maintain contacts in peaceful coexistence." [32] The view was supported by Liu Shao-ch'i, the man who was Mao's heir-apparent until his purge in 1966. In his report to the Eighth Congress of the Chinese Communist Party on September 15, 1956, Liu stated that the current international scene was favorable to China's application of peaceful coexistence in her foreign policy. He made it clear that peaceful coexistence would apply to Peking's relations with the United States if the latter was willing to reciprocate.[33] Ch'en Yi, the future foreign minister, appearing before the same party congress on September 25, gave the assurance that peaceful coexistence was *"absolutely not* a strategem of expediency [*chüeh fei ch'üan-yi chih chi*]." [34]

Mao Tse-tung himself gave unreserved endorsement to the idea, declaring: "We firmly maintain that all nations should practice the well-known Five Principles of . . . peaceful coexistence." [35] In his *Correct Handling of Contradictions Among the People* (February 27, 1957), Mao formally revised Stalin's early dichotomous division of the world, which Mao himself had accepted in 1949.[36] From the assumption of the coexistence of three camps, Mao reasoned that the CPR's foreign policy must follow three basic guidelines: First, the CPR must join in solidarity with nations of the socialist bloc. Secondly, it must empathize and align with the "peace-loving" Afro-Asian countries and peoples. And lastly, it must seek an understanding with the people of the "imperialist" countries, trying to prevent the outbreak of war by practicing peaceful coexistence with those countries.[37]

Until Peking's position hardened after 1958, it can be said that peaceful coexistence had been portrayed by Peking as a body of norms applicable to all international relations. Its attitudes changed after 1958 from exuberant enthusiasm to lukewarm interest to militant defiance, because of a combination of factors, including the fruitless nature of the CPR-United States Ambassadorial Talks, growing suspicion of Soviet intentions, and domestic setbacks during the Great Leap. As we shall see in the next chapter, Peking's changing attitudes on the applicability of peaceful coexistence, like those on proletarian internationalism, have followed closely the vicissitudes of its triangular relations with Moscow and Washington. In the section below we shall probe the legal significance of peaceful coexistence as CPR jurists envisaged it and the true import which Peking attached to the doctrine despite recent CPR-Soviet polemics.

Legal Significance of Peaceful Coexistence

An authoritative treatise expounding peaceful coexistence as the quintessence of "modern" international law was written by Professor Chou Keng-sheng in 1955. If Soviet writers have attempted to credit socialist influence with the doctrine's development and to rest the doctrine's universality on "agreement" between states, the Chinese jurist did not quite do so. In fact, he endeavored to find the basis for its universality in the fundamental principles generally accepted by states, as crystallized in the Charter of the United Nations and other conventions and in custom. Although only implicit in his arguments, Chou's assumption about the existence of a body of *jus cogens* seemed to bypass the element of "agreement," serving in a way to resolve the impasse of the CPR's exclusion from the United Nations and many multilateral treaties. Below is a summary of Chou Keng-sheng's discussion of the legal basis of the Five Principles, as found in general international law.[38]

(1) First, respect for territorial integrity and respect for sovereignty, which heads the list of the Five Principles, is mentioned as two separate precepts and as "mutually inclusive and complementary principles of *customary* international law" recognized in the Charter of the United Nations." Article 2 (4), for example, prohibits violations of the "territorial integrity of political independence of any state."

(2) Secondly, nonaggression, the second principle, is an obligation which Chou asserts is imposed by customary international law upon all states. He recalls the Kellogg-Briand Pact, the unanimous resolution passed on February 18, 1928, by the twenty-one American republics at the Sixth (Havana) Pan-American Conference, which declared that "war of aggression constitutes an international crime against the human species"; and the Charters and Principles formulated at the Nuremberg and the Tokyo trials. To Chou, the U.N. Charter, especially Article 39, represents a culmination of the world community's efforts to prevent aggression. Under Chapter VII of the U.N. Charter, the United Nations is provided with a body of measures for dealing with acts of aggression, as well as threats to the peace and breach of the peace. Aggression is proscribed under the U.N. Charter as a matter of principle; but, unfortunately, he adds, the Charter does not define what constitutes an aggression.

Chou then suggests that definitions of aggression can be sought elsewhere, such as the many international (unratified) treaties and pronouncements by governments prior to the 1933 London Convention for the Definition of Aggression, the London Convention itself, the recommendations of the special committees for the definition of aggression set up under the U.N. General Assembly, etc.

(3) Thirdly, nonintervention is introduced by Professor Chou as an obligation derived from the principle of respect for each other's sovereignty. As such, it is another principle of customary international law adopted in the U.N. Charter, as under Article 2 (7). "Imperialist" countries, he continues, frequently use indirect meth-

ods of intervention in the domestic affairs of other countries, such as those employed by Western powers in intervening in the Spanish War in 1936. United States' attempts to prevent the CPR's "liberation" of Taiwan by means of the so-called mutual defense treaty are condemned as "indirect intervention" in China's internal affairs.

(4) Fourthly, Chou considers "mutual benefit and equality," another principle of peaceful coexistence, as also part of customary international law in existence long before the Charter of the United Nations. Article 2 (1) of the Charter specifically emphasizes the principle of sovereign equality of states. Equality is inseparable from sovereignty, and mutual benefit is complementary to equality. Use of "unequal" treaties or nominally equal treaties to acquire privileged status or rights is, according to him, a violation of international law.

(5) Lastly, peaceful coexistence, the overall concept of the Five Principles, is characterized as a most fundamental principle of modern international law by which all international relations are or should be ordered. The traditional law of war, Professor Chou asserts, has lost its place to the new law of peaceful coexistence, and the latter is destined to assume increasing importance as peaceful relations in political, economic, and cultural arenas continue to grow among nations. Interestingly, Chou makes no mention of the question whether "imperialist" countries are excluded from the application of the law of peaceful coexistence. He merely states that peaceful coexistence must not be made a sheer shibboleth of propaganda. Talks about "first strike," "cold war," "nuclear deterrence," and "position of strength," Chou asserts, are detrimental to the promotion of peaceful coexistence, because they will only create an atmosphere of tension and mutual distrust.

It is significant that Chou Keng-sheng in this exposition invokes not only the Charter of the United Nations but, more important, customary international law and even norms contemplated in unratified conventions. Although Chou was writing in a period when the CPR was still actively seeking representation in the U.N., the very fact of her exclusion from the world organization would *ipso facto* put in doubt any claims that the Charter was the source of the norms she was promoting. The law of the Charter could be invoked as of universal validity under either of two conditions: (a) The CPR gives explicit consent, attributing an *opinio juris* to the provisions of the Charter; (b) She considers that the law embodied in the Charter only codifies principles and norms already in existence outside and independently of the Charter itself. Chou's repeated references to customary international law appears designed to establish the validity of the Five Principles as a body of peremptory norms which exist in their own right. His invocation of principles and norms embodied in unratified treaties may be seen in the same light.

Chou Keng-sheng's views are representative of many other mainland Chinese jurists,[39] but he was among the first to air them. The importance of his writing is twofold: First, he does not see the Five Principles of Peaceful Coexistence as a revolutionary innovation in international law. Secondly, his views were advanced back in 1955, one year before the Soviet Union officially endorsed the doctrine of peaceful coexistence. More important, Soviet theory in 1955 was still ambivalent on how claims of the universality of contemporary international law could be sustained in the absence of explicit agreement between states of different ideologies. Chou Keng-sheng bypassed the "agreement" dilemma and based his universality claims for the Five Principles on fundamental principles well established in customary international law, which presumptively transcend ideological and temporal differences.

In agreement with Chou, other mainland Chinese commentators have likewise claimed that "modern" international law is based on peaceful coexistence "among *all* states." At the same time they have insisted that only the "imperialists" have resisted and attempted to sabotage peaceful coexistence—a notion which in more recent years became a convenient excuse for denying peaceful coexistence to the "imperialists." [40] The word "modern" associated with the law of peaceful coexistence, as it is used in CPR literature, seems to suggest a *continuum* advancing from the traditional to the contemporary and anticipating the future. Mainland Chinese writers have claimed that "the reason why the Five Principles of Peaceful Coexistence have touched the [world's] people to their heart is precisely that they are compatible with the *historical trends* of our time." [41] It has also been stated that:

the Five Principles of Peaceful Coexistence have *replaced* many of the old, corrupt precepts of international law which have until now served the interests of imperialism; and they have become *new contents* of international law.[42]

Any norm not compatible with the "new contents" is either considered to have been replaced or to be on its way to oblivion. Reasoning in accordance with this continuum concept CPR writers have expressed confidence that modern international law is on the side of the socialist and anti-"imperialist" states.[43]

Semantics over Peaceful Coexistence

A prevailing impression gained from the post-1960 polemic exchanges between the Chinese Communist Party (CCP) and the Communist Party of the Soviet Union (CPSU) is that Peking is now opposed to peaceful coexistence. One Western analyst has suggested that the CCP "in its letter of June 14, 1963, attacked the policy of peaceful coexistence as a departure from revolutionary struggle, the true Marxist-Leninist path to world Communism." [44] Because of the great significance of the subject matter involved, we shall re-examine the CCP's letter of June 14, 1963, officially known as the "Sixth Comment on the 'Open Letter' of the CPSU." A careful reading of the document reveals a subtle threefold differentiation between states currently existing in the world: (a) socialist and capitalist; (b) nationalist and "imperialist"; and (c) "ordinary capitalist" and "imperialist" states.[45]

The purpose of the fine differentiation is to define that peaceful coexistence is applicable to all states but the "imperialist" group. Yet, the denial to the latter is not absolute. Under conditions favorable to the cause of socialism, the CCP document admits, "it is possible for socialist countries to compel one *imperialist* country or another to establish some sort of *peaceful coexistence*. . . ." But, so long as the "imperialists" persist in "policies of aggression and war," the CCP is bound by a "proletarian internationalist duty" to support the "national liberation movements" against "imperialism" throughout the world.[46] The CCP statement hastens to add that Peking *"perseveres* in peaceful coexistence with countries having different social systems." [47]

A few subtle points emerge from this semantic jugglery: First, the mention of a "proletarian internationalist duty" seems designed to needle the CPSU into acknowledging its "betrayal" of the cause of world Communism due to Moscow's bridge-building with the United States. Second, the denial of peaceful coexistence to the "imperialists" in the current situation is justified by the latter's policy of "aggression and war." Third, exceptions can nevertheless be made to extend peaceful coexistence to the "imperialists," but only to the extent that the interests of the socialist countries will not be jeopardized. Fourth, waging the "national liberation movements" against the "imperialists" means a suspension of peaceful coexistence justified by the latter's provocation. Last but not least, the suspension does not mean that the CCP leadership abandons its policy of "persevering" in peaceful coexistence with countries of different social systems.

Although its dual policy of pursuing peaceful coexistence with all other states but pressing continued struggle with the "imperialists" became all the more pronounced in the 1960s, Peking did not renounce peaceful coexistence as a whole. Nor did it advocate blind provocation in dealing with the United States. Instead, the Chinese attack was aimed at the Soviet brand of peaceful coexistence. Thus Wu Te-feng, president of the Chinese Association of Political Science and Law, had the following condemnation of the Soviet-United States' collusion practiced in the name of peaceful coexistence:

> Imperialism is the basic cause of modern war, and American imperialism, moreover, is the most ferocious and ambitious aggressor ever to exist in the history of mankind; and it is the most flagrant violator of the principles of modern international law. . . . However, modern revisionists never cease to make efforts to propagandize the practice of "peaceful coexistence" *with the imperialists* without any concern for principles, to spread the view that contemporary international law is

[this kind of] "law of peaceful coexistence," and to promote "full cooperation" with the American imperialists.[48]

Since the "true" international law of peaceful coexistence represents the aspirations of the majority of the peoples in "modern times," [49] its application must not undercut the realization of those aspirations, which are, according to Peking, essentially expressed in self-determination and anti-"imperialism." [50] So far as Peking is concerned, the applicability of peaceful coexistence will wane or wax in direct proportion to the degree of a given state's relative affinity with these aspirations.

To recapitulate, it is important to note that in Peking's usage peaceful coexistence always presupposes the existence of a sizable third camp of uncommitted countries, as well as the contention between the socialist and the "imperialist" camps. In the 1950s, peaceful coexistence was employed to break Peking's international isolation by cultivating friendship with the third camp. Increasingly in the 1960s the doctrine became the nexus of Peking's efforts to promote an "international united front" designed to encircle and isolate the United States.[51] As the Sino-Soviet feud deepened, the CPR conceived of itself as the head of a growing third bloc, within which the law of peaceful coexistence would continue to develop.[52] Here is a major difference with the Soviet concept of peaceful coexistence, which focuses on bipolarity and sees peaceful coexistence as mainly designed to apply between the socialist and the "imperialist" blocs. As for Peking, on the other hand, the "imperialists" never received more than peripheral considerations in the application of peaceful coexistence. Before we leave the present discussion, it may be pointed out that peaceful coexistence in CPR theory does have something in common with the Soviet concept in the negative sense. First of all, peaceful coexistence does not include arbitral or judicial determination of legal issues between states, as we have already noted. Secondly, peaceful coexistence does not *ipso facto* condemn war as such. National liberation wars or revolutionary civil wars have never been considered on the same footing as wars between states; only the latter is outlawed. In practice, Moscow and Peking may differ over the role and importance to be assigned to a given war of national liberation. But in theory they both accept this kind of war as just and legitimate. Thirdly, peaceful coexistence does not extend to the sphere of ideology, in which the class struggle continues, although Peking has stronger feelings about this than Moscow.[53]

III

Peaceful Coexistence and Proletarian Internationalism: Sino-Soviet Divergencies

LIKE THE Soviet Union, the CPR considers peaceful coexistence (PCX) and proletarian internationalism (PI) as the two most fundamental principles of contemporary international law. But she differs with the Soviet Union not only over the juridical basis of the two principles [1] but also over the specific extent of their applicability. Although to both countries international law is an adjunct of foreign policy, the policy needs behind Peking's endorsement of PCX and PI have always been different from those of Moscow. Since its policy needs have changed in the two decades since 1949, Peking's views regarding the two cardinal doctrines have also changed significantly. To assume a static view here, one would fail to understand the changing import of PCX and PI in different stages and would totally miss the interplay of law and policy. In a large sense, the specific interpretations and emphases which the two precepts received in any given stage reflected closely Peking's triangular relationships with Moscow and Washington.

In this chapter we shall review the significance and implications of the CPR's changing views in light of her evolving policy needs, and in comparison with those of the Soviet Union. Before we proceed any further, it may be appropriate to deal in brief with the evolution of Soviet views on the content of contemporary international law.

Soviet Views on Contemporary International Law

In the half century of its existence official views of the Soviet Union have gone through a few distinct stages of evolution. The early debate between Korovin (who in 1924 advocated the *separate* existence of a socialist system of international law) and Pashukanis and Vyshinsky (both attacked Korovin for his negation of a general international law) had fallen into a long period of quietude until 1948. In that year and again in 1951, Kozhevnikov brought back the once controversial view of a "socialist international law in the making." Between 1952 and 1954, however, this view was again discredited, although Korovin in 1954 alluded to the coexistence of socialist and general international law. From thereon the trend seemed to be in favor of a contemporary, general international law. But the position did not crystallize until after the Twentieth Party Congress, that is, after Stalinism had been debunked in doctrine. So far as its world view is concerned, Stalianism (at least in the earlier years) dichotomized two hostile camps, presupposing two separate systems of law. The alleged bipolar hostility had dramatized the need for bloc solidarity and had given Stalin a justification for the subordination of other socialist countries and parties to the primacy of Moscow. The denunciation of Stalinism in 1956 helped to absolve the dichotomy view, paving the way for the theory of a single body of international law.[2]

Between 1956 and 1958, however, Soviet literature was still ambivalent over the question whether the universality of this single body of general international law was founded on peaceful coexistence or proletarian internationalism. The dilemma arose from Soviet ideological orientation toward aloofness and a simultaneous desire to claim "socialist" contribution to the making of a new international law. In 1956, two years after the Chou-Nehru declaration of the Five Principles, Moscow pronounced PCX to be the hard core of its foreign policy. Soviet jurists began to modify the earlier standard definition of international law, to rid it of the imprint of Stalin and Vyshinsky's emphasis upon class struggle and use of force in international relations. But, PCX was not to apply to international relations within the socialist bloc. Furthermore, Soviet writers have long held the view that "agreements of states" are the principal source of international law. If PCX constituted the bulk of the new international law, "it cannot be socialist," as Tunkin pointed out, "since agreement on this basis is impossible between socialist and capitalist countries." [3] On the other hand, if the Soviets were to claim that proletarian internationalism, rather than PCX, had bridged the gulfs and made the new international law universal, then a different problem immediately arose. For, this claim would mock the Soviet assertion that PI was a "higher type" of international relations known only to socialist countries.[4]

Obviously aware of the dilemma, Korovin attempted to show that certain attributes of the new international law had developed along parallel lines to PI under the impact of the practice of socialist states. In other words, under the Soviet impact not only was a new framework of international relations instituted within the socialist bloc but also there emerged a *parallel* set of norms in general international relations. The implicit theory of parallel development thus bypassed the "agreement" hitch. The same "impact" view (as distinct from "agreement") was repeated by Tunkin in an introductory article to the *Soviet Yearbook of International Law* in 1959. However, Tunkin did not give as much prominence as Korovin did to the universality of PI, which for him, as for most other Soviet jurists, continued to govern relations exclusively within the socialist bloc. Instead, he shifted emphasis to PCX and described contemporary international law as a new law of the peaceful coexistence of states with opposing social systems. "With the appearance and strengthening of the socialist camp," Tunkin declared:

[The] development of international law *reflects* the increasing *influence* of the countries of *socialism*. The decisive superiority of the forces of peace and progress against the force of reaction and war, which will be the result of the economic successes of the Soviet Union and the other socialist countries and also the growth of the *forces of peace everywhere,* will also have a significiant *impact* on the future development of international law.[5] (Emphasis added)

Two underlying thoughts emerged between the lines: First, following the impact view, the new general international law of PCX by and large was a reflection of the influence of socialist forces. Secondly, the socialist countries shared the credit for the making of the new international law with the "forces of peace everywhere," which were already growing rapidly in 1959. Tunkin's explicit acknowledgement of the emerging third world suggests a new evaluation of world forces that departed from the early Stalinist dichotomy of two hostile camps.

With this re-evaluation, the once persistent theory that international law consisted in "struggle and cooperation"—which Tunkin adhered to as late as 1962—also began to evaporate. In a new definition of current international law, given in 1964 by the Soviet Institute of International Relations, the reference to "struggle and cooperation" was dropped. "Contemporary international law," it was stated:

has as its *principal content* the generally recognized principles and norms designed to regulate the most varied relations of sovereign wills between the subjects of international community on the basis and for the purpose of effectively securing international peace, and above all *peaceful coexistence* in some cases and *socialist internationalism* in others.

The degree and forms of such securing are determined by the very character of the given international legal order. Under the conditions of peaceful coexistence, the element of *coercion is greatly limited, but not excluded.* In the world system of socialism, all legal principles and norms, being based on socialist internationalism and therefore having a fundamentally different content, are invariably observed, and their securing is subordinated to this content.[6] (Emphasis added)

The qualitative difference between PCX and PI was maintained, but presumptively their contents could overlap and run parallel to each other. Furthermore, given the optimism imparted by their ideology, Soviet commentators seemed to believe that, although the current general international law was mainly conceived in the principles of PCX, its content would increasingly become more "progressive" and "democratic" as it acquired the "new spirit" of socialist internationalism practiced among socialist nations.[7] It is plain that the separateness of PCX and PI and the characterization of PI as a body of new socialist principles posed a dual challenge to the universality claims of the new general international law which is allegedly derived from these very principles. Soviet jurists were not unaware of the contradiction.[8] But, very possibly, the suggestion that the current international law, the equivalent of PCX, would become more progressive after the image of PI was offered as a solution to the contradiction. Furthermore, as the Soviets did not initiate, but merely adopted, the Five Principles of PCX, their insistence on the potential (although indirect) influence of socialist internationalism would reserve a ground for Soviet claims of contribution to the future development of general international law.

A number of points in the Soviet theory beyond 1964 are noteworthy. First, peaceful coexistence is a necessary product of the Soviet-United States nuclear stalemate, which has greatly curtailed the frequency of coercion while limiting its permissibility to the subnuclear level. Disagreeing with the Chinese, the Soviets insist that PCX is especially reserved for relations between socialist and capitalist countries. A corollary is that the law of PCX operates differently in relations between socialist and newly independent, nonaligned states—both sharing a community of interests in peace and socialism—from those between capitalist states *inter se* and between capitalist and socialist states.[9] Much uncertainty remains as to the specific ways in which PCX operates in these different groupings.

Secondly, the Soviets have been seeking codification of the law of PCX in various international forums, although its content still lacks definitive formulation. Unlike the Chinese, who appear to fall back on *jus cogens* or the concept of *ordre public,* the Soviets claim that near universal adherence to the Charter of the United Nations signifies a wide agreement by most countries on the acceptance of PCX. Codification is seen as a necessary step forward from this general endorsement.[10]

Thirdly, while socialist internationalism remains a "higher type" of law currently followed by socialist countries in their mutual relations, its observance *ipso facto* includes compliance with the lesser requirements of peaceful coexistence.[11]

Fourthly, although socialist internationalism has been interpreted to include "fraternal friendship, close collaboration, and mutual assistance," [12] it is never supposed to support the national interests of any individual socialist country over and above the "common interest" of the bloc as interpreted by Moscow. In fact, it has been openly suggested that "national interests, on occasion . . . be subordinated to the more important, international interests of the whole socialist commonwealth." [13]

And, lastly, until the World Conference of Communist Parties in June, 1969,[14] the harshness of anti-"imperialist" polemics was toned down, as new emphasis was given to peaceful competition. Between 1961 and the time of Khrushchev's downfall in 1964, the Soviet position was deliberately vague on whether peaceful coexistence debarred aids to wars of national liberation. Although Moscow never denied that such aids were legitimate, it did not go as far as Peking in advocating them in public.[15]

Does PCX Apply to Relations Between Socialist States?

Soon after its official pronouncement of PCX as the blueprint for all international relations in 1954, the CPR seemed to have attempted to make the Soviet Union accept the Five Principles as equally applicable within the socialist camp. If the Chinese were attempting to modify the existing framework built on proletarian internationalism, which sanctioned Soviet primacy, the motive was characteristic of Peking's aspirations in 1954–1956 to assert greater autonomy. In order to help us better assess the Chinese rethinking about Sino-Soviet relations in the period immediately after the death of Stalin, we shall examine briefly the status of those relations during the time.

Sino-Soviet Relations in 1954 Re-Examined

The earliest date of the conflicts between the two erstwhile Communist allies has often been given at 1957. But with the advantage of hindsight, the year 1954 was probably a better watershed. If this point can be sustained, then the timing of the CPR's proponency of PCX in the same year would have a new significance not understood heretofore. I have dealt with this question elsewhere,[16] and revelations during the Cultural Revolution (1966–1968) seem to support my view. We have of late learned from remarks attributed to Mao Tse-tung that in 1950 the CPR was impelled to intervene in the Korean War, because there was a strategic necessity to convince Stalin that Communist China would not follow the road of Titoism.[17] The surrounding circumstances and the aftermath of this historic episode appear, in retrospect, to have been the genesis of subsequent Chinese hostility toward the Soviet Union.

The CPR's intervention in Korea was apparently not anticipated by Mao himself at the Third Plenum of the Seventh Central Committee in the early part of June, 1950. Its entry in the war four months later deprived Peking of a golden chance to take Taiwan by force as had been planned. From their point of view, the Communist Chinese had every good reason to expect Soviet *quid pro quo* when they launched their campaign to "liberate" Taiwan in 1954. The laggard Soviet response aroused serious resentment in Peking.[18]

Mao already had had many grudges against the Soviet "Big Brothers." In July, 1949, Moscow signed a trade agreement directly with Kao Kang, the party boss in Manchuria, who headed a regional delegation to the Soviet Union. The deal was sufficient to arouse Mao's suspicion of Soviet interference in China's internal affairs. It was an open secret that Soviet relations with regional forces on the Chinese side of the Sino-Soviet border were of grave concern to Peking, and they constituted a central subject in Peking's talks with Moscow between 1950 and 1954.[19]

In May, 1950, the People's Government of the Inner Mongolian Autonomous Region had to be moved to Chang-chia-k'ou from Huhehot, where an allegedly Soviet-supported "Inner Mongolia

People's Revolutionary Party" was reported to be active and to be gaining strength.[20] Other sources of tension can be found in the long delays in the Soviet return of Port Arthur to Chinese jurisdiction, and Soviet direct control of the joint stock companies in China. The Politburo of the CCP in December, 1953, issued a call for "strengthening the Party's unity." Four months later, in February, 1954, Peking officially outlawed the "Inner Mongolian People's Revolutionary Party," apparently because of its secret ties with the Soviets.[21] Kao Kang was purged in the same year, along with Jao Shu-shih, the organization chief of the CCP. As part of its drive to eliminate "independent kingdoms" vulnerable to possible outside interference, Peking in 1954 abolished the six large administrative regions that had intervened between Peking and the various provinces.

During Khrushchev and Bulganin's trip to Peking in October, 1954, Mao even demanded that the two countries renegotiate the status of Outer Mongolia, formerly part of Imperial China's domains but independent since 1945 as a result of Soviet interference.[22] (Maps claiming Chinese territories lost to Czarist Russia began to appear in Chinese textbooks in 1954.[23]) Some of the agreements reached during Khruschev's visit were clearly concessions and other enticements to placate Mao. Among other things, Khrushchev agreed to the final withdrawal of Soviet troops from Port Arthur and the transfer of Sino-Soviet joint stock companies to Chinese ownership and jurisdiction. The latter measure meant, among other things, the termination of Soviet rights of exploiting uranium and other rare metals in Sinkiang province. As inducements, the Soviet Union promised long-term loans and assistance for the installation of industrial plants in China, a Sino-Soviet scientific-technical cooperation agreement, and Soviet assistance for the construction of railways linking the strategic Lanchow with Urumchi of Sinkiang, and Chining with Ulan Bator, capital of Outer Mongolia.[24]

The Soviet conciliatory gestures were only partially satisfactory to the Chinese, who were resentful of Soviet insistence that they must repay the aid extended during the Korean War. For what it may be worth, the first CPR loan ever granted to a foreign country was extended to Albania, on December 3, 1954, less than two months after Khrushchev's Peking visit.[25] Prolonged Sino-Soviet negotiations over the specific terms of Soviet assistance were conceivably responsible for the long delay in the finalization of Peking's First Five-Year Plan. Although officially launched in 1953, the plan's details were not formulated and announced until mid-1955.

This rather spotty list of possible areas of Sino-Soviet tension in 1954 is sufficient to raise the question whether the earliest date of the Sino-Soviet conflict should not be pushed back from 1957 to 1954. With this background in view, it will be easier to appreciate why Peking attempted in 1954–1956 to substitute PCX for the more authoritarian PI in the international relations between socialist countries, especially between the CPR and the Soviet Union.

PCX in Peking's Struggle for Greater Autonomy

At the end of Mao's 1954 talks with Khrushchev, a joint declaration was issued, which, when viewed from the vantage point of the late 1960's, was rather revealing of the possible tussle that had transpired. Under the title "Sino-Soviet Joint Declaration on Various Questions Concerning the International Situation," the two sides stated their positions in following terms:

> The Governments of the two countries deem it necessary to declare that the People's Republic of China and the Union of Soviet Socialist Republics will continue to build their relations with countries in Asia and the Pacific region and other countries on the basis of a strict observance of the principles of *mutual respect for each other's sovereignty and territorial integrity, mutual non-aggression, mutual non-interference in each other's internal affairs, equality and mutual benefit,* and *peaceful coexistence. . . .*[26] (Emphasis added)
>
> The Governments [of the two countries] declare that the friendly relations already in existence between the two countries will be the basis for further cooperation between them in accordance with the principles of *equality, mutual benefit,* and *mutual respect for sovereignty and territorial integrity.*[27] (Emphasis added)

Although the Five Principles of PCX were given a blanket endorsement, on closer examination the following points become clear:

First, PCX was to apply only to relations with "countries in Asia and the Pacific and other countries," but not between the CPR and the Soviet Union. Secondly, Sino-Soviet relations were to be built on the basis of a different set of principles, namely, "equality, mutual benefit, and mutual respect for sovereignty and territorial integrity." These formed the triad laid down by Mao in 1949 as the cornerstone of China's foreign relations with *all* countries willing to reciprocate. It is puzzling why this triad was singled out in 1954 as the guideline for relations between the two Communist allies. Furthermore, the wording in the second passage quoted above is very tricky. It stated that the existing "friendly relations" between Peking and Moscow would be the "basis for further cooperation" in accordance with Mao's 1949 triad. Thus, pending the promised "further cooperation," Sino-Soviet relations in 1954 were not as yet up to the level envisaged by the triad. Could it be a circumspect way of admitting that thus far the CPR had been a lesser partner and bound to Soviet hegemony under the hierarchical ties forged in the Stalinist era (proletarian internationalism)?

One can only speculate as to whether Mao had attempted to inject greater equality into China's relations with the Soviet Union. But, it is clear that the Mao-Khruschev declaration omitted any mention of proletarian internationalism. The omission is significant in view of the fact that Moscow's relations with other "people's democracies" in Eastern Europe continued, beyond 1954, to be bound by the dicates of proletarian internationalism, as evidenced in Soviet bilateral treaties with them [28] and in the Warsaw Treaty.[29] Although CPR literature made references to proletarian internationalism, Chinese jurists took pains to stress that the principle did not submerge the national interests of individual Communist countries. They often attempted to insinuate a Soviet obligation, under the principle of PI, to aid less developed socialist nations (China included). Wei Liang, writing during this period, put forward the Chinese view with great subtlety:

> The socialist countries base their relations on the principles of complete equality, respect for one another's territorial integrity, respect for independence and sovereignty, and mutual non-interference in domestic affairs; and make mutual assistance an inalienable part of their relations

with one another. These relations of *mutual assistance* are a manifestation of proletarian internationalism.[30] (Emphasis added)

Not until 1956 did it become known that the CPR had advocated the adoption of PCX within the socialist orbit as well as outside it. If Mao had urged its adoption during Khrushchev's 1954 visit in Peking, the latter's rejection would be a foregone conclusion. The Soviet leader could have even insisted that the injection of PCX would debase the character of the relations between socialist countries, which should be governed by PI. The final separate endorsement of PCX in general (i.e., outside the socialist camp) and of Mao's 1949 triad for Sino-Soviet relations was probably a compromise, thus steering clear of both PCX and PI so far as bloc relations were concerned.

Despite the Mao-Khrushchev declaration of 1954, the Soviet government did not officially embrace the Five Principles of PCX until 1956. In his report to the Twentieth Party Congress of CPSU, in February that year, Khrushchev gave special credit to the CPR and India for having advanced the Five Principles as the "foundation of peaceful relations among all countries in all parts of the world." But he made it plain that PCX was to apply "between the two systems," without mentioning intrabloc relations.[31] After the outbreak of the Hungarian and Polish revolutions, however, the Soviet government on October 30, 1956, issued a statement entitled: "The Foundations of the Development and Further Consolidation of Friendship and Cooperation between the Soviet Union and Other Socialist States." In this historic document, Moscow conceded grave errors in its relations with other socialist states, promised amends, and called for the transformation of the Communist orbit into a commonwealth of socialist nations. The statement even pledged that "the Soviet Government is ready to discuss, together with the governments of other socialist states, measures . . . to remove the possibilities of violating the principle of national sovereignty and . . . equality." [32]

In this conciliatory move to play down Soviet supremacy, the Soviet statement declared:

The principle of *peaceful coexistence,* friendship, and cooperation among *all* states has always been and still is the unshakable foundation of the foreign relations of the U.S.S.R. This policy finds its most profound and *consistent expression* in relations with the *socialist countries*. United by the common ideal of building a socialist society and the principles of *proletarian internationalism,* the countries of the great commonwealth of socialist nations can build their relations *only* on the principle of full equality, respect for territorial integrity, state independence and sovereignty, and non-interference in one another's domestic affairs.[33] (Emphasis added)

The elevation of PCX and the redefinition of PI went hand in hand, as Moscow sought to reassure other socialist states, those in Eastern Europe especially, that it would pay greater respect to the latter's national aspirations. Although the statement did not directly admit that PCX was equally applicable to bloc relations, the acknowledgement that the policy of PCX "finds its most profound and consistent expression in [Soviet] relations with socialist countries" came very close to that position.

The CPR immediately commented on the Soviet statement of October 30, 1956. Seizing upon the *prima facie* Soviet enthusiasm for the universal application of PCX, the CPR government on November 1, 1956, issued the following statement:

The People's Republic of China *has always believed* [yi-hsiang jen-wei] that the Five Principles of mutual respect for sovereignty and territorial integrity, mutual non-aggression, mutual non-interference in internal affairs, equality and mutual benefit, and peaceful coexistence should become the uniform norms [chun-tse] for the establishment and development of mutual relations between all nations in the world. Socialist countries are all independent and sovereign nations and at the same time bound together by the common ideal of socialism and the spirit of proletarian internationalism. For this reason, *inter-relations between socialist nations should all the more be structured on the basis of the Five Principles.* Only in this way can socialist nations bring about brotherly friendship and unity and realize their common aspirations for economic advancement through mutual cooperation.[34] (Emphasis added)

Significantly, the CPR claimed that it always believed that PCX was universally applicable, all the more so within the socialist camp. The admission seems to substantiate our suspicion that during the 1954 Mao-Khrushchev talks Peking might have attempted to divest Sino-Soviet relations of their hierarchical attributes (PI) and redefine them within the PCX framework, which anticipated greater equality and mutuality. Also worthy of note is the insistence in the same Chinese comment that true mutual cooperation between socialist countries could materialize only when they accommodate each other in accordance with the principles of PCX.

After stating its agreement with the Soviet admission that relations between socialist countries were "not without mistakes," the CPR comment described as legitimate the Polish and Hungarian aspirations for democracy, independence and equality, and for enhanced material well-being. At the same time, it warned that a careful distinction must be made between "legitimate demands of the greatest majority of the people" and the "conspiratorial activities of an extremely small number of counterrevolutionaries." The CPR statement then plunged into a poignant condemnation of "big-nation chauvinism":

> Certain functionaries [kung-tso jen-yüan] in the socialist countries, because of the unanimity in their ideological structure and the aim of struggle, are often apt to *neglect the principle of equality* in the mutual relations between these countries. By nature this is a mistake of bourgeois chauvinism. Such a mistake, especially one of *big-nation chauvinism,* cannot but bring harmful effects to the unity and common cause of the socialist nations. . . . We must ceaselessly educate our functionaries and people to be resolutely opposed to big-nation chauvinism. If this kind of mistake has been found, it must be promptly corrected. This is a duty to which we must devote our utmost attention in order to strive for *peaceful coexistence with all nations* and to promote the cause of world peace.[35] (Emphasis added)

Big-nation chauvinism, ascribed to the Soviet stance, was thus seen as standing in the way of true equality between socialist states and "peaceful coexistence with all nations." Although the CPR continued to pay lip service to proletarian internationalism, the unveiled attack on big-nation chauvinism signified a redefinition of PI along the lines of mutual (horizontal) accommodation. It may be concluded, therefore, that between 1954 and 1956 the CPR attempted to modify the structure of intrabloc relations by relaxing the strait jacket of PI, inherited from the Stalinist era, and by injecting the principles of PCX within the bloc.

Impact of Changing Events on Peking's Views

1957–1961: PI Briefly Restressed

In less than two months following its November 1, 1956, statement, Peking moved slightly back toward supporting bloc unity, but did not abandon its criticisms of big-nation chauvinism.[36] On December 29 the official *People's Daily* published a long statement, described as a summary of discussions held in the CCP Politburo. Presumably cleared beforehand with Moscow, the document was immediately reproduced in full by the Soviet press. Among other things the Chinese statement condemned the extremes of both Stalinism and Titoism, but restressed Soviet leadership under the principle of PI. The shift underlined Peking's new role as the mediator in intrabloc conflicts. Largely on the basis of the new ideological framework outlined by the Chinese, the torn fabric of Eastern European Communism was mended in the early months of 1957.[37]

On his Eastern European swing in early 1957, Chou En-lai held talks with other top Communist leaders and signed a number of joint communiqués.[38] In these communiqués the following principles were set forth for regulating international relations: (a) In international life, peaceful coexistence should be followed. (b) Relations between socialist states should be built on the basis of proletarian internationalism and unity of ideology and goals. (c) As independent and sovereign states in their own right, the socialist countries should build their mutual relations upon the principles of respect for each other's sovereignty, mutual noninterference in internal affairs, and equality and mutual benefit.[39] In the Sino-Soviet joint statement, which Chou signed with Bulganin on January 18, "big-nation chauvinism, narrow nationalist sentiments, and residual misunderstanding between nations" were linked to "imperialist" intrigue.[40]

Although Peking exalted PI along with PCX, its position by early 1957 was that PI must not in any way violate the national independence and equality of other socialist countries. But it ceased to insist that PCX must equally apply to intrabloc relations. While PCX was once again reaffirmed as the fundamental principle of general international law, the threats of "imperialism" curtailing the universal application of PCX were repeatedly cited in the joint statements Chou signed. These points suggest a middle ground between Peking's position in 1954–1956 and that of the Soviets before the Eastern European revolts of October, 1956.

At the Moscow Conference of Communist Parties, November 16–19, 1957, Mao Tse-tung strongly supported Soviet leadership of the bloc. He was responsible for having Soviet primacy written into the declaration of the conference: "the socialist camp headed by the Soviet Union." [41] The emphasis on Soviet bloc leadership was a reversal of Chinese policy during 1956–1957 toward true equality of bloc relations, much to the chagrin of Gomulka and Kadar. Gomulka, the Polish leader, was reported to have reproached Mao with advocating Soviet leadership in exchange for Soviet economic and military aid.[42] Later revelations confirmed this point.

In 1958 Peking demanded samples of atomic weapons, but the Soviets refused to supply any.[43] Mao probably raised the question again during Khrushchev's second visit in Peking during the summer of that year. It is generally believed that the negotiations were bogged down by Soviet insistence on the retention of Soviet control of the warheads supplied, some measures of joint planning and joint command in the Far East, and Chinese assurances that no independent military initiatives would be taken over Taiwan.[44] Later Chinese claims that Moscow in 1958 put forward "unreasonable demands designed to bring China under [Soviet] military control" [45] were doubtless exaggerated. But it is clear that the question of nuclear sharing turned the focus back on the issue of equality and mutual assistance between Peking and Moscow. A joint communiqué issued on August 3, at the end of the Mao-Khrushchev talks, restressed that "countries of differing social systems must observe peaceful coexistence" and that Sino-Soviet relations were built upon the basis of *full equality* and *comradely mutual assistance.*" [46] Again, proletarian internationalism was not mentioned. Chinese support of Soviet bloc leadership, therefore, did not mean that their own relations with Moscow were to remain within the erstwhile hegemonial framework clamped down by Stalin. The Chinese lip service was either offered to salvage bloc unity, in the face of Eastern European unrest in 1956, or was used by Peking to bargain for more generous Soviet assistance.

In any event, Mao's brief re-endorsement of Soviet primacy within the bloc was part of a compromise reached with the Soviet leaders at the Moscow meeting in November, 1957. The final declaration reflected this compromise. It endorsed the Soviet view that "at present the forces of peace have so grown that there is a real possibility of averting wars . . ." and claimed that these powerful forces "can prevent the outbreak of war." On the other hand, it also stated that "so long as imperialism exists there will always be soil for aggressive wars," and that if the "imperialist maniacs" unleashed a war it would be doomed to destruction.[47] Pending the further deterioration of the Sino-Soviet split, the Chinese were ready to put up with the Soviet policy of "peaceful competition" with the United States.

Events between 1958 and 1963 were extremely critical in Sino-Soviet relations and were responsible for reshaping their respective views regarding PI and PCX. While PI lay dormant in Sino-Soviet relations during this period, the two countries' views on the application of PCX began to diverge drastically. Soviet response to the 1958 Taiwan crisis was far from satisfactory to Peking.[48] Chinese resentment and distrust brought the Sino-Soviet feud to the open. According to subsequent Chinese charges, Moscow, in June, 1959, "unilaterally tore up" the Sino-Soviet "agreement on new technology for national defense" concluded in October, 1957.[49] On August 3, 1959, it was announced that Khrushchev would meet with President Eisenhower in the United States. Almost simultaneously, Marshall P'eng Te-huai, Chinese Minister of Defense and a ranking member of the CCP Politburo, was dismissed. Documents made available during the Cultural Revolution (1966–1968) suggest that P'eng had been in league with Khrushchev against Mao's policies.[50] On August 7, 1957, the Sino-Indian border conflicts flared up. Moscow interpreted the incident as a Chinese device to frustrate the Khrushchev-Eisenhower meeting. After some heated exchange with Peking, the Soviets deplored the border conflict and virtually dissociated themselves from the CPR's actions.[51]

A few years later, Peking was to accuse the Soviet Union of having betrayed proletarian internationalism. But at the second conference of all Communist parties held in Moscow, in November, 1960, the Chinese concentrated their ideological fire on Soviet "big-nation chauvinism" and neglect of its obligations toward other socialist countries and parties.[52] The schism within the bloc was officially acknowledged by Khruschev in a widely publicized speech on January 6, 1961.[53] Proletarian internationalism never again means the same as it once did; and Moscow never again can dictate the law to the international Communist movement as before.

1961–1963: PCX Not Applicable to "Imperialists"

By the Twenty-second Party Congress of the CPSU, in October, 1961, Soviet primacy within the socialist bloc had been dethroned. If the Chinese had attempted to assert their leadership, they also had been rebuffed. The polarization saw the drifting of the Soviet Union toward greater détente with the United States, while allowing the widest latitude of autonomy to other Communist states in their relations with Moscow. The Soviet-United States détente prompted Peking to inject a restrictive interpretation of PCX; its ulterior motive was to avert further Soviet drifting toward the "imperialist" camp. The increasing autonomy of Eastern European states resulted in a *de facto* diminution of proletarian internationalism. Peking's only interest in PI lay in its polemic value. The doctrine could be twisted around to support its arguments why the Soviet Union must live up to its obligations toward the international Communist movement.[54]

The Sino-Indian border conflict and the Cuban missile crisis, both flaring up in October, 1962, had tremendous impact upon the CPR's evaluation of world politics. Despite the border war, Soviet military aid to India continued as before. As if to add insult to injury, Moscow accused Peking of failing to heed the voice of reason.[55] The Cuban missile crisis, on the other hand, showed Peking that Soviet capability of standing up to the nuclear teeth of the "imperialist paper-tiger" was highly dubious. Although it had pledged its support to the Soviet Union during the height of the Cuban crisis, on October 25, the CPR government subsequently accused Moscow of having first committed "adventurism" and then "capitulationism." [56] The two incidents in 1962 pointed up two things for the CPR: (a) that the Soviet Union could not be trusted as an ally for the defense of interests of the socialist countries; and (b) that the "imperialists" must not be handled too timidly or with too much temerity.

Soviet "infidelity" during the 1962 Sino-Indian border war topped a long list of Chinese grudges against the Soviet Union. Peking now recalled Moscow's siding with India during the 1959 border conflict. That act, Peking said, was "the first instance in history in which a socialist country, instead of condemning the armed provocations of the reactionaries of a capitalist country, condemned another fraternal socialist country when it was confronted with such armed provocation." [57] Soviet military aid to India during the 1962 Sino-Indian conflict gave Peking new evidence that Moscow openly "sold out" the interests of another socialist country in order to placate the "U.S. imperialists." As such, the Soviet Union was accused in *People's Daily* of "complete betrayal of proletarian internationalism." [58]

The CPR further recalled Soviet refusal to supply samples of atomic weapons and other nuclear assistance in 1958, insinuating a long-standing Soviet "betrayal of proletarian internationalism." [59] Unrelenting, the Soviets retorted that if the Chinese really had faith in PI they should know that China could always have relied upon Soviet nuclear power for her security. The Chinese endeavor to develop a separate nuclear capability, Moscow added, was motivated by a desire to start military adventures, which would be subversive and detrimental to Soviet interests. In the Soviet view, therefore, the CPR was the one that had rejected proletarian internationalism.[60]

The seriousness of the Sino-Soviet conflict can be seen in the Chinese tirades between 1962 and 1964 that treaties such as those of Aigun, Peking, and Ili signed with Czarist Russia were "unequal treaties" to be abolished and renegotiated.[61] The final open break came in mid-1963, when the treaty on partial nuclear test ban was negotiated and signed in Moscow. The CPR government had "warned" the Soviet Union against any such "deal" with the United States and Britain.[62] After its signing on July 25, the treaty was condemned by Peking as a "dirty fraud." In the first place, the treaty would in no way restrain the "U.S. policies of nuclear war preparation and nuclear blackmail," Peking claimed. Secondly, the central purpose of the treaty was, as Peking viewed it, "to prevent all the threatened peace-loving countries, including China, from increasing their defense capability. . . ." [63] The Test Ban Treaty was thought to be another Soviet sellout of the interests of international Communism.

The anticipated signing of the treaty brought forth a long series of polemic exchanges between the CCP and the CPSU, dealing with a whole range of issues of both domestic and international concern. Of direct relevance to our interest here is whether PCX was to be the "general line" to be followed in the foreign policy of socialist countries, or, to put it in plain language, whether PCX was universally applicable. The CPR now openly claimed that it was wrong for socialist countries to attempt indiscriminately to apply PCX in general international relations. The new CPR doctrine stressed that socialist states must adopt the following measures in their foreign policy: (a) promotion of friendship, mutual assistance, and cooperation with countries in the socialist bloc, under the principle of PI; (b) peaceful coexistence with countries of different social systems in accordance with the Five Principles, but continued struggle against the "imperialist" policies of "aggression and war"; and (c) support of the people's liberation wars of all oppressed peoples.[64]

In a fine differentiation, as we noted in the preceding chapter, PCX was redefined to be applicable to all countries except the "imperialists." [65] In Peking's view, all socialist countries must join hands under the compulsion of a "proletarian internationalist duty," to fight the practicing "imperialists." [66] The new restrictive interpretation of PCX thus went hand in hand with Peking's insistence that the Soviet Union was obligated under PI to look after the interests of other socialist states and to aid people's liberation wars. Just as PI changed its meaning in CPR usage, the import of PCX also turned full cycle. Whereas Peking endorsed PCX in 1954 out of a defensive need to break its own international isolation, the doctrine was turned by Khrushchev in 1954–1963 into a justification for Soviet-United States collaboration; and from 1963 on, Peking jealously guarded PCX as a sacred trust not to be shared with the "imperialists." Increasingly, PCX became an offensive weapon in Peking's foreign policy to encircle and isolate the United States.

1964–1969: Proletarian Internationalism Without the Soviet Union

After 1963 the previous Chinese fear of Soviet primacy was replaced by a new and more gruesome fear—that of Soviet collusion with the United States. Since its attempts in 1961–1963 to persuade a sense of "proletarian international duty" upon the CPSU toward the world Communist cause went nowhere, the CPR gradually shifted toward a new policy of PI that eventually excluded the Soviet Union.

The removal of Khrushchev in 1964 brought a brief lull in Sino-Soviet polemics. Since his successors did not seem to abandon Khrushchev's policies, Peking soon renewed its intense polemic war. Frequently citing Vietnam as evidence of Soviet perfidy, the Chinese maintained that Brezhnev and Kosygin pursued the same "criminal objective of Soviet-United States collaboration for the domination of the world." [67] They also charged that the new Soviet leaders were "pursuing the Khrushchev line of an anti-Chinese alliance with Nehru's successors." [68]

Partly due to Peking's needling and partly because it attempted to rerally bloc unity, Moscow once again restressed the anti-imperialist struggle and called for united action by fraternal socialist countries.[69] The CCP, however, rejected the call for united action out of hand, citing the continued Khrushchevian policies of the Soviet leaders and their collusion with the United States.[70] The Soviet attempt in 1965 to involve the CPR in greater military cooperation to support North Vietnam's war efforts was also given a cold shoulder. Although internal trouble and possible Chinese fear of another Korean-type war could have been in part responsible for Peking's intransigence, it is obvious that the Chinese were suspicious of the intentions behind Moscow's call for bloc unity at this time.[71] For one thing, the very idea of Soviet influence in Vietnam, at the southern gateway to China, was repulsive to a jealous and suspicious Mao. Besides, Peking had reasons to be apprehensive that, given the existing hostility between the two Communist giants, Moscow might use the CPR as a pawn in the Vietnam War, pitting Chinese military sinew against that of the United States.

In any event, Soviet commentaries during the post-1964 era manifested a rearoused interest in proletarian internationalism, reflecting Moscow's concern for bloc unity, which grew in intensity in the face of the centrifugal trends in Eastern Europe.[72] References to people's liberation wars also seemed to become more numerous from 1964 on. More explicitly than during the preceding period, Soviet writers denied that people's liberation wars constituted a form of aggression or unlawful intervention.[73]

The CPR remained adamant. Its policy beyond 1964 sought to undercut Soviet leadership, charging Moscow with "revisionism" and "collusion" with the "imperialists," to undermine the credibility of Soviet promises to defend the military security of its smaller allies, and to isolate the Soviet Union from the underdeveloped states and the revolutionary movements in Latin America, Asia, and Africa.[74] One of the greatest sources of Mao's ire was Soviet covert ties with the domestic "revisionists" in China, if Maoist polemics during the Cultural Revolution are to be trusted.[75] The Soviet intervention in Czechoslovakia in August, 1968, aroused great alarm and distaste in Peking. In an open criticism, Peking attacked the "shameless act" on three grounds: (a) Ideological issues should not be settled by forceful intervention (big-nation chauvinism); (b) Czech "revisionism" was the result of the bad example set by Soviet "revisionism"; and (c) Soviet invasion was no way to safeguard the fruits of socialism; it was not only a violation of proletarian internationalism but was also proof that the Soviet Union intended to establish a new colonial empire.[76]

Implicit in Peking's condemnation was a fear that the Soviet leadership might similarly resort to open intervention in China in a desperate attempt to resolve the Sino-Soviet dispute. The fear was openly aired subsequent to the border clash over Chenpao (Damansky) in March, 1969. The Chinese accused the Soviet Union of "revisionist social-imperialism." [77] The placing of the Soviet Union in the "imperialist" camp was the most dramatic turn in the long polemic war. It paved the way for the final exclusion of the Soviet Union from the socialist camp. The Maoist-controlled 12th Plenum of the Eighth Central Committee of the CCP, in October, 1968, made the exclusion official. A communiqué issued at the end of the Plenum declared that all revolutionary forces must band together in a general "international united front," in the spirit of proletarian internationalism, which would be directed against both the United States "imperialists" and the Soviet "revisionists." [78]

Lin Piao, Mao's heir-designate, outlined the new Maoist foreign policy in his important report to the Ninth Congress of the CCP, on April 1, 1969. Lin reiterated the CPR's foreign-policy goals: (a) to develop relations of friendship, mutual assistance, and cooperation with socialist countries on the principle of PI; (b) to support and assist the revolutionary struggles of all oppressed people and nations; and (c) PCX with countries of different social systems except the "imperialists" practicing "policies of aggression and war." This "proletarian" foreign policy was described as not an expediency but one of long standing.[79]

The bridge between PI and PCX was found in equality and noninterference, which Lin defined as the principles on which "the relations between all countries and between all parties, big or small, must be built." [80] A central principle which ran through the three foreign-policy goals outlined by Lin was independence, which provided the legal basis for the right of a socialist country, such as the CPR, to be "prosperous and powerful," the right of self-determination by all "oppressed" peoples, and their struggle against United States and Soviet "imperialism." [81]

Lin Piao read the Soviet Union off the camp of "genuine Marxism-Leninism," not only because it "colluded" with the United States but, more important, because Moscow was practicing a new brand of Czarism. Recalling Soviet occupation of Czechoslovakia and the Sino-Soviet border clashes at Chenpao, he accused Moscow of attempting to impose an "international dictatorship" over all other socialist countries. Soviet theory of "limited sovereignty," offered to justify the interests of the "socialist community," was denounced as worse than a plot to whitewash for recent Soviet "aggression and plunder." It was compared to Hitler's "New Order of Europe," the "Great East Asia Co-Prosperity Sphere of Japanese Militarism," and the "Free World Community of the United States." [82]

In short, Soviet collaboration with the United States was considered by the CPR as a rape of PCX; and Soviet practice of "international dictatorship," a total destruction of PI.[83] The exclusion of the Soviet Union from the bailiwick of both PCX and PI was made official by Peking.

In November, 1968, it was briefly reported that the CPR, in approaching Washington for resuming the suspended CPR-United States Warsaw talks, had vaguely proposed a pact on PCX with the United States.[84] Although the scheduled resumption of the talks for February 20, 1969, was later postponed, the very suggestion coming from the CPR about a pact of peaceful coexistence with the United States is food for thought. It appears that Peking was contemplating once again the use of PCX as a shield against possible encroachments on its interests that might result from Soviet-United States collaboration and as a necessary step to keep that collaboration in checks. If so, then PCX has landed where it once was in 1954, turning a complete cycle from defensive (1954–1963) to offensive (1963–1968) back to defensive again.

On the other hand, the Soviets at the World Conference of Communist Parties, in June, 1969, ostensibly skipped PCX, whipped up a renewed blistering attack on "imperialism," and attempted to justify their use of troops in Czechoslovakia under an expanded principle of proletarian internationalism.[85] Although the new anti-"imperialist" mood probably reflected a Soviet desire to consolidate bloc unity and to answer Chinese charges, the invocation of PI in the given circumstances recalled its erstwhile Stalinist connotations. In this light, the Soviet position on PI also has turned a complete cycle, returning to what it once was before 1954.

It may be concluded therefore that PCX and PI have always served the policy needs of Communist China as well as the Soviet Union, that the evolving meanings of the two doctrines have always followed the changing policy needs of the decision-makers, and that Sino-Soviet divergencies over the application of the two doctrines have always reflected deeper divergencies in policy. It would be simply impossible to understand correctly the significance of peaceful coexistence and proletarian internationalism—two fundamental principles of "modern" international law endorsed by both the CPR and the Soviet Union—outside this interplay of law and policy (which encompasses ideology and polemics).

IV

Sovereignty, Self-determination, and Equality

IN ADDITION to peaceful coexistence, CPR doctrine endorses absolute sovereignty, self-determination, and true equality as among the foremost principles of contemporary international law. CPR attitudes on these issues reflect both Soviet influence and China's own experience in modern history.

Illimitable Sovereignty

The traditional Soviet view that sovereignty is "the keystone of international law" and illimitable [1] is generally followed in Communist China. Like the Soviet Union, the CPR has used sovereignty both as a shield to protect her interests from interference by "imperialist" states and as a sword in her struggle with such states. Given their Marxist belief that any state is but a dictatorship by the ruling class, state sovereignty is considered by CPR writers to be a ploy originally used by "capitalist jurists" to conceal the class character of states. Nevertheless, in order to combat capitalist encroachments, they have endorsed state sovereignty for its utility. Thus sovereignty is viewed as the "core" of all fundamental principles of international law, such as noninterference, mutual nonaggression, equality and mutual benefit, etc. It is, furthermore, the legal foundation on which are based many institutions and norms of international law, including peaceful settlement of disputes, the binding force of treaties, and diplomatic privileges and immunities.[2]

In expounding the inviolability of sovereign independence, CPR jurists assert that "imperialists" have employed a full complement of "disguises" to cover up their acts of intervention and aggression. Among these "disguises" are:

a) the establishment of a puppet regime (e.g., the "Manchukuo"); [3]
b) the use of "mutual defense" pacts (e.g., United States treaty with Nationalist China) as a pretext for military occupation or acquiring foreign bases; [4]
c) the doctrine of "protecting nationals abroad" (e.g., United States and British warships' bombardment of Nanking in 1927; and Japanese massacre of over 3,000 innocent Chinese in Shantung, including Ts'ai Kung-shih, the Chinese government envoy, in the same year); [5]
d) the maintenance of "balance of power" (hence, the "Open Door Policy"); [6]
e) the gambit of "humanitarianism" (e.g., United States submission of the "Tibet Question" to the U.N. General Assembly).[7]

One can readily see the link between Peking's exaltation of state sovereignty and its yearnings to see China's sovereignty respected by the foreign powers after a century of Western domination.

There are three claims or component elements in the Communist Chinese doctrine: First, violation or infringement of CPR sovereignty by other countries shall not be tolerated. Second, the CPR claims that she is equally committed to respecting the sovereign prerogatives of other states. Third, she will never surrender her own sovereign interests or sell out those of other states in order to come to terms with the "imperialists." [8] By posing as the defender of the sovereignty of other states as well as her own, the CPR has used sovereignty as a sword for attacking the alleged interventions by "imperialist" countries. The following cases have been singled out as blatant violations of the sovereign rights of other states: United States "suppression" of the people's liberation movement in

Indochina, which was traced back to 1947; the Korean War; United States "armed suppression" of the revolutionary movement of the people in South Vietnam and United States "armed intervention" in Laos, which were described as a violation of the 1954 Geneva accords; landing of United States and British forces in Lebanon and Jordan in 1958; the Bay of Pigs invasion of 1961; and United States quarantine of Cuba in 1962.[9]

Although propagandistic motivations are doubtless behind these charges, the strong support which the CPR has given to the principle of sovereignty may also reflect an empathy for other underdeveloped nations which, in her eyes, have been subject to the same fate of "imperialist" domination as China was from 1840 on. The CPR's attempt to regain a status of autonomy from Soviet control after 1954 was already noted in the previous chapter. In 1964, when the Sino-Soviet rift had deteriorated beyond repair, Mao could no longer conceal his grudge against Moscow's pre-1945 intervention in Outer Mongolia, to the total disregard of Chinese sovereign rights in their former dependency. In an interview with a visiting Japanese-Socialist delegation, Mao was quoted as saying:

> In accordance with the Yalta agreement, the Soviet Union, under the pretext of assuring the independence of Mongolia, actually placed the land under its domination.[10]

Peking's resentment against what the Soviets had done to China found a vicarious outburst in its harsh condemnation of the Soviet occupation of Czechoslovakia in 1968.[11]

The incident shed new light on the correlation between a state's power status and its view on sovereignty. In the early years of its existence the Soviet Union had sought to build a legal barrier by the doctrine of absolute sovereignty, in order to circumvent the "capitalist encirclement." Even in more recent reflections on relations with Western powers, Soviet literature still showed apprehensions that the shield might be ripped apart by the "imperialist" attempt to reduce the extent of sovereignty guaranteed by existing international law. Although the Soviets in the 1960s were using sovereignty as a sword to advance the socialist cause in the developing areas, their opposition to curbs on sovereign rights nevertheless demonstrated a consciousness of the discrepancy in national strength between the Soviet Union and the United States. In denouncing those who advocated restrictions on sovereignty, a recent Soviet textbook on international law declared:

> The forcible restriction of the sovereignty of States which are members of the international community is impermissible, except following aggression. The subjection of small States to the will of large States, or the subordination of the former by the latter, is also impermissible. This is often cloaked by hypocritical reference to the weak states' "voluntary restriction of sovereignty." The utter untenability of such references is particularly manifest in the relations between the colonial Powers and the so-called non-self-governing territories—relations which are tantamount to annexation.[12]

Despite its earlier advocacy of unrestricted sovereignty, however, the Soviet Union in 1969 employed the theory of "limited sovereignty" to defend its intervention in Czechoslovakia, attempting to rest its case on the argument that the interests of the "socialist community" centered in Moscow were larger than the national interests or the independence of any single socialist nation. Peking, whose relative strength to Moscow is comparable to the latter's vis-à-vis the "imperialist" powers, has taken a strong issue with the Soviet "limited sovereignty" theory.[13] The Communist Chinese are obviously haunted by a fear of the restrictions that a powerful state like the Soviet Union can impose upon the weaker states. This apprehension was shared by Rumania's spokesman, President Nicolae Ceausescu, at the Moscow conference of world Communist parties in June, 1969. Disputing the Soviet claim that proletarian internationalism required Moscow's "fraternal aid" to Czechoslovakia, Ceausescu insisted that "independence and national sovereignty, equal rights and non-interference in the internal affairs" must not be sacrificed.[14] When the chips are down, it appears that national independence is priced over and above the ideological bonds even though only states like the CPR, Rumania, and Yugoslavia seem to have the minimal capability to take a stand vis-à-vis Moscow. But, it remains true that the weaker states are the more jealous about their sovereignty and this is no less true within the socialist camp than in the world community at large.

In CPR literature "imperialist" encroachments upon the sovereignty of other states are said to take three forms: (a) under the disguise of "interdependence," (b) advocating a "transnational law," and (c) through attempts to force a "world state" upon others. All three are imputed to United States practices in international relations. First, the Organization of American States (it is pointed out that the United States was able to ram through a number of anti-Castro decisions in the OAS), mutual defense pacts signed with a number of weaker states including the Southeast Asian Treaty Organization (SEATO), and foreign aid under the Marshall Plan and subsequent programs are all considered to be devices for furthering United States interests at the expense of the sovereign rights of other countries.[15]

Secondly, the "transnational law" concept advanced by Judge Philip Jessup (*Transnational law*) is viewed as an underhanded move to cut into state sovereignty by the elevation of individuals to a coequal status as "subjects" of international law. The CPR stands firm in its view that only states enjoy such pre-eminence, the individuals being only "objects" of international law with no *loci standi* internationally. The Jessup view, which has found support from Sir Hirsh Lauterpacht (Oppenheim, *International Law,* 8th ed.), Wilfred C. Jenks (*A Common Law of Mankind*), and others, contains germinal elements of a new law which would give greater recognition to the rights of individuals and treat questions of jurisdiction by competent international tribunals as procedural matters not involving national honor or sovereignty.[16] From Peking's point of view, the whole idea of a "transnational law" as such is to aid "imperialist" intervention in the domestic affairs of other states, abridging their authorities over their own nationals.[17]

On the other hand, the Chinese as well as the Soviets do not seem to object to the international delictual capacity of individuals. The CPR accepts the Nuremberg and the Tokyo charters as embodying principles of general international law. In so doing she has indicated endorsement of universal jurisdiction over "crimes against humanity" and "crimes against the law of nations." [18] The underlying thought is that individuals have international duties and that *delicta juris gentium* make them directly accountable to international law. Although possibly due to Soviet influence, this position also reflects a traditional Chinese legal precept that "offenders of the public order are punishable by whoever is able to exercise jurisdiction." [19]

Recalling the Soviet consciousness of the "capitalist encirclement," the Chinese Communist doctrine of sovereignty is opposed to the theory of "limited immunity," as advocated in the "Tate Letter" of 1952, which advised United States courts that they should henceforth take jurisdiction in suits involving the "private acts" of foreign states.[20] The Chinese have challenged the distinction between a state's public acts (*jure imperii*) and its private acts (*jure gestionis*). They see in this an "imperialist" conspiracy to curb the "expanding economic activities of the socialist states," which engage in state trading.[21]

Thirdly, in order to thwart "imperialist" domination, the CPR claims the United Nations must be forbidden to serve as a legitimating agent for "imperialist" acts of intervention and aggression.[22] Collective action of the United Nations must not be exploited by the "imperialists" and perverted into a cover-up for their own acts of intervention (e.g., the Korean War) infringing on the sovereignty of other states. Intervention under the pretext of concerns for "human rights" (e.g., Tibet, Hungary, etc.) must also be prohibited.[23] Included in the CPR bill of wrongs against the United Nations under the "imperialist" aegis are the "Uniting for Peace" resolution of 1950, under which the General Assembly may have competence over an issue concerning peace and security if the Security Council is blocked by veto from taking action, and the disarmament movement fomented by the United States, which is viewed as an attempt to freeze the existing American arms superiority.[24]

CPR doctrine is as jealous about the United Nations acquiring "international personality" as about individuals being considered as "subjects" of international law. She fears that if the United Nations is clothed with legal capabilities and sovereign prerogatives on a par with the sovereign states, the "imperialist" powers would then be able to dictate their will to others through the "world government" thus created.[25] A similar suspicion is found in the CPR's attitude toward the International Court of Justice (ICJ). In a semiofficial yearbook on international affairs, the ICJ is said to have been used by the Anglo-American bloc as "an instrument of aggression." One example cited is the *Anglo-Iranian Oil Co.* case of 1951, in which the ICJ was allegedly used to support the British "plundering of Iranian oil." Other examples of "imperialist" abuse of the ICJ include the *Corfu Channel* and the *Peace Treaty* cases.[26]

It has been suggested in Western literature that national sovereignty is today anachronistic, both because nationalism is a nineteenth-century European ideology and because its delayed and frantic implementation in the non-Western world, unlike the earlier nationalist movements, tends to create smaller rather than larger political units. The discrepancy between the legal symbols of sovereignty—expressed in the privileges and immunities of statehood and in the claim to "sovereign equality" with the world's peers—and the real sovereignty ensured by the resources and capabilities at the disposal of the new arrivals becomes greater everyday.[27] While this may be true from the viewpoint of Western powers that are already sufficiently developed to look ahead to a future of "transnational" cooperation, the former colonial nations who have recently gained statehood are both psychologically and physically unprepared to think along the same lines. To them national independence is only the beginning of internal political unity and development, and state sovereignty is the only guarantee available to them for protecting their national independence.[28]

More or less the same can be said of the CPR's jealous guarding of her own sovereign rights. In the first place, the CPR's exclusion from much of international life has made her hypersensitive to suggestions about a "world government" or any supranational organization in which the CPR either has no voice or is definitely to be outvoted. Secondly, the hostility directed at Peking from a ring of United States' foreign bases and United States-sponsored alliances has made CPR leaders suspicious of slogans of "mutual defense" and "interdependence," as well as of American foreign aid programs. Thirdly, CPR leaders are conscious of their social system being disliked by the Western democracies. Their Communist ideology values collective rather than individual well-being. Naturally, a "transnational law" that seeks to strengthen the position of individuals before international law runs counter to that premise.

CPR leaders have repeatedly stressed that peaceful coexistence is to ensure the right of individual states to determine their own domestic socio-political systems, and that the foremost principle of PCX is respect for the sovereignty of other states.[29] In Peking's lip service to sovereignty, one can see a self-consciousness of its international isolation, which only increased in the 1960s with its suspicion of a United States-Soviet collusion directed against it. If the same circumstances continue, Peking can be expected to continue to seize upon absolute sovereignty as both shield and sword in its two-front struggle against Washington and Moscow.

Self-Determination

A closely related principle to sovereignty is that of self-determination. The CPR asserts that self-determination is the sole criterion for admitting a new state or government into full membership in the world community. There are strong indications that the Chinese adopted the doctrine from Soviet theory,[30] and it has been used as shield and sword. It has been employed to support Peking's claims to being the sole legitimate government of China. Nonrecognition by other states on political grounds has been condemned as a denial of the CPR's right of self-determination.[31] Self-determination has also been invoked to support the struggle of "oppressed" peoples in Asia and Africa for independence and sovereign equality. At the 1954 Geneva Conference on Indochina, Chou En-lai declared that the Vietnamese people's demand for independence and self-determination was conceived in the same spirit as the American Declaration of Independence (1776) and the French Declaration of the Rights of Man (1791).[32]

In a statement made at the Plenary Session of the Afro-Asian Conference at Bandung, on April 19, 1955, Chou went even further, declaring: "All subjugated peoples are entitled to the right of self-determination, free from persecution and massacre." [33] The same theme was repeated by Chou in an important foreign policy report before the Second Session of the Second National Committee of the Chinese People's Political Consultative Conference, on

January 30, 1956. He reaffirmed that self-determination and equality for all states were two of the foremost principles guiding the CPR's foreign policy.[34]

Peking's obsession with its own brand of self-determination has found expression in the CPR Constitution. Under Article 99, the "right of asylum" is guaranteed to "any foreign national persecuted for supporting a just cause, for taking part in the peace movement, or for scientific activities." The implications are that all individuals seeking refuge from persecution for their part in the struggle against colonial and "imperialist" domination will find solace and legal protection in Communist China in recognition of the right of self-determination of the oppressed peoples. Parenthetically, the inclusion of the right of asylum in the CPR Constitution may suggest either the adoption of an international law by making it a definite right in municipal law or an attempt to strengthen that right as an international institution by first making it an affirmed right in the CPR's domestic legal structure. The latter intent is not impossible since the CPR advocates that municipal law be considered as a subsidiary "source" of international law.[35]

When forced to make a choice in practice, the CPR has shown a greater interest in supporting the right of self-determination of colonial peoples, such as those in Angola and Portuguese Guinea, than in cultivating relations with a colonial power like Portugal, whose recognition would presumably interest Peking.[36] Despite her border conflicts with India, the CPR in 1961 promptly and warmly congratulated India on the latter's "liberation" of Goa from Portuguese "imperialism." [37] In view of the tension in Macao and Hong Kong in 1967 and 1968, Peking's empathy for the right of other peoples to self-determination may reflect its own consciousness of the last vestiges of Western influence in China.

CPR concept of self-determination is generally equated with decolonization and anti-imperialism. These concerns have turned self-determination into a sword, justifying intervention on behalf of the "oppressed" peoples. Peking is known to have received permanent missions from national liberation movements abroad, such as the Palestine Liberation Organization, the Malayan National Liberation League, the South Vietnam National Liberation Front, etc.[38] To a certain extent, Peking's active support of these movements has something in common with the position held by Afro-Asian members in the United Nations that the prohibition of intervention in international law should be suspended in cases where intervention is specifically intended to terminate a situation contrary to self-determination.[39] CPR doctrine has warned against "imperialist interventions" masqueraded as United Nations collective actions. It remains to be seen whether the CPR will support U.N. interventions backed by Afro-Asian nations to advance the cause of self-determination (i.e., to oppose colonial rule and to further racial equality). The answer would probably depend on whether the Communist Chinese fear of "imperialist" exploitation of U.N. interventions outweighs their confidence in the forces of self-determination, or vice versa. In view of the wide popularity in which self-determination has been held among Afro-Asian nations,[40] the CPR would be expected to capitalize more on the issue. Yet, specific references to self-determination in CPR literature appear to have declined over the years.

In a content analysis of CPR literature, I have found that as the use of the term "self-determination" declines there is a proliferation of equivalents such as: national liberation struggle; national movement; national independence movement.[41] Whether these were meant to substitute for self-determination is unclear. But the change in terminology seems closely related to the CCP's deepening feud with the Soviet "revisionists" over what to do about the struggles of the colonial and semicolonial peoples.[42] The following speculation might be offered: In the first place, the term "self-determination" used by Lenin and by Woodrow Wilson meant different things. For Lenin, self-determination meant the liberation of the subjugated peoples in colonial and semicolonial areas. But for Wilson the use of the principle for the protection of national minorities was only proposed for application in Europe or, to be more exact, those parts of Europe previously under Germany and Austria-Hungary, now vanquished after World War I.[43] Furthermore, in its ideological disputes with Moscow on who should lead the revolutionary movements in the colonial and semicolonial areas, Peking has emphasized the hegemony of the "proletariat" from the first stage onward. Chinese polemics has cited Lenin to show the fallacy of Moscow's current "national democratic" strategy, which seeks to manipulate at the top rather than exerting pressure from below. The Soviet strategy calls for acquiescence by local Communists in (bourgeois) nationalist leadership, anticipating Communist take-over only during the second stage of the revolutionary movement.[44] In an important article commemorating the ninetieth birthday of Lenin, Shih Tsu-chi quoted extensively from Lenin to show that, although any national movement partook of a "national bourgeois" character, it did not follow that the leadership of colonial revolutions must be entrusted to the bourgeois-democratic class. The reason given by Lenin, Shih asserted, was that the specific demands of each revolutionary movement, "including national self-determination," were not isolated but part and parcel of "the world's over-all democratic (now socialist) movement."[45] It is not impossible, therefore, that the CPR's more recent inclination to use terms such as "national independence" or "national liberation" in lieu of "self-determination" arose from her disagreements with "modern revisionism" over the correct ideological stance and strategy for the world Communist movement.

Equality Between States

CPR pronouncements claim that true equality is a major principle governing the regime's foreign policy. Its inclusion in Mao's triad announced on October 1, 1949, has already been noted. Both the Common Program (Article 56), which served as a quasi-constitution until 1954, and the 1954 Constitution of the CPR have given a prominent place to the principle of equality. In this respect CPR doctrine follows generally the Soviet position, except that the Chinese have used even stronger language in its behalf. The greater emphasis may be in part attributed to China's "unequal" status from the 1840s to the 1940s. During that time Western powers (Czarist Russia included) enjoyed extraterritorial and other privileges in China guaranteed by treaties signed under unequal circumstances.[46]

For one thing, CPR writers are particularly bitter about the traditional Western precept that only "civilized nations" were qualified to participate in the prevailing international public order. They recall how the British extracted from Manchu China the right to exercise consular jurisdiction in cases involving British nationals. The British advanced the excuse that laws of non-Christian countries were inapplicable to nationals of Christian countries.[47] Chinese writers are also bitterly opposed to the principle of "international standards," which Western powers have insisted must be upheld in the treatment of aliens and their properties. A state that has failed to live up to those standards is often considered to have breached an international responsibility mandatory under traditional international law.[48] CPR jurists have challenged the principle on grounds of practical inequality, since the so-called international standards were enjoyed solely by Western nationals in the backward countries but not the other way around.[49]

Ch'ien Szu questioned the sincerity of the Western powers and cited the Chinese Exclusion Act (1882), which was not repealed until 1943, the more than fifteen different kinds of legislation providing for "discrimination against persons of Chinese descent" between 1882 and 1913, and the "discriminatory features" in the immigration law of the United States. He also vehemently condemned the *apartheid* practices of the Union of South Africa, as part of his effort to show that the "international standards" never applied to nonwhites in the practice of Western powers.[50]

In place of "international standards," the CPR has advanced the principle of "equal treatment," which would assure the same level of treatment to aliens as to nationals. One practical example is Peking's technical assistance agreements with African states, which specified that, among other things, Chinese technical assistance personnel were to be accorded living standards no higher than those accorded corresponding personnel of the host countries.[51] The CPR follows the Soviet view that the extensive application of the national treatment principle by "powerful imperialist states" in their trade agreements with small and weak nations merely serves to confer legality upon their encroachments on the latter's economy.[52] Thus, in CPR usage, the term "equal treatment" is in part designed to avoid the stigma of the overworked principle of national treatment. Another reason is the drastic differences in the nature of the CPR as a Communist state and its form of economy. Under the state monopoly system Chinese citizens themselves are denied the right to engage in private business with foreign countries. Furthermore, the domestic population is, under the existing constitutional scheme, divided into "people," "citizens," and "nationals," with decreasing political statuses. It is simply impossible to extend "national treatment," in the literal sense of the word, to a foreign treaty partner. The principle of "equal treatment," on the other hand, would suggest compatible, reasonable terms, though not strictly "national." [53]

Obviously, Peking is conscious of similar sentiments held by newly independent Afro-Asian nations, especially those which are small and weak, and of the propaganda value which appeals to equality can yield. At the Bandung Conference in 1955, Chou En-lai told an eager audience that his government believed that "states, large and small, strong and weak, must all enjoy *equality;* and their sovereignty and territorial integrity must be respected without fail." [54] Chou repeated the same assurance to Prince Norodom Sihanouk of Cambodia during the latter's visit in China in 1958.[55]

In CPR treaties signed with Afro-Asian states, the principle of equality was given habitual prominence. For example, the Sino-Burmese Boundary Treaty of 1960 proclaimed that the transfer of certain territories between the parties was to be effected "in view of the relations of *equality* and friendship between China and Burma." [56] Considerations for equality were said to support the return by Burma, in exchange for compatible CPR concessions, of the Meng-Mao triangular area (Namwan Assigned Tract) over which Burma had inherited rights of "perpetual lease" from Britain secured under an 1897 treaty with Manchu China.[57] Similarly, the Chinese side renounced its "rights of participation in mining enterprises at Lufang of Burma," obtained in a Sino-British exchange of notes on June 18, 1941, as inconsistent with the CPR's policy of opposing foreign prerogatives and respecting the sovereignty of other countries.[58]

In their professed advocacy of true (as opposed to nominal) equality, CPR jurists have taken pains to show the hidden "unequal" nature of many treaties signed with or by Western countries due to either the "exploitative" relationships thereby created or to the conditions of inequality surrounding their conclusion. The Sino-British Treaty of 1842, under which a defeated China signed away many concessions, including her right of tariff automony, is given as a typical example.[59] Another often-cited example is the Treaty of Friendship, Commerce, and Navigation, signed between the Republic of (Nationalist) China and the United States in 1946. It is pointed out that though its provisions appeared to be reciprocal, hence nominally equal, only American nationals could actually benefit from the investment privileges granted to each other's nationals because no Chinese private citizen would have the necessary financial resources to take advantage of the privileges granted him on paper.[60] This is no place to get into the subject of "unequal treaties," [61] but these examples serve to illustrate Peking's hairsplitting attitude toward inequality.

From the limited data available, CPR domestic laws and regulations concerning aliens in mainland China seem purposely to have avoided any possible sign of discrimination. Aliens and stateless persons are, as far as possible, promised equal treatment, although it is highly questionable whether acts like the taking of alien property could be defended in international law on grounds that the same expropriation measures were equally applied to Chinese nationals as well.[62]

Comparison with Pre-1949 China

The Chinese drive to erase their "unequal" international status and to reassert their sovereign independence from foreign domination dates back to several decades before the birth of the CPR. It was evident in the 1913 foreign policy platform of the Kuomintang (KMT) under Dr. Sun Yat-sen, which called for the abolition of China's unequal treaties.[63] Although no concrete results came until after the KMT government was established under Chiang Kai-shek in 1928, Chinese sentiments against foreign influence and prerogatives in their country were widespread and intense. In 1926, for instance, the then warlord Peking government made one of the first Chinese attempts to shake off "unequal" treaties by denouncing a Sino-Belgian treaty of 1865.[64] Between 1926 and 1943, when the last vestiges of the unequal treaties were removed, the country witnessed a prolonged battle with foreign powers, which was waged to accomplish the following aims: (a) abolition of foreign consular jurisdiction; (b) regaining of tariff autonomy; (c) liquidation of foreign rights to engage in coasting trade, to navigate in internal waters, to station warships in Chinese ports, and to maintain troops in China; and (d) recovering of sovereign rights in foreign settlements and leased territories in China.[65]

Chinese jurists at the time strongly supported the campaign to restore China's sovereign independence and equality. One KMT commentator, Liang Ching-ch'un, severely criticized Western consular jurisdiction on grounds that it constituted an invasion upon China's sovereignty and that it imposed inequality on China. Liang inveighed against the Western pretext that Chinese laws, like those of "uncivilized" societies, were inapplicable to nationals of Western powers.[66] In an extensive review of China's existing treaties that contained the "most-favored nation" clause, Liang found that, except for the United States, Japan, and Sweden, all other foreign powers were abusing that clause to claim and exercise the right of consular jurisdiction.[67] Drawing upon precepts and norms of existing international law, he further criticized the powers for overstepping the boundary of privileges guaranteed under treaty. Among the excesses singled out for attack were: the denial of jurisdiction to Chinese courts in litigations involving Chinese residing in foreign settlements, interference with the trial by Chinese courts of native criminals for offenses against nationals of the foreign powers, interference with the function of Chinese police attempting to arrest fugitives hiding inside foreign settlements, etc. The treaty basis and the origin of the foreign settlements, he pointed out, was that foreign merchants needed space for warehousing and accommodations due to trade in China. Whatever right was not signed away was retained by China, and the existence of foreign settlements did not mean that China had lost its sovereignty over the land itself. Noting the yearnings of the Chinese for sovereign equality and the KMT's platform for the liquidation of unequal treaties, the writer concluded that consular jurisdiction must be abolished through negotiation with the powers concerned.[68]

As early as 1926 the same Chou Keng-sheng, whose post-1949 writings we have quoted before, was voicing his objection to the "infringement of China's political integrity" posed by Western and Japanese "spheres of influence." [69] China's entry into World War I on the Allied side was motivated by the very desire to recover German interests in Shantung and to regain sovereign equality vis-à-vis the other powers.[70] To a certain extent the "betrayal" at Versailles by Western powers, transferring the erstwhile interests of defeated Germany to Japan, was responsible for the disillusionment of pro-West Chinese intellectuals and for redirecting their attention to Marxism with its hostility to Western capitalism and its promise of historical redemption.[71] Chou Tzu-ya, (we have already noted his post-1949 writings) speaking as a supporter of the KMT government in 1943, glorified the "Chinese drive to abolish the [unequal] treaties begun since the Versailles" as part of the nation's overall campaign against "imperialist aggression." [72]

Thus one finds a common anti-"imperialist" fervor behind China's sensitivity to her own sovereign independence and equality both before and after 1949. One noteworthy difference is that the KMT government ceased its agitation after 1943, whereas Communist China revived the issue from 1949 on, both because of its ideology and its unhappy relations with the United States. Another difference lies in the relative Chinese lack of attention to the right of self-determination until the Communists came to power. An explanation for this phenomenon may be that, until the question of nonrecognition on ideological grounds came up after 1949, the Chinese anti-"imperialist" focus was mainly on sovereignty and equality. Self-determination in Communist usage therefore was invariably linked to the ideological conflict. Like that of peaceful coexistence, the CPR's proponency of self-determination was motivated by a desire to justify its own existence as a Communist regime by claiming that all states have a right to determine their own internal social-political systems.[73]

In any event, the Chinese Communist leaders and the pre-1949 elites had more in common between themselves than with their counterpart in Imperial China, in that their distrust of the rest of the world was born out of one hundred years of humiliation in dealing with what one Western writer has called "the arrogance of the white man." [74] Traditional Chinese attitudes toward the outside world before the Western impact, on the other hand, manifested a very different kind of arrogance, one born out of a sense of superiority over the barbarians. Yet, on issues involving China's "historical rights" over Tibet, Taiwan, and Outer Mongolia, the differences in the attitudes of Communist and KMT elites and between them and earlier Chinese governments begin to evaporate.[75]

Whatever differences do exist, they are hardly related to vital issues involving national interests and, in some ways, differences are due to changed conditions in China's international position. The Communist leaders, for example, have relaxed the traditional Chinese stand on *jus sanguinis* in connection with the nationality question of Chinese born abroad.[76] Another departure from the past is the CPR's silence on the question of suzerainty. Although the CPR is known to have demanded that territories lost to the Czarist government under the Aigun (1858) and Peking (1860) treaties are subject to renegotiation, its leaders have not made claims or allusions to any Chinese territorial rights by virtue of suzerainty as past Chinese governments had done. The silence may be due either to the disappearance of the concept in modern international law, or to a purposeful avoidance of symbols of "great-nation chauvinism," a "crime" often laid at the doors of India and the Soviet Union.[77]

V

Some Evidence of International Law in CPR Policy Thinking

AFTER WE have examined Communist China's basic attitudes toward international law, we are now ready to probe into its actual practice, in order to see whether there is evidence that international law is taken into consideration in Peking's foreign policy, how it invokes international law for the protection of its interests abroad, and how it uses international law in the conduct of its foreign relations. This three-way investigation will spread out in the following chapters. Here we shall explore some evidence that international law does receive more than cursory attention in the CPR's foreign relations, to the extent that this can be found in (a) the citation of international law in Peking's international agreements, domestic court proceedings, and official statements; (b) the status accorded international law in Chinese domestic law; and (c) foreign policy commissions and omissions made with the consequences under international law in view. Needless to say, the general survey in this chapter is not intended to be exhaustive, but to pave the way for the more specific and detailed study to follow.

Citing International Law

One notable example of CPR "deference" to international law is found in the numerous references to the principles of the United

Nations Charter, which appeared in treaties signed with other states up to 1966. The preamble of the Sino-Soviet Treaty of Friendship, Alliance and Mutual Assistance, signed on February 14, 1950, declared that the two contracting parties were "imbued with the aims and principles of the United Nations." [1] The same allusion is found in the preamble of all the CPR's treaties of friendship and cooperation with other socialist states, e.g., East Germany (December 23, 1955), Czechoslovakia (March 27, 1957), and Hungary (May 6, 1959). Furthermore, an identical article in these treaties usually stipulates that both parties will "in conformity with the principles of the United Nations Charter, participate in all international actions devoted to preserving world peace and security of all peoples." [2]

In other treaties, such as the Sino-Afghan Treaty of Friendship and Non-Aggression (August 26, 1960), there is a pledge to respect each other's independence, sovereignty, and territorial integrity, couched in language similar to that of Article 2 (1) and (4) of the United Nations Charter. According to its preamble, the Sino-Afghan Treaty was concluded "in accordance with the fundamental principles of the U.N. Charter." [3]

As court proceedings and judgments in Communist China are normally not publicly available, the only evidence of international law being cited or heeded to by Chinese courts is found in the 1956 trials of Japanese "war criminals." According to CPR accounts, these consisted of 140 former Japanese war criminals captured during the course of the Chinese civil war (1945–1949) and 969 others captured in 1945 by the Soviet army in Manchuria and later turned over to the CPR. Minus 47 who died between 1949 and 1956, a total of 1,062 Japanese war criminals were being tried under rules and procedures laid down by the Standing Committee of the CPR National People's Congress (NPC).[4] In the end, 45 were indicted and sentenced to prison terms, and the remaining 1,017 were released and repatriated.[5]

Of direct relevance to our interest here is that the trials were conducted under the name of international law, in pursuance of a "Decision Concerning the Handling of Japanese Criminals During Japan's War of Aggression Against China Currently in China's Custody," adopted by the Standing Committee of the NPC on April 25, 1956. The preamble of the "Decision," which had the character of a legal enactment both under the CPR Constitution and by dint of its inclusion in the *Fa-kuei hui-pien* (Compendium of Laws and Regulations), declared:

> The Japanese war criminals now in China's custody, during the Japanese imperialist war of agression in China, flagrantly violated the norms of *international law* and *humanitarian principles*. . . . (Emphasis added) [6]

The war criminals were tried by an *Ad Hoc* Military Court, constituted by the Supreme People's Court in accordance with the "Decision." From what can be gathered in available materials, the procedure of the court followed somewhat that of the International Military Tribunal at Tokyo, which had tried the most celebrated Japanese war criminals between April 29 and June 4, 1946.[7] The resemblance was, perhaps, more than a coincidence, since Mei Juao, [8] the Chinese judge at the Tokyo trial, remained in mainland China after the Communist take-over, and there is evidence that he continued to function in the juridical field in the early 1950s.[9] A semblance of what might be called "international standards" was maintained during the 1956 trials. The defendants were given an open trial and permitted the rights of hearing the charges, confronting the witnesses, and of defense counsel.[10]

In language recalling that used at the Tokyo trial, the *Ad Hoc* Military Court raised the following charges: aggressive war, infractions of the laws and customs of war, and inhumanities against the civilian population. The court charged Suzuki Hirohisa and seven others with "resolutely prosecuting the Japanese imperialist *war of aggression* against China [and], during the war, flagrantly violating the *norms of international law* and *principles of humanity*.[11] Suzuki Hirohisa was specifically charged with the responsibility for the "massacre of over 1,280 peaceable residents and burning down of more than 1,000 civilian houses" at P'an-chia Village, on October 28, 1942, and for five other massacres in North China.[12] The prosecution recounted how the five other codefendants [13] had murdered and pillaged Chinese civilian populations, used captured

Chinese as "mine sweeping instruments" and "living targets for the shooting exercises of [Japanese] military recruits," and murdered Chinese prisoners of war (POWs). The prosecution further charged:

Funaki Fenjiro, in flagrant violation of the norms of *international law and humanitarian principles* . . . further ordered his troops in September, 1941, to use *poisonous gas* against [the population] of Tu-chia Village, victimizing 400 residents.[14] (Emphasis added)

Using more or less similar language, the court condemned Sakakibara Hideo [15] for having committed the following crimes:

The accused personally led his troops in the culturing of bacteria and the manufacturing of bacteriological weapons in Heilungkiang, engaged in *bacteriological warfare,* [and] during tests on the effectiveness of bacteriological weapons, killed four peaceable residents, all in violation of *international law and humanitarian principles.*[16] (Emphasis added)

In another trial the court convicted Takebe Rokuzo and twenty-seven others for offenses against the law of nations, on the ground that they "arrogated [to themselves on behalf of Japan] the sovereignty of the Chinese state" by directly or indirectly "manipulating and dominating the puppet Manchukuo." Furumi Nakayuki was singled out as the mastermind for the execution of Japan's narcotics-trafficking operations in northeastern China (Manchuria). The court quoted him as confessing to his "crime" against international law.[17] Similar indictments were made against many others.[18]

In all the charges and final verdicts, the *Ad Hoc* Military Court made no more than the general references to international law and humanitarian principles already noted. A few points, however, were patent. First, as already noted, the court was given the mandate by the NPC to try the war criminals in accordance with "norms of international law and humanitarian principles." Secondly, the prosecution raised broad charges in language that presupposed the existence of an international criminal law, reminiscent of the philosophy of the Nuremberg and Tokyo trials. Although both China and Japan at the time of World War II were parties to the 1907 Hague Convention (IV) Respecting the Laws and Customs of War on Land,[19] the Chinese court made no explicit reference to it, probably because it considered that the rules contained in the convention were merely declaratory of those already existing in customary international law. This declaratory view was held by the Nuremberg Tribunal.[20] Not only was there evidence that the CPR subscribed to this view [21] but there was a practical need for her to do so. The Chinese court, as we have seen, prosecuted a number of Japanese war criminals for having murdered Chinese POWs and for having engaged in bacteriological and chemical warfare. Japan was not a party to either the 1929 Geneva Convention of Prisoners of War,[22] or the 1925 Geneva Protocol Prohibiting the Use of War of Asphyxiating, Poisonous or Other Gases, and of Bacteriological Methods of Warfare.[23] By not naming the specific conventions, the court could more easily justify its rulings, as it appeared to be doing, by holding the Japanese war criminals responsible for rules of war of which the conventions were merely declaratory.

A third point worthy of note is that the concept of "crimes against humanity," invoked by the Chinese court, recalled Article 5 (c) of the Tokyo Charter, in that it had broader application than infractions of the laws and customs of war.[24] Unlike the latter, which took place in the course of the war, "crimes against humanity" in the court's usage appeared to denote criminal acts which occurred before as well as during the actual hostilities. The prosecution showed that the crimes against humanity, with which the defendants stood charged, were connected with a conspiracy to plan, initiate, prepare, and wage the Japanese aggressive war against China and also with the atrocities and cruelties perpetrated after the commencement of hostilities, such as multiple killing, wounding, enslaving, persecuting, and otherwise eliminating Chinese persons. A minor difference with the Tokyo trials, however, was that the defendants tried by the Chinese Military Court in 1956 were second-echelon Japanese leaders who had *personally* and *physically* committed crimes against humanity.[25]

Another noteworthy point about the Chinese trials of Japanese war criminals, insofar as international law is concerned, is the court's conviction that it had the right under international law to try and punish individuals for crimes against peace, conventional war crimes, and crimes against humanity. The defense raised the point that the defendants, though field commanders, were themselves subject to the commands of their superiors and that in their acts they were merely carrying out orders issued from above. The plea was disallowed by the court; but the public admission of guilt and the good conduct during pretrial detention of the defendants were taken into consideration in the final sentencing.[26] The concept of *delicta juris gentium* had always existed in international law and it was only rearoused at the Nuremberg and Tokyo trials.[27] The Chinese tribunal's insistence that criminal responsibility be imposed on the defendants as individuals meant the rejection of the Act of State doctrine, which was not accepted at Nuremberg nor at Tokyo.[28] It may be concluded that the proceedings of the *Ad Hoc* Military Court and the final verdicts it handed down in the CPR's 1956 trials of Japanese war criminals were conducted and couched very much within the framework of existing international law.

Another area where evidence is found of international law being cited by Peking is its official pronouncements bearing on vital international issues. In later chapters we shall examine more fully its invocation of rules of international law. Here we shall content ourselves with one example. In a statement condemning the initial Anglo-French-American attempts to "coerce Egypt into capitulating on the Suez nationalization issue," the CPR government on August 15, 1956, stated:

> The United States, Britain, and France have been brutally exerting coercion upon Egypt. They have frozen Egypt's properties and funds found within their territories. They have moved in troops, flaunting [possible] use of force and making threats of force. . . . Asian and African states and all peace-loving states and peoples cannot but vehemently condemn these acts, which gravely violate the *Charter of the United Nations* and the *norms of international law*.[29] (Emphasis added)

International Law in Chinese Domestic Law

We shall content ourselves here with the domestic significance of treaty provisions, certain "enabling legislations" for the internal implementation of treaty obligations, and compliance in municipal law with international law, as can be observed from the scanty data available.

(a) Domestic significance of treaty provisions. The CPR does not have a separate body of nationality laws.[30] But a number of treaties with provisions regarding nationality are, like other treaties and agreements, promulgated in the *Compendium of Laws and Regulations of the CPR.* The Sino-Indonesian Dual Nationality Treaty,[31] the Exchange of Notes Concerning the 1961 Sino-Burmese Boundary Treaty,[32] the Exchange of Notes Concerning the Option for Nationality, Trans-Frontier Cultivation, and Herds-Grazing by Border Inhabitants between the CPR and Nepal,[33] etc., may be read together as a cumulative body of legal principles regarding nationality. As we shall see elsewhere, the CPR has by these international agreements modified the *jus sanguinis* stand inherited from the past. Presumably, the impact of these agreements is that Chinese domestic law will give effect to the option taken under their provisions by Chinese who possessed dual nationality.

In addition to the *Compendium,* treaties and international agreements of the CPR are published in other volumes having very wide circulation. These include *Shih-chieh chih-shih nien-chien* [Yearbook of World Knowledge], *Jen-min shou-ts'e* [People's Handbook], *Shih-shih shou-ts'e* [Current Affairs Handbook], etc. In view of such prominent play given to treaties, and in view of the effect of the above agreements relating to nationality, there is some basis for speculating that perhaps the CPR, like the Soviet Union, intends to give her treaties and agreements the status of law once duly promulgated domestically.[34]

(b) "Enabling Legislation." Some laws or regulations of the CPR are intended to aid domestic implementation of treaty provisions. One such example is the "Regulations of the Ministry of Public Security Concerning the Procedure for Declaring Option for the Nationality of the People's Republic of China by Persons Who Simultaneously Possess Indonesian Nationality and the Nationality of the People's Republic of China," promulgated on April 25, 1961. As the language of the regulations suggested, they were intended to implement in China the relevant provisions of the Sino-Indonesia Dual Nationality Treaty. Article 9 (2) of the treaty provided: ". . . [D]etailed provisions of an administrative and technical nature can, without violating the Sino-Indonesia Dual Nationality Treaty, the Exchange of Notes between the Premiers of both countries, and provisions of the present Measures, be separately formulated by Governments of both countries, to be carried out upon promulgation." [35] The regulations were formulated in pursuance of this provision in the treaty, to facilitate the latter's implementation in China, although the validity of the treaty as domestic law did not seem to depend on the regulations.

(c) Compliance in municipal law with general international law. We shall merely mention one example. While no peace treaty has been signed between China and Germany since the end of World War II, the CPR government in 1955 unilaterally terminated the state of war existing between the two countries. The termination, effective and binding at least so far as the CPR is concerned, was effected by an "Order" of the CPR chairman, the chief of state.[36]

The order stipulated that the change thus unilaterally declared did not prejudice Germany's international status or obligations, nor the rights or obligations of the CPR with respect to Germany arising from international agreements. The language and spirit of this particular provision bespoke the caution with which the CPR government handled the delicate relationship between municipal and international law in this instance. It was careful not to alter any international status, rights, or obligations by a unilateral decree, which would have only domestic validity and applicability. For, as the Permanent Court of International Justice on many occasions stated regarding this type of problem, it is an established principle that, since in international relations the rights and obligations of a state are determined by international law, it is that law, and not the municipal law of the state, which provides the standards by which to determine the legality of its conduct.[37]

Decisions Taken with International Legal Consequences in View

Examples can be cited in which the CPR has made decisions or opted for restraint in foreign relations apparently because of the anticipated consequences under international law.

The CPR in the 1950s brought separate complaints to the United Nations against the United States. We shall single out two such complaints, one in 1950 and the other in 1955, for comparison.[38] In response to its first complaint, the Security Council on September 29, 1950, invited the CPR to participate in its deliberations over the alleged "armed invasion of Taiwan" by the United States Seventh Fleet.[39] A team led by Wu Hsiu-ch'uan, Peking's special envoy with the rank of Ambassador, arrived at the U.N. Headquarters in Lake Success, New York, to sit in the Security Council deliberations without vote and to press his government's complaint.[40] In 1955, Peking brought another complaint against "United States aggression" over Taiwan to the General Assembly, requesting that the Assembly urge the Security Council to call upon the United States to withdraw all its forces in the area. On January 31, 1955, the council decided to invite the CPR again, but in its invitation it dropped references to "U.S. aggression" and instead addressed itself to the fightings then going on between the Communist and the Nationalist Chinese forces at Yi-kiang-shan Islands, off the east China coast. Peking rejected the invitation, for fear that participation in the council debates would have implied recognition of the council's competence to intervene in its own campaign to force the Nationalist Chinese out of the Yi-kiang-shan, a matter which Peking considered to be "China's internal affairs." [41]

The CPR had brought the two complaints under the provisions of Article 35 (2) of the U.N. Charter, which reads:

> A state which is *not a Member* of the United Nations *may bring to the attention* of the Secretary Council or of the General Assembly any dispute to which it is a party *if it accepts in advance,* for the purposes of

the dispute, the *obligations of pacific settlement* provided in the present Charter. (Emphasis added)

Since acceptance of the council's invitation involved a prior obligation to accept in advance the council's recommendations for the pacific settlement of the situation brought before the U.N., the CPR was carefully making a vital distinction, on the two separate occasions, between accepting and rejecting U.N. competence. For obvious reasons, Peking could not accept the council's invitation in 1955 without obstructing its own Yi-kiang-shan war effort. The same caution may have been responsible for the fact that, although Wu Hsiu-ch'uan took part in the council's deliberations in 1950, he refused to discuss any matter outside the CPR's charges against United States "aggression" over Taiwan.[42]

Another example of CPR cautiousness in respect of consequences under international law can be found in the course of the CPR-United States Ambassadorial Talks at Geneva in 1955. On October 8, 1955, Ambassador U. Alexis Johnson stated to his Chinese counterpart that, in the face of the continuing CPR threats to take Taiwan by military force, progress in further discussions could not be expected. Johnson suggested that both sides agree to an open renunciation of the use of force generally and particularly in the Taiwan area "except defensively," and to settle their differences by peaceful means.[43] In a draft declaration proposed on October 27, the Chinese side showed willingness to renounce the use of force *in general,* stating *inter alia:*

3. In accordance with Article 2, Paragraph 4, of the Charter of the United Nations, "All Members shall refrain in their international relations from the threat or use of force against the territorial integrity or political independence of any state, or in any other manner inconsistent with the purpose of the United Nations";

4. The People's Republic of China and the United States of America agree that they should settle disputes between their two countries by peaceful means without resorting to the threat or use of force.[44]

The CPR draft purposely omitted the mention of Taiwan and the right of self-defense in that area. The omission was considered by the American side to be unacceptable.[45] The State Department in a subsequent statement implied a charge of bad faith and intransigency on Peking's part. However, the Chinese views are worth careful scrutiny:

The United States . . . demanded that the Chinese people recognize that she had, over Taiwan, the so-called "individual and collective right of self-defense." On the other hand, [the United States] demanded that the Chinese people "renounce the use of force" in the Taiwan area, our own territory. Our side sternly refuted these absurd ideas, which would mean *abandonment of our exercise of sovereignty* over Taiwan; and pointed out that the United States had no rights whatsoever in intervening in *China's internal affairs.*

China had not, in the Taiwan area, used force against the United States. On the contrary, it was the United States which had used its force to occupy China's Taiwan forcibly. Therefore, it was precisely the United States herself which needed to renounce the use of force.[46]

A careful reading of this CPR statement reveals two significant but subtle points. First, the omission of Taiwan in the CPR's draft, which proposed renouncing the use of force in general, did not necessarily imply that she was ready to use force in that area but probably indicated that she was afraid that its mention would amount to abandoning the CPR's claim to the title of sovereignty over the island.

Secondly, the Chinese Communist omission of the right of self-defense in the Taiwan area could be attributed to a fear that an agreement thereupon would explicitly confer on the United States the right to defend Taiwan against Peking itself. Under the maxim *pacta sunt servanda* (agreements must be observed), the agreement, if reached, would be legally binding upon Peking and would explicitly deny it the option to take Taiwan by force, if necessary and feasible. The CPR's draft may be said to have been drawn up with international law as well as policy considerations very much in mind.

LEWIS AND CLARK COLLEGE LIBRARY
PORTLAND, OREGON 97219

VI

Territorial Jurisdiction and Territorial Sovereignty

NEEDLESS TO SAY, a most basic function of international law is to prevent or minimize friction between states by delimiting the sphere of their authority. Although the principle is universally accepted that a state's authority is conterminous with its territorial extent, it is not always clear where one state's territorial jurisdiction ends and that of another state begins, mainly because of the conflicting claims made by states sharing common borders and by coastal states over the width of their territorial waters. Historical claims and demands for renegotiation about territories lost under past "unequal" treaties have further complicated the issues. The Sino-Indian border conflicts of 1959 and 1962 and the Sino-Soviet border clashes of 1969 are typical of international disputes arising from conflicting territorial claims. In order to understand these and other territorial disputes likely to occur in the future, it is necessary to understand the CPR's views and practice in this regard.

Territorial Jurisdiction in General

Under international law a state has jurisdiction over all persons and property within its territory; the territorial jurisdiction is, as Chief

Justice John Marshall stated in the *Schooner Exchange,* "necessarily exclusive and absolute." [1] The CPR's civil and criminal laws are by definition in force throughout the entire territorial domain of China, which in theory includes also Taiwan.[2] Except during the period of 1949–1954, when Dairen and Port Arthur were subject to a form of Sino-Soviet condominium,[3] the CPR government has been able to maintain full territorial jurisdiction over virtually all of China's domain with the sole exception of Taiwan. In the past, China had lost sovereignty or had accepted restrictions upon her sovereignty over certain territories through lease [4] or concession,[5] or because of the existence of foreign treaty rights (such as the right to navigate in China's internal rivers),[6] or that of foreign "spheres of influence." [7] This situation no longer prevails after 1949, although the status of Hong Kong and Macao is *sui generis.*[8]

A CPR textbook on criminal law defines China's "entire territorial domain" as comprising the following, "in accordance with universally accepted principles of international law":

1. The land within the country's boundaries;
2. National waters (internal waters, rivers, and lakes) and part of a river which forms a boundary with another state—the exact boundary line being equidistant from both banks, or, if it is a navigable river, the middle of the main channel used for navigation [thalweg];
3. Territorial waters; and
4. Airspace superjacent to China's territorial domain.[9]

Chinese warships or military aircraft sailing on or flying over the high seas, or anchored in a foreign port, and nonmilitary ships and aircraft sailing on or flying over the high seas under CPR flags, are considered to be subject to Chinese jurisdiction.[10] In a criminal offense which took place abroad but was consummated within the domain of China, or vice versa—such as planting a time-bomb to blow up a train that crosses international boundaries—a Chinese court will have jurisdiction as though the crime had been committed in China.[11]

By its victory in the civil war (1945–1949), the CPR has inherited the whole territorial domain previously under the control of the Republic of China after World War II, with the exception of Outer Mongolia, whose independence has been recognized by both the Kuomintang and the Communist governments since 1945.[12] The CPR has based her territorial and legitimacy claims alternately on state continuity and state succession, although the two principles are not at all times compatible.[13] This broad claim has proven useful in countering the territorial claims of India; [14] and by tracing the threads of continuity back to the Manchu Empire, the CPR has demanded that the Soviet Union renegotiate the vast territories which China had lost to Czarist Russia in 1858 and 1860.[15] Besides, the alternate claims of state continuity and state succession could be pressed either to demand the return of Hong Kong and Macao, or to rationalize their present retention by Britain and Portugal under treaties signed by Manchu China during the nineteenth century.[16]

In its territorial settlements with neighboring states, Peking has not only called in service rules of general international law governing the acquisition and loss of territory but has also referred to the doctrine of not taking advantage of the fruits of the "imperialist" policy of former rulers. Obviously because of its propaganda value, the doctrine as such has found expression, for example, in the Sino-Burmese Boundary Treaty of 1960.[17] What is more important in Peking's claim of state continuity is its insistence that, in the absence of a delineated boundary, there is a "traditional" boundary line with neighboring states. The Sino-Pakistani Boundary Agreement of 1963, for example, gave explicit recognition to a "traditional customary boundary line." [18] Although the CPR at times has also based its legitimacy on self-determination and state succession, it is apparent that it has not completely followed the Soviet theory that a state which has undergone fundamental social changes is not the same legal person as the one which it replaces.[19]

Maritime Belt

Territorial Waters

China is a country with coastlines extending to over 6,700 miles in total length. The regime of its territorial sea is of no small significance. Not until 1958 did the CPR formally abandon the traditional "cannon shot" rule that a state's territorial waters extended three miles seaward from the coast measured from low-water marks.[20] On September 4, 1958, Peking issued a Declaration Regarding Territorial Waters, which adopted the twelve-mile rule and the straight base-line method for measuring the territorial sea.[21] A few reasons may be ascribed to the decision and its timing. First, the United Nations Conference on the Law of the Seas at Geneva, in April, 1958, had failed to reach an agreement on the width of territorial waters. Although not a party to the convention, the CPR followed its proceedings quite closely. Apparently, it sensed the decline of the cannon-shot rule and took note of the fact that the convention recognized the straight base-line principle "where the coastline is deeply indented and cut into, or if there is a fringe of islands along the coast in the immediate vicinity." [22] The Soviet Union, which had from 1921 on indicated an interest in expanding its territorial waters, formally advocated the twelve-mile rule at the 1958 Geneva Conference, along with the straight base-line principle.[23] There may be some link between the Soviet advocacy—which was supported by a substantial number of states at the conference—and Peking's decision to announce formally its own extension of the territorial sea to twelve miles. Another consideration was the exploitation of ocean resources, although Peking's capabilities in this respect were still quite limited.[24]

The most immediate and urgent reason was probably the current Taiwan Strait crisis, which commenced with the prolonged Chinese Communist shellings on the offshore islands on August 23, 1958. The CPR Declaration Regarding Territorial Waters coincided with the September 4 statement by Secretary of State Dulles pledging

United States commitment to defend Kinmen and Matsu under the mutual security treaty signed with Nationalist China.[25] Explicitly, the CPR declaration placed Kinmen and Matsu within its "internal waters" inside the straight base line from which the twelve-mile territorial sea was measured. It is clear that Peking was attempting to keep off the United States Seventh Fleet, which was rendering logistic assistance to the Nationalist Chinese garrison forces on the offshore islands. In his September 6 reply to the Dulles statement, Chou En-lai restressed that Kinmen and Matsu were within the CPR's "internal waters," adding that "the Chinese people cannot tolerate [the] threat posed" by these offshore islands being held in hostile hands.[26] CPR commentators also focused on the needs of national defense as the overriding reason for claiming a twelve-mile belt of territorial sea.[27]

The United States and Britain immediately rejected the CPR claim,[28] although it was supported by the Soviet bloc countries and others like Indonesia.[29] In a deliberate challenge, the United States sent its Seventh Fleet warships to escort a convoy of Nationalist Chinese supply vessels to a distance of three miles off Kinmen on September 7. Whereas such escort missions had previously been carried out only at night, this time it was done in broad daylight. The action brought "serious warnings" from Peking and was condemned as a "senseless imperialist intervention" and "invasion upon the sovereignty" of China.[30]

Generally speaking, the CPR justified its twelve-mile claim on three grounds. First, every state has a "right" under international law to define its own territorial sea, generally not exceeding twelve nautical miles, in accordance with specific conditions.[31] Secondly, existing international law does not accept any uniform rule regarding the breadth of the territorial waters of a littoral state; even the United States, which has strongly supported the three-mile rule, has not always consistently followed it; and China has simply followed the precedent of many other states with similar coastline conditions which have adopted the twelve-mile limit.[32] Thirdly, the once common cannon-shot rule has now become obsolete, and even the United States and Britain have in practice extended their territorial sea to twelve miles if the so-called customs zone is included, although they have maintained the three-mile fiction.[33]

There seems to be some confusion between the territorial sea over which the coastal state has sovereignty, and the "customs zone" contiguous to territorial waters. In any event, CPR jurists see a sinister design in the United States and British efforts to keep the three-mile limit, because, in their view, the narrower the territorial waters of other states the easier it would be for them to carry out espionage, military aggression, and "economic plundering." The *Fisheries* case (ICJ, 1951) is taken as evidence that Britain sought unsuccessfully to restrict Norway's territorial sea in order to enable British trawlers to get closer to the fish stocks and other marine life off the Norwegian coast. The United States objection to the CPR's twelve-mile claim is also seen as an attempt to perpetuate its "military aggression" in the Taiwan Strait.[34]

Policy needs and propaganda aside, it is noteworthy that in defending the extension of its territorial sea the CPR did not rest its case solely on domestic decrees but sought to justify it in the name of international law. CPR jurists point out that the base line and the low-water mark principles are both accepted under international law, but that since China's coastlines are full of curvatures and indentures the former is a more practical method for adoption. They cite the decision of the ICJ in the Anglo-Norwegian *Fisheries* case to show that the straight base-line principle ("skaergaard") was widely accepted as part of international law even before the 1958 Geneva Convention.[35] Mainland Chinese writers have also claimed CPR sovereignty over its territorial waters in accordance with international law. Writing in the official *Peking Review,* Liu Tse-yung declares that "territorial sea is that part of the sea which is under [the] sovereignty . . . of a coastal state . . . this is a generally accepted principle of international law which even the imperialist countries dare not deny." Thus, the requirement that foreign warships obtain authorization prior to passage through Chinese territorial waters is defended by Liu on grounds of sovereignty.[36]

Internal Waters

The base lines drawn by Peking are generous enough to enclose the Po-hai Bay and the Ch'iung-chou Strait within China's "internal waters." The Po-hai Bay is the mouth to Peking and its strategic importance was attested to by the Anglo-French Expedition of 1858 and 1860. The largest opening of the Bay is 22.4 miles, and its headlands are well within Chinese territory. It has traditionally been considered by the Chinese as a "historic bay." In defending the 1958 official characterization of the Po-hai Bay as China's "internal waters," CPR commentators have tried to establish the presence of all the following factors: (a) Where the adoption of the straight base line is justified, a bay within the base line so drawn constitutes the internal waters of the littoral state; (b) The 1958 Geneva Convention has endorsed the principle that a bay whose natural entrance points are no more than twenty-four miles apart, measured from the low-water marks, is considered as internal waters; and (c) Certain bays which exceed the twenty-four mile limit in their natural entrance may, because of their special economic or strategic significance, be classified as "historic bays." [37] Although the last point reflects the Soviet view,[38] allusions are made to Article 7 (6) of the 1958 Geneva Convention to show that "historic bays" are widely accepted in international law and in state practices.[39] These points are offered in the alternative. Presumably, the presence of any of the factors could justify the CPR's claim of the Po-hai Bay as internal waters. The official CPR Declaration of 1958, nevertheless, falls on only one justification, namely, that the bay is within the straight base line drawn between its natural entrance points.[40]

The Ch'iung-chou Strait, which is also proclaimed to be part of China's internal waters, is roughly 9.8 to 19 miles wide and 50 miles long. Like the Po-hai Bay and other areas designated as internal waters, the strait is off-limits to all foreign warships and aircraft. It is a usual practice under international law to recognize in peacetime a right of passage through straits that are narrow enough to form part of a state's *territorial waters* but that also form a channel of navigation between one part of the high seas and another part of the high seas or the territorial waters of another state.[41] By declaring the Ch'iung-chou Strait part of China's internal waters, so defined because it is within the straight base lines drawn for measuring the territorial sea, the CPR intends to make it impossible for any state to claim the right of innocent passage. From CPR commentaries, one can be sure that this legal fine point was kept in mind when Peking drew up the 1958 CPR declaration. As Liu Tse-yung puts it:

The legal status of *internal waters* is exactly the same as that of land territory. The most marked difference between internal waters and territorial seas is that in internal waters the *right of innocent passage* of foreign vessels *does not exist*.[42]

The Question of "Innocent Passage"

The time-honored rule that foreign ships enjoy the right of innocent passage in peacetime through the territorial waters of the coastal state has been codified in the 1958 Geneva Convention. In state practices, however, whether foreign warships also enjoy the same right to the same extent has been subject to different interpretations. In the Draft Treaty on the Territorial Sea and the Contiguous Zone submitted by the International Law Commission to the General Assembly, there was an article which would permit the coastal state to make the passage of warships through its territorial sea subject to prior authorization or notification.[43] In the final convention the article was deleted, despite strenuous objections by the Soviet Union.[44]

Following the Soviet policy, the CPR stated in its 1958 Declaration Regarding Territorial Waters that no foreign warships or airplanes are permitted to enter the waters or fly over them within the twelve-mile belt of China's territorial sea, except by prior authorization. Commenting on this provision of the declaration, Fu Chu has noted that although certain states accept the innocent passage of foreign warships the right is not universally granted. W. E. Hall, the English jurist, even denied that such right was ever enjoyed by foreign warships, and L. Oppenheim also admitted that the right of innocent passage by foreign warships without prior authorization had not been universally recognized. Fu Chu also takes cognizance of the fact that Article 24 of the Draft Treaty of the International Law Commission noted above had explicitly required authorization.[45]

As to the right of innocent passage by foreign nonmilitary vessels, the CPR Declaration of 1958 was rather ambiguous in its wording. It did not deny such right, nor did it address itself directly to the matter. After stating that foreign warships and aircraft cannot enter Chinese territorial sea and its superjacent airspace without authorization, Paragraph (3) of the declaration stipulates: "*All* foreign vessels *while navigating* in China's territorial sea shall abide by all relevant laws and regulations of the [CPR] Government." Since nonmilitary foreign ships are not required to obtain prior permission, the phrase "while navigating in China's territorial sea" leaves room for interpretation. In his comment, Fu Chu acknowledges that the right of innocent passage by "foreign merchant vessels" is recognized under international law. But he hastens to add that such right is not unconditional or unlimited. In the first place, he notes, the passage must be "innocent" and must not involve smuggling, evasion of customs duties, sending ashore of espionage agents, gathering of intelligence, etc. Secondly, he adds, the foreign merchant vessels must obey relevant laws and regulations enacted by the coastal state. All civil and criminal cases which have occurred on board during passage through the territorial sea, with consequences extending to the coastal state, will in principle be subject to the jurisdiction of the coastal state.[46]

These points agree generally with provisions of the 1958 Geneva Convention on the Territorial Sea and the Contiguous Zone. Article 14 of the convention, which recognizes the right of innocent passage, defines "innocent" passage as being "not prejudicial to the peace, good order or security of the coastal State." Article 16 provides that "the coastal State may take the necessary steps in its territorial sea to prevent passage which is not innocent." Article 17 requires foreign ships exercising the right of innocent passage to "comply with the law and regulations enacted by the coastal State. . . ."

There are, however, two noticeable differences between the CPR position and the provisions of the 1958 Geneva Convention: First, the convention recognizes innocent passage for "ships of all states," with no restriction on warships except that submarines must surface, whereas the CPR permits only nonmilitary ships to have that right. Secondly, the convention puts the rights of the coastal state to regulate passage through its territorial sea in a rather negative context. For example, although foreign ships are required under Article 17 to comply with the laws and regulations of the coastal state, the same article also specifies that these laws and regulations must be "enacted in conformity with these Articles and other rules of international law." Article 19 lists four specific conditions under which the coastal state may assume criminal jurisdiction over a foreign ship lying in its territorial sea. Under Article 20, it is stated that:

the coastal State *may not* levy execution against or arrest the ship for the purpose of any civil proceedings, *save only* in respect of obligations or liabilities assumed or incurred by the ship itself in the course or for the purpose of its voyage through the waters of the coastal State.[47]

The CPR, on the other hand, has stated its position in positive and in maximum terms. As we have noted, the 1958 Declaration claims, without any qualification, that all foreign ships in Chinese territorial waters must obey all its "relevant laws and regulations." According to an authoritative commentator, the "relevant laws and regulation" include the CPR's Customs Regulations, Provisional Articles Relating to the Sea Ports, Regulations Relating to Health and Quarantine in International Transit, Measures Governing Foreign Vessels Entering and Departing from CPR Ports and Harbors, etc.[48] Of course, as we shall see, these enactments have been carefully drawn up so as not to conflict with international law in general.

The Contiguous Zone

The 1958 Declaration and subsequent commentaries are conspicuously silent about the contiguous zone, though the CPR, as we shall see below, has claimed exclusive fishery conservation zones contiguous to its territorial waters. In the Regulations Concerning Japanese Vessels Destined for China, laid down in 1952, a provision stated: "Within the sea area 15 nautical miles from the China coast, no hovering is permitted. . . . A Japanese vessel destined for China shall observe all Chinese maritime regulations upon entering the sea area 15 nautical miles from the China coast. . . . In case there is any suspicion on the part of a Chinese patrol boat against a Japanese vessel, the latter must obey orders and submit to the visit and search by the former." [49] But it is not known whether this "hovering law" has continued beyond 1958.

There may be some reason why the 1958 Declaration was silent about the contiguous zone. Article 24 (2) of the 1958 Geneva Convention on the Territorial Sea and the Contiguous Zone stipulates that "the contiguous zone may *not* extend beyond twelve miles from the base line from which the breadth of the territorial sea is measured." As the CPR claimed a twelve-mile belt of territorial sea measured from straight baselines, any further claims of a contiguous zone beyond that breadth would be a departure from this provision. The CPR is not a party to the convention, but it is not impossible that she deliberately avoided making claims that would run head on against the provisions of the convention.

Furthermore, the Soviet Union does not seem to claim a contiguous zone. Some Soviet writers even go so far as to suggest that: "in the USSR there are no contiguous zones in the common understanding of that term." [50] It is not impossible that the CPR silence was due to this Soviet influence.

The CPR has not made known its stand on the right of "hot pursuit," or on the question of continental shelf except very briefly in late 1970. Commenting on the alleged Japanese designs on the Tiao-yü-t'ai (or, in Japanese, Senkaku) islets, an article in the *People's Daily* signed by "Commentator," on December 29, 1970, declared that the "resources of the sea-bed and subsoil of the seas around these islands and of the shallow seas adjacent to other parts of China all belong to China." There was, however, no mention of the term "continental shelf," let alone a definition of its extent. The same paper on December 31, 1970, carried excerpts from an article by John Gittings, "Scramble for Oil in East China Sea," published in the British newspaper *Guardian* on December 18 of the same year, in which references were made to the sovereign rights of the coastal state over the continental shelf "to a depth of 200 metres or beyond that limit to where the depth of the waters admits of the exploitation of natural resources," as established by the 1958 Geneva Convention on the Continental Shelf. Since the *People's Daily* published the excerpts without comment, it is hard to ascertain the Chinese Communist attitude on the subject.

In a related area, the CPR has claimed special fishing and security zones beyond the territorial sea. A zone has been established along the coast from the Sino-Korean border to Chekiang, apparently extending seaward beyond the twelve-mile limit, in which no fishing by Chinese or foreign trawlers is permitted.[51] A regulation issued by the State Council on August 18, 1957, extended the prohibited zone from North 29th Parallel to North 27th Parallel.[52] The entire prohibited area was specified in the 1963 fishery agreement between CPR and Japanese fishery associations. One of these zones is at the mouth of Po-hai Bay, two in the huge indenture between the Shantung Peninsula and Haichow (Tunghai) in the Yellow Sea, one at the Yangtze estuary near the Chusan (Chou-Shan) Archipelago off Shanghai, and three along the southeast China coast, scattered between Ningpo, Chekiang, and Foochow, Fukien.[53] In the past, alleged intrusions by Japanese fishing vessels into the forbidden zones were often cause of disputes. These unhappy incidents, involving damage to life and property and arrests of Japanese vessels, some charged with espionage, led to the discontinuance of the fishery agreements after 1958. The new 1963 agreement was reached only after lengthy negotiations, and not before the Japanese had consented to respecting the Chinese prohibited zones.[54]

In defending these prohibited areas, CPR writers have cited as precedent the United States Presidential Proclamation of September 28, 1945, which claimed a right to establish fishery conservation zones in the areas of the high seas contiguous to United States coasts.[55] The similarity, however, is rather specious. Although the United States was also seeking to establish fishery conservation zones, its application was rather limited:

Where such activities have been or shall hereafter be developed and maintained *by its nationals alone,* the United States regards it as proper to establish explicitly bounded conservation zones in which fishing activities shall be subject to the regulation and the control of the United States.

Where such activities have been or shall hereafter be legitimately developed and maintained jointly *by nationals of the United and the nationals of other states,* explicitly bounded conservation zones may be established under agreements between the United States and such other states; and all fishing activities in such zones shall be subject to regulation and control as provided in such agreements.[56]

Thus, under the United States proclamation, the unilateral action of establishing special conservation zones applied only to those areas of the high seas where only United States nationals were engaged in fishing activities. In areas where other nationals were also engaged in such activities, the specific regulations pertaining to the establishment and control of the bonded zones would be meted out by agreement with the states concerned. These two principles have been adopted in the Convention on Fishing and Conservation of the Living Resources of the High Seas, adopted at Geneva in 1958.[57] At least in some of the prohibited zones which the CPR has established, the Japanese were also engaged in fishing, or at least the Japanese so claimed. Whether the CPR had a right to declare those areas closed to the Japanese is questionable, although the Japanese statement in 1963, which "pledged . . . to stop of her own accord the operation of Japanese motor-boat trawlers in the forbidden area," may be considered as the result of an "agreement" reached between the parties.[58]

Furthermore, if the 1945 United States proclamation attempted to extend the country's fishery rights, the fact is that the United States claimed only a territorial sea of three miles. Since 1963, the United States, as well as Canada, Britain, and New Zealand, has established a twelve-mile exclusive fishery limit along its coasts. But, the total expanse encompassing both the territorial waters and the special fishery zones still does not exceed twelve miles in total.[59] The CPR, on the contrary, claims a twelve-mile territorial sea, measured from straight base lines, to start with, and, on top of that, claims additional prohibited zones that further extend seaward. To use the United States example as precedent would be hardly appropriate.

Freedom of the High Seas

The CPR does not consider that the Taiwan Strait, which is between 83 and 140 nautical miles in width, is closed to international navigation. In the 1958 declaration, the Taiwan Strait is not included among the bays, straits, and offshore islands considered to be within China's "internal waters." In fact, in Paragraph (1) of the declaration, Taiwan is described as being "separated from the mainland by the high seas," although the CPR government reserves to itself the right to "liberate" Taiwan and the nearby Penghu from current "U.S. armed occupation." [60]

One commentator explicitly points out that, although on both sides of the Taiwan Strait are Chinese territories, the central strip of water separating the territorial sea on both sides is more than twice as wide as the twelve-mile limit claimed by China; hence, it is part of the high seas.[61]

Although the CPR, as noted above, has declared certain fishery zones in the high seas contiguous to its territorial waters as closed to other states, the CPR-Japanese fishery agreement of 1963, which acknowledged the existence of these restricted zones, stipulated that "the provisions . . . shall not restrict navigation in the agreed sea areas." [62] The freedom of the high seas is thus maintained even in the exclusive fishery zones; the provision shows that the CPR does not intend to extend sovereignty to these zones.

The official Peking press even explicitly stated that "the high seas are that part of the ocean or sea the use of which is shared by all states." It explained that the word "freedom" encompassed the right "to navigate, to fish, to hunt, and to engage in other maritime enterprises as well as to lay submarine cables." "The principle of the freedom of the seas," it was explained, "has been recognized by international law and all nations." [63]

Although it has condemned the United States nuclear tests in the Pacific as serious violations of the U. N. Charter and the freedom of the high seas,[64] the CPR itself has designated at least three areas on the high seas contiguous to Chinese territorial waters as security areas. Foreign vessels would either be barred from these areas, or would have to obtain permission to enter, or would be advised not to enter.[65] In the past, CPR commentators defended similar security areas designated in certain areas within Chinese territorial waters on defense grounds.[66] But it remains to be seen how the CPR defends the designation of military security areas that are within portions of the high seas adjacent to but outside its territorial waters.

Entry and Departure of Foreign Ships

The "Open" Ports

The CPR has issued special regulations governing foreign ships entering and leaving Chinese ports which have been formally approved as "open" to foreign vessels. The Measures Governing Foreign Vessels Entering and Departing from CPR Ports and Harbors (hereinafter referred to as the "Foreign Vessels Measures"), which came into effect as of March 14, 1957, are applicable to all foreign vessels in the "open" ports.[67] Given its present limited seagoing capabilities, the CPR has to rely on foreign ships in international transport. Available information shows that in 1958 Soviet and Eastern European vessels and those from some "capitalist countries" were undertaking a sizable part of Peking's sea transportation on the four main shipping routes linking China with other parts of the world.[68] From 1959 on, a large number of foreign ships were known to visit at seven recently expanded and modernized seaports, capable of accommodating vessels of 10,000 tons and up.[69] The seven—Dairen, Chinwangtao, Tientsin, Tsingtao, Shanghai, Canton, and Chankiang—are presumably among the seaports approved for international transport.

The 1957 Foreign Vessels Measures replaced the Provisional Measures Governing the Entry and Departure of Foreign Vessels promulgated by the CPR Ministry of Communications in 1952. In addition, foreign vessels in Chinese ports are also subject to CPR Provisional Customs Regulations "and other relevant laws and regulations."[70] According to the Foreign Vessels Measures, the captain of a foreign ship must apply for entry one week ahead of arrival or before sailing out from the port of departure. He must report the following data through the ship's local agent to the authorities of the port of destination: the scheduled arrival time, the ship's displacement, the amount of cargo, and number of passengers on board. Twenty-four hours before arrival, the captain must report to the port authorities through its local agent the ship's exact time of arrival.[71]

Both at entry and departure a foreign ship must fly or display the "various designated signs and flags" and during the daytime must fly the flag of the state of registry.[72] The ship will go through the quarantine inspection procedures pursuant to the Regulations Relating to Health and Quarantine in International Transit.[73] Unless guided by a pilot appointed from the port authorities the ship is not permitted to enter or leave the port or move in the harbor.[74] Its crew and passengers will also be subject to luggage inspections by the port authorities in conjunction with other officials concerned, in accordance with the provisions of the Provisional Rules Governing the Inspection of the Luggage of Crew and Passengers.[75]

After entry in port, the captain must report to the port authorities the nomenclature and quantity of weapons and ammunitions, radio equipment, message transmitters, radar and other reconnaissance equipment, pyrotechnics, etc. that are carried on board. Weapons and ammunitions will be sealed. Use of the other equipment will be prohibited while in port, except in times of distress or emergency; any such emergency use must be promptly reported to the port authorities.[76]

Upon anchoring in port, the captain of the ship will file to the port authorities the entry report form and furnish complete lists of the crew and passengers and the inbound cargoes on board. Before leaving port, he will go through similar procedures, to get clearance. While in port, the captain will also make available for examination documents certifying the nationality of the ship, navigation logs, engine-room logs, and other documents on board.[77]

Upon completion of the inspection procedures, members of the crew may, if necessary, apply to the frontier guard for shore-visit permits to go ashore.[78] Both crew and passengers are forbidden to take photographs or to make drawings while in port.[79] Except with the consent and under the supervision of the appointed pilot, the foreign vessel is not permitted to take fathoms during entry, voyage, or exit.[80] In case of maritime accident during voyage along

China's coasts, the captain of the foreign ship must report to the port authorities within forty-eight hours after entry; any accident that occurs in the port must be reported immediately.[81]

The Chinese port authorities may stop a foreign vessel from leaving the port of call in the following circumstances: (a) when the ship has violated relevant regulations concerning the documents on board, the seaworthiness of the ship, other safety measures relating to cargo, provisions, and equipment, etc.; (b) when the ship has failed to pay up the various fees for the use of the harbor, fines levied for violations of the relevant laws and regulations, and compensations for damages to harbor installations, markings guiding the sea routes, and other properties. However, if the ship has left sufficient security to match the total amount owed, it may be permitted to proceed on its voyage.[82]

The Ch'iung-chou Strait

In addition to the Foreign Vessels Measures of 1957, there are other regulations governing foreign ships sailing into and out of Chinese waters. One is the Rules Governing Passage Through the Ch'iung-chou Strait by Foreign Nonmilitary Vessels (hereinafter referred to as the "Ch'iung-chou Rules"), promulgated on June 8, 1964.[83] The Ch'iung-chou Strait separates Hainan Island and Liuchow Peninsula, where a major modern port has been built at Chankiang to serve as the gateway to southeast Asia and other parts of the world. The strategic importance of the Ch'iung-chou Strait is enhanced by the fact that it links Hong Kong and other parts of southeast China with Haiphong, in the Gulf of Tonkin. The timing of the promulgation of the Ch'iung-chou Rules in 1964 was clearly tied to the escalation of the Vietnam War, which had necessitated the heavier use of the Ch'iung-chou Strait and also precautions against "enemy" ships.

We have noted earlier that in the 1958 CPR Declaration Regarding Territorial Waters the Ch'iung-chou Strait was declared part of China's internal waters. Under the Ch'iung-chou Rules, foreign nonmilitary vessels may apply to the Ch'iung-chou Strait Administration for permission to sail through the strait, under terms similar to those laid down in the Foreign Vessels Measures.[84] Thus, although the right of innocent passage is not recognized with respect to the strait, the rules have made it possible to authorize passage for those friendly foreign nonmilitary ships which must use the strait as a major artery of navigation.

The Ch'iung-chou Rules are more stringent than the Foreign Vessels Measures in respect of security. Given the strategic importance of the strait, this is hardly surprising. Even after permission has already been granted, a foreign nonmilitary vessel may be barred from passage through the strait on moment's notice.[85] Authorized passage is limited to the daytime, and all foreign nonmilitary vessels must clear the strait before sunset.[86] All such vessels must sail through the middle channel during passage, unless given permission to do otherwise.[87] They must strictly abide by the designated hours and routes, and must immediately accede to requests signaled to them from the shore or from patrol boats.[88] Use of radar is not permitted during foggy weather or under poor visibility unless cleared with the Ch'iung-chou Strait Administration; taking photographs and fathoms is also prohibited.[89]

In case a foreign nonmilitary vessel has failed to comply with or has violated provisions of the rules, either of the following two courses of action may be taken: (a) If the vessel has not yet entered the main body of the strait (known as the "regulated area"), it may be barred from completing the passage and ordered back out from the strait and made to detour around the southern tip of Hainan Island; or it may be permitted to continue its passage upon completion of the application and related procedures. (b) If the ship has already entered the "regulated area," it may, when conditions warrant it, be ordered to stop and be escorted to a point near the sea for inspection. Appropriate punitive measures may be taken in light of the inspection results. Depending upon the individual situation, the ship may then be permitted to sail through the "regulated area," or be barred from it and ordered to leave the strait under escort.[90]

Border Rivers

A different body of regulations governs foreign vessels calling at ports and harbors on rivers forming borders between China and other countries or Chinese rivers flowing into or out of neighboring countries. The Regulations Governing Foreign Ships on Border Rivers, promulgated on April 19, 1966, follow the provisions of the 1957 Foreign Vessels Measures in general, but appear to be slightly more stringent. No foreign ship is permitted to enter or leave these ports and harbors "except in accordance with the *agreement* on commercial navigation signed between the government of China and the country to which the ship belongs, or with the approval of the Chinese Government." Every time a foreign ship enters or leaves a Chinese port or a river, it must apply for clearance with the Chinese port authorities before it departs from the last port of call.[91]

To my knowledge, the CPR signed two agreements with the Soviet Union on the navigational procedures, development and joint use of the Ussuri River, one on January 2, 1951, and the other on March 11, 1959. Two more agreements were signed with the Soviet Union, August 18, 1956, and April 17, 1962, concerning the joint development and joint survey of the Heilungkiang River. Likewise, the CPR reached six agreements with North Korea for the joint exploitation and utilization of the Yalu and the Tumen rivers. Two of these, dated May 23, 1960, and December 2, 1965, were explicitly concerned with navigation on the border rivers.[92] The 1966 Regulations Governing Foreign Ships on Border Rivers may very well have these agreements in mind. In view of the 1969 Sino-Soviet border conflict, much of it related to the use and exact boundary of the Ussuri River, these agreements have strategic significance. A standard clause in these bilateral agreements is that the ships of the other contracting party, while in Chinese ports and waters, must comply with the CPR's "relevant laws and regulations." [93]

Jurisdiction over Foreign Vessels

Very little is known about the CPR's policy and law regarding jurisdiction over foreign vessels in Chinese waters in respect of civil disputes on board. The various regulations we have examined thus far only have tangential provisions relating to such jurisdiction. The relative silence may be related to the CPR attitude that a foreign ship in Chinese waters remains under the jurisdiction of the flag state insofar as maintenance of order on board is concerned, except when consequences extend to the shores of the coastal state. The principle was codified in the Sino-Soviet Agreement on Merchant Marine Navigation on Rivers and Lakes Along Their Borders, signed on December 21, 1957.[94] It reappeared in the Agreement Concerning Navigation and Transport Cooperation on Border Rivers, signed by the CPR with North Korea on May 23, 1960, which provided, *inter alia:* "As regards the *internal order* of the vessels [in the waters of the other Contracting Party], the laws and regulations of the Contracting Party whose flag the vessels are flying shall be applicable." [95] The provision agrees with the general practice of other states, as affirmed in such cases as the *Regina v. Anderson* [96] and the *United States v. Flores,*[97] and as codified in the 1958 Geneva Convention on the Territorial Sea and the Contiguous Zone.[98]

Matters pertaining to "maritime accidents," however, fall under the jurisdiction of the CPR as the coastal state. These cases are dealt with under the Regulations Governing the Investigation of Maritime Accidents and Damages (hereinafter referred to as the "Maritime Accidents Regulations"), which came into effect on October 15, 1959.[99] A "maritime accident" of a ship is defined as one of the following cases resulting in the loss of property or business or injury or death to human life: (a) running into reefs, ashore, or aground; (b) collision or damage due to tidal waves; (c) fire or explosion; (d) impairment of a ship's capability to navigate, due to damage or diminution of equipment or vital parts; (e) natural disasters; (f) damage caused by a vessel to harbor installations and infra- and supra-structures; and (g) capsizing or disappearance.[100]

By these regulations, each local Chinese Harbor Administration, or its equivalent, has jurisdiction over the "investigation and disposal" of each of the listed cases when the matter of responsibility is involved; or otherwise it may exercise jurisdiction when warranted by conditions, or when instructed by its superiors or requested by the owner or captain of a vessel concerned.[101]

Although the Maritime Accidents Regulations are applicable in general to Chinese vessels, a foreign ship is subject to the same kind of investigations and/or handling either because: (a) it has caused property damage to a Chinese national; or (b) the accident has taken place in Chinese waters; or (c) the consul of the state of registry has requested such actions to be taken by the Chinese authorities.[102] Chinese jurisdiction over a foreign vessel in the given cases, therefore, is based either on the principle of "passive personality," or that of "territoriality," or that of "nationality." These are among the general principles accepted by many states for exercising jurisdiction over aliens with respect to crime. They were included with two others—the "protective" principle (determined by reference to the national interest injured by the offense) and the "universal" principle (such as the jurisdiction over piracy on the high seas)—in the Harvard Research Draft Convention on Jurisdiction with Respect to Crime (1935).[103]

The principle of "passive personality," which authorizes jurisdiction by reference to the nationality or national character of the person injured by the offense, has been the subject of controversy in more recent years; and state practices vary. Its absence from the provisions regarding national jurisdiction of the 1952 Brussels Convention and the 1958 Geneva Convention on the High Seas is indicative of the controversy.[104] It appears that the decision of the Permanent Court of International Justice in the famous *Lotus* case, which approved jurisdiction by the state of which the victim of a collision on the high seas was a national ("passive personality"), is losing support.

However, the three principles advanced by the Chinese Maritime Accidents Regulations, on closer examination, seem to be more closely patterned after Article 19 of the 1958 Convention on the Territorial Sea and the Contiguous Zone (as opposed to the Convention on the High Seas), under which the coastal state may assume criminal jurisdiction in the following cases:

a) if the consequences of the crime extend to the coastal state;
b) if the crime is of a kind to disturb the peace of the country or the good order of the territorial sea; or
c) if the assistance of the local authorities has been requested by the captain of the ship or by the consul of the country whose flag the ship flies.[105]

Although the Maritime Accidents Regulations are phrased broadly enough to extend the CPR's investigative authority and criminal jurisdiction to accidents that have occurred in areas of the high seas immediately contiguous to China's territorial waters, it is probably true that its provisions were drawn up essentially with accidents within the Chinese territorial waters in mind. It is doubtful, at least not clear, whether the Chinese endorsement of the principle of "passive personality" really extends to those parts of the high seas that are totally removed from the Chinese coasts.

Furthermore, assumption of criminal jurisdiction by a Chinese court under the "passive personality" principle does not mean, in CPR thinking, that its jurisdiction is exclusive. As Ni Cheng-ao suggests, if the foreign ship which has caused damage or injury to a Chinese national or vessel is found in the port of a third state subsequent to the accident on the high seas, nothing under international law can prevent a court of that foreign port from exercising jurisdiction if it so desires. Under the circumstances, he continues, the CPR can only request through diplomatic channels that the third state detain the vessel (or at least do so pending the posting of bond), investigate the accident, and/or initiate court proceedings.[106]

The Maritime Accidents Regulations confer investigative authority upon the port or harbor authorities (or their counterpart) nearest to the site of a maritime accident. One main purpose of the investigation is to determine the existence and extent of criminal responsibility. Once criminal responsibility is established, the investigating authorities will notify the "people's procuratorate concerned." [107] Depending upon the circumstances, the dispute arising from the accident may be settled by a number of means:

a) conciliation between the parties, at the recommendation of the investigating authorities; or
b) arbitration by the Maritime Arbitration Commission; or
c) proceedings before a competent people's court [presumably one in the nearest vicinity of the harbor administration or its equivalent which is undertaking the investigation].[108]

In view of the broad range of means of settlement—including even conciliation between the parties concerned—and the anticipation of concurrent jurisdiction by other states, it can be said that the manner in which the CPR's domestic law handles the question of criminal jurisdiction by Chinese courts over foreign ships indicates a combination of self-restraint, a concern lest the crime would go unpunished, and a desire to assist in the pacific settlement of disputes arising from offenses involving Chinese and foreign nationals.

Treatment of foreign vessels in distress seeking refuge has been spelled out in at least two agreements signed by the CPR with foreign countries. Under the Sino-Soviet Merchant Marine Navigation Agreement of December 21, 1957, it is stipulated that vessels of each party of any type, unless with prior permission, shall not stop and anchor off the coast of the other party other than in its ports, except under conditions of *force majeure*.[109] The Sino-Japanese Fishery Agreement of April 15, 1955, provided for assistance to be given the fishing vessels of the other party in case of distress, including their admittance into harbors for refuge and repairs.[110]

Whereas customary international law seems to recognize the immunity of foreign vessels admitted under circumstances of *force majeure* from the laws of the coastal state, it is not the case under the Sino-Japanese Fishery Agreement of 1955. Vessels of the other party admitted in distress, according to the terms of the agreement, were subject to the relevant laws and regulations, special instructions, or investigations by the authorities of the coastal state.[111]

As a whole, an identical consciousness of national security underscores the regime of the CPR's internal waters, territorial sea, contiguous zone, and border rivers. Traditional international law reflects a more open and generous attitude toward international navigation, which has grown from heavier use of the sea routes due to commercial interests and the development of sea power by the Western countries. The doctrines of the freedom of the high seas and innocent passage in the territorial waters of a coastal state are conceived in that liberal tradition. But jurists of the socialist countries insist that the Western powers have attempted to manipulate these norms to enhance their own economic and political interests at the expense of less developed states. Innocent passage by foreign merchant vessels, they claim, is justified only by the commercial advantages accruing from such passage. Following this logic, therefore, the same right must be denied to foreign warships, both because they bring no commercial advantages to the coastal state and because of security considerations.[112]

Similarly, the limited shipping interests of the CPR and its greater concern for security have colored its views in this respect. The gradual accommodation of foreign ships sailing into and out of CPR waters, nevertheless, represents a compromise between practical maritime needs and security considerations. The "opening" up in 1964 of the Ch'iung-chou Strait to navigation by authorized foreign nonmilitary ships, despite the 1958 declaration characterizing the strait as part of China's internal waters, is a good example of how practical needs could change Peking's attitudes. On the other hand, the CPR is not at all times consistent between what it demands from other states and what it does in regard to others. For example, it has occasionally protested that United States bombing of Chinese fishing vessels on the high seas constitutes a violation of the freedom of the high seas.[113] But, as we have noted, Peking itself has denied the same freedom to Japanese vessels attempting to fish in certain parts of the high seas contiguous to the Chinese coast which the CPR has declared off limits to nationals of other countries. Of course, given the present international tension, the same kind of obduracy and vigilance will continue to mark Peking's attitudes in this respect as in others.

Territorial Airspace and Outer Space

Airspace

It has been noted that the CPR does not recognize the right of innocent passage for foreign aircraft in airspace superjacent to its territorial waters. In accordance with Peking's 1958 declaration, all foreign aircraft must obtain prior permission before flying into Chinese airspace.[114] The policy is in agreement with a basic principle under general international law that a state possesses and exercises complete and exclusive national sovereignty in its territorial airspace.[115]

The jealousy with which the CPR guards its sovereignty in airspace can be seen in her frequent protests raised against alleged intrusions of foreign (mainly United States) aircraft.[116] Occasionally, downing of the "intruding" planes has been reported. On February 14, 1968, for example, the Department of Defense in Washington announced that an "unarmed" United States Navy Skyraider dive bomber, with one man aboard, had been shot down by a CPR MIG in Chinese airspace. According to the same announcement, it was the eighth United States plane lost over or near Chinese territory in three years. Interestingly enough, the plane shot down was one of two propeller dive bombers that allegedly "strayed" within five miles of Hainan, thus violating the CPR's twelve-mile territorial limit. Peking Radio condemned the "intrusion" as a "military provocation." [117]

The principle of sovereignty over a state's territorial airspace finds expression in a limited number of air transport agreements which the CPR has signed with foreign countries. The Sino-Burmese Air Transport Agreement (November 8, 1955), for instance, was "based on the principle of mutual respect to the sovereignty of either Contracting Party over the airspace above its territory." [118] The treaty further provides:

(a) The aircraft of the designated airline of one Contracting Party *shall comply with the laws and regulations of the other Contracting Party* relating to the admission to or departure from the territory of the other Contracting Party or to the operation, navigation or to prohibited or restricted areas within the territory of such other Contracting Party of civil aircraft engaged in international air navigation.

(b) *All laws, orders and regulations in force in the territory of one Contracting Party* such as relating to entry, departure, clearance, customs, passports, immigration, prevention of spread of disease, quarantine, and others *shall be complied with* by the crew members, passengers, baggage, cargo and mail carried by the aircraft of the other Contracting Party. Either Contracting Party shall avoid any unnecessary delay in enforcing the above laws, orders and regulations.[119] (Emphasis added)

It is also stipulated that "navigable airspace of the route specified" in the agreement within the territory of each contracting party "shall be prescribed by such Contracting Party." [120]

Viewed as a whole, the CPR's position regarding airspace appears to confirm the three simple but fundamental principles which have guided the legal and diplomatic framework within which international air transport has developed in general, namely: (a) Each State has sovereignty and jurisdiction over the airspace directly above its territory (including territorial waters); (b) Each State has complete discretion as to the admission or nonadmission of any aircraft to the airspace under its sovereignty; and (c) Airspace over the high seas, and over other parts of the earth's surface not subject to any state's jurisdiction, is free to the aircraft of all states.[121]

If one examines the CPR's bilateral air transport agreements with different countries, in which standard provisions such as the ones cited above are found almost in identical form, one will not fail to find that they follow very closely many of the standard provisions in bilateral air transport agreements signed by other states.[122] Under the 1944 Chicago Convention on International Civil Aviation, however, all aircraft of contracting states, other than those engaged in scheduled international air services, are permitted to "have the right . . . to make flights into or in transit non-stop across [each contracting party's] territory and to make stops for non-traffic purposes without the necessity of obtaining prior permission. . . ." [123] It is apparent that the CPR—not a party to this convention—does not accept such a "right" of foreign aircraft. In the circumstances, therefore, it is within the CPR's sovereign power to require, as it does, that any foreign aircraft must obtain prior permission before entry into Chinese airspace in the absence of a bilateral air transport agreement.[124]

Outer Space

In this connection, we may briefly ascertain the CPR's attitudes toward the law of outer space. Since she is not a party to any international undertaking concerned with the progressive development of outer space law—such as the work of the Committee on Peaceful Uses of Outer Space, of the U.N. General Assembly—CPR commentaries in this respect are scarce and offer no more than general comments. In a scholarly article written in 1959 and still the only one available on the subject, Liu Tse-jung outlined a position which took a middle ground between two opposite views attributed to international jurists in different countries. He did not accept, on the one hand, the theory alleging that the lack of protest or opposition from other states to Soviet and United States orbiting of satellites at altitudes ranging from 600 to 1,000 or more kilometers indicated a tacit recognition that such altitudes were beyond the outer extent of a state's territorial airspace.[125] On the other hand, he also brushed aside the theory that the sovereignty over territorial airspace recognized in existing conventions, such as the 1919 Paris Convention on Aerial Navigation and the 1944 Chicago Convention, did not extend to an altitude beyond the reach of ordinary flying machines.[126] The basis for his rejection of this view was that not all states were parties to these conventions. He used the same argument to refute suggestions that Soviet and United States orbiting of satellites, which flew over the territorial airspace of different countries, had been authorized by the International Geophysical Year.[127]

Liu, on his part, accepted the principle that a state's territorial airspace was limited. After reviewing various existing theories, he suggested that the theory which saw territorial airspace as coextensive with the atmospheric sphere was more widely accepted. The specific extent of territorial airspace, however, was yet to be defined pending further scientific advance and the progressive development of the law of outer space through "international negotiation." [128] At the present stage and in the future, Liu stressed, outer space can only be used for peaceful purposes. Although outer space did not belong to any state, he added, international law prohibited the use of outer space in such a way as to breach world peace, invade upon the sovereignty of other states, or threaten their security.[129] Since the CPR did not as yet possess the capability to explore outer space in its own right, the apprehension that its sovereignty and security might be threatened by the presence of man-made satellites in outer space belonging to its enemy is readily perceivable. Liu's position fell short of either unreservedly supporting outer space exploration or challenging the legality of such endeavoring, obviously anticipating the day when the CPR would have the capability to send its own satellites to outer space. (The CPR orbited its first man-made satellite on April 25, 1970.)

Between 1957 and 1967, the official Peking press carried commentaries relating to outer space law only on two occasions. One was a criticism, published on October 19, 1957, of the view expressed by Andrew Haley, a United States scholar on space law, that landings on the moon should require the prior permission of an appropriate international agency. Haley's view was expressed in the wake of the successful launching of the Sputnik by the Soviet Union.[130] The other commentary came in the form of Peking's denunciation of the Treaty Governing the Exploration and Use of Outer Space Including the Moon and Other Celestial Bodies, which had been unanimously approved by the U.N. General Assembly on December 19, 1966, and signed in Moscow by the United States, Britain, the Soviet Union, and several other nations on January 27, 1967. The gist of the essay was not so much a direct attack on the treaty as a suggestion that behind its making loomed large a United States-Soviet conspiracy to further their own space programs and to help their use of outer space for espionage against other states.[131]

The Peking press only occasionally reported on Soviet or United States activities of space exploration. Its omission of United Nations resolutions on legal and other problems relating to outer space shows that at least until the late 1960s the CPR government's interest in outer space law was at best lukewarm. But, Peking is not known to have raised any protest against space satellites orbiting over and above the territories of other states, including its own, as it has persistently done against the "intrusion" of foreign aircraft into its territorial airspace. The silence may indicate that the CPR government does not deny the principle that outer space is beyond the extent of a state's territorial airspace, hence, not subject to any state's territorial sovereignty.

Delimitation of Boundaries

The boundaries of a state, which mark the limits of its territorial domain, may be natural or artificial under international law.[132] The CPR's boundary treaties and agreements with neighboring states do not appear to deviate from the general practice.[133] As a whole, both natural and artificial boundary devices are made use of in CPR boundary demarcation. The following provision in the Sino-Burmese Boundary Treaty of 1960 shows the alignment of boundary according to natural devices, including watersheds:

> [The] boundary from high conical peak to the western extremity of the Sino-Burmese boundary . . . shall be fixed along the traditional customary line, i.e., from the high conical peak northwards along the *watershed* between the Taping, the Shweli and the Nu Rivers . . . to a point on the south bank of the Tulung (Taron) River . . . then further along the *watershed*. . . .[134]

In addition, the CPR boundary treaties and agreements also accept the principle of *thalweg* (as defined below) in determining the boundary when it runs along a navigable river. The Sino-Burmese Boundary Treaty reads in part:

> The Contracting Parties agree that wherever the boundary follows a river, the mid-stream line shall be the boundary in the case of an unnavigable river and the *middle line of the main navigational channel* (the deepest watercourse) [thalweg] shall be the boundary in the case of a navigable river. In case the boundary river changes its course, the boundary line between the two countries shall remain unchanged in the absence of other agreements between the two sides.[135]

The last part of this provision seems to depart somewhat from the general rule, as exemplified in the *Chamizal* case,[136] that the boundary remains in the old bed only when a boundary river shifts itself to a new bed so rapidly that the change is immediately noticeable (avulsion).

To avoid problems which might arise out of diversion by either side of water from boundary rivers, the Sino-Mongolian Boundary

Treaty of 1962 stipulates that such water resources will be shared by both sides and that details for sharing them will be worked out by further negotiations between the two governments.[137]

As in general international practice, CPR boundary treaties and agreements delimit artificial boundaries along astronomical or mathematical lines based on latitude or longitude or mountain height meters. The Sino-Pakistani Boundary Agreement of 1962 provides the following:

From the aforesaid point, the boundary line runs up the Kelechin River . . . along the middle line of its bed to its confluence (reference coordinates approximately longitude 76 degrees 02 minutes E. and *latitude* 36 degrees 26 minutes N.) with the Shorbulak Daria. . . .[138]

The Sino-Nepalese Boundary Treaty, signed on October 5, 1961, relies very heavily upon mountain height meters for boundary delimitation. For example, Article 1 (4) stipulates:

From height 6214.1 meters, the boundary line runs northeastwards along the mountain spur, passing through height 5025 meters and crossing the Angarchubo (Angarchhu) stream to height 5029 meters. . . .[139]

In CPR boundary treaties a uniform procedure for boundary demarcation is used. A joint boundary demarcation commission is constituted and charged with the responsibility of holding conferences and carrying out the tasks of:

a) conducting boundary surveys;
b) setting up boundary marks;
c) delineating the boundary line on jointly prepared maps;
d) drafting a protocol setting forth in detail the alignment of the entire boundary line and the location of all the boundary markers; and
e) preparing and getting printed detailed maps showing the boundary line and the location of the boundary markers.[140]

While the above indicates the general patterns by which the CPR has negotiated and worked out boundary settlements with neighboring states, it does not mean that any of the principles or methods used is immutable. The CPR, during her border dispute with

India, as discussed elsewhere, reiterated her opposition to the application of the watershed principle in the boundary alignment as proposed by the Indian side, on the ground that India had picked the wrong watershed.[141]

VII

Jurisdiction over Nationals Abroad and Treatment of Aliens

Nationals Abroad and "Overseas Chinese"

The CPR's civil laws are equally applicable to all Chinese nationals "irrespective of ethnic origin, sex, age, class origin, and religious creed." [1] Chinese nationals abroad, including the "overseas Chinese" who have CPR nationality, are exhorted at least officially to abide by the laws of their countries of residence. The Sino-Indonesian Dual Nationality Treaty of 1955, for example, spells out this basic attitude in Article 11:

> Each high contracting party agrees to encourage its own citizens residing in the other country . . . *to respect the laws and social customs of the country in which they reside* and not to take part in political activities of that country.[2] (Emphasis added)

During the prolonged negotiations preceding the much delayed exchange of ratifications of the treaty, the CPR maintained that "the Chinese Government has always encouraged the overseas Chinese to abide by the laws and decrees of the Indonesian Government. . . ." [3] As will be discussed later, the CPR also reciprocally demands that aliens in China obey Chinese laws and decrees. On the other hand, foreign laws are sometimes given effect in

China under circumstances not "detrimental to the public order of China." [4]

In criminal cases involving Chinese nationals abroad, the CPR accepts cojurisdiction between China (based on "nationality") and the state *loci delicti* ("territoriality"). This does not mean a waiver of her right to try the nationals who have been tried by foreign courts for crimes committed abroad. It means only that a Chinese court may take into consideration the punishments already meted out by the foreign courts which tried them while abroad. The Chinese court may then decide whether to commute or waive the penalty under Chinese law after such considerations. In this indirect way, the principle of "no double jeopardy" seems to be recognized in CPR municipal law. But when the Chinese nationals concerned do not return home after committing crimes abroad, the CPR can only seek their rendition through diplomatic channels in the absence of extradition treaties.[5]

CPR domestic laws confer certain political rights on either "overseas Chinese" or "Chinese who live abroad," [6] but no law is known to exist which imposes explicit duties on them, although whether conferring "rights" as such constitutes an imposition of "duties" remains an academic question. The Electoral Law of 1953 provides that, in pursuance of provisions of the CPR Constitution, thirty deputies to the National People's Congress shall be elected from among the overseas Chinese. But, according to Article 7 of the Electoral Law, regulations governing the election of overseas Chinese deputies (as well as those from among the armed forces) shall be "laid down separately." [7] It is not clear whether the separate regulations signify that the overseas Chinese enjoy a different legal status.

Whereas Article 23 of the CPR Constitution uses the term "Chinese who live abroad," in the Electoral Law the term has been uniformly changed to "overseas Chinese." Obviously, the two terms have the same meanings, namely, Chinese nationals abroad. The CPR Constitution further provides that the CPR "protects the just rights and interests of Chinese who live abroad." [8] Under international law, the right of a state to protect its nationals abroad is generally recognized.[9] The extension of the effect of municipal laws of a state to its nationals living in foreign countries, however, is accepted in international law only so long as it does not interfere with domestic public order of their countries of residence.[10] As noted elsewhere in this study, the CPR officially has not demanded more than the standard of "equal treatment" for Chinese nationals abroad from their host countries.[11] Nowhere is the term "overseas Chinese" or "Chinese who live abroad" ever defined in terms of their nationality or the passports they hold. During the Sino-Indian boundary conflict the CPR government even insisted that those Chinese in India who did not hold Chinese passports were nonetheless entitled to the right of repatriation as Chinese nationals.[12]

It may be said that the CPR, in the absence of a nationality law, still subscribes to the principle of *jus sanguinis,* which was accepted by all preceding Chinese governments before 1949.[13] But, with respect to Indonesia, Burma, and Nepal, the CPR has accepted limitations on her claims of nationality of overseas Chinese.[14] However, the option provisions in the CPR's agreements with these countries did not necessarily indicate a complete abandonment of the *jus sanguinis* principle. Even under the Sino-Indonesian Dual Nationality Treaty, which was intended to resolve problems arising from conflicting claims, the *jus sanguinis* basis of determining the nationality of those who should fail to take an option within the specified period was accepted in Article 5:

> The high contracting parties agree that the nationality of those persons who hold the two nationalities mentioned in Article I and who fail to choose their nationality within the period of two years prescribed in Article II shall be determined in the following manner: If *their fathers* are of Chinese origin, they shall be considered as having chosen the nationality of the People's Republic of China. . . .[15]

Jurisdiction over Aliens

Various regulations have been issued governing the status and movement of aliens within the CPR's borders. Before 1964, there were four sets of "provisional regulations" for such purposes. These were then replaced by the "Law Governing the Entry, Exit, Transit, Stay and Travel of Aliens" (hereinafter referred to as the "Alien Law"), which was passed by the NPC Standing Committee on March 13, 1964.[16] The Alien Law is as equally applicable to "stateless persons" as to foreign nationals who enter, leave, pass through, travel, or stay in China (Article 1). All aliens shall "abide by the laws and decrees of China when they are in the country" (Article 2).

All alien applications for visa or permission for travel must be made with CPR diplomatic missions and consular offices abroad, or public security offices within China (Articles 3 and 4). Applications by foreign diplomatic and consular and other governmental personnel accredited to or stationed in China will be accepted by the CPR Foreign Ministry or its branch offices. Other aliens holding diplomatic or official passports will apply to the CPR Foreign Ministry, its branch offices, or public security offices (Article 4). Aliens who are nationals of a state with which the CPR has an exemption-of-visa agreement will freely enter or leave China via ports "open to the outside." After entry they will inform the Chinese "inspection authorities" of their destinations in China and proceed forward by the specified type of carrier and route of transit (Article 9).[17]

Aliens who have violated the Alien Law will be subject to varying measures of penalty to be determined by the local public security authorities in accordance with the seriousness of each case. The punishment may range from warning, payment of fines, detention, compulsory departure within a specified time, to deportation. If criminal responsibility is involved, prosecution may be initiated (Article 17). In the case of diplomatic personnel, who enjoy immunities, the case of violations will be settled "through diplomatic channels" (Article 17). Thus, although aliens in China are subject to more stringent regulations than in a Western democracy, the Alien Law nevertheless shows minimum deference to the immunities and privileges which foreign diplomats enjoy under international law.

The CPR requires all aliens to observe Chinese civil and criminal law, including the household registration regulations applicable to citizens and aliens alike.[18] The conditions warranting the application of Chinese law in criminal cases are: (a) that the offense is found to be a crime by Chinese law, and (b) that the act constitutes an invasion of the interests of the CPR and/or her citizens. The extent of criminal responsibility in such cases will be determined on the same basis as would apply to a Chinese citizen having committed the same offense.[19]

When an alien or stateless person has already been tried and has received punishment in a foreign country for an offense committed in China, the matter will be handled by a CPR court according to the same principle as would apply to a Chinese national under similar circumstances.[20] The CPR may consider this policy as a practical application of the "equal treatment" principle.[21]

In some civil cases, such as marriage and property inheritance, involving foreign nationals in China, the CPR has shown to be quite eclectic in giving effect to foreign laws within China. While this subject falls within the bailiwick of *private* international law, it is nonetheless of interest to note that the reasons for Peking's giving extraterritorial effect to foreign laws are: (a) reciprocity (so that CPR laws may also be given effect in foreign countries in similar circumstances), and (b) practical considerations (so that, for example, no nullification of marriage or bigamy may occur).[22]

In actual practice, CPR treatment of aliens in China has manifested a conspicuous discrimination on the basis of the nationality of the aliens concerned. For example, at one time in the 1950s there were four British subjects being detained and another serving a prison term in China; [23] but American nationals imprisoned there by May, 1957, according to the Department of State, numbered more than 30.[24] This last figure probably surpasses that of aliens from any one country ever imprisoned or detained by the Chinese Communists. Furthermore, aliens from the same country may be treated differently in different periods, depending upon the existing relations between the CPR and their own government. Before 1958, for example, Russians in China were given the most generous treatment even to the point of obsequence.[25] But during the subsequent years when Sino-Soviet relations worsened, the generosity diminished rapidly and in 1967 members of the crew on board a Soviet freighter were seized and detained during a two-day Red Guard rampaging on the vessel.[26]

The CPR has entered into agreements with certain countries which set forth special terms for the treatment of each other's nationals. For example, an agreement with Denmark in 1961 exempted each other's students from taxation.[27] The CPR has bilateral trademark registration agreements with Britain (June 1, 1956), Switzerland (April 14, 1957), Sweden (April 8, 1957), Denmark (April 12, 1958), and Finland (January 26, 1967), under which the nationals of each party can obtain registration of trademarks and be granted exclusive use of such trademarks in the other country.[28] Certain agreements also provide for the exemption in full or in part of customs duties for the nationals of each party in the other's territory.[29] Aliens from countries with which the CPR has special agreements as such are entitled to certain special privileges and rights not enjoyed by nationals of other countries. Needless to say, this practice is in agreement with state practices in general.

Taking of Alien Property

As is well known, one of the foremost goals of the Chinese Communist revolution is the complete and radical socialization of economic life. The drive to nationalize private property affected aliens in mainland China as well. No systematic study of the CPR's expropriation of alien property has been made, and available information is scarcely sufficient to offer an overall, coherent picture. In the first year of its existence, between October 1, 1949, and late December, 1950, the CPR did not seem to have taken any systematic steps in this direction, except for the "confiscation" of American consular properties in Peking.[30] The Korean War, however, seemed to have precipitated later events. First, in December 1950—less than two months after Peking sent its troops to participate in the Korean War—the United States government froze all Chinese assets in the United States claimed by the CPR and its citizens.[31] The Chinese Communists retaliated two weeks later by seizing United States property and freezing American funds, both public and private, that were found in mainland China.[32]

The action followed a decree issued by Chou En-lai as head of the Government Administrative Council (GAC), dated December 28, 1950. The decree referred to the December 16, 1950, announcement by the United States government, which froze Chinese public and private assets in the United States and forbade all ships registered in the United States to sail into CPR ports. The GAC decree condemned the United States for attempting "to further plunder the Chinese people" by economic deprivation "following U.S. armed aggression in Taiwan, aerial bombing of Northeast China [Manchuria] and bombardments against Chinese merchant vessels." [33]

In view of "mounting U.S. agression and hostile acts" and in order to prevent "U.S. economic sabotage in China" and other activities "detrimental to the interests of the Chinese state and people," the same GAC decree laid down the following measures:

(a) All properties of the United States Government and private United States enterprises found within the domain of the People's Republic of China shall be subject to the *control* of the people's government in each locality, and shall be given a general accounting. They shall not be transferred or disposed of without the approval of the People's Government (Military Control Commission) of the Large Administrative Regions. (In case of a province or a municipality under the direct administration of the Central Government, such transfer and disposition shall be approved by the Commission on Finance and Economy of the Government Administrative Council.) Owners of these properties or their agents shall protect these properties against any damage or destruction.

(b) All United States public and private deposits in banks within the domain of the People's Republic of China shall be *frozen* forth-with. Funds necessary for maintaining normal operations and for personal living expenses shall be made available upon the approval of the people's government in each locality. The amounts of these funds shall be specified separately by the Commission on Finance and Economy of the Government Administrative Council.[34]

The key words in this decree are "control" and "freezing," and the general tone with which the decree was phrased is that the CPR and the United States were in some kind of a military conflict which made both parties opposing belligerents. International law recognizes the power of one belligerent, as an incident to its effort to weaken the enemy both militarily and economically, to confiscate the property of the enemy located within its national domain.[35] Although it may not confiscate enemy *private* property, a belligerent has the power under international law to "preserve" such property. The doctrine whereby a belligerent assumed the role as custodian of alien property found expression, for example, in the United States Trading with the Enemy Act. As A. Mitchell Palmer, Alien Property Custodian, stated it: "The broad purpose of Congress as expressed in the Trading with the Enemy Act is, first, to *preserve* enemy-owned property situated in the United States from loss and, secondly, to *prevent* every use of it which may be hostile or detrimental to the United States. . . ." [36] The United States freezing of CPR assets and its embargo against the CPR seemed to be likewise guided by this spirit. It is interesting to note that the CPR decree of December 28, 1950, avoided all references to "confiscation," "expropriation" or "nationalization," and gave the impression that the United States assets, both public and private, were to be held in trust. The exact legal status of these seized assets and their fate remain unclear.

Despite the legal haze, the fact is that United States interests and investments in mainland China were either eased out by various restrictions, including punitive taxes, or placed under "control" and "freezing," or taken over forthwith by the CPR government during the early 1950s. No compensation in any form was paid. Since the United States did not recognize the CPR, it delivered a diplomatic note to the Nationalist Chinese government seated in Taipei, Taiwan, in 1954, listing the properties in mainland China belonging to the United States government.[37] There is no agreement on the total value of private United States investments and interests appropriated in mainland China. One official report based on information received from the Department of State gave an estimate at $56,-000,000.[38] During a congressional hearing in 1966, however, a representative of the American and Foreign Power Company, which owned a majority interest in Shanghai Power Company, the leading electric power company in Shanghai, China, claimed that his company alone lost $60,000,000 as a result of the Chinese Communist confiscation in December, 1950. The figure, he further claimed, did not include the $2,000,000 representing the properties of its subsidiary, Western District Power Company in Shanghai.[39] Another independent source estimated the total value of United States investments in China toward the end of 1950 at $100-200 million.[40]

By the passage of an amendment to Title V of the International Claims Settlement Act of 1949, Congress in 1966 authorized the Foreign Claims Settlement Commission in Washington, D. C., to initiate a claims adjudication program for American claimants against the CPR on the same basis as the Cuban claims program authorized in Title V. Specifically, the commission was empowered to determine the amount and validity of claims against the CPR, arising since October 1, 1949, for losses resulting from the nationalization or other taking of property of United States nationals in violation of international law and claims for disability or death arising out of similar acts by the CPR.[41]

The period for filing the claims was set by the Foreign Claims Settlement Commission for January 6, 1968, through July 6, 1969.[42] In reply to my inquiries, Andrew T. McGuire, general counsel of the commission, reported that a total of 576 claims were filed under Public Law 89-780, primarily from Americans who had businesses in China, religious organizations, and from American missionaries. For all practical purposes the program has been completed. The commission approved 378 awards in the total amount of $196,309,559.33. A total of 195 claims were denied and 3 claims were withdrawn, according to Mr. McGuire.[43]

In the past, negotiations between the United States and certain Communist governments have resulted in claims settlement agreements whereby the expropriating government has agreed to pay the United States government a lump sum in settlement for the losses suffered by United States citizens. The first agreement of this nature was reached with the Yugoslav government in 1948.[44] The International Claims Settlement Act was enacted to implement this agreement by establishing a commission to adjudicate these claims and to provide certain adjudication procedures. The act also provided the machinery necessary to adjudicate claims of United States citizens included within the terms of any claims settlement agreement concluded thereafter between the United States government and a foreign government. The China claims program authorized by Congress in 1966 provided for the extension of the act to claims against the CPR in anticipation of a possible future settlement through bilateral negotiations with Peking.

If the CPR considered that its taking of American assets in China was effected in a state of belligerency against the United States, as we have speculated, then the settlement would have to await the termination of that status, which would mean, among other things, the prior settlement of the Taiwan impasse although President Nixon on June 10, 1971, lifted the United States embargo against mainland China. Much would also depend upon the size of the total CPR assets frozen in the United States and other conditions bearing on the bargaining position of the United States.

The CPR's taking of properties owned by nationals of other countries did not seem to follow the same pattern as the seizure of American assets. For instance, between 1951 and 1952, Peking "requisitioned" (*cheng-yung*) the properties of two British firms—the Asiatic Petroleum Company and the Shell Company—two British dockyards at Shanghai, the land belonging to the British-owned Shanghai and Tientsin Race Course Companies, and some houses and building land owned by British nationals.[45] In ordering the "requisition" of the assets of the Asiatic Petroleum Company, the CPR government specified that (a) the measure would affect only those assets *other than* the real estate occupied by the company's headquarters, branch offices, and sales offices in different parts of China, and (b) the Chinese government would "purchase" the company's "entire petroleum stock" in China.[46] According to the British government, however, the total value of British properties seized by Peking "without payment of rent or compensation" was 9,000,000 pounds up to October, 1952.[47]

Despite the dearth of specific information, it appears that some tentative conclusions may be drawn. First, the CPR did not seem to follow the Soviet example of issuing general nationalization decrees extending to all sectors of economic life upon the inauguration of the regime.[48] While the CPR's nationalization of domestic industry and commerce underwent a transition of public-private joint ownership and thereafter provided for the payment of fixed interests to members of the former "national bourgeoisie" for their appropriated properties,[49] its taking of alien property followed a more indirect procedure than outright confiscation.

Secondly, although official pronouncements were silent, there is evidence that CPR jurists were not unaware of the legal implications of the taking of alien property. A carefully documented article by Li Hao-p'ei, published in the *Cheng-fa yen-chiu* (Studies of Politics and Law) in 1958, stressed that nationalization of private property for public purposes was recognized under international law as a proper exercise of a state's sovereignty. Noting the change since 1917 and especially after World War II, Li suggested that the principle of respect for vested rights, which he attacked as "imperialist" in origin, now yielded to purposes of general welfare and a state's sovereignty over its natural resources and domestic mode of production. The new norm, he noted, was affirmed by the Permanent Court of International Justice in the *Chorzow Factory* case; and even Britain and France in objecting to the Egyptian nationalization of the Suez Canal Company could not deny its existence.[50]

After reviewing the various theories regarding nationalization, Li rejected the position stated in United States Secretary of State Hull's note to the Mexican government in 1938 [51] and reaffirmed in *The Rosemarie,* decided by a British court in Aden in 1953,[52] to the effect that expropriation must be accompanied by "prompt, adequate and effective payment" of compensation. Nor did he accept the compromise position proposed by Lauterpacht [53] and La Pradelle [54] that some partial compensation should be paid, calculated not so much by the extent of damage as by the capacity and good will of the nationalizing state. To the extent that nationalization is part of an all-reaching drive toward economic and social progress, such as is found in the socialist countries appearing after World War I, Li favored the view held by a third school which considered compensation as incompatible with the sovereignty of the nationalizing state and disruptive to its modernizing efforts. In addition to jurists from socialist countries, Li cited a number of Western publicists, including Sir John Fischer Williams [55] and S. Friedman,[56] as supporting this view.

After a lengthy review of cases involving the taking of alien property that had been decided by international and national courts and also of state practices dating from the Soviet and the Mexican nationalization efforts, the author found no uniform rule in international law regarding the payment of compensation, although for a variety of reasons compensations were paid at the discretion of the nationalizing states in many cases. He suggested, however, that the nationalizing state had an obligation not to discriminate between aliens and its own nationals. The principle that aliens could claim no better treatment than the same standards accorded to nationals, he stressed, was affirmed in the 1926 Report of the League of Nations Committee of Jurists on the Codification of the Law of the Responsibility of States,[57] and again in Article 11 of the Draft Convention on the Treatment of Foreigners proposed by the Economic Committee of the League of Nations in 1928.[58] This provision, which extended to measures of expropriation, was supported by a majority of states attending the International Conference on the Treatment of Foreigners at Paris in 1929, he further suggested.[59]

Li also cited Resolution 626 (VII) of the U.N. General Assembly, passed on December 21, 1952, in his attempt to show that each state enjoyed an inherent right of freely utilizing and exploiting its natural wealth and resources. He also invoked Article 1 of the Draft Convention on Human Rights passed by the Third Committee of the U.N. General Assembly at its twenty-ninth meeting in 1955, which affirmed a state's right of self-determination in the economic as well as social, political, and cultural spheres. The article provided that each nation may, for its own purposes, dispose of its natural wealth and resources in such a manner as not to contravene obligations assumed in the course of international economic cooperation on a reciprocal basis and in accordance with international law.[60] Li concluded that in the absence of specific requirements the payment of compensation would be only at the discretion of the state legitimately exercising its right of economic sovereignty.[61]

The article by Li Hao-p'ei was written before the passage by the General Assembly of a series of resolutions culminating in Resolution 1803 (XVII), December 14, 1962, which explicitly stated that the owner of the properties nationalized, expropriated, or requisitioned by a foreign state must be paid "appropriate compensation in accordance with the rules in force in the State taking such measures in the exercise of its sovereignty and in accordance with international law." [62] Nevertheless, despite his objection to the payment of compensation in principle, it is interesting to note that Li did not deny the fact that in practice some states did pay compensations at their own discretion, that a nationalization measure must not discriminate against aliens in favor of nationals, and that nationalization was within the province of public international law. Of course, it is impossible to know to what extent Li's views represent those of the CPR government, since his is the only article published on the subject thus far. Besides, he was dealing with nationalization in general and said nothing about the CPR's own policy.

Detention of Aliens

Various cases have occurred involving the detention of foreign nationals in mainland China since 1949. These cases can be generally classified under three categories: those convicted on spy charges, those held in a move of retaliation, and those held for alleged violations of Chinese law. The earliest "spy" case involved thirteen captured United States airmen whose planes were shot down in Chinese airspace during the Korean War. They were released in 1956 after many attempts by the United States and its allies to intercede on their behalf, including a personal trip to Peking by Dag Hammarskjold, the late secretary-general of the United Nations.[63] At least four Americans held over a long period of time are still in CPR prisons. The first two were taken in 1952. John Downey, of

New Britain, Connecticut, and Richard Fecteau, of Lynn, Massachusetts,* are officially described as civilian employees of the United States Army who were lost while flying from Korea to Japan. The Chinese say that they are intelligence agents shot down while dropping supplies to anti-Communist rebels in Northeast China [Manchuria], far from their alleged flight route. Fecteau was given a twenty-year sentence for espionage, due for release in 1972; and Downey was sentenced to life imprisonment.[64]

The other two prisoners are United States military pilots who strayed over China while on Vietnam duty and are being held as "flying bandits." Air Force Major Phillip Smith, of Roodhouse, Illinois, was downed in 1965, and Navy Lieutenant Robert Flynn, of Houston, Minnesota, was taken prisoner in 1967. Although it is not yet known whether either has been charged with a specific crime, they were exhibited at Red Guard rallies as "imperialist aggressors against the Vietnamese people." All these prisoners were allowed limited privileges of receiving from home two eleven-pound parcels per month and a trickle of mail, through the help of the Red Cross organizations in both countries.[65]

Formerly there had been two other prisoners. One was Hugh Redmond, Jr., of Yonkers, New York, arrested in 1951 in Shanghai, where he had represented Henningsen & Company, an American importing and exporting firm. Although the United States claimed that he was an innocent businessman illegally convicted, Peking said that he was a spy in secret contact with agents in Hong Kong. He was given a life sentence in 1954 but committed suicide on April 13, 1970, by slashing himself with a razor blade.[66] The other one was Bishop James Walsh, who had been given twenty years in 1958 after refusing to take advantage of Chinese permission to leave the country. A long-time missionary for the Maryknoll Brothers, Bishop Walsh chose to remain as a symbol of faith for Chinese Catholics. Because of his advanced age, the bishop's cell remained in the hospital section of the Shanghai prison. In an unannounced move, on July 10, 1970, the CPR released Bishop Walsh, at the age of 79. He reached Hong Kong the same day and

* As this had gone to print, on December 13, 1971, Peking announced the release of Fecteau and the reduction of Downey's life sentence to five more years. *New York Times*, December 14, 1971, pp 1, 7.

after a brief rest returned to the United States.[67] In a talk in New York, Bishop Walsh recounted that the charge for his arrest in 1958 was that he had helped a Chinese church board obtain remittances from Hong Kong, which, according to the financial laws of the CPR, was a criminal act.[68]

A recent case involving the arrest and trial of two agents of a British firm in China came up in 1968. In March, 1968, Peking press announced the arrest of George Watt, a Briton who arrived in China on December 14, 1966. "In the guise of an engineer" for the British Vickers-Zimmer, Ltd., the announcement said, Watt "engaged in espionage activities . . . and rendered active service to the British imperialist policy of aggression." During his stay in the country, Watt "spied out and stole important intelligence about China's military, political and economic affairs and the great proletarian cultural revolution, and had furtively taken many photographs of prohibited areas in China." [69]

Arrested along with Watt was Peter Deckart, a West German employed as an engineer by Vickers-Zimmer, Ltd., who "had also engaged in espionage activities in China." On March 15 the Intermediate People's Court in Lanchow, in a default judgment, handed down a three-year sentence for Watt. At the same time, the Lanchow Public Security Bureau ordered the immediate deportation of Deckart.[70] Subsequently in July, 1968, the Peking Municipal Intermediate People's Court convicted the Vickers-Zimmer firm for "fraud" and announced that its contract to construct a plant in China signed with the China National Technical Import Corporation on November 25, 1964, was annulled as of the date of the judgment. All personnel of the firm still in China were given ten days to leave the country, while Vickers-Zimmer, Ltd. was ordered to pay an indemnity of 650,000 British pounds for "economic losses" suffered by the China National Technical Import Corporation.[71]

On July 21, 1967, following the arrest of some CPR journalists by the British authorities in Hong Kong during the 1967 riots, Peking placed Anthony Grey, a British correspondent of Reuters news agency, under house arrest. Grey was kept in solitude for nine months before he was permitted to see for the first time two British Embassy officials.[72] The Chinese never suggested that Grey committed a crime, but on December 4, 1968, a CPR official in London made it clear that the British journalist was being held as a hostage for thirteen Chinese journalists being held in Hong Kong.[73] When finally Grey was released on October 4, 1969, the CPR Foreign Ministry told him that "since the Hong Kong British authorities had already released all the patriotic Chinese [leftist] journalists, his freedom of movement was restored to him." The CPR made it plain that Grey's detention in Peking was a retaliation for the British "unjustifiable persecution and imprisonment" of the leftist Chinese journalists in Hong Kong.[74]

On February 16, 1969, Chinese Communist gunboats captured three pleasure yachts, with two Americans and thirteen others aboard, on a holiday cruise near Hong Kong. For a time, it was speculated that these persons were taken in retaliation for the January 24 defection to the United States of Liao Ho-shu, chargé d'affaires of the CPR Legation in the Hague.[75] The thirteen other persons, including British, Norwegians, and Australians, and their Chinese crewmen, were released on April 2. But the two Americans—Simeon Baldwin, general manager of an aircraft parts company, Airstocks, Limited, and Mrs. Bessie Hope Donald, a divorcee secretary—were held until December 7, 1969. The two had thrown their passports overboard just before being captured in the hope of concealing their nationalities. This step turned out to have hurt their chance of quick release. According to a report by the official Chinese press agency, Hsinhua, Mr. Baldwin and Mrs. Donald had "at first adopted very dishonest attitude" but that they later "admitted their mistakes of trying to conceal their identities and intruding into China's territorial sea." [76] It became plain, therefore, that the original capture was on the ground of intrusion into Chinese territorial waters, which, according to the CPR, extend twelve miles seaward from the coast.

Toward the latter half of 1968, a total of thirteen Japanese newsmen and trading firm representatives were detained in mainland China. Attempts by the Japanese government to obtain their release did not get very far.[77] From the scanty information available, it became known that one of these, Masanobu Suzuki, a thirty-eight-year old resident official in Peking of Nikka Boeki Kogyo Company, Ltd., a Tokyo firm, had been arrested in February, 1968. A representative of the Association for Promotion of International Trade, Japan, who made the revelation in Peking, quoted an official of the Chinese Committee for Promotion of International Trade as saying that Suzuki's arrest was linked to evidence that he had violated China's laws and regulations. Although the specific violations were unknown, Suzuki was suspected of espionage activities of long standing. A total of sixty-four officials of fifty-five Japanese trading companies were then visiting in Peking and were staying at the Hsin Chiao Hotel. Suzuki reportedly had no close contacts with other trading company officials at the hotel. The Japanese Association official said that previously he had had no suspicion about Suzuki but it seemed now that Suzuki could have been involved in dubious activities.[78]

Obviously, as a Communist country the CPR is most sensitive to possible espionage activities. Similar arrests of foreign visitors are widely known in other Communist countries and take place only too frequently. In a celebrated case, Professor Frederick C. Barghoorn of Yale University was arrested in Moscow at the end of October, 1963, on espionage charges. He was later freed and expelled from the Soviet Union only after the personal intercession of President Kennedy.[79] Not long ago, a Columbia University instructor, Ronald Wiedenhoeft, was imprisoned for nine months in East Germany also on espionage charges. He was released in June, 1968, following long negotiations by Maxwell M. Rabb, a New York lawyer who had obtained the release of six other Americans held in East Germany.[80] But, there are other cases in which honest dialogues have averted misunderstandings that could otherwise have aroused suspicion of espionage. For example, Lisa Hobbs, of the San Francisco *Examiner*, told how she had obtained a visa to Communist China under false identity in 1965 and at the end of her trip she astonished her Chinese host by revealing her true identity. Li Tieh-fei, her official guide, was truly convinced of her honesty and her genuine desire to see China out of a belief that "some of us, from your country and from mine, at some level, away from an official table in Europe, must start talking to each other as members of the human race." In the end, after much pondering, Li said simply: "Thank you, Lisa, I assure you, I could guarantee, nothing will happen to you." Although she could have been held for espionage, she was allowed to leave as scheduled after a three-week trip in China.[81]

Concluding Remarks

A sovereign state enjoys unhindered freedom under international law, in matters concerning the entry of aliens and the rights and obligations of resident aliens in civic, economic, and political spheres. It can deny the entry of a foreign national and expel him even after an authorized entry. The same sovereign right extends to the control of a state's imports and exports and the laying down of tariff duties. The state may deny to aliens the right to own certain kinds of property, to engage in business or other gainful occupations, and to participate in political activity. International law does not forbid a state to discriminate between nationals of different foreign states or to discriminate in favor of its own nationals. But, in the protection of life, personal liberty, and property, and other similar matters of fundamental importance to the individual, a state is obligated generally to treat aliens at least as favorably as its own citizens. In the past, a large body of state practice and judicial and arbitral decisions supported the rule that a state must live up to an international minimum standard of treatment of aliens.[82]

Like the Soviet Union and other underdeveloped countries, [83] the CPR does not recognize the norm and the very concept of an international minimum standard. As we have observed elsewhere in this book, CPR commentators consider that "international standard" was but a tool employed by "imperialist" powers to assert the superiority of their nationals in China and other non-Western countries. The sentiment went back to the pre-Communist era. At the 1930 Hague Conference for the Codification of International Law, the delegate from the Republic of China, Dr. Wu Chao-chu, introduced a proposal which would substitute equal treatment of aliens for the "international standard" insisted by Western powers. The majority of the states attending the conference were from the more developed Western background. Although the proposal was supported by the less developed and capital-importing countries, it was defeated in the final vote by a small margin.[84] In a book written in

1940, a Chinese scholar on international law criticized the dual standard allegedly maintained by Western powers who demanded much higher standards of treatment for their own nationals in the less developed countries than they accorded the nationals from the latter.[85] He quoted the remarks by B. H. Williams, published in *Current History*,[86] that if the United States had been compelled to observe the same principles of liability which were required of China, many an American governor or sheriff would have gone to the gallows for acts of violence committed against aliens within their jurisdiction.[87] In the same discussion, the author supported this point by citing the following passage from E. M. Borchard's famous work:

> China, indeed, regardless of treaties, has in innumerable cases been held to a degree of responsibility amounting actually to a guarantee of the security of persons and property of aliens.[88]

It may be concluded that much of the CPR's attitude toward aliens and the outside world can be attributed equally to its Communist ideology and China's baneful past experience. The CPR's nationalization of alien property, as part of its overall socialization of economic life, is doubtless a product of its socialist structure. Many CPR restrictions on aliens also have precedence in the practice of Stalinist Russia. But its sensitivity toward possible alien superiority or defiance of Chinese sovereignty is unquestionably inseparable from China's past experience. Security considerations also figure prominently in the CPR's policy regarding the treatment of aliens within Chinese boundaries. But, part of its xenophobic manifestations is probably also due to the lingering influence of a traditional mentality, derived from the experience of a continental, agrarian, and largely self-sufficient society that had limited contacts with the outside. For example, being a sedentary, agrarian people unaccustomed to travel and commerce across national borders on a scale anywhere near that found in Western history, the Chinese always hold dear the thought that all brethren away from home are still tied to them by an inseparable bond of solidarity sealed by their common blood (*jus sanguinis*). Chinese nationals and persons of Chinese descent in foreign countries, except where treaties provide otherwise, are invariably regarded as "overseas Chinese" (*hua-ch'iao* [literally, Chinese transients abroad]), whose ties with the motherland are never severed, either sentimentally or legally.[89] The CPR Constitution, as we have seen, still reserved room for Chinese persons abroad to participate in the political life at home. Conversely, the Chinese also consider that aliens in China are never to be treated as though they had cut their ties with their home state. The United States regulations (promulgated in 1952) making aliens permanently resident in the country liable to military draft would be absolutely inconceivable to the Chinese. Aside from other implications, how could the aliens—who still owe their allegiance to their home state—be trusted if they ever were drafted in the Chinese armed forces? [90] Many of the spy charges against foreign nationals may reflect this very tradition-bound Chinese suspicion toward strangers in their midst. The sentiments, instead of being abated, would only be reinforced by the combined effect from the CPR's "closed" social system, frenzied revolutionary mentality enforced by Chairman Mao, and the country's continued international isolation.

VIII

Law Relating to Diplomatic Relations

Foreign Relations Powers under the CPR Constitution

The CPR's foreign relations powers are delineated under various provisions of the CPR Constitution. "The Chairman of the People's Republic of China *represents* the CPR in its foreign relations" and "receives foreign diplomatic representatives" (Article 41). In pursuance of "decisions" of the Standing Committee of the National People's Congress (NPC) made under Article 31 (11) and (12), the CPR Chairman "dispatches and recalls plenipotentiary representatives abroad and ratifies treaties concluded with foreign states" (Article 41).

In the event that the CPR Chairman is incapacitated, the above, as well as other functions and powers of the chairman, shall be exercised by the CPR Vice-Chairman (Article 46). It is apparently because of this constitutional provision that, during the upsurge of the 1966 Great Proletarian Cultural Revolution, Tung Pi-wu, in his capacity as the CPR's Vice-Chairman, received the new Polish Ambassador Witold Rikzinski in the presentation of his credentials, on November 2, 1966. (Liu Shao-ch'i, the head of state, was known to be in Peking but incapacitated at the time.)[1]

We shall see in a different chapter how the power of ratification of treaties is exercised by the CPR Chairman. An example of his exercise of the power of sending and recalling diplomatic envoys can be found in the following "order" of CPR Chairman Liu Shao-ch'i, of May 13, 1965:

Appoint Ma Tzu-ch'ing as the Ambassador Plentipotentiary of the People's Republic of China to the Republic of Mali.

Recall Lai Ya-li as the Ambassador Plenipotentiary of the People's Republic of China to the Republic of Mali.[2]

Many of the messages of felicitation exchanged during the presentation of credentials by CPR diplomats in foreign countries are reproduced verbatim in the *Chung-hua jen-min kung-ho-kuo tui-wai kuan-hsi wen-chien chi* [Collection of Documents Relating to the CPR's Foreign Relations]. They generally follow the established practice in diplomatic relations.[3]

Three clauses of the CPR Constitution govern the exercise of "state power" over matters of war and peace. By Article 27 (13) the NPC is empowered "to decide on questions of war and peace." When the NPC is not in session, its standing committee has the power, under Article 31 (16), "to decide . . . on the proclamation of a state of war in the event of an armed attack on the country."

In pursuance of such a "decision" by the NPC or its standing committee, the CPR Chairman "proclaims a state of war" in accordance with Article 40. No instance of a proclamation of "a state of war" has yet occurred. But, in 1959, when the armed conflict with India first erupted, the NPC Standing Committee was gripped with the problem in a three-day prolonged debate. A final resolution passed and prominently published seemed to endorse a "get-tough" policy for the State Council to follow. The question of the legal state of war, however, was not discussed.[4]

The NPC Standing Committee, under Article 31 (16) of the constitution, can bind the nation with decisions, "in case of necessity, to execute an international treaty for joint defense against aggression." Presumably this keeps the channels open to enable the NPC Standing Committee to have the power to declare treaties of a defense nature the supreme law of the land. But no instance of the NPC Standing Committee exercising this power is known.

A number of the CPR's laws and regulations purport to fill *lacunae* in the constitution with respect to foreign relations. By a resolution of the NPC Standing Committee, its chairman is authorized to "receive foreign diplomatic representatives" when both the CPR Chairman and the CPR Vice-Chairman [after 1959, Vice-Chairmen] are absent from the capital "either on vacation or on official duties." [5] Another resolution passed by the NPC Standing Committee spells out the types of treaties or agreements which must be ratified in pursuance of Articles 31 (12) and 41 of the CPR Constitution, and those others which need only be "approved" by the State Council. This enactment is followed in practice in CPR treaty making.[6]

The ultimate powers of the Central Committee of the Chinese Communist Party over the CPR's foreign relations, as over all other state functions, cannot be overstressed. However, no document laying down the exact relations between the policy-making leadership within the Chinese Communist Party and the implementation mechanisms within the State Council (the Cabinet) is known to exist.[7]

Diplomatic Practice, Immunities, and Privileges

Diplomatic Practice

By the end of 1969, twenty years after its birth, the CPR was recognized by fifty-three states and maintained diplomatic ties with forty-seven of them.[8] A breakthrough came when Canada and the CPR on October 13, 1970, reached an accord whereby Canada, which had until then recognized and maintained diplomatic relations with Nationalist China, switched recognition to Peking but did not commit herself to the Chinese Communist claim to the title of Taiwan itself. The Canadian formula seemed to set the pattern or otherwise inspired similar solutions in other cases (see Chapter XI below). Until the Cultural Revolution, it was a practice of the CPR to publish a complete list of both Chinese diplomatic missions abroad and foreign missions in China, which includes the names of the heads of missions.[9] The establishment of diplomatic relations between the CPR and foreign countries follows, *mutatis mutandis*, the procedure of: (a) diplomatic recognition,[10] (b) exchange of notes on the establishment of diplomatic missions in each other's capital,[11] (c) appointment and sending of envoys,[12] and (d) presentation of credentials by the envoys.[13]

Normally, all the CPR's diplomatic missions abroad are at the ambassadorial level, except in Britain and the Netherlands, where a chargé d'affaires is maintained. According to available information, the CPR's foreign service includes the ranks of: ambassador, counselor, commercial counselor, cultural counselor, first secretary, second secretary, third secretary, attaché, commercial attaché, military attaché, and assistant military attaché. The size of a CPR diplomatic mission abroad varies from country to country. The Chinese Embassy in North Vietnam in 1966 consisted of twenty-three persons, including two "economic representatives," a title not often used. The Chinese Embassy in Finland in 1966 was only a six-man mission. Until the abortive Communist coup in October, 1965, in Indonesia, the CPR maintained not only a twenty-nine-man embassy but also a consulate-general in Djakarta with five consular officers, and a consulate in Bandjarmasin, Makassar, and Medan.[14]

Diplomatic Immunities and Privileges

The State Council is known to have promulgated a number of regulations respecting the immunities and privileges of foreign diplomats and consular personnel in China. The following were promulgated on September 14, 1951:

a) Provisional Measures Relating to the Preferential Treatment of Foreign Diplomatic and Consular Personnel;
b) Provisional Measures Relating to the Exemption from Taxation of Foreign Diplomatic and Consular Personnel; and
c) Provisional Measures Relating to the Exemption from Inspection of the Luggage of Foreign Diplomatic and Consular Personnel upon Entry into and Departure from China.[15]

Article 2 (2) of the Provisional Measures Relating to the Preferential Treatment of Foreign Diplomatic and Consular Personnel provides: "Diplomats enjoy the privilege of exemption from the civil and criminal jurisdiction of China." A major Chinese textbook on civil law, in which the provision is cited, explains that in case of a dispute involving foreign diplomatic personnel the matter is to be resolved "through diplomatic channels, and our courts shall have no jurisdiction." [16]

However, the same textbook adds that, if a diplomat should be the plaintiff in a civil suit or if he should agree to waive his immunity, a Chinese court can then assume jurisdiction.[17] Another textbook on criminal law recognizes that Chinese courts will have no jurisdiction over foreign diplomats in cases involving criminal responsibility. The immunities and privileges of duly accredited foreign diplomats, it explains, guarantee that they are not subject to arrest, their official premises and private residence are not subject to search, and their mail and luggage are not to be inspected.[18] The course of remedy open to the Chinese government, the textbook continues, is to inform the home government of the diplomat involved and to obtain his recall or a consent from his home government to waive his immunities, so that he can be brought to the jurisdiction of a Chinese court. In cases of severe consequences, the diplomat directly responsible for the criminal act can even be told to leave China within a specified period.[19]

Persons enjoying diplomatic immunities and privileges are classified as follows: (a) the Chief of State or government officials of a country on an official visit to China, (b) diplomatic envoys of the rank of ambassador or minister, (c) members of a diplomatic mission below the ambassadorial or ministerial rank, including counselors, secretaries, military attachés, other attachés, and other personnel by prior agreement, and (d) the spouses and children (before reaching majority) of the above-mentioned personnel. Diplomatic immunities and privileges are, however, not granted to "service" personnel of a diplomatic mission in China.[20]

The textbook hastens to explain that immunities and privileges granted by the CPR to foreign diplomatic and other official personnel should not be confused with the rights of extraterritoriality (consular jurisdiction) which were once enjoyed by "imperialist" countries in China. A footnote states that the same immunities and privileges are granted to the spouses and children of foreign diplomats in order to guarantee the uninterrupted execution of diplomatic functions. Furthermore, such extension of immunities and privileges "is based on the principle of reciprocity and international comity, and has become international custom." [21] The Chinese sensitivity to the special privileges that Western powers enjoyed in pre-1943 China, such as consular jurisdiction, can be seen from this almost apologetic tone with which the textbook explains why and how the standard diplomatic privileges and immunities are extended to foreign diplomats without abridging Chinese sovereignty.

Many of the CPR domestic laws or regulations have shown *prima facie* respect for the immunities and privileges of foreign diplomatic personnel. Diplomats are given "preferential treatment" and exemption from the inspections provided for under the following public security regulations:

a) Provisional Rules Governing the Inspection of Ships, Their Crews, Passengers, and Luggage Upon Entry and Departure (promulgated by the Government Administrative Council on January 27, 1950);
b) Provisional Rules Governing the Inspection of Airplanes, Their Crews, Passengers, and Luggage upon Entry and Departure (May 24, 1951); and
c) Provisional Rules Governing the Inspection of Trains, Their Crews, Passengers, and Luggage upon Entry and Departure (May 24, 1951).[22]

A standard clause in these regulations reads: "Matters concerning the inspection of foreign diplomatic personnel shall be dealt with in accordance with the regulations laid down by the Ministry of Foreign Affairs of the Central People's Government." [23]

In Chapter VII we have seen that the Alien Law imposes certain penalties on aliens who have violated its provisions.[24] But the same provision contains a proviso in respect of foreign diplomats, which reads: "Cases concerning violations of these provisions by foreign diplomatic personnel, who enjoy diplomatic immunities, shall be dealt with through the diplomatic channels." [25]

The CPR's Provisional Customs Regulations also exempts foreign diplomats from customs duties, but it stipulates:

> Measures relating to the preferential treatment [i.e., immunities and exemptions, etc.] of the luggage and articles imported for official and personal use by foreign diplomatic officers and missions stationed in China shall be [separately] laid down by the Customs Administration in conjunction with the Ministry of Foreign Affairs.[26]

The separate regulations concerning the "preferential treatment" of diplomatic personnel, suggested in this provision, can not be located. But evidence of their existence is found in a later, more composite, version of the customs and luggage inspection regulations, "Revised Measures for Customs Inspection and Control of Luggage and Articles Carried by Travellers Entering or Leaving China," which came into effect as of October 15, 1958. Article 5 of the "Revised Measures" stipulates, in part:

> The luggage and articles carried by . . . foreign diplomatic and consular officials, foreign service couriers, experts invited to China, representatives of . . . foreign governments . . . shall be released [from Customs duties] in accordance with *relevant regulations*. (Emphasis added) [27]

It is apparent that what was promised in the early 1950s had by 1958 become existing "relevant regulations."

By another enactment, foreign diplomats, including those who come to China for visits, exhibits, negotiations, or conferences, and also "foreign dignitaries," are exempted from customs inspection insofar as "gift items" carried with them or shipped in or out of China for them are concerned.[28]

Consular treaties signed by the CPR with foreign countries usually contain references to diplomatic immunities and privileges as standards for comparison. The following clause from the Sino-Czech Consular Treaty of 1960 may be cited:

> Article 4 (2): Consuls shall enjoy the appropriate privileges and advantages arising out of this Treaty and prescribed by the legislation of the receiving state.
>
> Article 10: The baggage of consuls and articles imported for their use and for the use of consulates shall, subject to reciprocity, be ex-

empted from customs *to the extent to which such exemption is enjoyed by diplomatic officers and diplomatic missions.* (Emphasis added) [29]

It may be adduced from these provisions that the signatories of the treaty speak of diplomatic and consular privileges, "advantages," and "exemptions" as both prescribed by domestic legislation (Article 4 (2)) and established in state practices under international law (Article 10).

Consular rights, as a whole, are somewhat more restricted, as can be seen from CPR consular treaties with foreign countries. Part II of the Sino-Czech Consular Treaty, for example, deals with "Rights, Privileges, and Advantages of Consuls." In addition to the provisions already cited, the following is also stipulated:

(a) *"Consuls shall not be subject to the jurisdiction of the courts* of the receiving state in respect of acts performed in their official capacity." (Article 5) But, they shall be "required to attend as *witnesses* before the courts of the receiving state in proceedings not connected with their official duties." (Article 6)

(b) "Consular offices shall be inviolable. . . . The official document archives of consulates shall be inviolable. . . . Correspondence and telegrams dispatched and received by consuls in connection with their *official duties* shall be inviolable and *shall not be subject to inspection.*

(c) "Consuls and consular officers who are nationals of the sending state, and their spouses and minor children, *shall be exempt from personal and material service and from direct taxes."* (Article 9)

Of great interest is Article 20 of the same Consular Treaty, which stipulates:

The provisions of this Treaty concerning the rights and duties of consuls shall apply *mutatis mutandis* to officers of *diplomatic missions* who have been *assigned to consular functions.* This provision shall *not* affect the diplomatic privileges and advantages of such officers.

Summing up the discussion above and taking in view the CPR's practice,[30] we may venture the following basic conclusions:

(1) First, the CPR does adjust her state practice to the necessary amenities established under international law. She accords foreign diplomatic and consular personnel and missions rather broad immunities and affords them special protection under Chinese law:

Subject to minor exceptions, a foreign diplomat may not be arrested, prosecuted, sued, or taxed unless the sending state waives his immunities.

(2) Second, immunities and privileges granted to foreign consular personnel are more restricted than those given foreign diplomats. Consular rights are sometimes explicitly spelled out in bilateral consular treaties.[31] Immunities and privileges granted to foreign diplomatic officers and missions are in part prescribed in CPR domestic laws and regulations and indications are that they are more sweeping and broader than those enjoyed by consular officers, as is generally the case under international law.[32]

(3) Third, members of the families of both the diplomatic personnel, under customary international law, and the consular officers, by treaty, are generally accorded the immunities and privileges of the diplomatic and consular officers themselves. This extension is meant to assure that the latter will be able to perform their official duties and functions without interruption. While immunities are shared by all members of diplomatic rank independently of any treaty provisions or special agreements, personnel in the "service" category do not enjoy them unless otherwise specified.[33] Commercial representatives are either included as full-fledged members of a diplomatic mission with the rank of "commercial counselor" or are by special agreements accorded "full rights and privileges enjoyed by diplomatic personnel." [34]

(4) Fourth, the CPR seems to be well apprised of the diplomatic practices of other states [35] and the developing law relating to diplomatic and consular intercourse. Many of the measures adopted by the CPR, including the functional basis of diplomatic privileges and immunities, are in general agreement with the 1961 Vienna Convention on Diplomatic Relations and its counterpart, the Vienna Convention on Consular Relations, signed in 1963.[36] CPR consular treaties resemble, both in form and language, those signed by and between Western powers. (CPR use of diplomatic channels to protect the safety, interests, and properties of Chinese nationals abroad is discussed in a separate chapter and need not be repeated here.)

Worth mentioning in this connection is the unique device employed by the CPR to get around diplomatic obstacles presented by the lack of diplomatic recognition or the fact that a foreign state has accorded *de jure* recognition to the Republic of China government on Taiwan. In the "unofficial" Third Trade Agreement signed between trade organizations of the CPR and of Japan, on May 4, 1955, it was provided:

> Both parties agree to establish permanent commercial missions in each other's country. . . . The commercial mission and its personnel of each party shall enjoy in the other's country *the treatment and rights enjoyed by diplomatic officials.*[37]

CPR Record on Diplomatic Privileges and Immunities

In the initial years, roughly between 1949 and 1953, the CPR was quite ruthless in dealing with foreign diplomats and, more especially, consular personnel in China. The United States consul at Urumchi, D. S. Mackiernan, was charged in September, 1949, with "spying" because he had allegedly supplied funds to three Sinkiang chieftans and instigated them to resist the Communist take-over.[38] Under similar charges the United States consul-general in Mukden, Angus Ward, was put under arrest in November of the same year.[39] Both were permitted to leave China shortly afterward, however.[40] To the extent that Peking considered itself at war with the United States at the time, and given the fact that these consuls had been accredited to the Nationalist Chinese government, which was losing the civil war, their arrest and expulsion may have been exigencies. But out of international comity, at least, the CPR authorities would be expected to grant to these former United States consular officers the necessary time and facilities to leave mainland China and, during the interim, granted the respect due to them by reason of their official position.[41]

Before the Korean War broke out, nevertheless, the Chinese Communists seemed to be not so hostile to the official representatives and nationals of Western countries in China, with the exception of the maltreatment of American officials and nationals and the confiscation of American consular properties in Peking.[42] In February, 1950, the British consul-general in Shanghai, the city with the largest foreign population in China, was still able to praise the Chinese

Communists for their "honest and just treatment" of foreigners.[43] After the outbreak of the Korean conflict, Peking even expelled the former British consul in Mukden, L. Steventon [sic], for having allegedly obstructed the construction by CPR security forces of an air-raid shelter in his residence, as required by the Air Raid Regulations in force at the time.[44]

Over the years, as her own diplomatic contacts widened, the CPR has had occasions to worry about the safety and well-being of her own diplomatic and consular representatives abroad, such as in India and Indonesia during the early 1960s.[45] In 1966, the CPR had to protest to the military junta in Ghana, which had ousted the Nkrumah regime, for its alleged maltreatment of Chinese technical advisers sent to that African country under previous agreements.[46] On September 14, 1967, in Jakarta, Chinese Chargé d'Affaires ad interim, Lu Tzu-po and Second Secretary and Consul, Su Sheng were declared *personae non grata* and ordered to leave Indonesia on four days' notice. Shortly thereafter, on October 1, about one thousand Indonesian youths demonstrated at the Chinese Embassy and set fire to one building. At least six Chinese were injured and sent to the hospital.[47] In January, 1969, Peking reported that the CPR Embassy in New Delhi had been raided by "Indian ruffians and Tibetan traitor bandits" on December 30, 1968. The Chinese alleged that by its neglect to protect the embassy premises and its subsequent evasion of responsibilities the Indian government had violated "the principles governing international relations." [48] Perhaps as a result of these experiences, the CPR seems to have gradually become more sober, with some notable exceptions, in her own treatment of foreign envoys stationed in mainland China.

The first notable exception is Peking's attempt in late 1966 to hold the Netherlands chargé d'affaires as a "hostage" in order to ensure the return of an eight-man Chinese scientific delegation which had been in the Netherlands to attend a conference on the International Welding Institute.[49] The measure followed an incident in The Hague, where the Chinese chargé d'affaires on July 16, 1966, allegedly "abducted" Hsü Tzu-ts'ai, a member of the delegation, from a local hospital and rushed him back to the legation compounds. Earlier during the day, Hsü had been sent to the hospital after passers-by found him lying heavily injured on the sidewalk in front of the house where the Chinese delegation was staying. Apparently Hsü was hurt during an unsuccessful attempt to escape. Following the "abduction," the Chinese chargé refused to let Hsü be hospitalized or to offer an explanation when summoned by the Dutch Ministry of Foreign Affairs, insisting that the case was an "internal matter." The next day Hsü died in the Chinese chancery. The Dutch authorities ordered a judicial investigation to discover the facts in connection with Hsü's death. After refusing to cooperate and to permit the other members of the Chinese Welders' delegation to testify as witnesses, the Chinese chargé was declared *persona non grata* and requested to leave the Netherlands within twenty-four hours.[50] When Peking retaliated by declaring the Netherlands chargé *persona non grata,* in July, 1966, the Dutch government had begun a five-month "siege" of the Chinese Legation in The Hague, to prevent the eight Chinese welders from being smuggled out of the chancery. The siege ended in December, when a compromise was worked out whereby the Dutch public prosecutor visited the welders at the Chinese Legation and carried on "conversations" in lieu of a formal inquest. The welders were then permitted to leave for China. Only then did Peking permit the Netherlands chargé to leave China.[51]

A number of inter-related legal questions could be raised, although the one of direct concern to us here is the CPR detention of the Dutch diplomat. First, on what ground could the Chinese claim that the "abduction of Hsü Tzu-ts'ai was an act of "internal matter?" One author has suggested that the Chinese were apparently putting primacy on jurisdiction *in personam* (by reference to the nationality of Hsü), over and above the territorial jurisdiction to which the Netherlands was entitled, reversing the usual emphasis in state practices. The writer finds some similarity between the present case and the abduction of Dr. Sun Yat-sen in 1896 by the Chinese Legation in London on charges of conspiracy against the Manchu dynasty.[52] To the extent that the Chinese chargé considered that Hsü, apparently bent on escape, was in possession of state secrets, the forcible removal of Hsü and his subsequent refusal to permit the other members of the welders' delegation to testify could be considered as an emergency action taken in the course of protecting "national interests." [53]

Furthermore, one might venture some guesses as to whether the Chinese may have a different concept of jurisdiction, at least insofar as the powers of the head of a diplomatic mission over its own nationals are concerned. We do not profess to know the link, but in the practice of the various states in the ancient Chinese international system, during the Spring and Autumn period (722–481 B.C.) each diplomatic mission included a *ssu-ma* whose duty it was to maintain discipline among members of the mission and to punish any of them who had "violated the laws" or "committed violence or plundering." This "disciplinary privilege" enjoyed by a diplomatic mission over its own members was different from modern extraterritoriality, in the sense that it in no way imposed limitations on the sovereignty of the receiving state.[54] Could the CPR's chargé d'affaires in The Hague have felt that he somehow also enjoyed such disciplinary power over the members of his legation and, by extension, over the members of the visiting Chinese welders' delegation?

Coming back to our original question, what right did Peking possess in its detention of the Dutch chargé as a "hostage" for the return of the Chinese delegation? Although the reciprocal declaration of *persona non grata* is a habitual practice in diplomatic relations, the retention of a foreign diplomat after such declaration until certain conditions are met by the other state is rare in diplomatic history. Although the holding of foreign diplomats or other important personages as "hostages" to ensure the fulfillment of treaty commitments, such as an alliance, was an established practice between the various Chinese states during the Spring and Autumn period,[55] modern international law recognizes an envoy's right to leave upon the termination of his mission as part of the inviolable privileges and immunities guaranteed by his diplomatic status.[56] The only defense the CPR could find for its action is probably that the action was a reprisal against the Dutch detention of the Chinese welders. By definition, reprisals consist of "such injurious and otherwise internationally illegal acts of one State against another as are exceptionally permitted for the purpose of compelling the latter to consent to satisfactory settlement of a difference created by its own international delinquency."[57] The trouble for the Chinese is that they would have to prove that the Dutch detention of the Chinese welders, pending a judicial inquest into the circumstances surrounding the death of Hsü Tzu-ts'ai, was an "international delinquency."

On the other hand, the CPR appeared to maintain a distinction between the right to leave, which was the issue in the present case, and diplomatic inviolability. After the CPR had declared him *persona non grata,* the Dutch chargé d'affaires considered himself to have lost his diplomatic status and "felt like a prisoner," choosing not to leave the legation of his own volition.[58] As he recounted later after he had arrived in Hong Kong, the CPR government had not imposed on him any limitation of his freedom of movement between the *non-grata* declaration and his final departure from China.[59]

In fact, the withholding of exit permits to each other's diplomat was practiced reciprocally in a few other instances. For example, Indonesia announced the decision on August 24, 1967, to recall its diplomatic staff in Peking. Subsequently, the Indonesians complained that their embassy staff was being prevented from leaving. From available evidence, it appears that the Communist Chinese were initially attempting, by delaying tactics, to salvage their relations with Indonesia from a complete rupture and, after that effort had failed, wanted to ensure that their own embassy personnel in Jakarta would return safely.[60] Peking's relations with Britain dipped to a chilling low after the 1967 summer riots in Hong Kong, in which the British authorities arrested a number of leftist Chinese journalists and ordered the closedown of three leftist newspapers. In the subsequent tug of war, each side prohibited the diplomats of the other side from leaving the country without permission. The Chinese denial of an exit permit to Sir Donald Hopson, the British chargé d'affaires in Peking, appeared to be a retaliation in kind for an earlier London decision forbidding the fifty to sixty Chinese diplomats and officials in Britain to leave without permission. The Chinese personnel were also forbidden to travel more than five miles from Marble Arch, in the center of London, without giving the Foreign Office forty-eight hours' notice.[61] The Foreign Office action, which went beyond the denial of the exit permit, was in turn a retaliation against a Red Guard sacking and burning of the British chancery in Peking on August 23, 1967, which we shall discuss below. Although the Chinese for a time delayed the granting of an exit visa to Sir Donald and other members of his staff, some up to three months or more, it is not clear whether Peking also imposed similar restrictions upon the movement of the British diplomatic personnel as the Chinese envoys were subjected to in London. Upon his arrival in Hong Kong, on August 14, Sir Donald only reported the visa delays and that he had been denied access to or information about a number of Britons detained by the Chinese.[62]

Red Guard orgies against foreign diplomatic missions in Peking were another obvious exception to the trend of Peking's becoming more mellow over the years in respect of diplomatic immunities and privileges. A few notable events are worth mentioning here. First, the Red Guards staged a war of nerves against the Soviet diplomats in the latter part of 1966 and the spring of 1967, involving the siege of the Soviet Embassy and roughing up of Soviet diplomats and their dependents on their way to the airport for evacuation by air.[63] The Soviet Union in 1963 had expelled three Chinese diplomats and two students in Moscow for having distributed anti-Soviet polemics. But the CPR did not retaliate in kind.[64] In late 1966, the Soviets were reported to have insulted and inflicted brutality upon Chinese students in Moscow. At the time of the Red Guard demonstrations in early 1967, similar demonstrations were also staged by Russians outside the Chinese Embassy in Moscow.[65] Thus, the Red Guard campaigns against the Soviet Embassy and its staff could be a form of reprisal against the 1963 Soviet expulsion of Chinese diplomats and against the humility to which the Chinese Embassy personnel were alleged to have been subjected.

Whether the reprisal could be justified, Peking would have to cleanse itself of its obvious failure to provide proper protection to the diplomats of other countries. The Czech and East German chanceries in Peking were among those which suffered from a spillover of the Red Guard fury against the Soviets.[66] During the Soviet evacuation on February 14, 1967, some Western diplomats—including British Chargé d'Affaires Donald Hopson and Ambassador Lucien Paye of France—tried to link arms with diplomats from Communist states to make a passage for the Soviets to be evacuated by air, but they were reportedly jostled and roughed up by the Red Guard crowds.[67] David Oancia of the Toronto (Canada) *Globe and Mail* reported from Peking at the time that "the Chinese demonstrators seem to take great pains to insure that foreigners whose countries are not officially being attacked are not molested." [68]

Red Guard attacks persistently spread to other embassies. On June 14, 1967, hundreds of Red Guards beat and kicked two Indian diplomats at the Peking airport when they were leaving for Hong Kong after being ordered out of China as spies. Krishnan Raghunath, second secretary, and Padmanab Veejai, third secretary, were accused of having taken photographs on June 4, 1967, of what the Chinese described as "a prohibited military area." Raghunath had been tried *in absentia* by the Peking Municipal Higher People's Court, which, in a default judgment, convicted him of espionage. (It is a moot question whether the trial *in absentia* and the default judgment constituted a violation of the diplomat's immunities.) Indian officials described the charges as a fabrication and said that Raghunath had photographed places of cultural interest. The Red Guard manhandling provoked a strong protest from the Indian chargé d'affaires, Ram Sathe, alleging "inhuman treatment." [69] Chinese officials replied that the Indians had "provoked the masses" by refusing to hand over Mr. Raghunath to security authorities at the airport before leaving for Hong Kong, presumably for protection against Red Guard seizure. Nevertheless, the CPR government could hardly escape the responsibility incumbent upon a receiving state to protect with due diligence the inviolability of foreign diplomats against imminent mob action.[70]

The most bizarre of Red Guard antiforeign campaigns was the sacking and burning of the British Embassy compounds on August 23, 1967. The riot crowned a wave of Chinese protests against the British ban on three Communist newspapers and the arrest of leftist journalists in Hong Kong. It was the Red Guards' answer to the British rejection of a CPR ultimatum demanding that the ban be lifted. More than 10,000 Red Guard youths broke into the compounds, burned down the buildings and all automobiles, and seized all the British Embassy staff and their families, beating some of them before finally releasing them. The outrage strained Sino-British relations almost to the breaking point.[71] In this incident, however, Peking authorities tried actively to control the mob, to quell the fire, and to protect the safety of the embassy personnel. According to an Agence-France-Press dispatch, the fleeing Britons agreed that the Chinese policemen and soldiers—who had surrounded the chancery in an attempt to ward off the attackers—had tried to protect them from the Red Guards. They reported that some of the policemen were wounded trying to stem the fury of the crowd.[72]

The inviolability of the premises of a diplomatic mission, as well as of the diplomatic agent, has been universally recognized in the practice of states and is reaffirmed in the Vienna Convention of 1961.[73] The task of adequate protection may demand the taking of special precautionary measures by the receiving state, such as posting of police guards at the embassy premises or provision of an armed escort for the envoy.[74] Inadequate protection resulting in damages to person or property engages the responsibility of the receiving state. But, if the hostile act was unforeseeable or assumed unforeseeable proportions, the receiving state is free of any responsibility. In February, 1955, for example, the Romanian Legation in Berne was attacked by an armed group of Romanian refugees who took possession of the premises. The Swiss police had no warning for the totally unexpected event. Despite Romanian protests, the Swiss government could not be held responsible.[75] The Supreme Court of the United States in the *U.S. v. Hand* case expressed the view that an attack upon the mission premises is equivalent to an attack upon the person of the envoy himself, that precautions must be taken against mob violence, and failing that an apology was owed to the aggrieved state.[76] Under international law the receiving state has an obligation to intervene at the earliest possible chance to rescue the diplomat or mission premises when an attack breaks out. Where it has been impossible to forestall damage, the receiving state has the duty to repair the damage as early as possible.[77]

Whether the CPR could be held responsible for the Red Guard abuses would depend upon two criteria. The first is whether the Chinese authorities had taken the necessary precautions to protect the foreign diplomats and mission premises under attack. As we have seen, the answer varied from case to case. The CPR government could hardly escape responsibility for having failed to protect the two departing Indian diplomats from Red Guard manhandling. In the British Embassy case, Chinese police and soldiers had been posted outside the compounds but were overwhelmed. After the mobsters had broken into the chancery, these security men risked their lives to provide protection to the embassy staff and their families. The CPR's responsibility, therefore, would be limited to repairing the gutted compounds, plus an apology.

The other criterion for determining Peking's responsibilities is whether the Red Guard actions could be attributed to the willful prompting by the CPR authorities themselves. This would be most difficult to answer; yet, it is more important than the question raised above. From the vantage point of 1971, it appears that, although Red Guard activism owed its origin to an implicit encouragement from Chairman Mao himself at the outset of the Cultural Revolution, violence was from the very beginning prohibited.[78] After January, 1967, Mao reiterated the ban on violence and directed the People's Liberation Army to step in and help stop Red Guard anarchism.[79] It was more than a year before a semblance of order was restored. The ability of the CPR government to maintain effective control over the outbursts of the Red Guards at the time was at best questionable.

At the height of the chaos, some extremists even broke into the CPR Foreign Ministry and staged a "struggle" against Foreign Minister Ch'en Yi.[80] It did not become known until the spring of 1968 that a group of "radical leftist" leaders of the Cultural Revolution—Wang Li, Kuan-Feng, and Ch'i Pen-yu—had been personally responsible for the Red Guard attacks on the Soviet, Burmese, and British embassies in 1967.[81] The "Red Guard diplomacy" phase, which lasted till at least October, 1967, was evidently not sanctioned by Premier Chou En-lai and his foreign minister. In his conversation with Edgar Snow, the American writer, in December, 1970, Chairman Mao Tse-tung said he was not in control of the foreign ministry in 1967 and 1968. It was not until June, 1971, that it was confirmed that a "revolutionary group" was in control of the foreign ministry in August, 1967, when the office of the British chargé d'affaires was burned and attacks made on the Indonesian and Burmese embassies. Yao Teng-shan, former CPR chargé d'affaires in Indonesia, and an important member of the "revolutionary group," was purged and sent to prison on June 11, 1971. Premier Chou was reported to have expressed his regrets to John D. Denson, the new British chargé d'affaires in Peking.[82] These steps were meant to relieve the CPR government of whatever responsibility it had incurred.

It is tempting to compare the Red Guard defiance of diplomatic privileges and immunities with the notorious Boxer Uprising of 1900. In that earlier incident, Boxers besieged and attacked the Legation Quarters in Peking for two months; and, in the final count, death claimed the German Minister and a secretary of the Japanese Legation.[83] However, the similarities are more superficial than real. In the first place, the Boxers were supported by the Empress Dowager, the real power in the Machu government, who used the antiforeign sect to get even with Western powers after years of enforcing foreign privileges under unequal treaties. Secondly, the Boxers virtually declared war on the foreign missions and it was their avowed purpose to kill foreign envoys. The Empress Dowager even ordered that wherever in the empire a foreigner was found he had to be killed. The madness was stopped only after two courageous ministers had altered the outgoing telegrams so that for "kill" they read "protect." [84] Although the Red Guard antiforeign feelings were similarly strong and they had backing from some radical Cultural Revolution leaders, it is questionable whether they had been deliberately used by the CPR government to stage an extermination campaign against the entire diplomatic corps.

Perhaps it would be more correct to compare the Red Guard attacks with the frequent outbursts of anti-Western feelings in other

Afro-Asian countries. In May, 1960, for example, five hundred Indonesian students broke into the Dutch Legation and damaged furniture and valuable paintings.[85] In April, 1965, a mob of twenty thousand Cambodians attacked the American Embassy and ripped down the American flag.[86] The United States consulate-general in Alexandria, Egypt, was gutted, along with a nearby three-story building that housed the United States Information Service, shortly after the Arab-Israeli "June War" in 1967. American diplomatic and consular officers were expelled by Egypt under humiliating conditions for alleged United States support to Israel.[87] During the controversy over Sabah, in the fall of 1968, placard-waving Filipino students broke into the British Embassy residence in Manila, set fire to an adjoining cottage, and broke window panes before the riot police were called in.[88]

Actual violations of diplomatic immunities in state practices throughout the world are more numerous and more frequent than one realizes. In June, 1967, three Guinean diplomats, including the country's foreign minister and its permanent representative to the United Nations, were arrested in Ivory Coast during a stopover as they were returning home from a special session of the General Assembly. The third Guinean was an official of the Universal Postal Union; his family was traveling on the same plane and also arrested. The detention, Ivory Coast officials claimed, was a retaliation against earlier detention in Guinea of nationals and residents of Ivory Coast. The diplomats were not released until September 22, after prolonged efforts by U Thant, the U.N. secretary-general, to obtain their freedom. The seriousness of the case prompted the secretary-general to inscribe the question of diplomatic privileges and immunities of United Nations officials on the agenda of the Twenty-second General Assembly.[89] At the recommendation of the Sixth Committee, the General Assembly, on December 18, 1967, adopted a resolution deploring all departures from the rules of international law governing diplomatic privileges and immunities and those of the United Nations. Furthermore, the resolution urged all U. N. member states which had not yet done so to accede to the 1946 Convention on the Privileges and Immunities of the United Nations, and the Vienna Convention on Diplomatic Relations of

1961. It further urged all states, whether they were parties to the Vienna Convention or not, to "take every measure necessary to ensure the implementation of the rules of international law governing diplomatic relations and, in particular, to protect diplomatic missions and to enable diplomatic agents to fulfill tasks in conformity with international law." [90]

The United States has a "Headquarters Agreement" with the United Nations, signed on June 26, 1947,[91] but has refused to sign the more extensive Convention on the Privileges and Immunities of the United Nations, recommended by the General Assembly in 1946 for adoption by member states. Of course, the CPR is one of the many states, certainly not the only one, to which the General Assembly resolution could be addressed. It may be added, as *obiter dictum,* that the CPR was then ineligible to accede to the 1961 and the 1963 Vienna conventions, since only member states of the United Nations, its specialized agencies, the International Court of Justice, and other states specifically invited by the General Assembly may become parties to these conventions.[92] The Republic of (Nationalist) China was then seated in the United Nations and signed the two Vienna conventions in the name of "China." [93] Although Peking has now replaced Taipei in the U.N., its attitudes on this question remain to be seen.

IX

Practical Use of International Law (I)

AS WE HAVE already seen, the CPR not only recognizes the utility of international law but also makes practical use of it in the conduct of foreign affairs.[1] The main interest of this chapter and the next is to examine more methodically how she applies and invokes international law to accomplish certain basic aims in foreign relations. We shall, first of all, see how the CPR conducts herself in asserting claims and rights, defending official policy and conduct, and protecting nationals and official representatives abroad, including diplomatic and consular privileges and immunities. In the ensuing chapter, we shall carry on the study to instances in which the CPR accuses other states of violating international law and defends her territorial sovereignty and integrity by invoking international law.

Along these broad lines we hope to examine also how the CPR participates in the "game" of giving (or denying) consent and of creating (or preventing) "expectations." As already suggested, it is a basic belief accepted in this study that the ultimate basis of customary international law is "consensus" and "expectations" of states, of which practice is but one form of evidence. Other forms of evidence may include declarations with the intent to create a legal effect. "Actions" or "inaction," communication or noncommunication, may be equally relevant to the formulation of norms or legal obligations, insofar as they generate or preclude "expectations of continuation of the same kind of conduct." [2] It is in this context that the theory postulating acquiescence, consent, recognition, and good faith as the obligatory basis of international law is to be understood.[3]

In studying *how* the CPR takes part in the "game" of give and take under customary international law, one might profitably keep in mind the contrast between the CPR practice and that of the Manchu government. During most of the nineteenth century, until 1880, the Manchus, like the dynastic houses before, still viewed the world as divided between the civilized Chinese and the foreign barbarians, allowing little need for mutual accommodation. While nonintervention and nonexploitation of the "barbarians" guided Chinese thinking in general, the country's foreign policy (or lack of it) had essentially been one of inward-directed "segregation," ignoring the foreigners as much as possible.[4] It will be of interest to see to what extent the CPR has broken away from that tradition and whether it has taken any initiative to "accommodate" to the world rather than to avoid contacts.[5]

The present discussion will not touch upon CPR state practice regarding the law of treaties, which will be discussed in a separate chapter. Our discussion makes no pretensions of being exhaustive. At best, it will be illustrative and relatively brief. Oftentimes it may have to gloss over some "merits" of a given case. Of greater interest to us here is *how* the CPR uses international law and *what* rules of that law she is making use of.

Asserting Claims and Rights

The two most fundamental issues which the CPR believes affect her sovereign rights the most critically are the status of Taiwan and the larger but closely related question concerning her "right" to represent the whole of China in foreign relations, including full representation in the United Nations. Both issues have been extensively studied in existing literature.[6] We shall confine ourselves to the CPR's technical use of legal arguments to support her claims on these and a few other issues.

Although in the United Nations the Chinese "seat" problem has been treated variously either as the admission of a new state or simply as the problem of representation (which, in turn, could be viewed as a problem of credentials, state or government succession, etc.), the CPR government has taken a legal position which, except for the opposite purpose intended, is not too different from that taken by the Nationalist Chinese government and the United States. Conceiving of the question as purely one of representation, Peking has persistently claimed itself to be the "sole legal government . . . of China," [7] which alone can represent the country in the United Nations, and demanded the "expulsion" of the representatives of Nationalist China.[8]

In the years since 1949, the CPR's attitudes toward the United Nations have undergone seven distinct stages. From a favorable and, perhaps, naive attitude (1949–1950), the CPR became increasingly sophisticated, pessimistic, and antagonistic (1950–1953) since its initial bid to representation had failed. Hoping still to gain entry in the world organization, she turned to wooing patiently the Afro-Asian countries for votes (1954–1957); but, after that failed, her attitudes turned to deliberate arrogance (1958–1961), and finally, to an approach seemingly reflecting a conscious search for a substitute for the United Nations (1961–1965).[9] But Peking's interest in a substitute organization waned subsequent to the downfall in 1965 of the Sukarno regime in Indonesia, which had been the first to advance the notion. The notorious statement by Foreign Minister Ch'en Yi in October, 1965, demanding among other things drastic reforms of the United Nations as "conditions" for Peking's participation,[10] was probably an indication—however ironically—of continued interest.[11] From late 1969 on, Peking has openly and positively conveyed its revived interest in being seated in the United Nations, typifying an overall drive to end its diplomatic isolation and improve its relations with the outside world.[12]

Taking the Communist Chinese stand as a whole, it remains true that they have never treated the problem of their entry in the

United Nations as anything other than, or short of, the "restoration" of their right of representation.[13] In language which seems to incline toward state continuity as the basis of its claims to U. N. representation, Peking has repeatedly stated that "China is a member . . . and, moreover, one of its founding members, and a permanent member of the Security Council." Besides, seating CPR representatives in the United Nations has been viewed by Peking as a "procedural question," which, "according to the basic, accepted principles of international law . . . should have been settled long ago." [14]

The CPR has rejected the "two Chinas" solution in the United Nations, because she insists "Taiwan is an inalienable part of China's territory." [15] In November, 1966, reacting to the reported Canadian proposal which would have asked the General Assembly to seat representatives from both Peking and Taipei, the Chinese Communists attacked the idea as "exceedingly absurd" and "a grave provocation against the great Chinese people." [16] In an interview with a group of visiting American graduate students in Peking —shortly after the July 15, 1971, announcement of President Nixon's forthcoming visit to China—Premier Chou En-lai once again went on the record that the CPR would not take its seat at the United Nations under either a "two Chinas" or "one China and one Taiwan" formula.[17] Chou seemed to anticipate the announcement by Secretary of State William P. Rogers, on August 2, 1971, that the United States would support the seating of the CPR in the coming session of the United Nations, but not at the cost of Nationalist China's expulsion.[18] The Rogers' statement was promptly criticized in Peking as a "clumsy 'two Chinas' trick . . . absolutely illegal and futile." [19] While Peking made it known that President Nixon would still be welcome, the "two Chinas" question would continue, for some time to come, to highlight the difficult problems that have separated the CPR and the United States.* Solution to this question is invariably tied to the legal status of Taiwan.

The question of Taiwan's legal status did not occur until after

* The seating of Peking in the U.N., after the expulsion of the Nationalist Chinese in 1971, does not *ipso facto* obviate the "two Chinas" dilemma in American foreign policy.

the outbreak of the Korean War in 1950. The island had been retroceded to China in 1945, in pursuance of the Cairo Declaration signed by wartime Allies in 1943,[20] and the Potsdam Proclamation on postwar territorial and political rearrangements.[21] The transfer ended fifty years of Japanese rule of the island under the Shimonoseki Treaty of 1895 following China's defeat in the Sino-Japanese War the preceding year. In late 1949 the Nationalist Government, which had been administering Taiwan since 1945, lost the mainland to the Communists and rerallied itself on the island as its last stronghold. But as late as January, 1950, President Truman still considered that Taiwan had been duly returned to China (under President Chiang's government), in accordance with the Cairo and Potsdam declarations.[22] The view was supported and elaborated by Secretary of State Dean Acheson.[23] On June 27, 1950, in the wake of the outbreak of the Korean conflict, President Truman sent the United States Seventh Fleet to the Taiwan Strait to protect the Nationalist-held island from Chinese Communist take-over. Simultaneously, he announced that the "determination of the future status of Formosa [Taiwan] must await the restoration of security in the Pacific, a peace settlement with Japan, or consideration by the United Nations." [24] Communist China immediately responded to what was obviously a United States challenge to its bid to the title of Taiwan. On June 28, 1950, Chou En-lai declared:

On behalf of the Central People's Government of the People's Republic of China, I declare that, no matter what obstruction action the U.S. imperialists may take, the fact that Taiwan is part of China remains unchanged forever. This is not only a historical fact; it has also been confirmed by the Cairo and Potsdam Declarations and the situation since the surrender of Japan.[25]

The CPR even attempted to effectuate its claim through the United Nations. On August 24, 1950, it brought a complaint to the Security Council charging the United States with "open encroachment . . . and direct armed aggression on the territory of China." In the same cablegram to the Security Council, Chou reiterated that Peking's claim to the title of Taiwan was based on "historical fact," the actual surrender by Japan of the island, and the Cairo and Potsdam agreements, noting that "the United States Government has pledged itself to respect and observe" these agreements.[26] The complaint was typical of Peking's campaign since then to pressure the United States out of the Taiwan Strait, in order to facilitate its "liberation" of the island. Central to the CPR claim to Taiwan is a three-point argument that consists of: (a) an insistence that the island has been returned to the Chinese state both legally and factually following Japan's surrender in 1945, (b) a claim that the CPR is a continuation of the erstwhile Republic of China, entitled to all its rights and international status, including sovereignty over Taiwan, and (c) an accusation that the Chiang Kai-shek government seated in Taiwan has been spurned by the "Chinese people" and is a "stooge of U.S. imperialism." [27]

The CPR has considered the Taiwan question and that of Chinese representation in the United Nations as part of the same larger question of who represents the whole of China, including both the mainland and the island. All suggestions in and outside the United Nations that the Communist Chinese regime and the Nationalist authorities in Taiwan be considered as co-successors to the former "Republic of China"—whose name is explicitly mentioned in Article 23 of the U.N. Charter where it enumerates the five permanent members of the Security Council—has proven absolutely unacceptable to Peking (and to the Nationalists as well).[28]

Put in the simplest terms, the difficulty of the Taiwan issue does not lie in proving *de facto* Chinese exercise of authority after the island's retrocession in 1945. It lies in the lack of a legal devolution of sovereignty over Taiwan, since China was not represented by either the Nationalist or the Communist government at the signing of the 1951 Peace Treaty at San Francisco. The treaty, effective as from April 28, 1952, stripped Japan of "all right, title and claim to Formosa [Taiwan] and the Pescadores [Penghu]." But, it did not name China as the party to which the transfer of the title was to be made.[29]

If the legal limbo of Taiwan is equally embarrassing to the Kuomintang government in Taipei, it can at least take comfort in the fact that it is the party effectively administering the island despite the absence of a devolution of its status.[30] Peking has to rely more heavily on the Cairo and Potsdam declarations as the legal instrumentality by which the question has been resolved once and for all. To deny this fact, it maintains, is to breach an agreement already reached.[31] Although the argument cannot be dissociated from political motivations, the view somehow is in keeping with the CPR's inclination, perhaps even going beyond other socialist states, to ascribe to "declarations," communiqués, etc., a consensual character approximating the status of treaty. A CPR writer in the *Kuo-chi wen-t'i yen-chiu* [Studies of International Problems] elaborated on the view that the Cairo and the Potsdam declarations were not merely broad statements of policy, but were binding legal commitments made by the wartime Allies. To support his argument, he cited the following passage from Oppenheim's *International Law* (8th edition, Vol. I, p. 873): [32]

> Official statements in the form of Reports of Conferences signed by the Heads of States or Governments and embodying agreements reached therein may, in proportion as these agreements incorporate definite rules of conduct, be regarded as legally binding upon the States in question.

Both in the 1950 CPR complaint to the United Nations [33] and in other instances, the Chinese Communists have repeatedly claimed that prior to 1950 both the United States and Britain had recognized the binding force of the Cairo and Potsdam declarations and China's exercise of sovereignty over Taiwan.[34] An editorial of the *People's Daily* cited the statement by President Truman on January 5, 1950, as supporting Chinese sovereignty:

> For the past four years, the United States and the other Allied Powers have accepted the exercise of Chinese *authority* [as opposed to "sovereignty"] over the island [Taiwan].[35]

The *People's Daily* editorial also found support in a British statement which acknowledged the return of Taiwan to China: "Formosa [Taiwan] should be handed back to the Chinese Government, which was done [according to the Cairo Declaration]." [36]

Mainland Chinese commentators have addressed the issue in other ways. One writer has attempted to bypass the embarrassment that no Chinese government was represented at the 1951 San Francisco peace conference. Recalling that the wartime United Nations Declaration of January 1, 1942, explicitly forbade any of the Allies to sign a *separate* peace treaty with the enemy, Ch'en T'i-ch'iang considers the signing of the San Francisco treaty without China's participation as a violation of that agreement. He invokes the authority of Oppenheim's *International Law* to show that a state has, in the words of the original work:

> the duty not to conclude treaties inconsistent with the obligations of former treaties. The conclusion of such treaties is an illegal act which cannot produce legal results beneficial to the law breaker.[37]

Ignoring an obvious technicality as to whether the 1942 United Nations Declaration had the character of an actual "treaty" (as distinguished from an ordinary "international agreement," which requires no ratification in accordance with domestic constitutional procedures), Ch'en is insinuating that the validity of the 1951 Peace Treaty, being inconsistent with the earlier agreement, is very much in doubt.

Alternately, it has also been suggested that the retrocession of Taiwan was an *ipso facto* consequence of the abrogation by China on December 8, 1941, of all her treaties with Japan, including the Shimonoseki Treaty of 1895. The Cairo Declaration, therefore, merely confirmed this fact when it stated that the war aims of the Allies were "to restrain and punish the aggression of Japan" and to restore to China all "the territories Japan has stolen from the Chinese." By an analogy to municipal law, it is also suggested that when the "thief" surrenders the loot the original owner naturally regains possession.[38] In advancing alternate arguments a reference is made to the maxim *ex injuria jus non oritur* (a person cannot acquire a right through his illegal act) along with a citation from Lauterpacht (*Recognition in International Law*) that "acts contrary to international law are invalid and cannot be a source of legal rights for the wrong-doer." [39] The implication seems to be that Japan never acquired title to Taiwan, which legally has always belonged to China, despite the temporary Japanese rule of the island under a treaty imposed on China by force.

Thus, CPR writers have tried in various ways to show that

China's sovereign rights over Taiwan do not depend on any agreement [40] or a peace treaty.[41]

Defending Official Conduct

When one examines carefully the record of Peking's behavior in foreign relations, it becomes increasingly clear how wrong the general impression is that the regime is less interested than other states in cloaking their actions with the mantle of legality—especially those actions apparently not sanctioned by generally accepted international standards.[42] To those familiar with CPR literature there is scarcely any single Chinese policy action of questionable legality which is not carefully defended, despite the fact that the defense may not be couched strictly in lawyers' language and it may not argue exclusively in accordance with the norms accepted by Western jurists.

On January 5, 1950, the Department of State announced that United States consular properties in Peking had been seized by the Communist Chinese authorities and that this country was recalling its official personnel from mainland China. The Department of State condemned the Chinese seizure as an "unprecedented act" and "a flagrant violation of [U.S.] treaty rights and of the most elementary standards of international usage and conduct." [43] The Communist Chinese had a quite evasive answer in self-defense. A CPR Foreign Ministry spokesman said that the American recall was "blackmail," and that the Peking Military Control Commission had merely "taken back the real estate operated by the American military." [44] While the facts speak for themselves, it is significant that the CPR did not identify the properties seized as those belonging to the United States consulate-general in Peking; nor did it attempt to insinuate a right to seize foreign consular properties.

The same CPR spokesman discounted as "totally fabricated" a statement attributed to Secretary of State Acheson, made before the Senate Foreign Relations Committee on January 25, 1950, which alleged that Peking was detaining American nationals.[45] The Chinese spokesman gave his version of the story:

> Our Government not only will not prevent any American officials and their families from leaving China, but, in view of the espionage activities carried on by the former American consular officers in Shenyang [Mukden] and Ti-hua [Urumchi], will be more than willing to see them leave China at the earliest possible moment.[46]

After Chinese Communist troops had crossed the Yalu River to fight on the side of the North Koreans in late October, 1950, Peking defended the intervention as dictated by the urgent need to help North Korea repel "United States aggression." To bypass the legal technicalities, the Chinese troops were named as "volunteers" from the very beginning. In a statement circulated to the U.N. Security Council through the help of the Soviet delegation, Peking presented a long list of instances of alleged bombings and attacks by the "intruding" United States Air Force in northeast China [Manchuria]. Self-defense was very much played up to justify the sending of Chinese "volunteers" to the Korean battlefront. "To help Korea and to repel U.S. aggression," declared the CPR statement, "means to protect our own homes and our own country," and the "crimes committed by the U.S. armed forces . . . are violating the territorial sovereignty of China and threatening its security." [47] The Chinese compared their intervention in Korea to the French support to the American Independence War and Western assistance to "the Spanish people in their civil war against Franco." "The whole world," the Chinese statement asserted, "admitted that these [latter] acts were lawful," suggesting that the Chinese considered their own intervention in behalf of the North Koreans as equally "lawful." [48]

A wealth of instances of Peking's invocation of international law is found during its border conflict with India. One of the common arguments made in reference to international law is that its military actions were necessitated by self-defense. Countering a previous Indian charge of Chinese "invasion," the CPR Foreign Minister on January 19, 1963, protested:

It is known to the whole world that it was Indian troops which invaded and occupied large tracts of Chinese territory and made increasingly serious armed provocations, and it was after Prime Minister Nehru issued orders to "free" Chinese territory of the Chinese that they launched large-scale attacks on October 20, 1962. The Chinese frontier guards struck back in *self-defense* only when they were subjected to *repeated frenzied Indian attacks* and suffered heavy casualties and when they were *pressed beyond forbearance* and *left with no room to retreat*. (Emphasis added) [49]

The Chinese wording has a familiar ring of the language used in the oft-quoted doctrine of "necessity" with respect to self-defense formulated in the famous *Caroline* case.[50] It is to be noted that during the Sino-Soviet border clashes over Chen-pao in 1969 the Chinese also invoked self-defense to justify what they termed was a returning of fire against Soviet provocation along the disputed border on the Ussuri River.[51]

At one point during their border conflict with India in 1963, the Chinese were accused by India of holding 3,000 captured Indian troops as "hostages" and denying them "the benefit of the Geneva Convention." The CPR Foreign Ministry denied the charge and gave the following account of how the Indian POWs were treated:

The well-being of the captured Indian military personnel has been attended to and looked after in the best way possible in the local material conditions. Their religious beliefs and national customs have been properly respected. They have been given every facility to correspond by mail and cable with their families.

The sick and wounded among them were given first aid and effective medical care in good time. . . . That is why both during their captivity and at the time of their release and repatriation the captured Indian military personnel time and again praised and thanked the Chinese frontier guards and the Chinese Government for the good treatment accorded them.[52]

The kind of treatment which Peking claimed to have accorded the Indian POWs seems designed to indicate that the CPR met the requirements laid down in Articles 34, 71, and 15 of the 1949 Geneva Convention Relating to Treatment of POWs.[53]

Communist China has often been criticized for having refused to sign the 1963 Moscow Treaty on Partial Nuclear Ban. But Peking has, in turn, condemned the treaty as a collusion to monopolize nuclear destructive power, and has defended its own nuclear tests as a matter of an "inalienable right" accruing from state sovereignty and self-defense from "nuclear blackmail." An announcement following Peking's first successful atomic detonation on October 16, 1964, declared:

> To defend oneself is the *inalienable right* of every sovereign state. To safeguard world peace is the common task of all peace-loving countries. China cannot remain idle in the face of the ever-increasing nuclear threats from the United States. China is conducting nuclear tests and developing nuclear weapons under compulsion.[54]

Peking has repeatedly publicized its fruitless efforts to seek "complete prohibition and destruction of nuclear weapons" through the conclusion of treaties with the world's nuclear powers. It has also used the absence of CPR representation as a pretext why it feels itself not bound by an agreement reached or to be reached at any disarmament talks. Using a language not unfamiliar to the principle of *pacta tertiis* in the law of treaties,[55] Peking has stated its position as follows:

> Just as the Chinese Government has time and again emphatically stated, it will not undertake any obligation regarding disarmament agreement or other international agreements in the discussion of which no Chinese representative has taken part and which no Chinese representative has signed.[56]

This attitude applied also to the United Nations Eighteen-Nation Geneva Disarmament Conference.[57]

Protecting Nationals and Official Representatives Abroad

In the early 1950s foreign countries had trouble protecting their nationals and official representatives in mainland China.[58] Ironically, the CPR in the early 1960s began to confront more serious problems of protecting her own nationals and official interests abroad. The most recent predicament came up in Indonesia following the failure of the Communist *coup* of October, 1965.

In the midst of deteriorating relations, Peking charged the new Indonesian government with persecuting the local Chinese population. According to Peking's charges, the general patterns of violence against Chinese nationals in Indonesia fell under five categories: (a) ransacking and seizing premises of Chinese schools and organizations; (b) ransacking stores and residences of Chinese nationals; (c) "illegal subpoenaing, arresting, manhandling, and beating up" of Chinese; (d) burning down and tearing up of Chinese national flags and "portraits of Chinese leaders"; and (e) nonsuppression, and even instigating, of mob actions against Chinese nationals by the Indonesian Army.[59] These "outrages," Peking protested, were:

> a brutal encroachment upon the proper rights and interests of the Chinese nationals and their personal safety and a gross violation of the *accepted principles of international law* and practice. (Emphasis added) [60]

In its many protests Peking repeatedly "demanded" that the Indonesian government take the following measures of "redress": (a) "severely punish those who persecuted the Chinese nationals and those who instigated the persecutions"; (b) "release all the Chinese nationals who have been unwarrantedly arrested"; (c) "compensate for all the losses of property suffered by the Chinese nationals"; (d) "truly protect their proper rights and interests and personal safety"; (e) "check all the outrageous persecutions of Chinese nationals"; and (f) "apologize for the incidents. . . ." [61]

The CPR not only based her charges against Indonesia on damages caused by individual Indonesian mobsters, for which the Indonesian government would already have a share of responsibility under international law, but also raised the question of nonsuppression of mob violence by the Indonesian "army personnel on the scene." When the anti-Chinese riots broke out in Semarang, Peking charged, the Indonesian Army "far from checking the outrages, used their guns to drive passers-by to join in damaging and smashing the property of Chinese nationals." [62] It is quite obvious that Peking was attempting to engage the responsibility of the Indonesian government for nonpunishment and nonsuppression of the delictual acts.[63] In another protest against the Indonesian government's failure to act when the local Chinese consul requested help, Peking expressly charged that "the Indonesian Government has an unshirkable responsibility." [64]

The question of protecting the person and properties of Chinese nationals in India arose during the height of the Sino-Indian border conflict. One significant case involved India's seizure of branches of the Bank of China in Calcutta and Bombay. The Indian government had defended its actions on the ground that they were "in conformity with Indian law" and asserted that the matters were "within the sovereign jurisdiction" of India. The argument was refuted by Peking as "completely untenable":

> According to accepted norms of international law, every country is obliged to grant full protection to peaceful and law-abiding foreign nationals and foreign juridical persons, and *it is not permitted to deny their human rights and fundamental freedoms by recourse to its national laws,* much less to infringe at will on their living, property, and security. It is obvious that the above-mentioned wanton persecution by the Indian authorities is in serious violation of the norms of international law. (Emphasis added) [65]

If anything can be adduced from this statement, there seems to be an implicit assumption that international law takes precedence over domestic laws. This was certainly not the position held by Peking in the initial years of its existence, when it seized foreign properties by decrees.[66] Nor did the Soviets before Stalin's death accept the primacy of international law. It remains to be seen whether the Chinese have lately switched their position, as the Soviets seem to have, to what one writer has labeled a "reconciliation" view regarding international and domestic systems of law.[67]

In another connection, the CPR charged the Indian government with violating in two main instances the Geneva Conventions of 1949 and "principles of international law." First, some Chinese nationals held in Indian concentration camps had allegedly become sick or died of maltreatment, lack of adequate food and even starvation, poor sanitation, and denial of medical care. Second, New Delhi had refused to provide a list of Chinese internees and permit Chinese officials to visit them.[68]

The CPR government often insists that to protect Chinese nationals abroad is a "right" of the CPR as a sovereign state under international law. A typical example of this view is the following statement:

> In asking the Indian Government to provide a list of the interned Chinese nationals, arranging visits to them, and registration of the victimized Chinese wishing to return to China . . . , the Chinese Embassy was exercising the internationally acknowledged *right* of protecting one's own nationals.[69]

During the course of the CPR's difficulties with India and Indonesia, the question of defending Chinese diplomatic consular rights also arose. This experience may have some sobering effect on Peking, which in the early 1950s was none-too-kind to foreign diplomats and consular officers. Arrest and expulsion of Western (including American and British) consuls were reported more than once at the time.[70]

Peking, in May, 1960, had to face the hard fact that its own consul at Bandjarmasin, Indonesia, was put under house arrest by the local military authorities. The CPR Embassy protested the act as a violation of the "universally acknowledged international norms." [71] In November, 1965, the Chinese Consulate in Medan was raided and damaged by Indonesian rioters allegedly "organized by Indonesia Rightwing forces." A protest from the CPR Foreign Ministry charged that the outrage

> constituted a gross violation of *accepted principles of international law* and a rude encroachment on the privileges enjoyed by the Chinese Consulate and the personal safety of its personnel.[72]

In October, 1965, according to the Chinese, armed Indonesian troops broke into the compounds of the CPR Embassy in Djakarta and conducted an "inspection." The embassy protested strongly to the Indonesian government against this "violation" of its "diplomatic privileges." [73]

In these and similar cases, Peking's protests normally stressed that the outrages "obstructed the functioning" [74] or "placed restrictions on the right . . . to exercise . . . normal functions" [75] of the Chinese diplomatic or consular officers. The consistency with which this assertion reappeared confirms a CPR endorsement of the "functional" interpretation of the juridical basis of diplomatic and consular immunities and privileges, as we have earlier suggested.[76]

X

Practical Use of International Law (II)

WE SHALL continue our study of how the CPR makes practical use of international law in the fulfillment of basic foreign-policy aims. In this chapter we shall focus on Chinese accusations of alleged illegal acts by other states and their efforts to defend China's territorial integrity.

Accusing Others of Violating International Law

While charges of Peking's violations of international agreements and custom have often appeared in Western official literature,[1] the CPR government has also charged other states with similar violations. In some instances these charges are accompanied by citations of specific international agreements or customary norms. One such occasion arose during the concluding phase of the Korean War, when Peking attacked American "connivance" at the detention and reorganization by South Korea of 27,000 Chinese and North Korean ex-POWs on and after June 18, 1953. The United States-South Korean action was consummated within ten days after the signing of the Armistice Agreement. Premier Chou En-lai, at the 1954 Geneva Conference on Korea, declared that in accordance with the

1949 Geneva Convention relating to POWs all the ex-POWs of the Korean War should have been released and repatriated immediately upon the cessation of conflicts. The detention and reorganization by South Korea, with the support of the United States, of CPR and North Korean POWs, he charged, was a breach not only of the Korean Armistice Agreement but also of the Geneva Convention (III) of 1949.[2]

Since the United States at the time had not ratified the Geneva Convention in question, Chou's charge of United States violation of its provisions seemed to suggest that the CPR considered these provisions to be declaratory of customary norms already in existence even without the convention.

The declaratory view seemed to underscore Peking's condemnation in 1965 of alleged United States "gas warfare," which, it declared, was a "complete contempt for international law" and, more specifically, violated the 1925 Geneva Protocol prohibiting gas warfare. The official *Peking Review* quoted an Associated Press dispatch from Saigon as reporting American use of gases against the Vietcong, which it said was later confirmed by White House Press Secretary George Reedy. The Chinese comment declared:

> Since the 1925 Geneva Protocol prohibiting gas warfare, no country, however aggressive, has yet dared to publicly admit, let alone defend, its use of gas on such a large scale. Now Johnson's United States has gone one better than Hitler's Germany in its savagery, and Mussolini's Italy or Tojo's Japan in its complete contempt for international law.[3]

The statement appeared to suggest that, although the United States was not a party to the 1925 Geneva Protocol, there was no excuse for resorting to the use of gases in the Vietnam War, since the ban on gas warfare was part of general international law only reaffirmed in the protocol. The *Peking Review* went on to say that even Senator Wayne Morse (Democrat-Oregon) had publicly admitted that the United States gas warfare in Vietnam was a violation of international law.[4] To my knowledge, however, although Peking repeatedly accused the United States of having committed atrocities in Vietnam,[5] nothing was said about possible violations of the laws and customs of war such as laid down in the Hague Regulations of

1907. The Lawyers Committee on American Policy Towards Vietnam (New York), for instance, charged in 1966 that Washington was violating "every aspect of the rule of proportionality" respecting reprisal and that its bombing of nonbelligerents during the Vietnam War was "abhorent to international law" and a clear violation of the laws and customs of war laid down in the 1907 Hague Regulations.[6]

The CPR has persistently denounced the United States war efforts in South Vietnam and aerial bombings of North Vietnam as "savage crimes" and "naked aggression," in violation of the 1954 Geneva Agreement.[7] In a special volume, *Mei-kuo tui yüeh-nan nan-fang te kan-she ho ch'ing-lüeh cheng-ts'e* (The United States Policy of Intervention and Aggression in the Southern Part of Vietnam), the CPR noted that the use of force was as a matter of principle prohibited under Article 2 (4) of the United Nations Charter, and that Paragraph 12 of the Final Declaration of the Geneva Conference on July 21, 1954, explicitly stipulated:

In their relations with Cambodia, Laos, and Vietnam, each member of the Geneva Conference undertakes to respect the sovereignty, the independence, the unity, and the territorial integrity of the above-mentioned states, and to refrain from any interference in their internal affairs.[8]

The authors then pointed out that the United States delegate, at the final session of the Geneva Conference, not only accepted the various paragraphs (except the last paragraph [9]) of the Final Declaration but also made a two-fold pledge with respect to the accords just reached:

(i) [The United States] will refrain from the threat or the use of force to disturb them, in accordance with Article 2 (Section 4) of the Charter of the United Nations dealing with the obligation of Members to refrain in their international relations from the threat or use of force; and

(ii) it would view any renewal of the aggression in violation of the aforesaid Agreements with grave concern and as seriously threatening international peace and security.[10]

Technically, the United States did not formally join the other major powers at Geneva—namely France (Mendes-France), the

CPR (Chou En-lai), Britain (Eden), and the Soviet Union (Molotov)—in signing the Final Declaration. The above statement cited by the Chinese writers was contained in a separate unilateral declaration by Bedell Smith, the United States delegate, appended to the Final Declaration jointly signed by the other delegates. Needless to say, given the CPR's general position regarding treaties,[11] it is clear that the Chinese held the United States, by dint of its unilateral declaration as such, obligated to the same (or nearly the same) extent as the other signatories to the Final Declaration to respect the provisions of the accords, including the commitment on noninterference.

The CPR sought to establish a case of duplicity by tracing a United States intention to flout the Geneva accords to the very beginning. "On the following day [of the signing of the 1954 accords]," the *Peking Review* asserted, "the then U.S. President Eisenhower brazenly declared the United States not bound by any decisions of the Geneva Conference." [12] The United States support for the Ngo Dinh Diem regime, the increasing United States military buildup after 1961, and the final full-fledged United States entry in the Vietnam War were thus considered as a natural extension of a policy of "intervention and aggression" formulated as early as 1954. The dual pledge made by the United States delegate at the Geneva Conference, as noted above, was therefore considered by the Chinese as an intentional deception.[13]

Furthermore, Peking also endeavored to point up an inconsistency in the United States stand on Vietnam. "U.S. President Johnson," it stated, "sees [it] fit to pass himself off as a protector of the [1954] Agreement. He said in his March 25 [1965] statement that the United States seeks 'no more than a return to the essentials of the Agreement of 1954.' " [14] In other words, as Peking saw it, the United States was both posing as a "protector" of the 1954 accords and attempting to escape from the obligations accruing from them. The reasoning is that the one would estop the other; and Peking was in effect employing the principle of "equitable estoppel" from customary international law in accusing the United States of proverbially blowing hot and cold (*allegans contraria non audiendus est*).[15]

Building its case on the thesis that declarations between governments have a legal binding character *inter se,* Peking in 1951 charged that the United States, in sponsoring the Japanese Peace Treaty, violated her wartime obligations toward China under the Cairo Declaration. The coming into force of the peace treaty without China's cosignature and the subsequent deactivation of the Allied Council for Japan and the Far Eastern Commission were all considered to be "illegal." In a statement Premier Chou En-lai declared that such actions violated the letter and spirit of the 1942 United Nations Declaration, the Cairo Declaration, the Yalta Agreement, the decisions of the 1945 Moscow Foreign Ministers' Conference (on the establishment of the Allied Council), and the basic policy decisions of the Far Eastern Commission concerning postwar Japan.[16] The tone in Chou's statement suggests that his government considered the cited documents to have a binding force approximating that of duly consummated treaties. It may be maintained in this connection that Peking has on many occasions seized upon the maxim *pacta sunt servanda* (international agreements must be observed) as a legal weapon against other governments. A more recent example is Peking's charge against India in 1963 that the latter was guilty of "unilateral tearing up of the Sino-Indian agreement on the mutual establishment of consulates-general in disregard of international good faith." [17]

The most frequent charges the CPR has made against Western powers are those of "aggression" and "intervention." We shall mention a few of the more important cases which the CPR held to be clear-cut examples of Western (and Soviet) "aggression" and "intervention":

(a) The United Nations intervention in Korea in 1950 was, in Peking's eyes, a cover-up for "United States armed aggression and . . . intervention in the internal affairs of Korea in violation of world peace." [18]

(b) The presence of the United States Seventh Fleet in the Taiwan Strait is, as Peking views it, a blatant "aggression" against China.[19] Premier Chou En-lai in 1954 attacked the United States mutual security pact with Nationalist China as an illegal "treaty of war and aggression," adding:

By the treaty, the U.S. Government attempts to legalize its armed seizure of China's territory of Taiwan, and with Taiwan as a base, to extend its aggression against China and prepare for a new war.[20]

(c) The Anglo-French intervention in the Suez in 1956 provoked vehement criticisms and protests from Peking. An official CPR statement on November 11, 1956, called the military actions of British and French forces in the Suez "acts of armed aggression," [21] and declared CPR support to Egypt in the latter's fight to maintain sovereign and territorial integrity.[22] In direct protests to the British and the French governments, Peking accused them of "brutal violations of the United Nations Charter," demanded withdrawal of Anglo-French-Israeli forces behind cease-fire lines, and suggested that navigation on the Suez be settled by peaceful negotiation.[23]

(d) To the 1958 dispatch of American and British forces to Lebanon and Jordan, respectively, Peking reacted with similar acrimony and forcefulness. It called the acts "crimes in violation of international law and the U.N. Charter." The pretexts of "protecting American nationals" and "safeguarding the sovereignty of Lebanon," Peking asserted, "cannot cover up the naked acts of aggression. . . ." [24]

Peking called the British pretext for sending forces to Jordan—to help resist an external aggression—a "lame excuse" because the supposed "external aggression" did not exist. It was Britain who committed "aggression" by violating Jordan's sovereignty, the CPR charged in a protest on July 18, 1958.[25] In Peking, a symposium was held the next day by some of the most well-known CPR international lawyers and publicists. All participants expressed their disapproval because the American and British actions in the Middle East contravened international law.[26]

(e) The United Nations operations in the Congo (ONUC) were attacked by Peking in ways showing its basic suspicion of the United Nations. It contended that ONUC was but another instance of United States "aggression" perpetrated in the name of the world organization, and an "imperialist" intervention in the internal affairs of Congo in defiance of Article 2 (7) of the U.N. Charter.[27] By contrast, despite apparent contradiction, the CPR defended the

Soviet intervention in Hungary in 1956. The argument used was that the Warsaw Pact contained a provision for such action, thus suggesting a constructive endorsement by members of the pact of the Soviet action.[28]

(f) The United States quarantine of Cuba in October, 1962, was condemned by Peking as an intervention calculated to deny to the Cubans their right of self-defense, and an act of piracy. A typical attack came in the CPR government's statement on October 24, 1962:

> The excuse for the United States aggressive action that Cuba had gained "offensive weapons" is a most shameful one. The U.S. piratical act constitutes an *intervention* in the internal affairs of Cuba, and a *denial to Cuba of her right of self-defense*. The blockade is the most flagrant act of *piracy* on the high seas.
>
> In intercepting ships bound for Cuba and in enforcing the quarantine over Cuba, the United States is violating one of the most fundamental norms governing the relations of nations. . . . What kinds of weapons are in Cuba's possession is a matter entirely within the country's sovereign jurisdiction, which the United States has no right to question or interfere into. . . . All the acts of aggression and intervention of U.S. imperialism will be doomed.[29]

(g) The Soviet military occupation of Czechoslovakia in August, 1968, drew similar denunciatory fire from Peking. Premier Chou En-lai harshly condemned the Soviets for their "crime of aggression" and intervention, which he likened to Hitler's aggression against Czechoslovakia and the United States role in Vietnam. He charged that the Soviet "crime of aggression," designed to "create puppets with the help of guns," had the blessings of the United States in an open collusion to "redivide the world" into exclusive spheres of influence between them.[30]

Defending Territorial Sovereignty and Integrity

In Chapter VI above we noted the Chinese attitudes toward territorial jurisdiction and territorial sovereignty. Here we will examine how the CPR has made use of international law in efforts to defend its territorial integrity against alleged infringements by other states.

Territorial Waters and Airspace

The CPR has persistently raised protests against "intrusions" into its territorial waters and airspace. On December 15, 1966, for instance, the CPR Foreign Ministry issued what it called the "418th serious warning against . . . U.S. military provocations" caused by the alleged intrusion of six United States warships and two United States planes into Chinese territorial waters and airspace.[31] In a number of similar cases, Washington's practice normally was to deny the Chinese allegations but, when necessary, it would retract previous denials and suggest "a possibility that some inadvertent intrusions of Communist China may have taken place." [32]

Some other concrete cases of "intrusions" have been given by Peking, including those by U-2 flights over the interior of China and by other American reconnaissance flights over Chou-shan and other islands (as far out as the Paracels) and over coastal regions such as Kiangsu, Chekiang, Fukien, Kiangsi, Kwangtung, and other provinces.[33]

Aside from these alleged flights directly over the mainland, many other "intrusions" may have been due to the conflicting claims concerning the width of the territorial sea. In protesting the "intrusions" by foreign warships and planes into its twelve-mile belt of territorial waters drawn from straight base lines, Peking has claimed that every state has the "sovereign right" to declare the extent of its territorial sea. At the same time, it has claimed an obligation by each state to respect the width of the territorial sea of other states (presumably when reasonably drawn). "Intrusions" into the territorial waters and their superjacent airspace of another state, Peking maintains, would only create "great chaos in the world." [34]

Boundary Alignment and Inviolability

Boundary questions are considered by Peking as "matters of major importance, which involve the sovereignty and territory of a country." [35] The major principles of international law governing the formation of boundary alignment are conceived by Peking as follows:

1. "A formally delimited boundary must be jointly negotiated (sometimes also jointly surveyed) by the countries concerned and with its alignment and location explicitly and concretely defined in a certain treaty form (usually the conclusion of a boundary treaty or agreement)."

2. A traditional customary line, that is, a line formed in the absence of a treaty, is gradually formed and made certain "through a long process of historical development according to the extent to which each side has all along *exercised administrative jurisdiction* . . . not mechanically defined or predetermined by some geographical principle [like that of watershed]." [36]

With these fundamental principles laid down, the CPR set out to show during the Sino-Indian boundary dispute that there had been no treaty delimiting the boundaries between the two countries [37] and, yet, all Chinese claims were based on effective control through the exercise of administrative responsibility and jurisdiction.[38] Despite the lengthy debates, Peking's views on the Sino-Indian boundary question can be summed up as follows:

First, it insists that the 1914 Simla Treaty, which was not signed (though initialed) by the Chinese representative, is not legally binding upon China. The "McMahon Line," which resulted from the Simla Conference, is "illegal" from Peking's point of view and there is no basis for accepting that line as the boundary. There has been no other treaty whatsoever which purports to settle the boundary problem.[39]

Secondly, while both sides agree there is a general customary boundary line, the boundary claimed by India in the eastern and western sectors far exceeds the actual extent of Indian administrative jurisdiction. Only in the middle sector, i.e., from the eastern terminus of the western sector to the tri-junction of China, India, and Nepal, can it be said that the Indian territorial claims conform to the general conditions of effective control.[40]

The CPR government took great pains to produce what it claimed to be evidence of China's continued administration and jurisdiction of the territories under dispute. The following are some of the "evidences" they produced:

1. the establishment of Chinese administrative organs, like the *She-chih-chü* (Preparatory Hsien) at Shahidulla, in the western sector, in 1927, and the various local government units at the *tso* and *din* levels, etc.;
2. tax collection, exaction of corvée, household census, conferring of fiefs by Chinese authorities in the territories under their effective control;
3. exercise of judicial power, such as passing judgments in cases of dispute and punishing offenders and officials who neglected their duties;
4. suppression of revolts, e.g., the 1927 suppression of the revolt by the Pome chieftain in the Loyul area (in the eastern sector); and
5. taking up frontier defense, and exercising entry and exit control.[41]

Furthermore, the Chinese claimed evidence of China's taking up the responsibility of suppressing many revolts, from 1853 to 1927, in the areas between what the Chinese consider to be the traditional boundary line and the "McMahon Line," which is considered by India as the correct boundary. It is plain that the purpose is to attempt to dispute the Indian claim that the territory immediately south of the McMahon Line was ever under effective Indian control in history.[42]

Peking's stress on effective control (through "administration and jurisdiction"), besides, may have been an attempt to challenge or override India's territorial claims based on the principle of *watershed,* which was used in the McMahon Line. Peking did not deny that the watershed principle was accepted under international law and in fact acknowledged its merits. But, it argued that the McMahon Line picked the wrong watershed, one deep in "China's territory." Employing an analogy, Peking stated that boundary delimitation sometimes follows the principle of *thalweg* (the middle of the navigation channel of a river) under international law. Would India, it asked, accept the *thalweg* of the Brahmaputra River (well within Indian territory) as the Sino-Indian boundary simply because it follows an accepted principle of international law and has its merits? [43]

The legal adviser of the Indian Ministry of External Affairs had argued that the watershed principle was accepted by China in a number of treaties made in and before the nineteenth century.[44] Peking's argument here seems to be a direct answer: It did not oppose the watershed principle, but the particular watershed picked for drawing up the McMahon Line was a wrong watershed.[45]

In the dispute over the legality of the McMahon Line, the CPR also resisted Indian territorial claims based on state succession. It pointed out that India cannot have succeeded to any rights which had not been lawfully acquired by the British, from whom India obtained independence in 1947.[46] This is clearly an allusion to a fundamental principle concerning state succession in international law. In the *Palmas* arbitration (1928), for instance, the tribunal of the Permanent Court of Arbitration denied the United States claim that she had derived title to the Palmas Island from Spain by way of cession under the Treaty of Paris. It ruled that the United States could not have received more rights than Spain had possessed, and the Treaty of Paris, being a treaty between third parties not including the Netherlands, could not have derogated from the Netherlands title of sovereignty acquired by "continuous and peaceful display of state authority during a long period of time." [47]

During the Sino-Soviet border conflicts in the spring of 1969, the Chinese challenged the Soviet claim that the contended Chen-pao Island in the Ussuri River was an "inalienable part of Soviet territory." According to the Sino-Russian Treaty signed in Peking in 1860, the Chinese pointed out, the boundary between the two countries in the disputed areas runs along the Ussuri River. In a reference to the principle of *thalweg,* Peking declared:

> According to established principles of international law, in the case of navigable boundary rivers, the central line of the main channel [thalweg] should form the boundary line, which determines the ownership of islands.[48]

Thus, the Chinese claimed that since the "Chen-pao Island is situated on the Chinese side of the central line of the main channel of the Ussuri River" and "has always been under Chinese jurisdiction," it was "indisputable Chinese territory." [49]

How the CPR Participates in the "Game" of Customary International Law

Use of Acquiescence and Estoppel Against Another State

In international law, as in any legal system, one party's failure to act or acquiesce in certain situations may prejudice his rights against another who has been misled by the party's inaction or silence. Sometimes, when there is a postulated duty to speak out or act, the silence of the party concerned may even operate like an estoppel.[50]

In its dispute with India over the repatriation of Chinese nationals from India, during the boundary conflict, Peking repeatedly used previous Indian acquiescence or consent as the basis of its claims of rights. A case in point is the exchange which followed India's announcement that repatriation facilities would be "limited to holders of passports" issued by the CPR government. The CPR Foreign Ministry protested:

> The Indian Government is *clearly aware* that . . . many Chinese nationals do not hold Chinese passports. However, this does not change their status as Chinese nationals. And, the Indian Government has never raised any objection to this. . . .[51]

On another occasion, when the question of the waiver of exit permits for nondiplomatic staff of the Chinese Embassy to leave India came in dispute, the embassy invoked an exchange of correspondence with Mr. Subramanian, deputy chief of protocol of the Indian Ministry of External Affairs. The exchange, it claimed, "*confirmed* that members of the Chinese Embassy and Consulates holding service passports 'are not required to obtain leave permits from the police, while leaving India.' "[52] The Chinese concluded:

> Therefore, for all the years since then, the nondiplomatic staff of the Chinese Embassy and Consulates, *in accordance with the correspondence exchanged,* did not follow formalities for exit permit and the Indian authorities concerned too *never had any objection.*[53]

The Chinese were suggesting that the Indian government was debarred from now taking a position contrary to the established practice based on the express consent given by its own officials.

In an effort to refute the Indian claim that the Sino-Indian boundary had been defined, Peking called attention to the different position held by India before 1959. It recalled that as late as August 28, 1959, Prime Minister Nehru told the Indian Lok Sabha (Parliament), in reference to the western section, that "this was the boundary of the old Kashmir state with Tibet and Chinese Turkistan [Sinkiang]. *Nobody had marked it.*" [54] The Chinese also cited a letter from Nehru to Chou En-lai, dated March 22, 1959, in an effort to show that the Indian leader "only mentioned geographical and traditional basis . . . and *did not say that there was treaty basis for it.*" "This," according to the Chinese, "is clearly at variance with the later [Indian] assertions. . . ." [55]

To further advance its case, Peking charged that Indian troops at certain times even crossed the McMahon Line, the very line which India had claimed to be the correct boundary. These troops, it protested, entered "the southern part of Miguitun (including Long-ju) and Tamaden, the latter being a place which even the Indian government admitted to be north of the alignment claimed by India." [56] Obviously, the Chinese were again invoking the principle of *allegans contraria non audiendus est* (no party can blow hot and cold at the same time).[57]

Denying Consent and Precluding Expectation

The CPR has shown conscious efforts to prevent possible reliance by other states on any construed consent or "expectations" which might accrue from her actions or nonaction.

In handling the release of American airmen in 1955, after direct talks between Premier Chou En-lai and Dag Hammarskjold, the U.N. secretary-general, the CPR made every effort to avoid its being taken as a precedent. She never admitted any relationship between the release and the Hammarskjold mission. At one time Peking used the word "deportation" for release since the airmen had been "convicted" as "spies." [58] Furthermore, its disclaimers were probably necessary to prevent any reading of the release as a tacit

CPR acceptance of the mandate of the General Assembly resolution which, besides authorizing Hammarskjold's intercession, had also condemned Peking for violating the Korean Armistice Agreement.[59]

Prime Minister Nehru once tactfully suggested that the Sino-Indian border dispute be submitted to "an international body like the International Court of Justice at the Hague." [60] Premier Chou promptly rejected the idea. "The Chinese Government," Chou stated, "has never agreed to refer the Sino-Indian boundary dispute to international arbitration, nor will it ever do so." [61] The use of the term "international arbitration" seems to exclude even submission to any other international tribunal. Chou gave the reason as follows:

> The Chinese Government is of the opinion that complicated questions involving sovereignty, such as the Sino-Indian boundary question, can be settled *only through direct negotiations between the two parties* concerned, and absolutely not through any form of arbitration.[62]

A generally accepted principle regarding the law of treaties is that a treaty applies only between the parties but not to or with respect of third states unless with the latter's consent.[63] When South Korea and Japan signed the 1965 Treaty of Basic Relations, Peking promptly denounced it as having no effect on the future status of Korea. "This," it declared, "is a grave step taken by the United States imperialism in its attempt to perpetuate the division of Korea. . . ." [64] Among the provisions of the treaty objectionable to Peking is Article 3, which reads that "it is confirmed that the Government of the Republic of Korea is *the only lawful Government* of Korea as specified in Resolution 195 (III) of the United Nations General Assembly." [65] Acceptance of this and other provisions would no doubt prejudice the legal status of the Pyongyang regime in North Korea, which Peking supports as the lawful government of all Korea. Thus viewed, the CPR's denunciation of the South Korea-Japan Treaty is not much different from United States opposition to Soviet attempts to conclude a separate peace treaty with East Germany, which, as the United States views it, would undermine the legal position of the Bonn regime.

Giving Consent and Creating Expectation

After concluding the boundary agreement of March 2, 1963, with Pakistan, Peking was confronted with Indian protests over the ownership of Kashmir. Peking made it plain that "the Agreement is of a *provisional* character and it has nothing to do with the ownership of Kashmir." Furthermore, Peking declared, "the dispute over Kashmir is solely the business of India and Pakistan themselves . . . in which *China will never interfere*." [66]

An intention to commit China to noninterference with the Kashmir question is embodied in a provision in the Sino-Pakistani Agreement, which reads:

> The two parties have agreed that *after* the settlement of the Kashmir dispute between Pakistan and India, the sovereign authority concerned will *reopen negotiations* with the Government of the People's Republic of China on the boundary . . . so as to sign a formal boundary treaty *to replace* the present Agreement.[67] (Emphasis added)

Since its first successful atomic explosion, Peking has repeatedly asserted a positive interest in some kind of a nuclear disarmament agreement that would provide a "no first use" clause. "The Chinese Government," said an official statement, "hereby solemnly declares that China *will never* at any time under any circumstances be the first to use nuclear weapons." [68] To what extent Peking's unilateral declarations like this can be relied upon is, of course, an open question. But it has proposed, perhaps as an interim measure, that the United States and China make parallel declarations, to guarantee not to be the first to use nuclear weapons—since a "no first use" treaty is not in sight. If Peking accepts parallel (but nevertheless unilateral) declarations as a modality of international commitment, as it usually professes to do, then its voluntary declaration above may imply some intention to induce expectation by other states that it will not be the first user of nuclear power. Peking, on the other hand, refused to sign the 1963 treaty on partial nuclear ban. The reason may be that, since it viewed the treaty as a United States-Soviet attempt to seal their existing nuclear superiority and to deny to other states the right to develop their own nuclear capabilities, there was no point in signing the treaty with which it knew it could not comply in good faith, at least for the moment. It may be suggested therefore that Peking did show, in these instances, a consciousness of the distinction between inducing and precluding expectation by other states.

By Way of Conclusion: A Tentative Evaluation

It can be concluded that the CPR's consciousness of international law has figured in the shaping of her foreign policy.[69] In our study of CPR use of international law, we have gained the impression that she quite consciously endeavors to maintain at least a semblance of self-consistency on a given issue. Although the CPR is found sometimes to bend or stretch international law to suit her own purposes, it is nevertheless true that she has also shown a concern for some measure of stability and continuity in the application of certain norms of international conduct. While she accepts international law for its utility, the CPR has manifested an awareness of the need to maintain its usefulness.

Just as the desire for a minimum measure of security, stability, and continuity in world public order engages the service of some rules of the game in international relations, the companion desire to keep the rules functioning requires the least possible destruction of their functional value. For the individual state, such as the CPR, there exists an obligation, out of practical calculations, to keep the law functioning and to maintain a minimum measure of "credibility" on its part so as to be able to benefit from the law's usefulness. The CPR, it seems, is not totally unaware of these fundamentals regarding international law and order when viewed from her actual conduct of foreign relations.

Saying this is not denying the fact that the CPR's practice still leaves much to be desired and that there is still a wide gap between what she expects of other states and what she herself actually does with respect to international law. We have, for example, witnessed strong CPR protests to India and Indonesia, in 1962 and 1966, respectively, against maltreatment (including arrests) of Chinese consular officers and nationals resident in these two countries. This does not mean that the CPR herself has always given foreign official representatives and private citizens the same kind of minimum treatment that she demanded for her own from India and Indonesia.

Despite her disclaimers or evasive answers, the CPR in January of 1950 did confiscate American consular properties in Peking, and since then she has detained American nationals, including airmen, without much regard for the proper procedural justice and minimum standards of a fair trial that she would want other countries to extend to Chinese nationals. In condemning India's expropriation of the properties of Chinese banks in that country, Peking quite correctly pointed out that no state should use its domestic laws as a bar to a legitimate claim of another state supported by international law. But, with respect to foreign properties expropriated in China during the 1950s, the CPR government has yet to convince one that it has lived up to what it preaches.

In its deteriorating relations with the Soviet Union, a rupture came in the form of Peking's closure of Soviet consulates in Sinkiang and other parts of China—perhaps not without some serious reasons. The Chinese act amounted to the "tearing up" of an agreement, comparable to the breach which Peking laid to the Indians when they closed CPR consular offices in India as a result of the Sino-Indian dispute.

XI

CPR Recognition Practice and International Law

ALTHOUGH NUMEROUS works have appeared on whether the CPR should or should not be accorded diplomatic recognition,[1] no serious study has yet appeared on the CPR's own view of the recognition question and her practice in the recognition of other states.[2] The importance of recognition in international law cannot be gainsaid. No system of law can function efficiently if it is not clear who are recognized as its subjects, entitled to the rights and bound by the obligations which it prescribes. Yet, recognition is a more complicated issue than it appears to be. For, although an entity answering the general definition of a sovereign state [3] would appear entitled to being accepted by the international community as such, it nevertheless cannot function effectively in relation to states which do not recognize its existence or that of its government. The discrepancy between a political fact and a legal fact has led jurists to diverge on whether recognition legally creates a new entity (the "constitutive" theory) or merely declares its existence (the "declaratory" theory). Some jurists, like Lauterpacht, have attempted to reconcile the two theories by making recognition constitutive but placing existing states under a legal obligation to recognize an entity which answers the definition of a sovereign state.[4] The debate is by no means settled. In our study of the CPR's recognition practice, we shall also attempt to investigate its views on this and other related issues.

Evolution of CPR Recognition Practice

The Initial Years (1949–1955)

In Peking's official notices to foreign states on the establishment of the CPR on October 1, 1949, and in subsequent communications, mention was made only of a desire to establish diplomatic relations; there was no specific request for recognition.[5] One wonders if the omission was due to an unawareness of the need for diplomatic recognition or whether the CPR leaders confused recognition with diplomatic relations. Upon closer examination it appears that Peking was far from unaware of the recognition question. At least one instance can be mentioned. When the Soviet Union responded to the CPR message on October 2, 1949, it declared a reciprocal willingness to establish diplomatic relations with the new Chinese Communist government. Like the responses from all other Socialist states (except the Democratic Republic of Vietnam [6]), the Soviet note omitted mention of recognition.[7]

In his acknowledgement, however, Premier Chou En-lai specifically thanked the Soviet government for being "the first friendly state to *recognize* the People's Republic of China." [8] This was possibly the only instance in which an *implied* recognition was explicitly acknowledged by Peking; but it is sufficient to indicate a Chinese appreciation for the legal nature and implications of recognition. Under international law, as a classic writer put it, "recognition is not necessarily expressed, it may be implied." [9] Although it cannot be accomplished by inference only,[10] recognition is essentially a matter of intention.[11] The Soviet express willingness to establish diplomatic relations clearly conveyed an intention to recognize the CPR, and Chou quite correctly inferred an implied recognition. (It may be noted that, unlike its official communications, published domestic CPR literature, such as *Jen-min shou-ts'e*

[People's Handbook], has always used the term "recognition" freely when listing countries that have recognized the CPR.)

The omission of recognition in outgoing CPR communications, between 1949 and 1955, was probably an indication of a general inclination to play down the recognition issue. There may be some reasons for this de-emphasis. First, the earlier experience of the "phantom Republic" [12] of 1912, from which foreign powers exacted political concessions as a price for their diplomatic recognition, may very well have been in the minds of the CPR leaders.[13] Thus, in his October 1, 1949, proclamation, Mao explicitly laid down three principles—"equality, mutual benefit, and mutual respect for territorial sovereignty"—as the basis on which the CPR was willing to establish foreign relations with other states.[14] Besides, the CPR may have adopted the Soviet view that recognition no more than declares the existence of a new government or state and that its more substantive meaning lies in the establishment of diplomatic relations.[15]

Another reason why Peking during this period played down recognition could be the "two Chinas" dilemma, which was becoming increasingly obvious. Peking might be apprehensive that if it forced the issue many states probably would recognize both regimes, possibly one *de jure* and the other *de facto,* thus petrifying the "two Chinas" impasse. By skirting recognition *per se* and focusing on diplomatic relations, Peking could probably expect to win more friends among the uncommitted countries. The maintenance of effective diplomatic relations, besides, is a semblance of *de jure* recognition hardly contestable under international law.

The CPR at the time was so preoccupied with diplomatic relations that it was not much interested in merely being recognized by any state that was not ready to enter into diplomatic ties. Its response to the recognition from Israel (January 9, 1950) and Afghanistan (January 12, 1950), neither of which showed a concomitant interest in diplomatic ties, was at best lukewarm, merely thanking them for their "decision." [16]

In establishing diplomatic relations, the CPR as a standard practice insisted on certain general conditions. First, the other party must sever its diplomatic relations with the Nationalist Chinese authorities on Taiwan or promise never to maintain such ties if none already existed.[17] In Peking's parlance, severance of diplomatic relations with Nationalist China also meant withdrawal of recognition.[18] Furthermore, a foreign government having diplomatic relations with the CPR was expected to support the latter's exclusive right to represent all of China both in the United Nations and in the international community at large. In the initial months of its existence, Peking circulated a uniform questionnaire which asked governments with which it had diplomatic ties to break relations with the Nationalist Chinese and to support the CPR as the sole legitimate government of China.[19]

Careful negotiations were therefore necessary to ensure that this set of conditions and the triad of "equality, mutual benefit, and mutual respect for territorial sovereignty" (laid down by Mao, as noted above) will be respected.[20] We know at least that the reluctance of the Netherlands government to support Peking's claims to exclusive representation in the United Nations was responsible for a suspension of the talks between the two countries from 1950 to 1954. The subsequent Chinese reluctance to expand diplomatic relations with the Netherlands beyond the chargé d'affaires level was in part due to this reason.[21]

The CPR, during the years 1949–1955, reserved the right to accept or reject diplomatic relations with a recognizing state, depending upon the outcome of the *ad hoc* negotiations. Results of such negotiations, which usually followed the recognition by a foreign government, were, as a rule, embodied in a joint communiqué. The only exceptions were: (a) when the recognizing state was from the Communist bloc; (b) when a state merely recognized Peking but professed no interest in having diplomatic ties; [22] and (c) possibly when a package negotiation (including both recognition and the terms for diplomatic ties) had preceded the announcement of a state's recognition of the CPR.[23] In state practices in general, if conditions are attached at the time of recognition they usually originate from the state granting recognition, not from the state being recognized. The CPR practice is a departure, which at least in part reflects the hostile international climate in which she has lived.

The practice of *ad hoc* negotiations seems to have continued till this day.[24] One of the latest cases is Canada. Until a settlement was reached on October 13, 1970, negotiations with Peking dragged on for a considerable time and, in August, 1969, were reported to have been stalled. The main hitch was Peking's insistence that Canada also recognize its claim to Taiwan and sever all ties, including those commercial and quasi-diplomatic in nature, with the Nationalist Chinese. The close-down of the Nationalist Chinese Embassy in Ottawa and the consulate-general in Vancouver was demanded by Peking as the precondition for the establishment of diplomatic relations between the CPR and Canada.[25] Although the final settlement was, as we shall see below, a compromise on the legal status of Taiwan, Canada finally agreed to sever its ties with Nationalist China.

Still another reason why Peking played down recognition in the initial period was probably its acrimonious reaction to the United States policy of nonrecognition. The impact of the United States denial of recognition was so great that CPR writers have denounced nonrecognition due to political motivations as an act tantamount to aggression.[26] After the United States-CPR Ambassadorial Talks began in August, 1955, the question of recognition became further complicated. Under international law such contacts could create a presumption of recognition unless rebutted by an explicit denial of intention. The United States from the beginning of the talks explicitly denied any such intention, and the "rituals" subsequently developed in the course of the talks were also so designed as to preclude any presumption to the contrary.[27] It is conceivable that Peking felt it necessary to discount recognition as a necessary legal amenity for establishing contacts with a nonrecognizing state.[28]

In any event, between October 1, 1949, and the end of 1955, the CPR was—according to its official registry—recognized by twenty-four of the world's pre-existing states. On the other hand, it greeted the independence of three new states.[29] Peking's view on recognition at the time was thus almost exclusively formulated by its own concern about other states' recognition of itself (i.e., a self-directed perspective). In all its replies to the recognition by other states (except the Soviet Union), Peking avoided the express use of the term "recognition," but merely conveyed, as the occasion arose, a reciprocal willingness to develop diplomatic or other ties.

The first occasion for the CPR itself to recognize another state arose with the formation of the German Democratic Republic on October 25, 1949. Premier Chou En-lai sent a congratulatory message in which he raised the question of diplomatic ties but did not expressly mention recognition.[30] On January 18, 1950, when greeting the birth of the Democratic Republic of Vietnam (DRV), Peking made no explicit mention of recognition, though it considered the DRV to be "the *legitimate government* representing the will of the Vietnamese people." [31] The omission of the word "recognition" is all the more interesting in view of the fact that the DRV, on its part, had, in a note dated January 15, expressly *recognized* the CPR.[32] At the time of Indonesia's independence, Chou En-lai, on March 28, 1950, informed Premier Mohammed Hatta that the CPR was willing to establish diplomatic relations with his new government. As before, no mention of recognition was made.[33]

The Transitional Period (1956–1959)

A few newly independent states emerged on the international horizon, including Sudan, Ghana, and Guinea, whose gaining of statehood heralded an upsurge of anticolonial tides soon to sweep across the African continent. Increasingly, the CPR was impelled to face more seriously the problem of recognizing other states and to weigh its implications. In other words, the CPR had to view the recognition issue increasingly from an outward-directed perspective, unknown during the previous period. It became less restrained in the express use of the term "recognition" in its responses to the independence of the new states.

In greeting the independence of the Republic of Sudan, on January 4, 1956, Peking not only expressed the hope of entering into diplomatic relations but explicitly "recognized" the new African state.[34] This was probably the first time Peking ever *expressly* extended its recognition to a new state. But it did not immediately repeat the practice when Morocco and Tunisia gained independence three months later. A message sent to each from Chou En-lai, on

April 4, 1956, merely offered felicitations and expressed a wish to "see the development of friendly and cooperative relations between our two countries." [35]

The CPR then on August 2, 1957, expressly recognized Tunisia, after the latter had dissolved its monarchy and adopted a republican form of government in July.[36] But, this act of express recognition should not be construed as anticipating immediate diplomatic relations, for it was not until January, 1964, that the two governments reached an agreement to establish diplomatic relations.[37] In 1957, Peking was understood to be seeking a new base for continent-wide activities in Africa, including aid to the Algerian revolutionaries, the usefulness of Cairo as a base having been somewhat reduced by the increasing anti-Communist stand of Nasser. Peking even feared that Nasser would reach a reconciliation with the "imperialists." [38] While Morocco was willing, Tunisia was hesitant about establishing full diplomatic ties with Peking at the time. Most probably, the CPR's express recognition—which in 1957 was quite an unusual act in view of its previous practice—was intended as a friendly gesture to win Tunisia's goodwill.

The express recognition did not necessarily indicate Chinese approval of Tunisia's turning to a republic. The CPR was known to separate recognition from approval in many cases, including that of Morocco, which was a semiautocratic Islamic monarchy, though with a strong left-wing nationalist movement based on trade unions. Despite its monarchical system, Peking recognized Morocco in October, 1958, possibly because of substantial trade interest and a common sympathy for the FLN movement in neighboring Algeria.[39] Diplomatic relations were soon established between the two countries.[40] It appears certain that practical interests—rather than approval of the domestic form of government of a given country—came increasingly to guide the CPR's policy of recognition at least so far as the nonaligned states are concerned.

Peking's responses to the independence of Afro-Asian states during this period varied with different cases. When Ghana became an autonomous dominion in 1957, Chou En-lai offered his felicitations and sent a special envoy to attend the celebrations at Accra. Although recognition was implied, Peking did not expressly address the question.[41] On the independence of Malaya, on August 30, 1957, Peking extended its express recognition but, except for a vaguely phrased wish for "friendly relations," did not explicitly suggest diplomatic ties.[42]

Similarly, recognition was expressly granted by Peking on February 23, 1958, to the newly formed United Arab Republic,[43] and on July 16, 1958, to Kassem's new republican government in Iraq after deposing the royal house in a bloody coup.[44] The CPR responded rather exuberantly to the formation on September 15, 1958, of the Algerian Provisional Government (GPRA). Three days later, in reply to a personal letter from Premier Abbas Ferhat, Mao Tse-tung himself, as the chief of state, and Premier Chou En-lai sent warm felicitations, followed by an express recognition extended by Foreign Minister Ch'en Yi.[45] The lack of mention of diplomatic ties in Ch'en's message was not surprising since the GPRA was a government-in-exile fighting an underground revolutionary war against the French colonial rule. Nevertheless, the CPR recognition heralded the stationing in Peking of an Algerian mission with full diplomatic status.[46]

At the time of Guinea's independence, Premier Sekou Touré addressed a personal letter to Chairman Mao, dated October 4, 1958, requesting the establishment of diplomatic relations. On October 7, Mao and Chou sent their felicitations in two separate messages. Foreign Minister Ch'en Yi expressly complied on the recognition request and expressed his government's readiness to negotiate the question of diplomatic ties.[47]

The general relaxation in attitude reflected the CPR's attempt to circumvent the impact of the United States nonrecognition through the cultivation of friendship with the nonaligned states. Although similar attempts had been made before, as in Peking's "unofficial" trade relations with Japan,[48] the 1956–1959 period saw a more self-assured CPR extending its contacts from the immediate surrounding regions to the Middle East, Africa, and other parts of the world.

Chou En-lai's approaches at the Bandung Conference of 1955 had paved the way for the expansion. In a few cases, trade and other informal relations eventually led to recognition and the establishment of formal diplomatic relations.[49] Evidently, Peking was consciously exploiting the subdiplomatic ties, technically bypassing the recognition question. In a report to the National People's Congress, on July 15, 1957, for instance, Vice-Foreign Minister Chang Han-fu stated that despite the United States "obstruction" the CPR had by then established diplomatic ties with twenty-seven countries, "semidiplomatic" ties with two, trade relations with sixty-eight (including nongovernmental trade), and "friendly contacts" with a total of one hundred one countries. Chang described relations short of express recognition as a "new form of diplomatic relations, the people's diplomacy." [50]

As Peking began this more subtle maneuver, a number of states began to switch recognition from Taiwan. Among the first to do so during this period was Egypt, which on May 16, 1956, announced that it was recognizing the CPR and simultaneously withdrawing its recognition of the Nationalist Chinese government in Taiwan. Peking *expressly* acknowledged Cairo's recognition and indicated a warm reciprocal desire to enter into diplomatic relations.[51] On three other occasions, when recognized by Syria (July 3, 1956),[52] Yemen (August 21, 1956),[53] and Cambodia (July 18, 1958),[54] Peking likewise expressly acknowledged their recognition.

It is apparent that the CPR now departed from its earlier practice by its express extension of recognition to the new states and also by its express acknowledgement of recognition by other states.

The Post-1960 Period

An identifiable pattern has emerged after 1960 in CPR recognition practice with regard to newly independent Afro-Asian states. On each occasion, Premier Chou En-lai would offer the CPR's felicitations, and Foreign Minister Ch'en Yi would extend express recognition on behalf of the CPR government.[55] As a rule, Chou's message would hail the independence of a former colony as a "great victory" of the native population against "imperialism and colonialism." [56] Ch'en's message would be more terse, to the point, and matter-of-factly confining itself to recognition and the pursuit of friendly relations.[57] Occasionally, Liu Shao-ch'i, as the head of state (between 1959 and mid-1966) would also send his own congratulatory messages.[58]

On the formal establishment of the Republic of Ghana, on July 1, 1960, however, the CPR merely sent warm greetings without reference to recognition.[59] This was not necessarily an exception to Peking's standard practice after 1960. Ghana had first become an autonomous dominion within the British Commonwealth in 1957. On that occasion, as noted above, the CPR had sent a special envoy to observe the celebrations at Accra.[60] That event took place during the transitional period (1956–1959) in which the CPR still resorted to *tacit* recognition. To the extent that the CPR felt that it had already recognized Ghana back in 1957, there was conceivably no need for repeating recognition in 1960. Under international law, only when there is obvious disruption in the political make-up of a state does it become necessary for other states to extend recognition anew.[61] There was no perceptible change in the political make-up of Ghana when in 1960 it became a republic under the same head of state, Kwame Nkrumah.

As a whole, the CPR practice of extending express recognition to newly independent states has been consistently followed in the post-1960 period, with only one or two exceptions.[62] The CPR may be consciously seeking to break its diplomatic isolation by cultivating good will and ties with the newly independent countries. Furthermore, since the independence of former colonies is a welcome indicator of the receding influence of (Western) colonialism, recognition could serve as a vote of confidence for the forces of self-determination. On the other hand, Peking during the same period maintained a rigid stance toward states that recognized Nationalist China and even toward states such as Canada and Italy that were willing to recognize the CPR short of accepting her legal claim to Taiwan. Solutions to the deadlock was to be left to the 1970s under a compromise formula, which we shall discuss separately below.

Legal Issues of Recognition

Recognition of States and Governments

Recognition of a state and recognition of its government are not the same in general international law, though it is oftentimes difficult to draw a distinction and, in a majority of cases, recognition of a new state also means recognition of its government. "The state is perpetual and survives the form of government," as *Lehigh Valley Railroad Co. v. the State of Russia* has indicated.[63] The recognition of a state continues beyond changes in its government. A classical view, which by and large still holds good, is that "the recognition of a new government within a State arises in practice only when a government has been changed or established by revolution or *coup d'etat.*" [64]

The question of recognition of a new government arises as a practical consequence of the fact that, although rights under international law are attributable to the state rather than to its government, the emergence of a new regime by other than peaceful means creates uncertainty as to its effectiveness, stability, and ability, as well as willingness, to commit the state to the observance of international obligations. Furthermore, in a world divided by differing social systems and ideologies, the question becomes more complicated as a new government may adopt a social system or ideological stance so completely different that the world is in effect confronted with almost a new entity. The law seems still fluid on this score, as it has been, since the appearance of the Soviet Union in 1917.

In doctrine, as we have already noted, the CPR does not seem to endorse fully the view that a drastic change in the domestic social system results in a new state.[65] In practice she has extended recognition anew to new governments within already recognized states where they have undergone drastic reorganization or changed in ideological complexion. For example, in 1962, the CPR once again recognized the new government in Yemen, now reorganized as a republic, although she had recognized the old Yemeni monarchy in 1956.[66] Similarly, on March 6, 1962, soon after the military regime under General Ne Win was installed in Burma, Foreign Minister Ch'en Yi notified General Ne Win of Peking's decision to recognize his new regime, though Burma and the CPR had exchanged recognition in October, 1949.[67]

Four days after the Kassem regime in Iraq was violently overthrown by the Ba'athists on February 8, 1963, Peking expressly recognized the new Iraqi government.[68] In November of the same year, President Aref expelled the Ba'athist elements from his government, but the action did not affect the CPR's recognition, apparently because no serious break of continuity resulted. In July, 1956, Peking had exchanged recognition with Syria.[69] On September 28, 1961, the Arab Republic of Syria was proclaimed and, in a note sent two days later, it requested Peking's recognition, which was granted on October 11. A new Ba'athist government was formed in Syria on March 8, 1963; a week later the CPR accorded it recognition.[70] Peking recognized the Republic of Zanzibar on December 9, 1963. Shortly afterward, a *coup* placed a leftist government in power. Foreign Minister Ch'en Yi extended anew his government's recognition on January 17, 1964.[71]

In these cases, Peking's practice did not depart much from that of most other states. Each time Peking appeared to imply that its recognition was extended to the new government. The question remains, however, whether the recognition could also apply to the state where drastic changes had put its continuity in doubt. Considering its position regarding the perpetuity of the state of China, one would assume that Peking probably endorses the theory that, while the emergence of a new government marking a clear break from the past gives rise to an occasion for recognition, the state being perpetual in nature remained recognized as before.

De facto and de jure Recognition

The distinction between *de facto* and *de jure* recognition was first drawn in the British practice in the nineteenth century, to accommodate the conflicting claims of the independence movements in Latin America and the European parent states. The terms fell into disuse for a time until readopted in the present century.[72] Even Soviet juristic vocabulary has adopted these terms, showing how widely the distinction has been accepted in international practice.[73] But, the legal consequences of the distinction are far from clear. While it is generally agreed that recognition *de jure* implies an unconditional acceptance of the stability, effectiveness, and legitimacy of the recognized entity or government, it is also a fact that regimes tottering on the brink of extinction are sometimes accorded recognition *de jure* for political reasons.

Most scholars agree that it is hard to tell whether an expressly accorded *de facto* recognition differs much in legal consequences from those of *de jure* recognition.[74] In *Luther v. Sagor,* the British Court of Appeals found that Her Majesty's government had explicitly recognized the Soviet government *de facto* and noted that, although *de facto* recognition was "for some purposes" distinct from *de jure* recognition, "for the present purpose . . . no distinction can be drawn." [75] As a result of the thin distinction, the two terms have often been confused or used interchangeably even by distinguished legal authorities.[76] The situation led McNair to suggest that "it is not the recognition which is *de jure* or *de facto,* but the Government or situation." [77] Even then, the confusion does not end, because in cases of cleavage between a *de jure* authority in jeopardy and a newly recognized *de facto* authority in the same country, foreign courts (especially British) in settling conflicting claims have at times decided in favor of the latter. *Arantzazu Mendi* (1939) and *Bank of Ethiopia v. National Bank of Egypt and Liquori* (1937) have demonstrated that the rights and status of an authority recognized *de jure* do not always prevail over those of another recognized *de facto.*[78]

Precisely because of the confusion, some states—India, for example—avoid expressly granting recognition *de facto.*[79] The CPR, to my knowledge, has never expressly recognized any state or government *de facto.* Whether *de facto* recognition exists in tacit form is hard to tell from avilable evidence. Given the fact that the CPR in 1949–1955 avoided all mention of recognition, one wonders whether her acknowledgement to the express recognition by foreign governments implied at least a reciprocal recognition *de facto*. One may also question whether the formal contacts made between the CPR and countries like Ethiopia—to which Premier Chou made a state visit in 1964 though no formal recognition had been extended between the two countries [80]—implied in any way a tacit *de facto* recognition. (As we shall see below, no express mention of recognition was made even when the CPR and Ethiopia jointly announced on November 24, 1970, that they would henceforth establish diplomatic relations.)

In extending recognition to other states, the CPR has also shunned the word *de jure*. Occasionally, it refers to the "sole legitimate government" of a state, especially with reference to itself.[81] After the murder of Premier Patrice Lumumba in the Congo (Leopoldville), Peking withdrew its recognition from the central government under President Joseph Kasavubu on February 19, 1961, and declared that it now recognized the Stanleyville regime of Antoine Gizenga as the "sole legitimate government of the Congo." [82] In these instances, of course, the references were made to a *de jure* authority rather than *de jure* recognition of a given authority.

In the CPR view, recognition of one regime, where there are two contending regimes in a country, as in the Congo case above, means the automatic withdrawal of recognition from the other if previously recognized. For a time after France had recognized the CPR she continued to maintain simultaneous diplomatic relations with Taiwan. Peking protested to the French government:

> According to international practice, recognition of the new government of a country naturally implies *ceasing to recognize the old ruling group* overthrown by the people of that country.[83]

While the CPR's view on the switching of recognition clearly reflects its distaste for the "two Chinas" idea, it accords generally with that of the Soviet Union.[84] However, while the Soviets assert that the "simultaneous *de facto* or *de jure* recognition of two governments in one and the same state cannot be considered normal," they nevertheless still consider such a situation acceptable.[85] The CPR insists, at least doctrinally, that *only* the "sole legitimate government" of a state is to be recognized. Yet in practice, the question is not so clear-cut. Although it recognizes the East German regime, Peking simultaneously maintains serious trade ties with West Germany, which remains the only major European trading partner that has not exchanged recognition with Peking or at least has not done so expressly. While Peking has openly admitted the coexistence of "two Germanys," [86] it is a moot question whether its simultaneous relations with both of them could possibly be considered the simultaneous recognition of two governments in one abstract German state.

Tension in the CPR Recognition Practice

A Coherent Body of Doctrine?

Although CPR writers seldom discuss in great detail implications of recognition in international law, a rather systematic treatment of the question appeared in an article by K'ung Meng.[87] The author gave a scathing critique of what he called "the bourgeois doctrine," as he outlined the CPR's own recognition doctrine. Analyzing the question from the Marxist framework of class struggle, he traced to the constitutive theory an intent to submit newly independent states to the certification by a capitalist-dominated world community. He considered "conditional recognition" and nonrecognition as thinly disguised forms of blackmail or, in some serious cases, even transmuted "aggression." Without arguing specifically for the acceptance of the declaratory theory, K'ung Meng laid down four basic principles regarding recognition which, he claimed, constituted "generally accepted norms of international law." These are:

a) That a state becomes an international person when its internal socio-political system is supported by its people exercising their right of *self-determination;*
b) That the independent and *effective exercise of authority* in a territory is the symbol of a state's existence internationally.
c) That no state can either use premature recognition or *withhold recognition* from another for the purpose of enforcing illegitimate interests. To do so would be tantamount to committing *aggression.*

d) To recognize a new state or government, either through individual or collective action, is a *right* enjoyed by all states *not to be abridged* by anyone. Any state coercing other states either to influence their recognition policy or to obstruct their recognition of a new state is committing an act of intervention.[88]

The trouble with this doctrine is that it was conceived in what we have called the CPR's "self-oriented" perspective, seeing the question almost exclusively from a concern for its own recognition by other states. These subjectively conceived tenets cannot always be followed even in Peking's own practice in regard to other states. For all its relatively consistent recognition practice since 1960, Peking has openly professed a nonrecognition policy toward Israel as a result of the "June War" of 1967.[89] Its doctrine of effective control regardless, Peking refuses to recognize Nationalist China's existence (although for obvious reasons). In a number of cases, which we shall note below, it appeared even to use premature recognition for political purposes. We possess no information as to whether the CPR has also engaged in coercing other states with a view to influencing their recognition policy; but we assume that she does not yet possess the capability to do so effectively.

Premature Recognition and Intervention?

Although the CPR doctrine equally condemns premature recognition and politically motivated nonrecognition, its own practice is not completely spotless on this score. As we have noted, it recognized the Algerian provisional government (GPRA)—a regime in exile—three days after its formation in 1958. By "normal" standards, the recognition would be considered as both premature and hostile to the parent state—France, in this case—against which the revolutionary regime was directed. Traditional international law would permit third states to recognize a conflict of the Algerian type as an insurgency or belligerency; but it would also require them to stay neutral. Neither an insurgent nor a belligerent would be regarded as competent to request military assistance in the name of the state, and the offering of such assistance by an outside state would be regarded as an act of intervention. Not until the insurgent or belligerent group had established general control or an armistice line had been accepted would the occasion arise for recognition by outside states.[90]

At the time of its formation, the GPRA had its headquarters in Cairo, far from Algerian soil. Not without reason the French government viewed the GPRA as an "artificial" creation.[91] Both because of the political complications and the legally shaky grounds of the GPRA's legitimacy, the United States and Britain were among many states (mainly Western) which refrained from recognizing it. The CPR's desire to assist the Algerian revolution and to make it a model for all colonial Africa apparently overrode other considerations. Almost simultaneously, a visiting Algerian delegation headed by Ben Khedda, and including Mahmoud Cerif, minister of armaments and supplies, was negotiating in Peking for arms supplies.[92] Later, as a result of mutual agreement reached in October, 1960, the GPRA stationed in Peking a "representative organ," [93] which was subsequently described in official Chinese literature as the Algerian "diplomatic delegation." [94] Although Peking's lack of diplomatic relations with France—which continued to recognize the Nationalist Chinese until January, 1964—made its support of the GPRA less embarrassing, the fact remains that its recognition was prematurely granted for political reasons.[95]

A number of revolutionary movements in foreign countries are known to have permanent missions in Peking. These missions possibly enjoy a special diplomatic or quasi-diplomatic status. There is a Mission of the Palestine Liberation Organization (PLO), sent from its headquarters in Cairo. Peking press suggests that the mission's head and deputy head have access to the CPR's foreign minister.[96] The Malayan National Liberation League also maintains a mission in Peking.[97] Most spectacular of all is the Permanent Mission of the South Vietnam National Liberation Front, whose new head, Nguyen Van Quang, according to Peking press, presented his "letter of appointment" to Premier Chou En-lai on December 4, 1967.[98] This appears to be a diluted version of the presentation of credentials by duly accredited diplomatic envoys.

Peking's acceptance of these missions seems to suggest a recognition *sui generis* of the revolutionary movements they represent. In some cases these movements are aimed at overthrowing regimes which Peking does not recognize, such as the Saigon regime in South Vietnam and Israel. In others, their targets are governments which Peking has explicitly recognized, such as in Somalia,[99] Burundi,[100] Indonesia,[101] etc. One wonders whether the quasi-diplomatic status enjoyed by foreign revolutionary movements—especially those from countries whose national governments have been formally recognized by Peking (either *de jure* or *de facto*)—cannot be viewed as flowing from a recognition *de ideologica*. In retrospect, recognition *de ideologica* has actually been practiced more widely and longer than one realizes. A ready example is the Soviet Union's triangular relations during the 1920s with the then Peking warlord government (*de jure*), the Kuomintang opposition government in Canton (*de facto*), and the nascent Communist movement in China (*de ideologica*).[102]

In any event, CPR recognition practice does not at all times measure up to its own recognition doctrine. The paradox may be summed up as follows: The CPR's recognition *doctrine* was conceived in an era when the world was still bipolarly divided by the ideological conflict characteristic of the Cold War. For that reason, its content was *by default* relatively ideology-free since Peking was anxious to argue why ideological differences should not bar its own recognition by other states. Yet Peking's recognition *practice* toward other states during the initial period was highly ambivalent, showing a much keener ideological concern than its own doctrine said any state should. It was only after the gradual collapse of the bipolar era that it became increasingly possible for CPR practice to stay relatively neutral and less ideological, thus more closely conforming to its own recognition doctrine. Even then, the CPR has not succeeded in making its practice fully comply with the doctrine of its own making. The difficulty bespeaks, in a nutshell, the clash between two different perspectives: what the CPR *expects* others should do to it, on the one hand; and, on the other, what it itself *can* or is willing to do to others.

Recognition as the "Sole Legal Government of China"

Despite the changing attitudes of Peking toward recognition, it has never relaxed its claim to being the "sole legal government of China," which means among other things possessing exclusive sovereign rights over Taiwan. The insistence has complicated matters for many a state which would be willing to recognize the CPR but not go as far as endorsing her Taiwan claim or abandoning the Nationalist Chinese. From Peking's point, the refusal to accept its claim to Taiwan is part and parcel of a larger "two Chinas" conspiracy that is totally unacceptable. As noted before, countries that attempted to recognize both Communist and Nationalist China invariably met with rebuff. Nigeria, before February 10, 1971, recognized both Peking and Taipei but was unable to maintain diplomatic relations with either. Senegal unilaterally recognized the CPR but established diplomatic relations with the Republic of China in Taiwan; for that reason the CPR refused to recognize Senegal.

The Taiwan impasse seemed for a long time to have closed the door on the CPR's being recognized by countries like Canada and Italy. The recognition negotiation with Canada dragged on for nearly two years because Peking insisted that recognition meant *ipso facto* acceptance of its claim to the title of Taiwan. Finally, on October 13, 1970, a more flexible formula was worked out which was acceptable to Peking but did not commit Canada on the Taiwan issue one way or the other. A joint communiqué announced that Canada recognized the CPR government as the "sole legal government of China" but added:

> The Chinese Government reaffirms that Taiwan is an inalienable part of the territory of the People's Republic of China. The Canadian Government *takes note* of this position of the Chinese Government.[103]

The "take note" formula was soon named after Canada as its author. It is noteworthy that the announcement spoke of "mutual recognition," implying an exchange, rather than unilateral extension, of recognition. In view of Peking's past practice of shunning explicit acknowledgment or reciprocation of recognition, the announced "mutual recognition" appeared to be a clear departure. The agreement also stipulated the immediate establishment of diplomatic relations in accordance with "the principles of mutual respect for sovereignty and territorial integrity, non-interference in each other's internal affairs, and equality and mutual benefit." [104] These recall the triad laid down by Chairman Mao in 1949 as the guiding principles for the foreign relations of the newly proclaimed CPR.[105]

The Canadian formula was promptly repeated in a number of cases. In the CPR's agreements with Italy (November 6, 1970), and with Chile (December 15, 1970), almost identical language was used.[106] The "sole legal government of China" clause, the "take note" form of dispensing with the Taiwan issue, and the three principles embodied in Mao's triad were all included. As minor variations, the agreement with Italy stipulated a three-month limit within which ambassadors were to be exchanged; and the agreement with Chile omitted the mention of "mutual recognition."

The CPR's agreement with Austria of May 26, 1971, followed the "mutual recognition" pattern and announced Austria's recognition of Peking as the "sole legal government of China." There was, however, no mention of the Taiwan question and therefore no "take note" provision. The same three principles cited in the agreement with Canada were spelled out here as the principles to govern the relations between the CPR and Austria. In addition, the CPR pledged to respect the status of Austria's neutrality.[107]

A few other agreements reached by the CPR with other states after October 13, 1970, seemed to contain greater variations, though they were obviously inspired by the Canadian formula. In its separate accords with Equatorial Guinea (October 15, 1970), Ethiopia (November 24, 1970), Nigeria (February 10, 1971), Kuwait (March 22, 1971), Cameroon (March 26, 1971), San Marino (May 14, 1971), Sierra Leone (July 29, 1971), etc.,[108] the CPR secured a common recognition as "the sole legal government of

China," although the Taiwan issue was not explicitly raised. In all these and the above instances, the word "recognize" was specifically used, with the sole exception of the CPR-Ethiopian agreement, which used the term "affirm." [109] In its agreements with Equatorial Guinea, Ethiopia, Nigeria, Cameroon, and Sierra Leone, the CPR was further identified as "representing the entire Chinese people," which seemed to imply the inclusion of Taiwan as well. In the same agreements, the "five principles" of peaceful coexistence, in contrast to the triad, were named as the guiding principles for diplomatic relations. Parenthetically, Peking's recognition accords with Kuwait and San Marino made mention of neither set of principles, but they seemed to be an exception.

It is not clear why the triad was cited in one group of the recognition agreements and the "five principles" in another. One might suggest that the "five principles" were reserved for states or governments that showed a greater affinity for the CPR. One is, however, immediately baffled by an editorial in the *People's Daily,* on October 15, 1970, which made enthusiastic references to the "five principles" in commenting on the CPR-Canadian exchange of recognition.[110] Was the editorial suggesting that the triad amounted to the same as the "five principles?" Or was it expressing an unrealized hope that the accord, minus the "take note" clause, would have come close to embodying the spirit of the "five principles?" In other words, do the differences, if any, between the two sets of principles hinge upon the Taiwan issue?

Besides invoking the "five principles," the CPR's accords with African countries such as Equatorial Guinea, Ethiopia, Nigeria, Cameroon, and Sierra Leone contained a standing clause expressing the CPR's support for the other party's struggle against "imperialism, colonialism, and neo-colonialism." One wonders if there was any link between the "five principles" and the anti-imperialist and anticolonial struggle. There can be no clear-cut answer, especially in view of the fact that in the agreement with Kuwait, which mentioned neither the "five principles" nor the triad, the CPR pledged support for the "Arab struggle against imperialism and Zionism." What made things even more complicated was an editorial in the *People's Daily,* which hailed the CPR-Kuwait accord as paving the way for diplomatic and other relations "on the basis of the Five Principles of . . . peaceful coexistence." [111]

Weighing the variations in wording among these recognition accords, one might venture to speculate a hierarchy of varying types of relations between the CPR and its cosignatories, probably determined by three considerations. The first consideration seemed to be ideological, in that by and large the five principles of peaceful coexistence were explicitly cited with relative consistency in accords reached with African states, those which were unmistakably anticolonial and anti-imperialist. By the same token, the triad was equally consistently reserved for Western countries. The second consideration was the individual state's previous position on Taiwan and, for that matter, the extent of United States influence on that score. It appeared that states which had to accept the "take note" formula —Canada, Italy, and Chile—were the ones which, conceivably out of deference to the United States, had continued to recognize and maintain diplomatic relations with Nationalist China until they switched recognition to Peking. The third consideration might be called the principle of default. When a state fell under neither of the two groups above, the recognition agreement made no mention of either the triad or the five principles, as was the case with San Marino and Kuwait.

What mattered, in the final analysis, was the recognition of the CPR as the "sole legal government of China," which was consistently found throughout the agreements noted above. A further test of ideological, if not practical, affinity seemed to be the acceptance of Peking as "representing the entire Chinese people." This blanket endorsement would seem to obviate the dispute over Taiwan's legal status and, for that reason, was probably held dearer by Peking than either the silence or the "take note" posture adopted by the other states.

One last note before we leave the subject: The increasing number of states that have recognized or switched recognition to the CPR after October 13, 1970, should not be blindly attributed to the Canadian "breakthrough" alone. As we have seen, a relatively few states have explicitly followed the "take note" formula. The single most significant factor responsible for the "recognize Peking" band wagon, as it were, has been the relaxation of the international climate accompanying the critical change in United States policy toward the CPR, which became unmistakably evident in mid-1971 with the announcement of President Nixon's planned visit to Peking and of the United States willingness to seat Peking in the United Nations. The CPR's acceptance of the "take note" compromise in the Canadian formula may have anticipated the forthcoming thaw. The subsequent plethora of recognition accords which Peking has been able to secure serves to substantiate the thaw's actual on-coming, without which the same signatory states probably would have been less willing to go as far as accepting the CPR as the "sole legal government of China," with all its awesome implications under international law.

XII

The Law of Treaties in CPR Practice

THE PRESENT section of the study will be concerned with the CPR's attitudes, policy, and practice with respect to treaties and international agreements. In the present chapter we shall attempt a systematic evaluation of the CPR's views regarding the nature and function of treaties, and also the principles and norms followed in CPR practice concerning the conclusion, application, and termination of treaties. In the following chapter we shall probe into the policy implications behind the CPR's treaty making.

General Conception of Treaties

(a) Definition. As a socialist state, the CPR views treaties as one of the least objectionable features of international law. In an important work on the subject, treaties are described as "*an* important source . . . [and] an important *manifestation* of international law." [1] Two implicit points are worth noting in this definition. First, the word "an" is used advisedly. As we have earlier suggested, [2] the CPR's exclusion from most of the multilateral conventions having a legislative character makes it impossible for her to claim, as the Soviet Union does, that treaties are "*the* main source of international law." [3] Secondly, as a logical corollary to the first, the CPR has to assert that many of the norms embodied in international conventions, including those from which she is excluded, already exist in customary law and are only given a "manifestation" in treaty form. As we have observed, CPR jurists have even attempted to find antecedents in general international law (as distinct from specific agreements) for the Five Principles of Peaceful Coexistence.[4]

A Chinese textbook defines treaties as "documents relating to the establishment, modification, or termination of the sovereign rights and obligations between two or more States." "Treaties," it continues, "represent a typical and most common legal amenity for regulating relations in the political, economic, and other spheres between States. All types of relations between States may constitute the content of treaties." [5]

International organizations—which under modern international law are generally accepted as possessing the capacity to become parties to agreements—are conspicuously absent from this definition. The omission is not surprising since the CPR does not support the view that international organizations such as the United Nations are imbued with an international personality comparable to that of states.[6] In this respect, the CPR continues to follow the position held until recently by the Soviet Union.[7]

The above definition is also silent about the capacity of dependent states to conclude treaties. Western jurists are not in complete agreement as to the validity of treaties concluded with a dependent state. The prevailing view, nevertheless, seems to be that such treaties would be void if they prove unacceptable to the suzerain or protector state.[8] During the Sino-Indian border dispute, the Chinese insisted that no agreement signed by the Tibetan "local authorities" with Britain could bind China.[9] The objection, however, was raised on two grounds: The first is lack of Chinese recognition of any agreements negotiated by the British with the Tibetan regional authorities. The second, and more important here, is that China considered, and still considers, Tibet to be no more than an autonomous region whose legal status might be likened to that of

Puerto Rico vis-à-vis the United States. Thus viewed, Peking's position regarding Tibet in no way shows an objection to a dependent state having the capacity to conclude treaties with foreign countries when properly approved by the parent or protector state. In fact, the CPR recognizes the treaty signed by Outer Mongolia, while still a Chinese dependency in 1936, with the Soviet Union,[10] although lately Peking was reported to have grumbled about Soviet coercion at the time.[11] Elsewhere we have seen that Peking concluded agreements of grave political and military importance with the provisional government of Algeria prior to the Algerian independence in 1962.[12] Presumably, a revolutionary group aimed at the overthrow of a colonial power could be recognized as having the capacity to enter into agreements with foreign states.

(b) Nature and character of treaties. CPR writers generally accept the view—described as Marxist-Leninist in origin—that treaties possess both utilitarian values (such as those concluded between or by socialist and nonexploitative states) and a class character (those concluded between an "oppressor" and an "oppressed" state).[13] There is no clear indication as to the class character of treaties formulated between a socialist and a capitalist state, or between two or more "oppressor" or "oppressed" states.

In an ideologically divided world, it has been suggested in CPR literature, treaties assume a peculiar significance. Given the basic difference in their internal systems, states can hope to develop political, economic, cultural, and other relations only on the basis of agreements. Since treaties embody agreements to create legally binding norms (i.e., legislative in nature), compliance with treaty terms will be *sine qua non* for ensuring stable international relations between states of different ideologies.[14] But, although a treaty can be a legislative enactment when the parties intend to create new norms, all norms so created must follow the Five Principles of peaceful Coexistence (PCX).[15] Just as they profess a belief in the existence of certain peremptory norms in general international law,[16] CPR writers thus hold the principles of PCX as a body of *jus cogens* in treaty law from which no derogation is permitted. Since the universal validity of PCX—the *jus cogens* for treaty law

—is itself predicated upon certain peremptory customary norms, the logical conclusion one could draw is that treaties are concluded and operate within the framework of customary norms. If this is true, CPR doctrine seems to rely more on customary law than do Soviet jurists.[17] In practice, however, there is evidence that the CPR feels more compelled to comply with norms created by treaties which it has concluded, acceded to, or supported, than other norms that exist in custom, especially where practical interests are at stake.[18]

Again in doctrine, it has been contended that treaties between socialist states, like their relations in general, belong to a higher category, to be regulated by proletarian internationalism.[19] But, in practice, CPR treaties afford only some qualified evidence of anything which might be strictly called "socialist" provisions. References to Marxism-Leninism or proletarian internationalism are found mostly in the preambular part of these treaties.[20] What stand out more significantly in these as distinct from treaties with other states are the usually longer duration they are intended for and the subject matter covered by them (e.g., commerce and navigation, nuclear assistance, etc.) [21]

CPR Treaties [22] in Existence

The CPR has since 1949 signed or acceded to hundreds of treaties and the exact number would be hard to ascertain. The 13 volumes of *T'iao-yüeh chi* (TYC), the official Treaty Series, publishes a total of 782 treaties, including 26 multilateral treaties, 37 semiofficial treaties (one of them the Armistice Agreement with the United Nations Command), and bilateral treaties with fifty-three countries. These are classified under fourteen headings: political, legal (including consular and nationality treaties), boundary, border relations (e.g., use of rivers or lakes shared with another country), economic, cultural, scientific and technical, agricultural and forestry, fishery, health and sanitation, postal and telecommunications, transport, the law of war (the four Geneva Red Cross Conventions of 1949, and the 1925 Geneva Protocol), and military (the Korean Armistice Agreement).[23]

An independent study by Johnston and Ch'iu lists a total of 2,-292 treaties, though the listing reflects "multilateral contacts" as well. (In other words, a treaty or agreement signed by the CPR with two other countries are counted twice, one under each country.) These are divided into twenty categories (as opposed to fourteen in the *TYC*); and about seventy countries are involved (as opposed to fifty-three in the *TYC*).[24]

The only agreement with the United States is the "agreed announcement" of September 10, 1955, regarding the repatriation of Chinese and American civilians in each other's country." [25] This is, as one veteran American diplomat put it, "the only transaction successfully concluded between Washington and Peking in the prolonged [Ambassadorial] Talks" since 1955, first at Geneva and then at Warsaw.[26] The Korean Armistice Agreement of July 27, 1953, marks the only one signed by the CPR with the United Nations; but, technically speaking, it was signed between the commander of the Chinese People's Volunteers (P'eng Te-huai) and the supreme commander of the (North) Korean People's Army (Kim Il Sung), on the one side, and the United Nations Command, on the other.[27] The most important treaties of a "political" nature included in the *TYC* listings are the 17 treaties of friendship, cooperation, mutual assistance, and/or nonagression, concluded between 1949 and 1965. Six of these were with socialist states and 11 with nonaligned states.[28] An analysis of their characteristics and significance will follow in the next chapter.

By far the largest body of existing treaties are trade agreements, which in the official *TYC* number 356, or 46 per cent of the total treaties included therein.[29] The second largest group in the *TYC* are the "political" treaties, numbering 132, followed by the "cultural" treaties at a total of 65. According to the *TYC*, Nort Vietnam ranks first as the country having signed the largest number of treaties with the CPR (47), followed in decreasing order by: the Soviet Union (40), Hungary (40), North Korea (39), Czechoslovakia

(37), Rumania (36), Poland (35), Outer Mongolia (32), Burma (31), Bulgaria (30), Cambodia (25), etc.[30]

If one goes by Johnston and Ch'iu, the largest body of CPR treaties are still in the trade category, totaling 620, or slightly over 22 per cent of the total 2,292 included in their calendar of CPR treaties. The second largest group consists of "cultural" agreements (317), followed by those related to scientific and technical cooperation (260), those concerning economic assistance (215), and "political" (including friendship) agreements (167). According to the same study, the Soviet Union has signed the largest number (totaling 218) of treaties with the CPR among all the latter's treaty partners, with North Vietnam ranking second (163), followed by North Korea (151), Poland (116), Albania (113), East Germany (113), Outer Mongolia (105), and Czechoslovakia (104).[31] The main reasons for the differences shown in the Johnston and Ch'iu study are twofold: First, whereas the *TYC* covers only the period of 1949–1964, their study extends to 1967; and, secondly, the authors have employed a combination of criteria by which additional agreements not published in the *TYC* are also included.[32]

By conventional Western standards, the treaty character of many of the agreements included in the *TYC* may be highly questionable. To mention one example, the official collection includes 102 joint announcements, communiqués, or declarations, which would not be considered as treaties, let alone included in official treaty series, in Western state practices. But, if one understands that the Communist Chinese, going even beyond the Soviet views on this,[33] look to the consensual intent rather than the specific modality or form of an agreement as the source of its binding force, then the inclusion of these "lesser" documents in the *TYC* is not so surprising. For example, the one agreement between the CPR and the United States mentioned above was purposely phrased in English, by the ingenuity of the United States delegation at the Geneva Talks, as "agreed announcement," unilaterally issued but identical in wording, so designed as to eschew diplomatic recognition. In its Chinese counterpart, however, the term is *"hsieh-yi te sheng-ming,"* literally, "the declaration of [an] agreement." The implication appears to be that the "agreement" which has been reached is only now openly "declared" and its character as an agreement transcends the form in which it is presented. Cynics may suggest that the CPR was attempting to boost its own international standing by upgrading the agreement with the United States into a more dignified document. But the CPR must also be aware of the added burden of obligation such "upgrading" would have cast upon her.

The real answer can be obtained only by observing CPR practice in broad context, which appears to support the consensuality principle posited above. At the end of the 1954 Geneva Conference on Indochina, after the United States refused to endorse the Final Declaration pledging the intention of the sponsoring states to respect the agreements on the settlement of the Indochina problem, Premier Chou En-lai demanded that the United States make a unilateral declaration that she would not disturb the implementation of the accords. This the United States did, and Chou accepted the unilateral declaration. On account of that, the CPR has persistently held the United States bound by the Geneva accords.[34] In 1960, the CPR explicitly stated that it would no longer accept an agreement between two states in the form of separate unilateral declarations (meant mainly to pressure the United States).[35] The very fact that they announced the intended change suggests that they had accepted unilateral declarations as a form of agreement until then. In practice, Peking has not completely broken away from that tradition. Following its first successful atomic explosion in October, 1964, Peking first proposed a treaty with the United States banning the use of nuclear weapons; but, that having been rejected by Washington, it then proposed—as an interim measure—parallel unilateral declarations by both sides pledging not to be the first user of nuclear weapons.[36]

Of the various agreements included in the *TYC* less than thirty-two are formally given the most formal designation *t'iao-yüeh,* or "treaty." The others are given a variety of titles including: (a) *hsieh-ting,* or "agreements," some requiring ratification as treaties; (b) exchange of notes; (c) joint declarations; (d) joint communiqués; (e) *shih-shih pan-fa,* or "measures for implementation"; (f) protocols; (g) memoranda; (h) "exchange of correspondences" (that convey commitments), etc.[37] Some of the agreements listed in *TYC* were actually concluded by what purported to be unofficial or, at best, semiofficial organizations of the CPR and their foreign counterparts. In the absence of diplomatic relations, the CPR's trade and fishery agreements with Japan were signed by semiofficial organizations in both countries. The Third Trade Agreement between the CPR and Japanese trade organizations, signed on May 4, 1955, even specified that the trade mission from one side would be accorded the "treatment and rights of diplomatic officers" by the other.[38]

In view of the established CPR practice of clothing joint declarations and other forms of interstate communications with a legal character tantamount to treaties, it is not hard to see why the CPR has insisted that the Cairo and the Potsdam Declarations were legally binding upon the wartime allies who issued them. In a textbook joint "declarations" between two or more states are included as a common type of treaty. They are described as documents which usually state or reaffirm general principles regulating international relations or certain norms of international law accepted by the parties as binding upon them, though in some cases a declaration could deal with more specific topics. The Declaration of Paris of 1856, relating to rules of naval warfare and the Cairo Declaration of December 1, 1943, are cited in the same volume as examples of declarations with the force of treaties.[39]

The CPR has signed very few multilateral treaties as a result of its exclusion from the United Nations family and limited participation in international organizations. Until 1971 its participation was mainly limited to those organizations established within the Communist bloc, such as the Organization for International Railway Cooperation,[40] the Organization for Socialist Countries in Postal and Telecommunications Cooperation,[41] and the Fisheries Research Commission for the Western Pacific.[42] The CPR is a charter member in these three organizations, being a party to the agreements under which they were established. Between the mid-1950s and 1962, Peking also sent observers to meetings of the Council on Mutual Economic Aid (Comecon) and the Warsaw Treaty Organization.[43] These contacts were interrupted by the

Sino-Soviet split. At one time, the CPR was a member of the Joint Institute of Nuclear Research, established in 1956 under Soviet sponsorship for countries in the Communist bloc.[44] In 1966, however, it withdrew from the organization, charging Soviet perfidy and use of the institute to spy on the Chinese nuclear program.[45] It is obscure whether the withdrawal from membership also signified that the CPR has repudiated the agreement which created the institute.[46]

Among the existing multilateral conventions acceded to [47] by the CPR are: (a) The Protocol for Prohibition of the Use in War of Asphyxiating, Poisonous or Other Gases of Bacteriological Methods of Warfare (Geneva, 1925); [48] (b) The Convention for the Amelioration of the Conditions of the Wounded, Sick and Shipwrecked Members of the Armed Forces at Sea (Geneva, 1949); (d) The Convention Relative to the Treatment of Prisoners of War (Geneva, 1949); (e) The Convention Relative to the Protection of Civilian Persons in Time of War (Geneva, 1949); [49] (f) The Warsaw Convention for the Unification of Certain Rules Relating to International Carriage by Air (Warsaw, 1929); [50] (g) The International Load Line Convention (1930); [51] and (h) The International Regulations for Preventing Collisions at Sea (1948).[52]

The CPR's acceptance of the last mentioned convention was deposited on January 27, 1958, with Britain as the depository power. But the British depositary function was transferred on July 13, 1959, to the Intergovernmental Maritime Consultative Organization (IMCO), in which China was represented by the Nationalist government. An official listing of parties to the 1948 Regulations published by the IMCO in November, 1959, did not include the CPR. The Nationalist Chinese, on the other hand, deposited their acceptance of the Regulations with the IMCO on November 21, 1966. Whether the CPR is officially a party to the 1948 Regulations for Preventing Collisions at Sea, therefore, seems unclear.[53] According to British sources, the deposit of the CPR acceptance was recorded on January 29, 1959.[54] In a list published by the United States Department of State in 1964, the CPR is included among the parties to the Regulations.[55] Incidentally, a collision involving a United States ship and a mainland Chinese fishing vessel took place on

May 15, 1961, resulting in the sinking of the latter. The company owning the United States ship denied any responsibility when the Chinese invoked the 1948 Regulations.[56]

The Treaty-Making Process

In CPR practice, treaties are concluded through a series of steps including negotiation, signing, ratification (if required by the terms of the treaty), and—when ratification is required—the exchange of ratifications. The place for the exchange of ratifications is usually the capital of the other party if the signing is done in Peking, or *vice versa.*[57] The Communist Chinese have won a universal distinction of being tough negotiators.[58] The toughness only in part reflects their ideological stance and their intransigence over the "two Chinas" dilemma.[59] In part it reflects a seriousness attached to the terms with which they have to comply once an agreement is reached. As one scholar has concluded from a study of the original documents in the possession of the United Nations Command in Korea, Peking's tough posture during the negotiations for the Armistice Agreement and the subsequent record of its rather truthful compliance with the terms of the agreement had a more than casual correlation.[60]

(a) The power to sign treaties. A formal CPR treaty is negotiated and signed by a plenipotentiary deputed with "full powers" to undertake such a task. The plenipotentiary may be the chief of state himself,[61] or the premier,[62] or the foreign minister,[63] or other officials designated by the chief of state.[64] The negotiator's appointment by the chief of state is approved by the Standing Committee of the National People's Congress, in pursuance of Articles 31 (11) and (12) of the CPR Constitution. His full powers are also derived from the authorization of the NPC Standing Committee. This procedure applies even to the case of the chief of state himself signing a treaty.[65]

Treaties signed by a plenipotentiary other than the chief of state himself contain in the preamble the standard clause that the plenipotentiaries from both sides, designated by their respective chiefs of state, "having exchanged and examined each other's *full powers,* found in good and due form, have agreed upon the following . . . ." [66] As is true of the general international practice, the procedure of the examination of "full powers" is obviated when a treaty is signed by the CPR's chief of state with his counterpart from another state.[67]

The Communist Chinese follow the general theory that initialing on a treaty, or signature *ad referendum,* by a negotiator does not bind his government. The point was much played up during the Sino-Indian border conflict when the validity of the so-called McMahon Line was in dispute. Peking noted that the Chinese representative at the 1914 Simla Conference only *initialed* his name on a draft treaty proposed by the British, on April 4, 1914. The initialing was immediately repudiated by the Chinese government in a formal note to Britain dated May 1, 1914.[68] "Initialling and formal signature," wrote one CPR jurist, "are two completely different matters." He noted that initialing "merely indicates that the initialling representative temporarily *endorsed* [ch'ien-shu] and *acknowledged* [jen-cheng] the draft; but he cannot sign it until his government has formally given its consent." [69]

(b) Ratification. CPR practice in treaty making disposes of ratification in three different ways. First, treaties of peace, mutual nonaggression, friendship, alliance and mutual assistance, and other treaties or agreements by whose terms ratification is required must be ratified by the CPR chairman (the chief of state) in pursuance of the "decisions" of the NPC Standing Committee (under Articles 31 (12) and 41 of the CPR Constitution). Secondly, all other agreements, protocols, etc., not in the above category, must be "approved" by the State Council (the Cabinet). These two procedures were established by a resolution passed by the NPC Standing Committee on October 16, 1954.[70]

A third procedure, introduced in more recent years, is to obtain prior authorization from the NPC Standing Committee so that the CPR chairman can conclude treaties effective upon signing—provided the drafts have been reviewed by the NPC Standing Committee before the actual signing. For instance, by a resolution of the NPC Standing Committee on October 5, 1961, CPR Chairman Liu Shao-ch'i was authorized to conclude the Sino-Nepalese Boundary Treaty, to come into force "upon signing." [71]

It is unknown whether the new procedure was in any way tied to the presidency of Liu Shao-ch'i or whether it has survived his purge by Mao, the party chairman, during the Cultural Revolution. Few agreements have been signed since 1966. But on March 14, 1967, the State Council approved the Sino-Mauritanian Agreement on Economic and Technical Cooperation, signed on February 16, 1967.[72] At least, the two-point procedure established in 1954 seems to be still in practice.

(c) Accessions to multilateral conventions. As noted in a previous section, the CPR has acceded to a number of multilateral conventions. In practice, the acceptance is signified by a resolution of the NPC Standing Committee. The state council, through its foreign ministry, acting upon the resolution, transmits the instrument of accession to the depository. Reservations may be attached at the time of accession, such as the CPR's reservation to Article 85 of the 1949 Geneva Convention relating to POWs.[73] It is not clear what specific attitude the CPR may have on the validity and effect of reservations attached to these accessions, or on reservations to multilateral conventions in general. One wonders whether the CPR follows the Soviet position that a state has the sovereign right to make reservations without the consent of the other contracting parties. An official Chinese publication, reproducing the texts of the four Geneva Red Cross Conventions of 1949, lists all the contracting parties and adhering states without differentiation as to reservations.[74] There is no indication of the CPR's attitude toward the so-called Pan-American rule whereby a convention is considered not in force between a state which has ratified it with certain reservations and another state which is already a party but rejects the reservations.

(d) Recognition of pre-1949 treaties. The CPR seems to maintain a distinction between treaties signed by the Kuomintang government (before 1949) and others by earlier Chinese governments. Even though it has not taken a positive stand regarding the latter, the CPR has not formally nullified any specific treaty concluded by a pre-Kuomintang government.

On the other hand, the CPR has been much more hostile toward treaties concluded by the Kuomintang government before the Communist take-over. On February 1, 1947, when the outcome of the civil war was far from certain, the Central Committee of the Chinese Communist Party declared that it would never recognize any foreign loans or any treaties "which disgrace China and strip away its rights" or any understandings to be entered into by the Kuomintang government after January 10, 1946.[75] Article 55 of the Common Program (1949), which served as a quasi Constitution until 1954, stipulated that the CPR reserved for itself the right to "recognize, abrogate, revise, or renegotiate" treaties previously concluded by the Kuomintang government with foreign states.[76] No guidelines for these options were ever made known, however. We only know two possible considerations in the recognition of past treaties: (a) Where China's vital rights are involved, such as representation in the United Nations, the CPR has insisted that the treaties concluded in the name of China by the Kuomintang government before 1949 have devolved upon it by dint of its take-over of the mainland; (b) The same attitude applies to "executed" or "dispositive" treaties signed by Kuomintang as well as earlier Chinese governments (such as those relating to boundary). The CPR, for instance, has not contested the validity of Sino-Burmese boundary treaties signed in 1894, 1897, 1935 and 1941—the last two signed during the Kuomintang administration—although the CPR's 1960 boundary treaty with Burma has replaced all these previous treaties.[77]

Not all treaties of the pre-1949 Kuomintang vintage are automatically nullified.[78] The Treaty of Friendship and Alliance and the Agreements on the Chinese Ch'ang-ch'un Railway, Dairen and Port Arthur, signed between the Republic of (Nationalist) China and the Soviet Union on August 1, 1945, for example, were recognized by the CPR to be valid until replaced by a new treaty and a new agreement concluded by the CPR with the Soviet government on February 14, 1950. The exchange of notes between Peking and

Moscow that announced the coming into force of the new documents also announced the abrogation of the old treaty and agreements.[79]

Effect of Treaties

(a) *Pacta sunt servanda.* Mainland Chinese commentators claim that a good Marxist-Leninist should honor treaty obligations under international law.[80] This seems to be a theoretical acceptance of the principle *pacta sunt servanda,* i.e., a treaty in force is binding upon the parties and must be performed in food faith. The Sino-Hungarian Treaty of Friendship and Cooperation, signed on May 6, 1959, has a clause stipulating that the treaty's provisions shall not prejudice the obligations which either party has separately assumed toward other states.[81] Although it is unknown what the clause alludes to, the spirit in which it is conceived manifests a concern for treaty obligations already contracted.

(b) *Pacta tertiis nec nocent nec prosunt.* Both CPR government and writers readily endorse the principle, generally accepted under international law, that a treaty applies only between the parties and has no effect upon third states. Liu Tse-jung alluded to the *pacta tertiis* principle when he rejected the argument that the orbiting by the United States and the Soviet Union of man-made satellites over the airspace of other countries could be justified by the fact that the satellites were launched under the International Geophysical Year (IGY) Program. Even if the authorization had been granted by the IGY, he argued, it could not be binding upon states not a party to the agreement which inaugurated the IGY.[82]

Yu Fan, another CPR writer, has invoked the same principle in his attack on alleged British attempts to restrict Chinese sovereignty over Tibet. In the Anglo-Russian Convention relating to Persia, Afghanistan, and Tibet, signed on August 31, 1907, he noted, an article provided:

> In conformity with the admitted principle of the *suzerainty of China over Tibet,* Great Britain and Russia engage not to enter into negotia-

tions with Tibet except through the intermediary of the Chinese Government. . . .[83]

Since China, he argued, had direct sovereignty over Tibet—although the latter enjoyed autonomous power—the treaty's characterization of China's rights as merely those of "suzerainty" was clearly an impairment of Chinese sovereignty. In his denunciatory commentary, Yu Fan said that the treaty had no effect whatsoever on China in accordance with the principle of *pacta tertiis:*

This Convention . . . was concluded between Britain and Russia and can only be effective between Britain and Russia. Since China was not a contracting party, according to the principle of *pacta tertiis nec nocent nec prosunt* of the law of treaties, this Convention naturally cannot bind China. How can it impose the fictitious "suzerainty" on the relationship between China and Tibet by a convention of which China was ignorant.[84]

It is a moot question whether the CPR would have raised the objection had the Anglo-Russian Convention conferred certain rights upon China. Under international law, it is not impossible for a treaty between two or more parties to confer rights (but not obligations) upon a third state.

The CPR has maintained that no international agreement on arms control to which it is not a party will be binding upon it.[85] It has also insisted that treaties or agreements contracted in the name of China by the Nationalist Chinese (in Taiwan after 1949) will have "no legal basis whatever" and are "null and void" so far as the CPR is concerned.[86] For example, in 1957, Nationalist China signed and ratified the 1954 Hague Convention for the Preservation of Cultural Property in the Event of Armed Conflict, and its related documents. The CPR declared that the Nationalist act was "illegal" and had "no effect upon China." [87]

Western jurists have begun to take the view that some treaties with an objective legislative character may have an effect beyond their immediate contracting parties. This would apply, for example, to those cases where a treaty creates an international situation (e.g., the Suez Canal Convention of 1888 and the clauses of the Versailles Treaty concerning the Kiel Canal, both of which converted the canals into international waterways) or where an entity binding upon all states is created (e.g., the United Nations).[88] Article 2 (6) of the Charter of the United Nations clearly states an intention to extend its principles to nonmembers.[89] Besides, in its Advisory Opinion rendered in the *Reparations* case (1949) the International Court of Justice held that states not members of the United Nations (i.e., not a party to the U.N. Charter) had nonetheless an obligation to respect the "objective international personality" of the organization originally established by fifty states "representing the vast majority of the members of the international community." [90]

The CPR, however, has invoked *pacta tertiis* whenever it rejects resolutions or decisions by the United Nations, claiming that these would not bind states with no representation. Wu Hsiu-ch'üan, Peking's special representative, told the Security Council in November, 1950, that "without the participation of the lawful delegates of the People's Republic of China, the Chinese people have no obligation to abide by the resolutions and decision of the United Nations." [91]

In its own treaty making, the CPR seems to take the necessary precaution not to abridge the rights of third states. The Sino-Pakistan Boundary Agreement of 1963 contains a special provision purporting to guarantee that the terms of the agreement will not prejudice India's interests pending a final settlement between her and Pakistan over Kashmir. Article 6 of the agreement reads:

> The two parties have agreed that *after* the settlement of the Kashmir dispute between Pakistan and India, *the sovereign authority* concerned will *reopen negotiations* with the Government of the People's Republic of China on the boundary . . . so as to sign a formal boundary treaty to *replace* the present Agreement.[92]

Entry into Force and Duration of Treaties

CPR treaties which require ratification, in most cases, come into force upon the exchange of ratifications.[93] A nontreaty agreement, unless ratification is explicitly required by its own terms, becomes effective from the date of signing.[94] In some cases, a nontreaty agreement does not come into force until the date of the subsequent exchange of notes after it has gone through the internal constitutional procedures of the contracting parties. For example, the Sino-Indonesian Agreement of Cultural Cooperation of 1961, by its own terms, "shall come into force upon the date of the *exchange of notes* between the two Contracting Parties after going through the *constitutional procedures* in their respective countries." [95]

The duration of a treaty or agreement may be left open, as in the Treaty of Friendship, Cooperation and Mutual Assistance between the CPR and North Korea, signed on July 11, 1961.[96] Or it may be limited to a definite number of years but renewable under specified conditions. The 1961 Sino-Indonesian Cultural Cooperation, according to its own provisions, "shall be valid for a period of five years," but renewable for another five years if neither side requests its termination "at least six months before its expiration." [97]

Validity and Registration

(a) Validity of a treaty. CPR writers have made an exception in the application of the principle *pacta sunt servanda*. Treaties of an "aggressive or enslaving nature," they maintain, are "not protected by international law." [98] Practically no information is available as to what treaties have actually been repudiated on the ground that they are "aggressive or enslaving" in nature.

Along the same line of argument, CPR commentators have insisted that treaties concluded under "unequal" conditions (presumably including coercion) or containing "unequal" provisions (e.g., creating an "exploitative" relationship) are subject to repudiation.[99] But in practice many of the treaties signed by previous Chinese governments do not seem to have been invalidated merely by the fact that they are now considered by Peking to be "unequal treaties." The CPR has named the following as among the "unequal treaties": the Sino-British Treaty of Nanking (1842); the Sino-Russian Treaty of Aigun (1858); the Treaties of Tientsin (1858) and Peking (1860) with Britain, France, the United States, and Russia; the Sino-Russian Treaty of Ili (1881); the Protocol of Lisbon (1887); the Sino-Japanese Treaty of Shimonoseki (1895); the Sino-British Convention for the Extension of Hong Kong (1898); and the International Protocol (1901) signed with eight foreign powers following the Boxer Uprising. But, the CPR has simultaneously declared that "pending future *negotiation,* the status quo should be maintained." [100]

There are obviously wide gaps between what is "repudiable" and what is actually repudiated. The asserted Chinese readiness to renegotiate the treaties indicates that Peking has not fully translated into practice the doctrine that "unequal treaties" are invalid *ab initio.* At the Third Afro-Asian People's Solidarity Conference, held in Tanzania in February, 1963, the CPR lent its name to a resolution which endorsed the doctrine. The "Resolution Concerning Treaties Signed with Colonial States," passed by the conference, declared that all treaties signed under duress or conditions tantamount to duress or before the departure of the colonial rulers when the local population had no freely elected representative government of their own would not be binding after their "liberation." [101] Although the authorship of this specific resolution is unknown, Peking's influence in the shaping of some of the resolutions passed by the conference was obvious. For example, one resolution which supported the CPR's "lawful rights in the United Nations" and its right to "liberate Taiwan by whatever means at the discretion of the Chinese people" clearly bore the imprint of Peking's initiative.[102] Regardless of its doctrinal *ab initio* denunciation of "unequal treaties," the CPR has tolerated the continued British control of Hong Kong, Portuguese control of Macao, and, of course, Soviet control of erstwhile Chinese territories now constituting Soviet maritime provinces.[103] The reality has made it practically impossible for the CPR to declare as null and void *ab initio* those past treaties that had sanctioned the cession or lease of the said territories.

On one occasion, the CPR invoked the principle that a treaty inconsistent with obligations of an earlier treaty has no validity.[104] On another it cited Article 103 of the Charter of the United Nations to show that no member states can contract obligations inconsistent with those already assumed under the Charter.[105] Of course, these arguments were used to attack treaties considered to be undesirable or unacceptable by Peking; they may or may not reflect its true conviction or actual practice in general. From the limited information available, the CPR seems to be rather careful thus far not to contract obligations that would contravene other obligations derived from earlier treaties. While it has signed a treaty of alliance or friendship with three of the four Communist states surrounding China, Peking is not known to have signed one with North Vietnam, possibly out of considerations for the 1954 Geneva agreement, which pledged to respect the neutrality of the three Indochinese states.[106]

(b) Registration of treaties. Some of the CPR's bilateral treaties with states that are members of the United Nations have been registered by the latter with the United Nations Secretariat, in pursuance of Article 102 of the Charter.[107] For example, the CPR's instruments of ratification of the Geneva Red Cross conventions (1949), along with its reservations, were deposited with the Swiss Federal Council, the depository, which in turn registered a "certified statement" to that effect with the United Nations Secretariat.[108] For obvious reasons, the CPR had not on its own initiative registered any of its treaties with the United Nations before 1971 when it first gained representation in the organization.

Termination or Suspension of Treaties

(a) By express notification. The Sino-Indonesian Treaty of Friendship of April 1, 1961, provided that within the specified ten years in which it was in force "each Contracting Party has the right to *notify* the other [of its intention] to terminate this Treaty, and the Treaty shall cease to be in force six months after the day of such notification." [109] The Agreement on Cooperation in Saving Lives and Aiding Ships and Aircraft in Distress at Sea, signed between the CPR, North Korea, and the Soviet Union on July 3, 1956, contained a similar provision, though phrased slightly differently: "If none of the Contracting Parties *declares* its abrogation of this Agreement six months before the expiration of the effective period, it shall remain effective for another year."[110] The CPR Foreign Ministry, on June 24, 1967, notified the Soviet Embassy in Peking of its intention not to extend the present agreement, which was to expire on January 1, 1968. When Izvestia, on July 19, 1967, criticized the Chinese notification as contrary to the spirit of international cooperation, the CPR defended its action not only by reference to the provisions in the agreement but also by reference to general state practice.[111]

(b) By express consent. The 1961 Treaty of Friendship, Cooperation and Mutual Assistance between the CPR and North Korea, according to its own provisions, will "remain in force until the Contracting Parties *agree* on its amendment or *termination.*"[112] While the "notification" procedure above means that the treaty can be terminated unilaterally after the lapse of the specified time upon the serving of the termination notice by one party, termination by "agreement" seems to require the mutual consent of both parties to a bilateral treaty.

(c) By unilateral "abrogation." We have noted that the CPR from the very beginning of its existence has reserved the right to "abrogate" (as well as take other actions upon) treaties previously concluded by the Nationalist government. In theory, "abrogation" remains a form of treaty termination. But, aside from the fact that the CPR has indicated support for the 1941 abrogation by the Nationalist government of the Shimonoseki Treaty of 1895, we know of no specific instance of unilateral abrogation. Again, even in the Shimonoseki case, it is highly debatable whether the treaty was terminated in consequence of the Sino-Japanese war then going on, or whether it was terminated by China's unilateral abrogation.[113] Another equally intriguing question is what effect the current Sino-Soviet split has upon the 1950 alliance treaty between the two Communist states. Would the existing state of near war terminate or suspend that treaty? Neither side has openly abrogated it or given any indication one way or another.

(d) Replacement by a later or renegotiated treaty. The Sino-Afghan Treaty of Friendship and Mutual Non-Agression of 1960, according to its appended exchange of notes, terminated the 1944 Treaty of Friendship signed by Afghanistan with Nationalist China.[114] In 1964, a second Sino-Yemeni Treaty of Friendship was signed. According to its provisions (Article 4), upon the coming into force of the new treaty, the first Treaty of Friendship signed between the two countries in 1958 would become inoperative.[115]

(e) *Rebus sic stantibus* (changed circumstances). Almost all modern jurists, though some with reluctance, admit the existence in international law of the principle that a fundamental change of circumstances may be a ground for terminating or withdrawing from a treaty.[116] But like many other states, the CPR has not actually terminated any treaty by unilateral act on the ground of *rebus sic stantibus*. The principle, nevertheless, has been invoked as a justification for the *revision* (not termination) of past treaties incompatible with state sovereignty or present conditions. In the 1950 Sino-Soviet Agreement Concerning Chinese Ch'ang Ch'un Railway, Port Arthur and Dairen, which provided for the Soviet relinquishment of certain privileges guaranteed by a 1945 treaty, references were made to changed circumstances after the birth of a Communist government in China in 1949. But, the doctrine was invoked here not so much as a ground for terminating the old treaty as for the conclusion of the new agreement.[117]

Similarly, when the new Sino-Burmese boundary treaty was being negotiated, Premier Chou En-lai told the National People's Congress on July 9, 1957, that the conclusion of a new boundary treaty with Burma was necessary in view of "historical changes," including Burma's independence from British colonial rule and the establishment of the CPR.[118] Chinese commentators have likewise raised *rebus sic stantibus* in supporting Egypt's proposal in 1956 to revise the 1888 Constantinople Convention regarding the use of the Suez Canal.[119] It appears that *rebus sic stantibus* has been as a rule invoked in CPR practice and commentaries only in connection with treaty revisions or the conclusion of new treaties to replace old ones.

(f) Impossibility of Performance. Modern international law accepts the doctrine that a treaty may be terminated or suspended in consequence of the permanent or temporary total disappearance or destruction of an object indispensable for its execution.[120] Of course, as the International Law Commission has commented in its Draft Articles on the Law of Treaties, the principle must be invoked in good faith.[121] During the Cultural Revolution, when Chinese schools and universities were closed down, the CPR Ministry of Higher Education notified the Soviet Embassy in Peking that Soviet as well as all other foreign students in China were to suspend their studies for one year. The Soviet Union considered the suspension a breach of the Sino-Soviet Cultural Cooperation Agreement of 1956 and retaliated by ordering all Chinese students in the Soviet Union to return home.[122] Peking's response was that the Chinese suspension of studies affected all students, both Chinese and foreign, and was in no way a discrimination against the Soviet students alone, whereas the Soviet expulsion of Chinese students was unwarranted discrimination since it affected no other foreign students and the Soviet Union was not carrying on a Cultural Revolution and its schools were not closed. Furthermore, the Chinese claimed that their emergency action had been explained to the Soviet Union and proper assistance to the Soviet students involved was being given through consultation with the Soviet Embassy. On the other hand, they claimed, the Soviet government had not consulted the Chinese government on the expulsion of Chinese students.[123]

In the Chinese view, therefore, their suspension of studies affecting foreign students without discrimination was not a breach of the existing cultural agreements, but a temporary suspension due to a *bona fide* supervening impossibility of performance during a national emergency. As such, their action should be no cause for the Soviet suspension of the operation of the same agreements. In international law a material breach of a bilateral treaty by one of the contracting parties entitles the other to terminate the treaty or suspend its operation consequent upon the breach. The Chinese in this case were claiming that their action was not a breach justifying the Soviet retaliatory measure. It may be noted in this connection that the Chinese do not deny the principle that a prior breach justifies the termination or suspension of a treaty by the other party. In 1963, for example, the CPR revealed for the first time that the Soviet Union in 1959 "unilaterally tore up" the Sino-Soviet agreement on nuclear sharing signed on October 15, 1957, and suggested that the Soviet breach had led to the termination of the said agreement.[124]

Internal Execution of Treaties

It is not clear what status treaties are accorded in the domestic legal system in mainland China. Many of the treaties and agreements signed with foreign countries are published in the *Fa-kuei hui-pien* [Compendium of Laws and Regulations], such as the Sino-German Consular Treaty of 1959, the Dual Nationality Treaty with Indonesia signed in 1955, the CPR's accessions to the Geneva Red Cross conventions of 1949.[125] One may speculate that some legal effect is intended in terms of internal execution when treaties are promulgated in the statute books. As we have suggested, many of the CPR's agreements are not published in the official *T'iao-yüeh chi* (TYC) [Treaty Series]. It is obscure what legal distinction exists, if any, between treaties and agreements reported in the *TYC* and those that are not.

Some of the CPR's domestic regulations are intended to assist in translating treaty provisions into action. For example, the Ministry of Public Security in 1960 promulgated a body of regulations for implementing the provisions of the Sino-Indonesian Dual Nationality Treaty.[126] The Bureau of Ship Inspection in 1959 published a Manual for Load Lines of Oceanfaring Ships,[127] purporting to promulgate and give effect to the 1930 International Load Line Convention, to which the CPR acceded in 1955. Article 1 of the convention requires each party "to promulgate all regulations, and to take all other steps which may be necessary to give this Convention full and complete effect." [128]

Another example that the CPR endeavors to execute treaty obligations internally is the establishment of a Foreign Trade Arbitration Tribunal attached to the CPR's Council for the Promotion of Foreign Trade. By a resolution of the Government Administrative Council, passed on May 6, 1954, under which the tribunal was established, it is stipulated that the tribunal "has the mission of deciding in disputes arising out of foreign trade and business transactions. . . ." [129]

Other Technicalities

In some instances, a clause regarding treaty revision is included in the provisions of a treaty. Article 7 of the Treaty of Friendship and Cooperation signed between the CPR and East Germany in 1955 provided that the treaty would be revised or terminated when Germany should become reunited or when both parties should agree on its revision or termination.[130] As noted earlier, the Sino-Pakistan Boundary Agreement of 1962 also contained a clause calling for revision or, if necessary, the conclusion of a new treaty, when a settlement was reached between Pakistan and India on Kashmir.[131]

Very little is known regarding actual CPR practice in the interpretation of treaties. At one time the debate over the universality of international law found its expression in the question of the proper interpretation of treaties.[132] Some agencies established by certain treaties for executing their provisions are known to have the competence to interpret the treaties in question.[133] Some treaties have a provision calling for "negotiation" by the parties as a means for settling disputes "arising out of interpretation or application." [134] Authenticity of a treaty is usually provided for in the "final clause" of a treaty. CPR bilateral treaties are usually done in duplicates, in Chinese and in the official language of the other party (and sometimes an English version is provided when the latter is not English). The "final clause" usually provides that both texts are "equally authentic." [135]

Unequal Treaties

Because of its significance, we would further explore the question of "unequal treaties" in historical perspective. The earliest Chinese attacks on unequal treaties dates back to the 1920s when China demanded the abolition of treaties that conferred upon Western powers such privileges as extraterritoriality and tariff control, which encroached upon Chinese sovereignty.[136]

The Nationalist Chinese government carried on a tenacious battle in the 1930s to undo the many treaties that clearly placed China in an unequal status vis-à-vis the powers. Not until 1943, when the Pacific War was in full blast and China was fighting on the Allied side, was the last of the unequal treaties abolished.[137] Without going into detail, I would like to make a few generalizations regarding the Communist Chinese position on unequal treaties in comparison with that of the pre-1949 Nationalist government.

First of all, while the Nationalists based their objection to unequal treaties on the latter's infringements upon Chinese sovereignty,[138] the Communist Chinese have suggested coercion and exploitation (e.g., "aggressive" and "enslaving") and also derogation from the Five Principles of Peaceful Coexistence as the grounds for their objection.[139] Under international law, coercion of a representative or coercion of a state by the threat or use of force in order to procure the signature or ratification of a treaty is considered to be a factor vitiating the validity of the treaty in question.[140] The CPR position agrees with this principle but goes beyond it. The concept of exploitation in interstate relations sealed by treaties has much broader application than coercion in the conclusion of treaties. Furthermore, mere nominal or verbal reciprocity, in CPR views, does not make a treaty truly equal. CPR commentators have cited nominal reciprocity but actual inequality as the ground for their denunciation of the 1946 Treaty of Friendship, Commerce and Navigation signed between the Nationalist Chinese government and the United States.[141]

Another marked difference between the Nationalists and the Communists is that, while the former was solely concerned with the abolition of China's own unequal treaties, the latter has used the doctrine as a sword for attacking treaties concluded between other states to which China is not a party. The CPR has labeled the following as "unequal treaties": (a) the 1956 United States-Swiss agreement regarding cooperation in the civil use of atomic energy

—unequal because the United States retained all control over the equipment and materials supplied to Switzerland and their utilization; [142] (b) the Anglo-Jordanian treaty of alliance signed in 1948, which, until abolished in 1956, granted Britain two military bases and the right to send troops to Jordan in time of war; [143] (c) the Status of Forces Agreement signed between the Nationalist Chinese government and the United States in 1965, which unilaterally granted to American servicemen in Taiwan certain broad privileges; [144] (d) the United States-Philippine trade agreement of July 6, 1946, which imposed restrictions on Philippine exports to the United States but not vice versa; [145] and (e) the United States-Japan mutual security treaty, signed on September 8, 1951, which, according to Peking, was unequal because the United States could, at will, bring Japan to the "brink of war." [146]

Both the Nationalist government in its pre-1943 fight to abolish unequal treaties and the CPR in its present doctrine have regarded renegotiation as the best solution to resolve the *status quo* already created under unequal treaties. But, whereas the Nationalists were silent about treaties under which Chinese territories had been ceded to foreign powers, such as the 1842 Nanking Treaty, which ceded Hong Kong to the British; [147] the Communist leaders have included these among the unequal treaties to be renegotiated.[148] On the other hand, while the Nationalists began in 1949 to denounce the 1945 Sino-Soviet Treaty of Friendship and Alliance and the Sino-Russian Tientsin (1858) and Peking (1860) treaties, the Communist Chinese did not do so until later. In fact, the 1945 treaty was replaced by a new one in February, 1950, as already noted. The CPR did not openly extend the list of unequal treaties to the 1858 and 1860 treaties until about 1962,[149] although Mao was reported in Russian press to have demanded the return of Outer Mongolia during Khrushchev's visit to Peking in 1954.[150]

In marked contrast to the Nationalist government, Peking has extended the concept of unequal treaties to multilateral conventions as well. In 1963, for instance, Peking branded the Partial Nuclear Test Ban Treaty as an unequal treaty, because it created disparate statuses, placing the three big nuclear powers—the United States, Britain, and the Soviet Union—in a privileged position without "identical and reciprocal" obligations vis-à-vis the other contracting parties. The three superpowers, Peking maintained, could continue nuclear tests underground while the other countries whose nuclear technology was not so advanced would be barred from the preliminary methods of testing, in the atmosphere, in space, and under water.[151]

One perceptive writer has pointed out that Peking's doctrine of "identical and reciprocal" obligations is not applied to all multilateral conventions on an indiscriminate basis. Anticipating the day when it would be seated in the United Nations in the name of China, Peking had frequently criticized the alleged attempt by "U.S. imperialists" to eliminate the veto power enjoyed by the permanent members of the Security Council.[152] Obviously, it did not view the veto privilege as a derogation from the doctrine of "identical and reciprocal" obligations.[153]

By and large, in its bilateral treaty relations, the CPR has taken great pains to eliminate or eschew provisions that would too obviously place China in a privileged position over the other country. The careful drafting of the 1960 Sino-Burmese Boundary Treaty is a ready example.[154]

The CPR has also abrogated an unreciprocated right secured by the Nationalist government in 1946 to maintain a special zone in Haiphong, Indochina, with warehousing and docking facilities under exclusive Chinese customs jurisdiction.[155] The privilege was dropped in a new agreement signed by the CPR and North Vietnam on April 12, 1957, governing transborder transit.[156] One scholarly source, drawing upon information received from a third state which maintained a consulate-general in Haiphong, suggested that the omission was a deliberate effort to terminate an unreciprocated right flowing from what might be called an unequal treaty.[157]

XIII

Policy in Treaty Making and Treaty Compliance

FOLLOWING THE discussion above of the legal technicalities of CPR practice in the field of treaties, we are ready to explore CPR policy in treaty making and its record of compliance, to the extent permitted by available evidence. It goes without saying that treaties reflect a state's foreign relations and policy. It is our belief that by examining the contents of the treaties, as well as the conditions in which they are made, one can gain some insights into the practical considerations occupying the minds of the decision-makers, the power configuration obtaining between the contracting parties, and the way the decision-makers manage their foreign relations with the given resources at their disposal. Much can be derived also from a state's treaty compliance record. In the case of the CPR, that record is of exceeding empirical value to those concerned with the question whether the Chinese Communists can live up to their international responsibility.

Some Major Issues in CPR Treaty Relations

The major issues covered in, or settled by, CPR treaties can be grouped under the following headings: (a) friendship and cooperation (including "mutual assistance," which means, *inter alia,* mutual defense and "mutual nonagression"); (b) foreign trade (including navigation); (c) consular matters; (d) nationality questions; (e) boundaries; (f) border questions (e.g., use of international rivers and lakes); (g) transport, etc. Our study here will be confined to the first two categories, namely, treaties of friendship and cooperation, and those concerning foreign trade. Most of the other topics either have been discussed elsewhere in the book or bear no direct relevance.

Treaties of Friendship and Cooperation

As already noted, the CPR up to 1965 had signed seventeen treaties of friendship and cooperation, including six with Communist states (Soviet Union, February 14, 1950; East Germany, December 25, 1955; Czechoslovakia, March 27, 1957; Hungary, May 6, 1959; Outer Mongolia, May 31, 1960; and North Korea, July 11, 1961), and eleven with nonaligned states (Burma, January 28, 1960; Nepal, April 28, 1960; Afghanistan, August 26, 1960; Cambodia, December 19, 1960; Indonesia, April 1, 1964; Yemen, June 9, 1964; Guinea, September 13, 1960; Ghana, August 18, 1961; Congo (B), October 2, 1964; Mali, November 3, 1964; and Tanzania, February 20, 1965).[1]

In order to ascertain the policy thinking behind the making of these treaties of extreme political importance, it is necessary to examine their contents and to compare their differences and similarities.

(a) Friendship treaties with Communist states. Four common clauses in more or less identical language are found in the six treaties of friendship and cooperation signed with Communist countries.

First, a declaration of the readiness of both parties to participate in international undertakings "aimed at ensuring peace and security throughout the world" appears in Article 1 of all the six treaties. In the Sino-Soviet treaty (Article 1) and the Sino-North Korean Treaty (Article 2), both of which have an alliance character, there is a provision for immediate military and other assistance by all means at each party's disposal when the other party is subjected to an armed attack from a third state.

Second, a standard clause in all the six treaties provides for bilateral consultation between the contracting parties on all important international problems affecting their common interests. The clause appears in Article 4 of the Sino-Soviet and Sino-North Korean treaties, but in Article 2 of the other four treaties.

Third, all six treaties contain a clause pledging economic, cultural, scientific, and technical cooperation, although phrased somewhat differently from case to case, reflecting the relative stages of development of the parties and the existing relations between them, and scattered in different articles.

The fourth standard clause is a pledge to respect each other's sovereignty, independence, and equality. Again, the actual wording varies slightly with each case. The 1950 Sino-Soviet Treaty of Friendship, Alliance and Mutual Assistance provides for "conformity with principles of equality, mutual benefit and mutual respect for the national sovereignty and territorial integrity, and non-interference in the internal affairs" of each other (Article 5). The treaties with North Korea (Article 5), Hungary (Article 3), and Czechoslovakia (Article 3) make references to "mutual respect for sovereignty, non-interference in each other's internal affairs, equality and mutual benefit."

To facilitate our comparisons in the next section, we shall identify these four common clauses by the shorthand labels of (a) the "preservation of peace" clause, (b) the "consultation" clause, (c) the "cooperation" clause, and (d) the "respect" clause.

Before we leave the subject, a few other generalizations may be offered concerning policy implications behind the CPR's friendship treaties with Communist bloc states. In the first place, the structure of these treaties bears a formal resemblance to that of the bilateral friendship treaties signed by Stalinist Russia with the "people's democracies" between 1945 and 1950. The most obvious similarity lies not only in the layout of the treaty provisions but also in the fact that despite the designation "friendship" the treaties are far more political than they appear and encapsule the more formal relations between the contracting parties.[2] But, the actual uses made of the device are different. Stalinist Russia had used the bilateral friendship treaties to absorb the individual "people's democracies" into the Soviet orbit, to make sure that the ties of each of them individually with the Soviet Union were closer than those between any of them, and to maintain a façade of equality while Soviet supremacy was ensured through less formal channels, such as the Communist party and Stalin's manipulations in the politics of these satellite states.[3]

Just as the Soviet friendship treaties did not reflect the less formal ties, the CPR friendship treaties deal with no other than state-level relations. Despite the fact that the Chinese Communist party maintains probably the most cordial ties with the Albanian Communist party, the two countries have not signed a friendship treaty.[4] The timing of the conclusion of the CPR's six friendship treaties with Communist countries is revealing of the political purposes they each serve. Between 1949 and the end of 1955, the CPR signed a treaty of friendship only with the Soviet Union. The 1950 Sino-Soviet Treaty of Friendship, Alliance, and Mutual Assistance conformed generally to the pattern of Soviet bilateral friendship treaties signed with other Communist states.[5] To this day, it remains the only "alliance" treaty the CPR has ever signed with another country.[6] Although some mutual concessions were made in two subsidiary agreements signed on the same day, the Sino-Soviet Treaty rather truthfully reflected Peking's heavy dependence upon the Soviet Union.

During the same period, the CPR had no formal political ties with any of the other Communist states in Eastern Europe, having only a *cultural cooperation* agreement with each.[7] The first friendship treaty signed between the CPR and states of this group was the Sino-East German Treaty of Friendship and Mutual Assistance, December 25, 1955,[8] which was followed by two others, Czechoslovakia (March 27, 1957) [9] and Hungary (May 6, 1959).[10] These treaties coincided with the CPR's shift from the earlier singular dependence upon the Soviet "Big Brother" to a policy of seeking greater autonomy and cultivating closer ties with other socialist countries. The fact that the Sino-East German friendship treaty was signed in late 1955 seemed to substantiate our suggestion made elsewhere that the real beginning of the Sino-Soviet conflict should be traced back to 1954 rather than 1957.[11]

The two other CPR friendship treaties subsequently signed—one with Outer Mongolia (May 31, 1960), and the other with North Korea (July 11, 1961)—were, by the same token, inseparable from the Sino-Soviet tangle. As far back as 1946, the Soviet Union already had a treaty of friendship and mutual assistance with Outer Mongolia.[12] The CPR treaty with Mongolia in 1960 probably represented an attempt to neutralize Outer Mongolia as a buffer state. The Sino-North Korean Treaty of Friendship, Cooperation, and Mutual Assistance was even more blatantly a by-product of the Sino-Soviet conflict, coming as it did only five days after the Soviet Union had signed a similar treaty with North Korea.[13]

(b) Friendship treaties with non-Communist states. The four standard clauses found in the CPR's friendship treaties with Communist countries appear also in those signed with non-Communist states. But some modifications are introduced in these clauses, and they usually appear in less schematic fashion. On the other hand, certain new clauses in more or less identical form are found exclusively in the present group but not in the previous group.

First, the "preservation of peace" clause appears in those of Peking's friendship treaties with non-Communist countries which bear the additional title of "mutual non-aggression." [14] While CPR treaties with Communist states provide for a mutual endeavor to promote world peace in general, these treaties focus more narrowly on "everlasting peace . . . *between* the Contracting Parties." [15]

Second, the "consultation" clause is contained in most of the treaties in this group as well, but its import is slightly different from the first group. "Consultation" used in the CPR's friendship treaties with Communist countries encompasses "all important international problems" affecting the contracting parties. But in those with non-Communist states, "consultation" is limited in its application to "disputes between [the parties]," and in some cases the wording is changed to "negotiation." [16]

Third, the "cooperation" clause is also common in the present group as before, but the application is slightly different. In the friendship treaties between the CPR and states within the Communist bloc, the contracting parties pledge to render each other economic and cultural (sometimes including technical and scientific) aid and cooperation. In treaties with states outside the bloc, the clause provides only for the development and strengthening of "economic and cultural ties." [17]

The fourth clause—the "respect" clause—finds a universal expression in all the CPR's friendship treaties, but with slight variations in language. In the treaties signed with non-Communist countries, the parties pledge to respect each other's "independence, sovereignty and territorial integrity." [18]

One may assume that the universal inclusion of the "respect" clause signifies a standing policy in the CPR's relations with countries of different ideological backgrounds. The same may be said of the inclusion of the other three standard clauses. The slight variations in their application may suggest that the CPR's relations with the Communist countries usually envisage broader commitments than those with non-Communist countries.

Like the first group, the friendship treaties with states in the non-Communist group are also products of specific policy needs in the CPR's foreign relations. Again, the timing of the various treaties is very informative. The first one signed was the Sino-Burmese Treaty of Friendship and Mutual Non-Aggression, of January 1, 1960. In rapid succession, within the same year, the CPR concluded four others, three of them with China's neighbors: Nepal (April 28), Afghanistan (August 26), and Cambodia (December 19).[19] All these countries, except Cambodia, have common borders with China and there was a practical reason why all the friendship treaties were all concluded in 1960. The Sino-Burmese friendship treaty preceded the Sino-Burmese agreement on boundary questions of January 28, 1960, by only three weeks; and in nine months the Sino-Burmese Boundary Treaty was signed (October 1, 1960).[20] The Sino-Nepalese friendship treaty, which was preceded by the Sino-Nepalese boundary agreement of March 21, 1960, heralded the signing of the Sino-Nepalese Boundary Treaty on October 5, 1961.[21] All these interlocking treaties came after the 1959

Sino-Indian border conflict, anticipating the more serious repetition of the conflict in 1962.

The other friendship treaty made in 1960 was signed with Guinea on September 13. It was part of Peking's serious drive to extend formal political ties to the African continent. Similar treaties were signed with Ghana (1961), Congo (Brazzaville) (1964), Mali (1964), and Tanzania (1965), plus another with an Asian country, Indonesia (1964). The expansion of CPR treaty relations to more remote areas coincided with the conclusion of similar treaties with two Asian Communist neighbors, Mongolia (1960) and North Korea (1961), as already noted. Doubtless, these treaty-making efforts were an outgrowth of the Sino-Soviet conflict which, further complicated by the East-West conflict, made of Africa both a "battleground" to "test out" the Chinese ideological formulations and an ideal area from which to win friends.

Trade Treaties and Agreements

As already noted, the importance of trade treaties and agreements can be seen from the fact that over 46 per cent of the total number of treaties listed in the official Treaty Series are concerned with trade. A breakdown shows that 11 of them are treaties of commerce and navigation (CN), 256 concern trade and payment (including 19 "semiofficial" agreements), and 87 are related to general conditions for the delivery of goods (including 2 "semiofficial").[22]

The goals underlying the multiplication of Peking's trade treaties are depicted in a textbook as follows: (a) to promote trade with countries in the Communist bloc; (b) to facilitate "normal international economic relations"; (c) to promote Chinese exports; and (d) to surmount the United States embargo against mainland China.[23] As one writer has pointed out, the CPR's foreign trade is part and parcel of the country's planned economy; and the trade agreements are concluded under the CPR's system of state monopoly of foreign trade although, unlike in the domestic scene, the regime has no comparable control over the international market.[24]

Trade agreements have been consciously employed by Peking as a first step toward the establishment of normal diplomatic relations. Wang Yao-t'ien, a professor at the Institute of Foreign Trade in Peking, has best summed up the official policy:

> Under international custom, trade treaties and agreements can be concluded between two states which have not yet established diplomatic relations. Therefore, concluding trade treaties and agreements can *lay the groundwork for the establishment of diplomatic relations*. China's [diplomatic] relations with Ceylon and Egypt were developed in this way.[25]

The reference was made to Egypt's switch of recognition from Taipei in 1956, following nine months of preliminary trade relations with Peking. The transition from trade to diplomatic ties was hailed by Yeh Chi-chuang, minister of foreign trade, as a great victory in Peking's foreign-trade policy.[26]

No matter whether the trade agreements are concluded at the state or corporational or associational level, they are always politically tinged. The case of Japan may be offered as an example. From 1952 to 1958 the CPR had four "nongovernmental" or "semiofficial" trade agreements with Japan, signed between the Chinese Council for the Promotion of International Trade and its Japanese counterpart.[27] Under the 1953 agreement, permanent trade missions were established in Tokyo and Peking,[28] and under the 1955 agreement these missions were given "diplomatic treatment and rights." [29] Under a 1958 agreement, the status of the trade missions was modified and defined as "private" delegations, but the rights to use ciphers for the conduct of business and to fly national flags on the buildings of the trade missions were granted.[30] After the 1958 Nagasaki incident,[31] Sino-Japanese trade was disrupted for several years and in subsequent negotiations the trend was toward less formality as typified by the so-called L-T memorandum formula [32] (from 1970 on known simply as "memorandum trade," or MT), accompanied by a steady shift of business to private Japanese firms (mostly of medium and small sizes) designated by Peking as "friendly." [33] Nevertheless, trade remains state-sponsored and trade agreements remain a method by which the CPR attempts to hinder Japan's ties with Nationalist China, while for Japan the trade relations represent, in Premier Sato's words, the "only pipeline" his government has to Peking.[34]

The two triads of principles linking trade to politics formulated by Premier Chou En-lai in 1960 for the resumption of Sino-Japanese trade talks seem to reflect Peking's thinking on foreign trade in general. The "three trading principles" called for the conclusion of governmental agreements, private contracts, and individual transactions. The "three political principles" required that the trading nation must desist from a hostile stance toward the CPR, must not join the United States "conspiracy to create two Chinas," and must not obstruct the normalization of relations between the two countries.[35]

By 1959, the year a $2,000,000,000 annual volume of Sino-Soviet trade was reached,[36] the CPR had already entered into trade relations with 80 countries under either official or "unofficial" aegis. Some 70 of these were "capitalist" or nonaligned countries, including Britain, France, Japan, Italy, and West Germany. Trade treaties had been concluded at the governmental level with 20 countries, such as India, Afghanistan, Ceylon, Burma, Indonesia, Cambodia, Egypt, Syria, Lebanon, Finland, Sweden, Denmark, Norway, Yemen, and Pakistan.[37]

As Peking's trade with the non-Communist world has been on the increase since 1960,[38] a comparative study of some of the important patterns of her trade agreements may be of no small interest. There are both similarities and differences in the form and content of CPR trade treaties signed with Communist and non-Communist states. The CPR has concluded CN (commerce and navigation) treaties with the Soviet Union (April 23, 1958), East Germany (January 18, 1960), Albania (February 2, 1961), Mongolia (April 26, 1961), North Korea (January 5, 1962), and North Vietnam (December 5, 1962).[39] No CN treaty has been signed with any country outside the Communist bloc. As a whole, trade agreements signed between the CPR and bloc countries are for longer periods of time, usually four years.[40] On the other hand, those with non-Communist countries are mostly on a year-to-year basis, such as the Sino-Indonesian Trade Agreement of November

30, 1953, which was good for one year but renewable.[41] There are also exceptions. The Sino-Ceylonese Trade and Payment Agreement, signed on September 19, 1957, was to "remain in force for a period of five years." [42] The Sino-Burmese Trade Agreement of January 27, 1961, was also for five years.[43]

Peking's CN treaties provide for broad guidelines and general legal principles governing matters of commerce and navigation between the two countries, with the details regarding transactions, shipping, and payment spelled out in a number of successive agreements. The formal and enduring nature of the CN treaties is attested to by the use of the nomenclature *"t'iao-yüeh,"* the term reserved for the most formal treaties. Certain standard clauses in the CN treaties and their subsidiary agreements, as a rule, are the following: (a) the types of commodities and their volumes to be bought and sold between the parties; (b) the state organs in charge of the execution of trade, including the signing of contracts and their fulfillment; and (c) the standard procedure for payment and liquidation of indebtedness. Aside from these, further details concerning specific transactions are delineated in separate protocols relating to "general conditions of delivery." [44]

Among other things, CN treaties provide for the establishment of trade delegations,[45] whose legal status and functions are spelled out in detail in an appended protocol. The main provisions in the latter stipulate that the trade delegation will be considered as an integral part of the embassy of the sending state, and that the trade representative and his deputy enjoy all privileges granted to diplomatic personnel, inviolability, and the right to use code and cipher.[46] Trade agreements signed in the name of the trade delegation by authorized members will be binding upon the sending state.[47]

In CPR trade relations with non-Communist states, on the other hand, there is no counterpart of a CN treaty. Trade and payment agreements are signed on an *ad hoc* basis; none purports to offer a coherent body of general principles or long-range plans regarding trade. There is no standing protocol governing the legal status and function of the trade missions, but some scattered provisions are found in a few individual cases. For example, the trade agreements with Syria (November 30, 1955) and Lebanon (December 31, 1955) recognized the diplomatic functions of the trade missions.[48] At least in two cases where there were diplomatic relations, trade missions performed consular functions under provisions of trade agreements. Under the Sino-Indian Agreement on Trade and Intercourse Between Tibet Region of China and India, signed on April 29, 1954, trade agencies (*shang-wu tai-li ch'u*) were established, whose members not only enjoyed freedom from arrest and other privileges analogous to those generally granted to consular officers but also had access to their nationals involved in civil or criminal cases.[49] Similar arrangements were provided for under the Sino-Nepalese agreement of September 20, 1956.[50]

A major distinction must be drawn, however, between the appended protocol to the CN treaties and the specific provisions in the other trade agreements governing the diplomatic or consular statuses of trade missions. In the former case, the appended protocol is designed to facilitate the trade functions of the trade delegations by clothing them with diplomatic privileges and immunities, while diplomatic representations remains exclusively within the bailiwick of the embassy to which the trade delegation is attached. In the cases of Syria and Lebanon, the trade missions were designed to fill in the diplomatic functions where no formal diplomatic ties had been established. At the time the trade agreements were signed, neither Syria nor Lebanon recognized the CPR.[51] It is significant that despite the nomenclature ("trade agreement") used, neither agreement defined the trade functions of the trade missions. The trade agencies established under Peking's 1954 agreements with India and Nepal were given concurrent consular functions mainly to accommodate Indian and Nepalese relations with Tibet, whose legal status is a very ticklish issue in their relations with the CPR. Perhaps for this reason the Sino-Indian and Sino-Nepalese agreements were classified in the *TYC* as "political," rather than "trade," agreements.

Many important CPR trade agreements with foreign countries, both Communist and non-Communist (including capitalist states), contain a "most-favored-nation" clause. CPR commentators regard the use of this clause as a most vital device for surmounting the embargo imposed upon mainland China.[52] The first instance of its use was in the Sino-Egyptian trade agreement of August 22, 1954, in which both countries agreed to grant most-favored-nation treatment in matters concerning the issuance of import and export licenses and customs duties. In subsequent trade agreements with other countries, the clause was given wider application, though confined to navigation and commerce proper since individuals play an insignificant role in the state-trading practice of the CPR. By 1968, the CPR had most-favored-nation arrangements with twenty-nine countries out of a total of forty-eight governmental and non-governmental trade-treaty partners.[53]

In CPR literature, the most-favored-nation clause is defined as follows: "When one of the contracting parties (for instance, state A) grants certain preferential terms to a third party, the other contracting party (state B) will automatically enjoy the same privileges." [54] The most-favored-nation arrangement in CPR's trade with Communist countries is usually provided for in the CN treaties. Like other clauses, the most-favored-nation clause in these treaties is more general and sweeping in its application than that in agreements signed with non-Communist states. One of the best examples is found in the 1958 Sino-Soviet Treaty of Commerce and Navigation, in which ten out of the total seventeen articles deal with most-favored-nation treatment applicable to "*all matters* relating to trade, navigation and other economic relations between the two States." [55] All the following matters are covered under the clause: (a) all customs matters relating to the import or export of natural and manufactured goods (Article 3 and 4); (b) internal taxation or charges (Article 6); (c) ships and their cargoes (Article 8); (d) conveyance of goods, passengers and luggage by internal railways, roads, or waterways (Article 11); (e) goods in transit (Article 12); and (f) the legal status of natural and juristic persons (Article 14). In more or less the same language, the most-favored-nation clause is included in the other five CN treaties,[56] and also in the Sino-Cuban Agreement of Trade and Payment of July 23, 1960. In the latter, however, the clause is only concerned with customs matters and taxation.[57]

The most-favored-nation clause is found in a number of Peking's trade agreements with the non-Communist trading partners as well. The *TYC* lists twelve of them: Norway (agreement signed on June 4, 1958), Tunisia (September 25, 1958), United Arab Republic (December 15, 1958, expanding an agreement signed on August 22, 1955 with Egypt), Iraq (January 3, 1959, and September 23, 1964), Guinea (September 13, 1960), Mali (February 28, 1961), Ghana (August 18, 1961, and March 26, 1963), Sudan (May 23, 1962), Somalia (May 15, 1963), Congo (Brazzaville) (July 23, 1964, and October 2, 1964), Central African Republic (September 29, 1964), and Burundi (October 22, 1964).[58] The selective nature characterizing the inclusion of the most-favored-nation clause is true of the CPR's trade agreements with Communist and non-Communist nations alike. Just as no such clause is found in treaties with Bulgaria, Czechoslovakia, Hungary, Poland, and Rumania among the Communist group, it is also lacking in the CPR's agreements with certain non-Communist trading partners such as Afghanistan, Algeria, Austria, Burma, Cambodia, France, West Germany, India, Japan, Nepal, Nigeria, Singapore, Malaysia, Switzerland, and Britain. There is no indication as to why these countries do not have most-favored-nation arrangements with the CPR. One writer has suggested that the absence is probably due to the particular nature of the relations existing between the CPR and the individual countries and is not necessarily a phenomenon of restraint of trade. All these five Communist states maintained normal trade relations with the CPR, and West Germany and Japan have been among the CPR's largest trading partners in the non-Communist world.[59] In view of Peking's conscious effort to circumvent the United States embargo by the use of the most-favored-nation clause in its trade relations with non-Communist states, could it be that close allies of the United States, such as West Germany and Japan, felt restrained not to connive openly at such a maneuver? Of course, trade volume probably also explains the absence of the most-favored-nation clause in the CPR's trade agreements with Afghanistan, Nepal, etc.

In practice, the most-favored-nation clause in CPR trade agreements with non-Communist nations is at times more restricted in its application. The areas of restriction vary with individual cases but include the following: (a) privileges granted exclusively to "contiguous countries" (e.g., Article 8 of the Sino-Ceylonese Trade and Payment Agreement, 1957); (b) privileges granted exclusively between Arab countries (e.g., CPR trade agreements with Egypt, Syria, Lebanon, Yemen, etc.); (C) special areas protected by domestic law out of considerations of public health (e.g., Article 3 of the Sino-Egyptian Trade Agreement, 1955); and (d) privileges granted exclusively between Scandinavian countries (e.g., CPR trade agreements with Denmark and Sweden). Restrictions on the application of the most-favored-nation clause are not unknown to CPR trade treaties with Communist states. Even in the Sino-Soviet CN treaty, with the widest application possible, that clause is suspended in regard to goods prohibited from import or export due to security and public health reasons,[60] and it does not apply to "frontier trade" between the two countries.[61]

In comparison, there are wider restrictions in the trade agreements with non-Communist countries. But, as a whole, the clause still has rather wide application. For example, in the 1957 Sino-Ceylonese agreement the clause was to apply "in respect of the issuance of import and export licenses, and the levy of customs duties, taxes, and any other charges imposed on or in connection with the importation, exportation and shipment of commodities." [62] In some instances, such as the Sino-Finnish exchange of notes on March 31, 1956, the most-favored-nation clause has been extended to the regular and incidental charges for the entry of ships, their crews, and their cargoes in the absence of a treaty of commerce and navigation.[63] Agreements of this nature are, significantly, considered by the Chinese as analogous to CN treaties, and in the official *TYC* they are listed in the same group as the latter.[64]

The discrepancy in the application of the most-favored-nation clause to states whose trade is carried on by private traders and states which conduct their own trade, through the government itself or state-controlled corporations, is a most complicated problem.[65] There is some evidence that the CPR is aware of this problem and in its agreements it has attempted to resolve it. For example, in the Sino-Ceylonese Trade and Payment Agreement, signed on September 19, 1957, under which trade between the two countries was covered by the most-favored-nation clause, a provision stipulated: "The two Contracting Parties agree that trade under this Agreement . . . may be conducted through the *state trading organizations* of China and Ceylon as well as through other [private] *importers and exporters* in the two countries." [66] In an exchange of notes accompanying the agreement, the Ceylonese ambassador in Peking made a special reference to import regulations enacted to enable (private) Ceylonese traders to participate to a greater extent in the country's trade. In the same note the ambassador also offered his government's help in the event the CPR's state exporting organizations should have difficulties in appointing (private) Ceylonese importers or exporters to handle particular commodities.[67] Despite the differences between socialist and capitalist economies, the wide use of the most-favored-nation clause in CPR trade with "capitalist" countries has been hailed as a most effective way to combat the "discriminatory policies" of these countries, just as its application in trade with Communist bloc states is conducive to achieving "economic equality, mutual assistance, and friendly cooperation" between them.[68]

Another common clause in CPR trade treaties with the bloc countries is the provision for the arbitral settlement of disputes arising from the implementation of trade agreements. Under the arbitration clause, all such disputes are referred to arbitral proceedings before a competent tribunal, i.e., either an arbitral tribunal established for the purpose or, if no such tribunal is yet in existence, a designated ordinary court, usually in the country whose trader or trading organization is the defendant.[69] Although not in all cases, the arbitration clause appears also in some of Peking's trade agreements with countries outside the bloc, such as the Fourth Sino-Japanese Trade Agreement of March 5, 1958.[70] In other cases, in the lack of an arbitration clause, similar disputes are to be settled through "consultation" between the parties.[71]

Conversely, certain provisions appear exclusively in CPR trade agreements with "capitalist" and Afro-Asian countries but not in those with Communist bloc countries. First of all, there is a standard clause concerning the "balance of values" between the imports and exports of the two parties.[72] In some cases involving principal trading partners, the total value of the commodities to be bought or sold by each party is set at fixed amounts.[73]

A second exclusive feature in the trade agreements of the present group is an attached "open" listing of the import and export commodities. The listing, however, does not specify the volume and monetary value of the commodities to be exported or imported, although in exceptional cases the additional information is also provided, as in the Sino-Indonesian Trade Protocol of September 1, 1954.[74] The significance of the "open" listing is either (a) that each contracting party undertakes to give special consideration to the applications for licenses by traders or trading agencies of the other party wishing to import or export the commodities enumerated in the listing,[75] or (b) that each party is under a special obligation to grant the necessary licenses for the import or export of the listed commodities in accordance with prevailing domestic regulations.[76]

Among other provisions which appear exclusively in CPR trade agreements with non-Communist nations are "commodity inspection" and "trade fair" clauses, as can be found in the agreements with Egypt (August 22, 1955) and Lebanon (December 31, 1955), respectively. The purpose of "commodity inspection," which in practice is specified in detail in each contract, is to ensure that the commodities imported meet the specifications. The "trade fair" clause, on the other hand, guarantees that each party's commodities will receive all necessary facility to be exhibited in trade fairs or expositions in the other country.[77] Another provision, which may be called the "commodity restriction" clause, excludes from trading any commodities which are prohibited by the prevailing laws and religious code of either party.[78]

Another principle—"equal treatment"—may be mentioned in this connection. Although it is not explicitly included in CPR trade agreements with non-Communist countries, it figures rather prominently in the almost standardized "Eight Principles" governing the treatment accorded to CPR technical and other assistance personnel in their host countries (mostly Afro-Asian).[79] This should not be confused with the "national treatment" principle widely advocated in the West. Like other Communist countries, the CPR does not accept that principle, considering it an infringement upon one's sovereignty.[80] The only known exception is in the event of a shipwreck when, as provided for in the Sino-Soviet CN treaty, the same rescuing assistance will be rendered as though to one's own nationals.[81]

In reviewing the CPR's trade treaties and agreements signed over the past two decades, some trends indicative of changing policy come to light. First, CPR trade protocols with the Soviet Union after 1960 showed a conspicuous omission of references to the volumes of trade contemplated, representing a departure from the practice between the two countries between 1955 and 1960. The omission is hardly surprising in view of the uncertainties and the drastic decline in the value of Sino-Soviet trade since 1959. This recalls CPR practice of not mentioning the expected volume of trade in agreements signed with non-Communist countries that are not her principal trading partners.

Secondly, the CPR did not sign any CN treaties with her immediate Asian Communist neighbors—North Korea, Outer Mongolia, and North Vietnam—until 1962, nearing the peak of the Sino-Soviet dispute the next year. All Peking's CN treaties with the Soviet Union and the other East European Communist states were concluded before 1961. The timing indicates that practical and political considerations also played a part in shaping CPR trade treaties and agreements even with Communist bloc countries.

To sum up, sufficient evidence suggests that CPR practice regarding trade treaties and agreements follows these policy assumptions or patterns:

(a) Trade relations can be established with countries with different political and social systems, insofar as they are feasible and physically possible. Trade agreements can be used as a first step to normalize relations with countries even in the "capitalist" camp.

(b) Matters of general legal character are contained in CN treaties with Communist countries, but are scattered in individual trade and payment agreements or protocols, on a more or less *ad hoc* basis, with non-Communist countries. The CPR does not have a CN treaty with any of the non-Communist countries, although there are substitutes.

(c) The most-favored-nation clause is found in trade treaties or agreements with both Communist and non-Communist countries. While its inclusion is guided by political and practical considerations in both cases, its application is broader in trade with Communist nations.

(d) There is an awareness of, accompanied by efforts to overcome, the difficulties of carrying out trade with a country which permits private trading. Because of the differences in domestic socio-political and economic systems, there cannot be standard provisions which can apply equally to trade with Communist and non-Communist countries alike. While common provisions are found in agreements with countries in both groups, differences also exist. But, they are not all ideological in nature or origin, and, in fact, a great deal of realism is manifest, which cuts across ideological lines.

A comparison between Peking's CN treaties and the FCN (friendship, commerce, and navigation) treaties concluded by the United States with foreign countries may be offered here, even though pending further study the comparison is sketchy and tentative.

In the first place, the CN treaties do not contain the additional title and provisions regarding "friendship" as do the FCN treaties signed by the United States. The separate (non-CN) "friendship" treaties which the CPR has concluded with both Communist and nonaligned countries in various forms are a separate entity.

Secondly, though the most-favored-nation clause is found in both Chinese CN treaties and American FCN treaties, it has different implications. For the former, the clause provides an instrumentality for overcoming the strategic embargo imposed upon her and for minimizing Western-inspired discrimination against CPR trade in the treaty countries. For the American FCN treaties, the clause tends to obligate the governments concerned to refrain from imposing obstacles to trade flowing between private parties. Following the Soviet theory, CPR writers have made a sharp distinction between "capitalist" and Socialist practices in the use of the most-favored-nation clause. Whereas in the latter's use it remains a "progressive" institution for increasing trade, they maintain the clause has been perverted in the hands of the "imperialists" into a tool for economic aggression and enslavement of small and weak nations. The FCN treaty signed between the United States and Nationalist China in 1946 had been singled out as an example: While Article 21 of the treaty obligated Nationalist China to open all coastal ports and inland waters to United States nationals, Article 27 excepted Panama Canal Zone from the "reciprocal" treatment granted to Chinese nationals.[82]

Thirdly, the "national treatment" clause, which occupies a prominent position in American FCN treaties, is condemned by the Chinese Communists as a subterfuge for obtaining *de facto* unequal rights for American nationals. No nationals of any country, they argue, can compete with United States nationals in matters involving financial investment. When the FCN treaties provide that "nationals of *both* countries" are entitled to certain rights or privileges, it in fact means that *only* United States nationals will enjoy them.[83]

Peking's CN treaties and related agreements do not employ the terminology of "national treatment" and, whenever an "equal (as opposed to national) treatment" clause is included or implied, it is put in a more "negative" way. Rather than providing positively that "nationals of both countries" shall have certain rights, these agreements specify that the "treatment" to be granted to the nationals of one party shall be "equal to" or "no less than" (and sometimes "no more than") that which is accorded the other party's own nationals "under similar circumstances." This more negative guarantee is, as the Chinese see it, designed to prevent the conferment of any special privileges upon foreign nationals which one's own nationals cannot enjoy or receive in return.[84]

Tentative Conclusions on CPR Treaty Practice

On the basis of our study of CPR treaty practice in general (including trade treaties) and the policy implicit in it, the following tentative conclusions may be drawn:

First, treaties are an important means for facilitating the CPR's foreign relations and achieving certain policy ends. Because of the utilitarian value of treaties, like international law in general, the CPR has found that it pays to follow generally the treaty practices of most other states.

Secondly, ideology is not the sole factor shaping the conclusion and composition of CPR treaties and agreements with foreign countries, though it is unquestionably an important factor. While references to Marxism-Leninism and "proletarian internationalism" are found in the preambles of CPR treaties with Communist states, one does not find provisions in the operative part which may be exclusively labeled "Socialist provisions."

Thirdly, while certain standard clauses are contained in CPR treaties—such as those relating to friendship and cooperation—with Communist countries, they are also included in those with other countries, though in a somewhat modified form. The difference is more or less one of degree, or at least not as great as might be expected.

Fourthly, a great degree of flexibility and realism is evident, especially in CPR trade agreements with the non-Communist countries. The importance of these agreements can be expected to increase as the CPR drifts further away from trading with the Soviet Union.

And, fifthly, national interest—however defined—is obviously an overriding factor in the CPR's position on historical treaties which she considers detrimental to her interests and concluded under "unequal" conditions. The ideological bond in the early years might have contributed to a temporary silence on Peking's part with respect to treaties signed in the last century and earlier between China and Czarist Russia. But, as that bond weakens, the strength of national interest begins to reassert itself.

CPR Treaty Compliance

It would be extremely difficult to assess objectively the CPR's record of compliance with its treaty obligations, because of a combination of factors, including: the lack of sufficient information, different conceptualizations of world order held by the CPR, different legal precepts, as well as cultural-ideological perspectives, and even semantic difficulties affecting the interpretation of treaty provisions, and the prevailing confusion resulting from the mutual exchange of accusations, more often than not exaggerated, between the CPR and its adversaries regarding treaty violations. What we attempt to do here is only a tentative probe into the problem, more in the nature of demonstrating the difficulties involved in making an adequate evaluation than a definitive answer, much less an exercise in polemics one way or the other. As a point of departure, it may be well to cite a list of cases provided by the United States Department of State in 1963 in a study of CPR treaty violations. The following is a summary of the cases supplied:

a) The Chinese Communists have introduced new types of equipment into North Korea and done so in violation of the 1953 Armistice Agreement and at ports of entry other than those specified in the agreement. According to the provisions of the agreement, both sides (the Chinese and Korean Communists, on the one hand, and the U.N. Command, on the other) shall cease the introduction into Korea of combat equipment except on a one-for-one replacement basis.
b) Communist China captured thirteen American airmen whose plane was shot down near the Yalu River in January, 1953, and did not release them until after two years of illegal detention, and not before U.N. Secretary-General Hammarskjold had negotiated with the Chinese authorities. The detention was a violation of the Korean Armistice provision calling for the expeditious return of POWs desiring repatriation.
c) The Peking regime has repeatedly violated the spirit and letter of the April 29, 1954, agreement with India on trade and intercourse between Tibet and India and the October 14, 1954, trade agreement between India and China. In 1959 and subsequently, Peking harassed and discouraged religious pilgrims from India, in outright contravention of the April 29, 1954, agreement, which provided for free transit by Indians to Hindu holy places in Tibet. The latter 1954 agreement

was clearly violated by Peking when it insisted in 1959 that trade transactions by Indian traders in Tibet be adjusted in Chinese currency. The alternative media of payment provided for in the agreement were denied by the Chinese. Since 1959, the Chinese have also violated the spirit of both agreements by restricting the activities of Indian trade and consular agencies in Tibet.

d) The CPR has failed to fulfill the September 10, 1955, agreement with the United States to permit all American citizens in Communist China who wished to leave to do so expeditiously. By December, 1955, Peking had released sixteen American civilians (but not those in Chinese prisons), but thereafter no American has been freed except upon completion of the full sentence handed down by the Chinese courts or, in one case, when death in prison was imminent.[85]

Let us now examine some of the broader implications of the above cases in order to make an appraisal of the CPR's record of treaty performance. For convenience sake, we shall begin with the last one—repatriation of American prisoners—and proceed in reverse order with the remaining cases.

(a) The repatriation question. It is to be recalled that the original agreement signed between the CPR and the United States, on September 10, 1955, during the initial rounds of the Ambassadorial Talks at Geneva, took the form of "unilateral but identical" announcements—or, to be more exact, an "agreed announcement." The awkward form was only matched by the ambiguity in language, reflecting the complexity and touchiness of the issues involved, not the least of which were the questions of diplomatic recognition, and the political use each side wanted to make of this first agreement. Officially billed as an agreement on the "exchange of civilians," the provisions of the agreement stipulated that "Chinese" and "Americans" currently in the other country who wished to return to their country "are entitled to do so" with the assistance of the embassy of a third state (India for the CPR, and Britain for the United States). Both governments pledged to adopt "appropriate measures" so that the nationals concerned would "expeditiously exercise their right to return." [86] Nowhere were the terms "civilians," "Americans," and "Chinese" defined, and disputes arose during the implementation stage over the question whether American "prisoners" in China were also included among those to be expeditiously repatriated.

To be true, the repatriation of Americans in China was the heart of the purpose for which the United States government, in the absence of diplomatic representation, consented to the talks. For Peking, on the other hand, the issue of repatriation was only a first step toward what it hoped would be a broader negotiation with the United States on such politically sensitive issues as the status of Taiwan, representation in the United Nations, lifting of United States embargo, etc. The United States won the first round of the negotiations when its agenda listing the repatriation question first, shunting the rest to Item 2—"other practical matters now at issue" —was accepted by the CPR, reversing the order of priorities preferred by the Chinese side. The agreement on repatriation was reached rather speedily, after only fourteen sessions in forty-one days from the first meeting on August 1 that year. It showed that the Communist Chinese were anxious to move on to the next item on the agenda.[87]

Immediately after the agreement was announced, the Communist Chinese side pressed for opening discussion on the other "practical matters." But, the American side insisted that the United States would not consider moving to any other substantive question, particularly the proposed foreign ministers' meeting, until all the Americans in mainland China had been repatriated.[88] The Chinese announced that, among the total sixty-six Americans in mainland China, nineteen had violated Chinese law and were serving prison terms, and the forty-seven others were free to leave any time when they applied for exit visas.[89] The question of whether "prisoners" were also covered by the repatriation agreement then came up. The United States side claimed that the word "civilians" used in the title of the agreement and the term "Americans" in the text were "generic" terms without any exception as to "prisoners." [90]

The deadlock radicalized the position of both sides, trading charges and countercharges. The CPR maintained that the agreement on repatriation had been intended solely for "ordinary American residents" and charged that the United States was purposely obstructing progress of the Ambassadorial Talks by interpolating the "prisoners" question.[91] Although some of the American convicts had actually been freed before serving their sentences, Peking insisted, American prisoners remaining in mainland China did not have a right of repatriation under the agreement.[92] To counter the American claim, Peking raised the question why the United States had not taken any action to release Chinese prisoners long after Chinese students and scientists had been repatriated. Although the United States subsequently (toward the end of 1956) ordered the release of Chinese prisoners, the fact that this occurred only after other Chinese nationals had been repatriated a year before would raise a reasonable doubt over the exact scope within which the repatriation agreement was originally intended to apply.[93]

In 1957, the United States Department of State, in its own account of the fourteen sessions of the Ambassadorial Talks leading toward the repatriation agreement, made the following admissions: (a) No distinction between Americans in or out of prisons in mainland China was ever made or implied by either side; (b) Wang Pingnan, the CPR ambassador who signed the agreement, had insisted on inserting an identical operative "expeditious return" paragraph into the agreement to make the United States reciprocally obligated to repatriate Chinese nationals in that country; (c) during the fourteen sessions Wang never mentioned Chinese prisoners in America; and (d) the Chinese side, accordingly, never indicated that the agreement of September 10, 1955, was intended also to cover prisoners.[94]

The Department of State thus belatedly corroborated the Chinese side of the story.[95] This suggests that Wang did negotiate in good faith and that, by the absolute reciprocal basis on which the agreement was reached, the lack of mention of Chinese prisoners meant that American prisoners were not included among the repatriates. The State Department admissions also lent credence to CPR allegations, made in the weeks immediately following the announcement of the agreement and subsequently, that Secretary of State Dulles was deliberately "dragging out" the talks at Geneva to block progress toward discussion of the vital issues in Item 2 of the agenda, on which Peking wanted to reach a settlement.[96]

The whole controversy, viewed from hindsight and with the detachment afforded by the lapse of a decade and a half, may perhaps be better characterized as one growing out of mutual suspicion and distrust, with attendant difficulties in the interpretation of the specific provisions of the agreement reached by the two adversaries. As such, it is a case falling more under conflicts arising from treaty interpretation than outright treaty violations.

(b) The 1954 Sino-Indian agreement. The apparent failure by Peking to live up to the provisions of the agreement on trade and intercourse between the two countries in the Tibet region brings us closer to an example of treaty violation. But the deterioration of relations between the CPR and India cannot be dissociated from the very problem at hand. The alleged violations dated from 1959, the year in which the first Sino-Indian boundary dispute erupted. The dispute was complicated by the alleged Indian attempts to exert political influence in the internal politics of Tibet (partly substantiated by the subsequent flight of Dalai Lama, the theocratic leader, and the political asylum granted to him by India in 1959), a spillover of the growing Sino-Soviet conflict (which in 1958 led Khrushchev to suggest replacing China by India as a permanent member of the U.N. Security Council), and the competition between Peking and Delhi to be the spokesman of the "third world." [97] The actual armed hostilities in 1959 and again in 1962 were in no way compatible with the spirit and provisions of the 1954 agreement governing trade and visits by Indian pilgrims to Tibet as well as other peaceable relations. Despite the fact that a semblance of diplomatic relations was maintained during the fighting, the actual use of force was accompanied by mutual violations of certain rights of the other side. The termination by Peking of the agreement to stem the flow of visitors in and out of the trouble spot would be a logical outcome of the war situation. In the circumstances, one would have to make a most careful inquiry, demanding the greatest judicious exercise of reason and impartiality, in order to determine whether certain mutual violations were not a form of retortion or reprisal against each other and, above all, whether the suspension or termination of the said agreement was justified by conditions approximating war.

(c) Detention of American airmen. Whether the CPR detention of the thirteen American airmen in 1953–1955 was "illegal" would first of all depend upon the conditions of their capture, which are by no means certain from available information. The United States government merely announced that the airmen were captured after their plane was shot down fifteen miles south of the Yalu River in January, 1953. The Communist Chinese, however, have accused them of being United States "spies." [98] The following cable sent by Premier Chou En-lai to Secretary-General Dag Hammarskjold of the United Nations may serve to sum up the Communist Chinese version of the story:

> The said 11 United States spies and two other intruded into Chinese territory and were caught in China. After examining evidences which conclusively proved that they had conducted *espionage* activities in China, the Chinese court on 23 November 1954 passed judgments on them accordingly. To convict *foreign spies* caught in China is China's internal affairs. . . . The case of these United States spies *has nothing to do with the question of the prisoners of war in Korea.*[99]

The Korean Armistice Agreement was not signed until June 27, 1953, or about five months after the airmen were captured, but the United States charged that Peking's continued detention of the men violated provisions in the agreement calling for the expeditious repatriation of prisoners of war. Chou's answer deliberately made a distinction between "spies" and POWs. In the same cable, Chou charged in return that the United Nations Command and the United States were indeed guilty of having violated the same provision, alluding to the release in June, 1953, of 27,000 North Korean and Chinese POWs by President Syngman Rhee of South Korea, which, according to Chou, was an "open violation of the agreement on the repatriation of prisoners of war." [100] Thus, to determine whether the Chinese detention of the thirteen American airmen was a violation of the Korean Armistice Agreement, one would have to investigate (i) whether the "spy" charge could be substantiated and, if so, whether "spies" were covered by the agreement on POW repatriation; and (ii) whether the release of North Korean and Communist Chinese POWs by the South Korean president was a breach of the agreement and, if so, to what extent the responsibility can be imputed to the United Nations Command and the United States and, further, whether this earlier breach could justify subsequent comparable breaches of the same agreement by the other side. Given the existing circumstances, no honest man can come up with any definitive answer to these questions, if he believes that the kind of truth treasured by an objective scholar is different from the concern of "law officers" or legal advisors in the employ of foreign ministries.[101]

(d) Introduction of additional combat equipment into North Korea subsequent to the Armistice Agreement of July 27, 1953. Again, the answer is unfortunately not so clear-cut as one might assume. The records of the Military Armistice Commission in Seoul, Korea, relating to armistice compliance and complaints of violations had escaped public scrutiny until recently. According to a study made by Dr. Luke Lee of these records, supplemented by interviews with responsible officials, including those of the Neutral Nations Supervisory Commission, there have actually been violations by both sides.[102]

On the one hand, contrary to Paragraph 13 (d) of the Armistice Agreement, which requires both side to report incoming and outgoing combat aircraft, the Chinese and Korean Communists have not submitted a single report. During an investigation by a Mobile Inspection Team sent by the Neutral Nations Supervisory Commission on October 12, 1953, the North Korean field commander of an airfield near Uiju, where newly arrived aircraft were reportedly located, took the team's members on a strictly guarded trip, refusing to let them conduct a free inspection. Although the team could find no direct evidence of aircraft crates, one may raise a reasonable doubt regarding the reasons behind the secrecy clamped on the airfield, which would seem to substantiate reports that new aircraft had arrived in violation of the Armistice Agreement.[103]

On the other hand, the actual compliance record of the United Nations Command side was, according to the same study, not above reproach even before it unilaterally suspended the operation of Paragraph 13 (d) on June 21, 1957.[104] For instance, personnel of the Neutral Nations Inspection Teams (there are ten of these, assisting the Neutral Nations Supervisory Commission, five working in the territories under the control of each of the two sides) were prevented from boarding American vessels to inspect boxes reportedly containing combat materials,[105] from carrying out inspection in the harbor of Inchon,[106] and from conducting spot-check inspections in Pusan on August 20, 1955, and in Taegu on August 8, 1955, except by helicopters.[107]

The question about violations of the Armistice Agreement in Korea has been further compounded by the undeterminable origin of the new combat equipment that did arrive in North Korea. There was only unsubstantiated rumors that the new consignment of MIG aircraft came from the Soviet Union. Beside general suspicions, according to Dr. Lee's study, in none of the incidents has it been possible to nail down any specific Chinese violation of the Korean Armistice Agreement with respect to the introduction of new combat equipment.[108]

As one can see, no definitive answer can be supplied in any of the above cases if one exercises the greatest caution and impartiality required by objective scholarship. Any study of the CPR's treaty compliance record on politically sensitive issues such as the ones above is at best a perilous enterprise. If one leaves the politically sensitive areas, however, the task is easier to cope with. For example, the CPR is not known to have violated any of the boundary treaties signed with its neighbors. In fact, Burmese officials have indicated that they have had no occasion to regret the signing of the Sino-Burmese boundary and friendship treaties or to complain of any violation.[109] In the views of one Burmese official familiar with the boundary situation, the Chinese Communists could have exploited the peripatetic presence of remnant Nationalist Chinese forces along the Sino-Burmese borders. Despite many provocations by the Nationalist Chinese irregulars, he reported, the Chinese Communists had not moved their troops across an undelimited boundary either in "hot pursuit" or in retaliation.[110]

In foreign trade, the CPR is generally regarded as having a better than average international credit standing. It has not only met its financial obligations promptly in transactions with Japan but it has also honored its payment of debts to the Soviet Union and obligations under wheat purchase agreements with Canada and Australia.[111] In 1958, Peking canceled its trade agreement with Japan on the ground that the Japanese government "obstructed" the establishment of a CPR trade mission and denied the mission its right to display the CPR's national flag in Tokyo. The acts of omission by the Japanese government, it maintained, constituted a breach of substantive parts of the 1958 Sino-Japanese agreement, which had guaranteed these rights.[112] The breach was all the more inexcusable, it was pointed out, since a Japanese negotiator had interrupted a session in Peking in order to return home for consultation with his government when the provisions regarding these rights were being negotiated.[113] Some reports indicate that, in the history of CPR-Japanese trade, Japan is the party which more than once failed to live up to the agreements signed. Although each of the first three trade agreements between 1952 and 1955 provided for a total two-way trade volume of 60 million pounds sterling, the actual transactions amounted to only 5.05, 38.8, and 75.12 per cent, respectively.[114] As these agreements were concluded under fictitious "private" or "semiofficial" sponsorship, the CPR could only vent its grievances by blaming United States "imperialism" for the Japanese failure to live up to their trade obligations.[115]

On the other hand, during the turmoil of the Cultural Revolution, loading and unloading of ships in Shanghai and other Chinese ports were greatly delayed. In one instance, a Japanese ship had to remain in port for twenty days before the loading and unloading was completed, almost ten times the normal period.[116] In almost all recent trade agreements and contracts signed between the CPR and Japan, a *force majeure* clause is included, as under the so-called L-T trade contract, which provides, *inter alia:*

Force Majeure. In no event shall Seller be liable for non-delivery or delays in making deliveries caused by state of war, severe floods, fires, natural disasters or *any other causes beyond the control of Seller* whether or not such unavoidable accident occurs during *production, shipping or transportation* of the goods. However, Seller *shall* notify Buyer by telegram of such accident immediately after Seller has known such accident.[117]

The same clause is found also in private trade contracts signed between state-controlled corporations in mainland China and Japanese companies.[118] Whether the loading and unloading disruptions during the Cultural Revolution turmoil fell within this *force majeure* clause, the burden of proof would rest with the CPR, which, in making the plea, would also be obligated to show that it had properly notified its trading partners of the delays.

It may be noted that during the height of the Sino-Soviet polemic war in 1963, three Chinese diplomats and two students were expelled from the Soviet Union on charges of having distributed anti-Soviet polemic literature.[119] In another incident in 1960, the Castro government requested the CPR Embassy in Cuba to cease its zealous distribution of anti-Soviet propaganda.[120] To the CPR, it appeared, the distribution of polemic literature was either a right guaranteed by existing bilateral cultural agreements between the countries[121] or a reciprocal right enjoyed under international comity.[122] In 1967, the CPR's economic assistance personnel (at a total of 390) in Burma and embassy staff in Indonesia were expelled for allegedly attempting to export the Cultural Revolution to Burma and interference in Indonesian politics connected with the abortive 1965 coup.[123] The disputed activities would constitute a breach of the noninterference provision in the existing friendship treaties with these countries.[124] But, what complicates the issue, here as elsewhere, is that the CPR seems to adhere to a different doctrine which contends that distribution of propaganda literature and export of ideas and ideology (as distinct from export of Chinese "Che" Gueveras or Chinese GIs) are not acts of interference or intervention.[125]

XIV

Force, Restraint, and Pacific Settlement of Disputes

War: Dogma vs. Reality

Inevitability of War?

In the favorite intellectual game of speculating on Maoist China's world view, it has often been suggested that Peking embraces an "ideological commitment to war." A typical example of this argument is put forth in a report prepared for the House Committee on Foreign Affairs in 1963, entitled: *The Conduct of Communist China,* which states, among other things:

> The Chinese Communists in a series of ideological pronouncements have made clear their belief in the *inevitability of war* and their apparent willingness to enmesh humanity in a *nuclear holocaust* for the sake of advancing their fortunes of the "proletarian revolution." [1]

The publication produces five quotations from Chinese Communist documentary sources to substantiate its argument about the CPR's war craze. Because of the importance of the topic, we propose to examine each on its merits:

(a) The first quotation was taken from a work by Mao Tse-tung in 1938—the "Problems of War and Strategy (November 6, 1938)"—in which he stated: "Whoever has an army has power, for war settles everything." [2] If one examines the context, one finds that Mao was discussing the "war history of the Kuomintang," the particular statement quoted here being his criticism of Chiang Kai-shek, leader of the Nationalist party and Mao's political adversary. To quote Mao out of context in this fashion would be no more convincing than to build a case against George Washington as a war zealot on the following passages summarily culled from his writings:

> . . . without a decisive *Naval force* we can do nothing definitive. And with it, everything honourable and glorious.[3]
>
> To *be prepared for war* is one of the most effectual means of preserving peace.[4]

(b) The report then quoted a statement from a 1960 article in the *Red Flag,* the official ideological journal of the Chinese Communist Party (CCP). "We believe," it said, "in absolute correctness of Lenin's thinking: War is the inevitable outcome of the systems of exploitation and the imperialist system is the source of modern wars." [5] Quite contrary to the belief of the authors who cited it, the *Red Flag* is crediting the "imperialist system" with being the source of war.

(c) Also quoted was a remark made by Liu Ch'ang-sheng, member of the CCP Central Committee, on June 14, 1963, to wit: "Only when the Socialist revolution is victorious throughout the world can there be a world free from war, a world without armament." [6] There was no indication as to the context of the statement, but from what was given it is clear that the reference showed no "ideological commitment to war," as the report alleged.

(d) The fourth quotation was from the CCP's famous letter of June 14, 1963, addressed to the Communist Party of the Soviet Union, which stated: ". . . Marx and Lenin did raise the possibility that revolutions may develop peacefully . . . [but] as a matter of fact there is no historical precedent for peaceful transition from capitalism to socialism." [7] The background of the CCP-CPSU polemic exchange is that the Chinese Communists were suggesting that the future of Communism depended largely on development in the underdeveloped countries (the "revolutionary struggles of the people of these areas") rather than the growing strength of the existing socialist camp, as Khrushchev asserted. Needless to say, the "revolutionary struggles" of the local populations in the underdeveloped areas are different from the "nuclear holocaust" which Peking was said to bring to humanity. In the original CCP letter, in fact, the above statement was followed by an explanatory sentence, which should not have been omitted from the quote: "The anti-imperialist revolutionary struggles of the people in Asia, Africa, and Latin America . . . are a mighty force in defense of *world peace*." [8]

(e) The last quotation given in the *Conduct of Communist China* came from the *Red Flag,* in another issue of 1960, stating: "on the debris of a dead imperialism, the victorious people would create with extreme rapidity a civilization thousands of times higher than the capitalist system and a truly beautiful future for themselves." [9] As the report correctly implied, the Chinese statement here was a reference to "the aftermath of a nuclear war" which the *Red Flag* said would be started by the "imperialists."

Two distinct points emerge from these quoted pronouncements. One is a deep dissatisfaction with the existing *status quo* prevailing in the international scene. Not unlike the domestic ferment in the United States during the 1960s, much of the discontent is directed against an "establishment," imagined or real. Invariably, this international "establishment" is identified as "imperialism." Although the label "imperialism" (rather than any other name-calling) reflects Marxist-Leninist influence, the cause for the discontent is rooted in China's modern history of political subjugation long before Marxism was even introduced in the country.[10] Again, not unlike the domestic struggle against the "establishment," much of the rhetoric is doubtless exaggerated and irrational. There is a familiar militant ring in what the Chinese Communists say about "imperialism" and what the civil rights leaders say in their struggle against racist bigotry ("We shall overcome" and "Burn, baby, burn").[11] It hardly needs pointing out that one would have to look beneath the surface of the emotionally charged inflammatory statements and into the "sociological" and psychological backgrounds from which the bellicose mentality was conceived. A CPR propagandist could easily cull suitable passages out of context from the Report to the National Commission on Causes and Prevention of Violence, *The History of Violence in America* (1969), to show that the United States is a country full of violence of various sorts, "free-lance multiple murder," "political assassinations," "gangster vendettas," "urban riots," etc., etc. What constructive purpose does this "trading" of intellectual superficiality serve?

The other point is that there is a deep-seated fear among CPR leaders that mainland China is vulnerable and subject to the political tempers of the United States with its surrounding ring of military bases and atomic warheads pinpointed at Chinese cities and other strategic points.[12] The talk about the "debris of a dead imperialism" brought about by the destructive nuclear power at the disposal of the "imperialists" themselves is typical of Peking's fear, especially before 1964, when it did not have any nuclear capability to speak of. The big talk reminds one of a lone nightwalker whistling in the dark as if to assure himself that he is not scared.

In any event, none of the five quotations used in the government report prepared for the House Committee is as reckless as the label "ideological commitment to war" insinuates. Although the pronouncements are highly militant, none is as irresponsible as the "confrontation" policy staged by Sukarno's Indonesia against Malaysia, or any more bold than the assertion "armed struggle is legal" made by Jordan's former Premier Abdel Monem Rifai in reference to Palestinian commando raids against Israel.[13]

When it comes to practical action, the CPR has actually failed to live up to its own militant rhetoric. The discrepancy lent itself to a malicious taunt by Nikita Khrushchev during a speech before the Supreme Soviet on December 12, 1962. Contrary to their advocacy of a showdown with the United States during the 1962 Cuban missile crisis, the Soviet leader retorted, the Chinese themselves had not taken the same bellicose stance in regard to Hong Kong and Macao.[14] The Communist Party of the United States on January 9, 1963, echoed the ridicule and questioned the Chinese Communists "why this double-standard approach?" [15] In its reply the CCP deliberately eschewed war or use of force as the right solution to China's "outstanding issues" with foreign countries. It stressed, instead, the role of "peaceful negotiation" in settling such issues as

Hong Kong, Macao, and even Taiwan. The CCP reply, which appeared in the official *Jen-min jih-pao* [People's Daily], stated:

With regard to the outstanding issues, which are a legacy from the past, we have *always* held that, when conditions are ripe, they *should be settled peacefully through negotiations* and that, the status quo should be maintained, pending a settlement.

Within this category are the questions of Hongkong, Kowloon, and Macao and the question of all those boundaries which have not been delimited in each case by the parties concerned. . . . We Chinese people are determined to exercise our sovereign right to liberate our territory of Taiwan; at the same time, through the *Ambassadorial talks* between China and the United States in Warsaw, we are striving to solve the question of effecting the withdrawal of United States armed forces from Taiwan and the Taiwan Strait.[16]

"National Liberation Wars"

One may look at the possible reasons for the discrepancy between rhetoric and real action and its attendant problems from the following perspective: First, while class struggle within domestic societies is accepted as a necessary form of human progress in the Marxist ideology, it is not so readily reconciled or reconcilable, on the international scene, to the reality and concept of state sovereignty. Unlike in the domestic scene, the espousal of class war in the international society must face the challenge and opposition of the other legally coequal entities, which exercise exclusive sovereignty in their own right within their own territorial confines.

This throws into relief the second consideration, namely, the physical restrictions and consequences to be confronted should a state actually start a war, especially if directed against another state which possesses stronger military might. In the simplest terms, when outright use of force does not pay because of the overwhelming strength of the foe, something less direct and more evasive would be necessary and considered more desirable than outright war.

As a result, the CPR has confined its ideological "commitment" only to the peculiar kind of war called the "national (or people's) liberation war." [17] Presumably, such a war answers four basic doctrinal requirements: (a) the anti-imperialist ("national") or the proletarian origin of the war (the "people"); (b) limitation of the war to within the boundary of a single state or a colonial area, to avoid provoking outside opposing interference; (c) keeping the door open for Communist infiltration and control; and (d) condemnation of any non-Communist interference as an infringment on the people's right of national self-determination ("liberation").

The whole concept of "national liberation wars" is inseparable from the Communist anti-"imperialist" dogma and is considered to be a necessary form of struggle by subjugated peoples exercising their right of self-determination. Quoting Lenin's *Imperialism: The Highest Stage of Capitalism* (1916), an important article published in Peking declared that the basic aggressive nature of "imperialism" was not a bit abated, its sugar-coated assertions to the contrary notwithstanding. No peaceful alternative could achieve national independence and equality for the peoples in the underdeveloped areas; and the "national liberation struggle" was hailed as part of a world-wide movement to assert the inalienable right of national self-determination against colonial rule and "imperialist" domination.[18] As such, the concept bears a *pro forma* resemblance to the Declaration on the Granting of Independence to Colonial Countries and Peoples, adopted by the U.N. General Assembly in 1960, which declared *inter alia:*

1. The subjection of peoples to *alien subjugation,* domination and exploitation constitutes a denial of fundamental human rights, *is contrary to the Charter of the United Nations* and is an impediment to the promotion of world peace and cooperation.
2. All peoples have the *right to self-determination;* by virtue of that right they freely determine their political status and freely pursue their economic, social and cultural development.[19] (Emphasis added)

But, there are two major differences in the CPR theory. First, the declaration above professed (at least formally) an awareness of, and an intent to preclude, the increasing conflicts resulting from the denial of or impediments in the way of the freedom of the subjugated peoples, which constitute a serious threat to world peace. The doctrine of "national liberation wars," on the contrary, preached that the use of force by the "oppressed" peoples to overthrow "imperialism," colonialism, and neocolonialism, even to the extent of threatening world peace, is justified. Secondly, while the CPR doctrine also openly endorses the freedom of all peoples freely to determine their own socio-political systems, in practice it is used to justify her own Communist system and to espouse the same for other underdeveloped countries.[20]

The simultaneous exaltation of the right of self-determination and espousal of the socialist system for all peoples is a most fundamental contradiction from which the Chinese Communists cannot easily free themselves due to their Marxist ideology. Yet, as it is originally conceived, the "national liberation struggle" is essentially a commitment to revolutionary changes (as distinct from war pure and simple) in *domestic* political systems. It becomes an international conflict only when caught in the crossfire from opposing interventions in the Cold War context.[21] Just like other types of civil strife, the Chinese Communists do not consider "national liberation wars" to be a challenge to the outlawry of interstate war (involving the moving of one nation's armed forces across the boundary of another) under modern international law. It is to be recalled that existing norms guaranteeing the right of self-determination, as embodied in the United Nations Charter, were not originally intended to apply to the colonies of the Western powers. By its argument that armed struggle is the only means for subjugated peoples to assert their right of self-determination, Peking is not only pointing up this discrepancy but even espousing implicitly that international law should give colonial peoples full protection.[22] The doctrine is similar to the position held by many Afro-Asian countries in the United Nations but it is much broader in application, extending to the struggles against "reactionary" regimes staged by the domestic "proletariat" of postcolonial and noncolonial nations as well. The CPR is known to have supported extremist groups professing revolutionary and anti-"imperialist" goals in postcolonial countries ranging from Sudan, Nigeria, Somalia, and Burundi, to Indonesia.[23]

While the CPR exhorts fellow revolutionaries fighting "national liberation wars" in underdeveloped areas to be "self-reliant," it has also pledged its moral and material support to struggles against "imperialism, modern revisionism, and reactionary regimes." [24] The CPR considers itself to be under an "international duty" to aid these struggles, suggesting that such struggles are justified by the prior delictual acts by the "oppressors" of the world's proletariats. The principles inherent in these arguments could be at best considered *de lege ferenda,* but certainly are not supported by existing international law (*de lege lata*) which proscribes not only the use of force in interstate relations but also interference in the domestic affairs of other countries.

In actual practice, again, CPR interference has fallen far below the level of the militancy its doctrine seems to convey. The gap is partly due to the limited capabilities at its disposal thus far. If a United States air force plane could return Emperor Haile Selassie to power after a palace *coup* had deposed him during his trip abroad, and if the American ambassador could act as "more consul than an envoy" during the Dominican Republic crisis,[25] Peking's capability to perform any feat nearly as impressive is at best questionable. Partly the gap derives from another more fundamental reason. Given its strong conviction that a revolution must be supported by the local masses in order to succeed, Peking has objected to the Guevara strategy of exporting armed bands to revolutionary-prone areas abroad.[26] A central part of Mao's leadership doctrine is its strong belief in the dispensing of "correct" ideology and offering of practical exemplification to encourage "spontaneous" mass participation, as distinct from clamping down a revolution upon an unprepared population.[27] Applied to the international scene, it means that the native revolutionaries mainly will have to rely on their own resources, and China will provide a "model" plus some aid and comfort but is not going to "make" a revolution or do the fighting for them.[28] This tenet of ideological leadership is part of Mao's conceptualization of a world hierarchial order in which nations that are the ideologically inferior must follow the ideologically more advanced, recalling a parallel (albeit different) hierarchial view of the world in traditional China based on the concept of relative proximity to Confucian *li*.[29]

Thus, both by reason of its limited resources and its "self-reliance" dictum, Peking's role in regard of "national liberation struggles" has been largely confined to one of advocate, instigator, coach, and in some instances supplier of limited material assistance. It is in this sense of limited physical involvement (but unrestricted verbal proselytizing) that Premier Chou En-lai and Vice-Foreign Minister Chang Han-fu made their pronouncements that China would not "export revolution." [30] And it is also in this spirit that Peking has opposed the Soviet intervention in Czechoslovakia in 1968, considering its use of armed forces to occupy physically another independent country to be an inexcusable violation of international law. In the Chinese view the "degeneration" of Communism under Dubcek was the result of Moscow's own ideological depravity, which could never be corrected by the use of brute force.[31]

Legal Use of Force

By a common-sense respect for the dictum of reciprocity—which is still the obligatory basis of international law—the CPR actually avoids any open espousal of *interstate* war or use of force as an instrument of policy. In a few concrete instances, CPR leaders invoked the idiom of "just war," but only to rally support for resisting a war started by their foes. The earliest mention of a "just war" by Mao was made in 1938, when he declared that the Japanese and Nazi aggression had given the Allied side a "just cause" for resistance. "All just wars," he stated, "must support each other. . . . In the present nation-wide anti-Japanese upsurge and the world-wide anti-fascist upsurge, *just wars* will spread all over China and the globe." [32] The idea of defensive "just war"—no doubt ideologically conceived and ringing with a strong sense of moral self-righteousness—has since been repeated in Chinese Communist attacks on "imperialist aggression." [33] Most recently, in 1965, Chou En-lai characterized the North Vietnamese struggle against the United States a "just struggle." [34]

By its asserted "defensive" nature, the concept of "just war" invoked by the Chinese Communist leaders appears to be different from the medieval European doctrine of *bellum justum,* drawn by jurists from the corpus of natural law to restrict the right of a state to *wage* war to those instances in which it had a "just cause." [35] To date, Peking has not claimed a right to wage an offensive war by invoking a "just cause." In its effort to protect itself from "imperialist" superior power, Peking has found it useful to subscribe to the ban on the use of force in interstate relations. War in the traditional sense (the "national liberation war" not included) is illegal not only by virtue of the Kellogg-Briand Pact and the United Nations Charter but also by virtue of the five principles of peaceful coexistence.[36] To maintain self-consistency, Peking has employed various means to avoid being accused of resorting to illegal use of force. Its boundary conflict with India was characterized as an exercise of self-defense against preemptive Indian invasion.[37] The same justification was used against the Soviet Union in the 1969 border clashes over the Issuri River.[38] The Taiwan Strait conflicts of 1954 and 1958 were defined as an "internal problem" in the sense of a continuation of the unfinished civil war.[39] The use of force to pacify unrest in Tibet is, from the Chinese point of view, another case of internal strife, perhaps an exaggerated version of President Eisenhower's sending of federal marshals to Little Rock, Arkansas. Peking's participation in the Korean War (1950–1953) was deliberately transmuted into an act by Chinese "volunteers"—a device seemingly borrowed from Western practice during the Spanish Civil War—to give the appearance that the CPR government was not directly at war with the United Nations.[40]

In the face of Peking's verbal militancy, it is of particular importance to see what it has not done or has not espoused. First, it has not resorted to commando raids against any of its neighbors, even in its conflicts with India. Nor does it espouse the legality of their use.[41] Secondly, it has not resorted to "preventive war" nor publicly endorsed the idea. The Soviet Union was reported in late summer, 1969, to be sounding out fellow Communist leaders in Eastern and Western Europe on what would be a pre-emptive air strike by Moscow against Peking's nuclear facilities. Some reports even suggested a very real possibility of a Soviet armed attack against Communist

China.[42] Its hard-line assertions notwithstanding, the CPR has never attempted or supported a pre-emptive strike. On the contrary, perhaps because of its limited capabilities, it has consciously tried to avert possible pre-emptive attacks from external sources. Amidst rumors of imminent Soviet attacks, Communist China was reported to be moving its nuclear installations from the frontier Sinkiang province to a "safer place" in northern Tibet.[43] In 1965, when the Soviet Union—then on slightly better terms with Peking—requested an air base in South China to aid the war in Vietnam, the Chinese brusquely rejected the idea, most possibly out of a fear that it would give the United States an excuse for striking China. During the 1965 domestic debate on the correct strategy toward the escalation of the Vietnamese war, Lo Jui-ch'ing, then Chief of staff, advocated direct Chinese intervention on behalf of North Vietnam in order to preclude possible crippling United states preemptive strikes against China. Lo was purged shortly thereafter, and his proposed strategy bowed to Lin Piao's more subdued approach.[44]

As a corollary to its endorsement of "national liberation struggles," the CPR claims that any outside intervention to prevent the exercise by native populations of their right of self-determination is an act of aggression. Like other Communist states, it has branded the United States an aggressor in Vietnam and holds the United States responsible for "crimes against humanity" by the latter's use of napalm and chemical means of waging war.[45] Elsewhere we have noted CPR charges that the United States in the course of the Vietnam War violated the 1925 Geneva Protocol banning gas warfare. Similar charges had been raised during the Korean War. In 1952, Peking officially acceded to the 1925 Geneva Protocol and the four Geneva Red Cross conventions of 1949. As we have observed in an earlier chapter, Peking invoked the latter conventions both at the end of the Korean War and during the Sino-Indian conflict in regard to India's treatment of Chinese POWs and detained Chinese nationals. From its charges against the United States during the Vietnam War, it appears that in Peking's eyes the latest conflict was legally on a par with the Korean and the Sino-Indian border conflicts. In other words, the United States "intervention" turned the "national liberation struggle" within Vietnam from a civil strife into an international war in which the usual customs and laws relating to warfare became applicable.

As a whole, self-defense and "national liberation" are the only two principles justifying the use of force in CPR doctrine, but the latter is supposedly limited to a domestic milieu. If therefore "national liberation" is excluded from consideration—because it approximates a civil war status—the only legal use of force in interstate relations remains that for self-defense. If this is true, then the position is in general agreement with the existing international law on the use of force.

Neutralism, Nonalignment, and Mutual Abstention

From its actual experience the CPR has found it feasible to make use of neutral third states to serve as buffer or cushion between the two opposing camps in the Cold War, especially where acute tension exists. This attitude can be seen in the great reluctance with which Peking in 1955 accepted the requests by Sweden and Switzerland for a reduction of their personnel on the Neutral Nations Supervisory Commission, established under the Armistice Agreement in Korea. At least outwardly, Peking gave the impression that it fully valued the peace-keeping role played by neutral nations.[46] From the mid-1950s on, CPR foreign policy has consciously, though with different emphases in varying stages, promoted nonalignment among Afro-Asian countries. Noting the increasing numbers of states adopting the nonalignment policy, Ch'en-Yi, in a report to the Eighth Party Congress in 1956, expressed the official view that neutralism was a growing tide of the day and "absolutely not an immoral act" as United States Secretary of State Dulles alleged.[47]

Strictly from the ideological point of view, nonalignment by Afro-Asian nations falls short of what Peking would otherwise have wished. But realistic appraisal of world power configurations has called for a rejection of the dogmatic notion that "those who are not with us are against us." Out of strategic considerations, the Communist Chinese have reconciled themselves to a policy based on the premise that those who are not against them are potentially for them. Their own continued international isolation has led them to perceive the role which a growing third world could play in mitigating the acute tension of the Cold War. Thus, Cambodia's "honest" neutralism before Sihanouk's downfall was hailed by Premier Chou as "not only conducive to preserving the Kingdom's independence but also to the maintenance of peace in Asia and the world." [48]

Nonalignment in Southeast Asia, especially in the Indochina region, has been a central policy which the CPR has been promoting in its efforts to liquidate Western influence from China's backyard. At the 1954 Geneva Conference to settle the Indochina war, Premier Chou En-lai stressed that Asian countries should settle their own fate and all foreign troops must be withdrawn and foreign bases removed from the surface of the Asian continent.[49] It was here that he first made known his concept of what subsequently became the five principles of peaceful coexistence. In an address on May 12, 1954, Chou maintained that only by settling their own fate under the principles of peaceful coexistence would the Asian countries be spared the catastrophe of "Asians fighting Asians" at the instigation of neocolonialists.[50] Although the CPR's promotion of nonalignment in Indochina boiled down to the keeping out of Western influence, its acceptance of the Geneva agreement, which forbade the Indochinese states to enter into military alliance with any foreign country, meant ultimately an endorsement of mutual disengagement.[51]

The same arrangement was repeated in 1962, when the CPR joined twelve other countries—among them the Soviet Union, France, Britain, and the United States—in an agreement to neutralize Laos. The CPR had actively sought to maintain a neutralist Laotian government. After Captain Kong Le overthrew the pro-United States government of Premier Tiao Somasanith and General Phoumi Nosavan in August, 1960, and proclaimed a neutral foreign policy, Peking immediately gave Kong Le's policy its warm endorsement and encouraged him to form a coalition government with the Pathet Lao against Phoumi Nosavan's right-wing groups.[52] Then neutralist Prince Souvanna Phouma was reinstated as premier in September. Immediately, Premier Chou En-lai sent a congratulatory message and expressed the hope that friendly and peaceful relations would develop between the two countries.[53]

In mid-December, 1960, however, General Phoumi Nosavan occupied Vientiane and installed a new pro-United States government under Premier Boun Oum, plunging Laos back into civil war. The warring factions were aided by the United States and the Soviet Union on opposing sides. Peking also threatened "proper measures" against massive American military supplies to the Boun Oum regime.[54] However, although Peking permitted Soviet airlifts of arms supplies via China, it pursued a course of self-restraint and avoided any direct risky adventures in Laos. A fourteen-nation Geneva Conference on Laos, proposed by Prince Sihanouk of Cambodia, was accepted by the CPR along with the Soviet Union and North Vietnam in January, 1961. The United States, after some initial opposition, also endorsed the idea.[55] It is not within our interest to review the conference proceedings, but the views stated by the CPR's delegation threw some light on the Chinese concept of neutrality. Ch'en Yi told the conference that a neutral Laos would (a) refrain from accepting any military alliance or protection, (b) enjoy absolute independence (not to be interfered with by either individual foreign states or any international machinery), and (c) pursue a neutral foreign policy, establishing friendly relations with *all* states.[56] The last condition meant in effect that a truly neutral Laos must be friendly to the CPR.[57]

At the end of the conference, on July 23, 1962, the fourteen participating countries (including Laos) signed a Declaration on the Neutrality of Laos, with an accompanying explanatory protocol. In essence it embodied an agreement on the neutralization of Laos and the establishment of a tripartite coalition government in that crisis-torn kingdom. The Laotian government pledged to build "a peaceful, neutral, independent, democratic, unified and prosperous Laos" and to apply the five principles of peaceful coexistence in its foreign relations. The guaranteeing nations promised to respect the sovereignty, neutrality, unity, and territorial integrity of Laos, and assumed a wide range of obligations.[58] One of the most important features of the agreement is the renunciation by Laos of the "protection of any alliance or military coalition, including the SEATO." This was a success for Peking, though not necessarily cause for elation. Alluding to the United States troops in Thailand on the Laotian border, Ch'en Yi, at the final meeting of the conference on July 21, declared that the permanent neutrality of Laos would depend on an effectual noninterference by outside powers.[59] Although the neutralization of Laos fit in with Chinese policy needs, it also placed Peking under a reciprocal obligation to observe abstention once the agreement was signed.

An important common feature of the 1954 and 1962 settlements is the obligation by the guaranteeing powers mutually to disengage. But mutuality does not necessarily mean equal obligations or equal sacrifices, considering the disparate "prices" paid by the various parties. One would not fully appreciate this point without considering other analogous situations. In 1962, for instance, when Khrushchev installed missiles in Cuba, the United States uncompromisingly demanded the withdrawal of the lethal weapons. The Soviet counterproposal that the United States also withdraw its missiles from Turkey was rejected for lack of *quid pro quo:* The United States had a particular claim to the Caribbean which the Soviets did not have to Turkey. The final settlement was unilateral, not mutual.[60] Over the prolonged Middle East tension the United States in 1969 proposed a mutual agreement by all major powers concerned to abstain from supplying armaments to the Arab states and Israel. The suggestion was swiftly rejected by Soviet Foreign Minister Andrei Gromyko. Although Israeli occupation of Arab territories was given as the official reason, Gromyko's rejection betrayed an attitude of exclusive Soviet interests in the Middle East by geographic propinquity. This was the essence of his statement that the Soviet Union was "not only a European but also an *Asian* state."[61] To the extent that Indochina is considered an area in which China has a special interest, the CPR's willingness to accept the mutual abstention arrangements worked out at Geneva in 1954 and 1962 implied a great concession on its part. It illustrated that Peking's anxiousness to seek the disengagement of the other foreign powers overtook its own concern for a claim to special predominance in the area. Given the prevailing circumstances of disparate power, the concession was "defensive" (as opposed to "expansive") in nature. Mutual abstention under the 1954 and the 1962 arrangements was tantamount to a Chinese renunciation of any real or imagined "Monroe Doctrine" toward Indochina. In this light, it is unfortunate that later developments denied neutralization and mutual disengagement a chance to prove their practicability.

It is beyond the interest of this study to affix the responsibility for the collapse of the 1954 accords or, in other words, who violated international law in the Vietnam War.[62] But, it may be of interest to note that, on its part, the CPR has exercised deliberate caution not to violate directly or unilaterally the principal obligation under the 1954 agreement that "each member of the Geneva Conference undertakes . . . to refrain from any interference in [the] internal affairs" of the Indochina states.[63] It has also shunned any straightforward military commitment to North Vietnam. As noted elsewhere, the CPR has concluded a treaty of friendship and mutual assistance—which means, among other things mutual defense—with three of the four Communist countries surrounding China: the Soviet Union (1950), Outer Mongolia (1960), and North Korea (1961). The missing link with respect to North Vietnam is obvious.[64] Of course, any such treaty with Hanoi would be incompatible with the obligations assumed under the 1954 Geneva agreement. Even after the Vietnam conflict had become an open international war after 1965, the CPR refrained from sending combat troops. By September, 1969, when plans for the withdrawal of United States troops had barely been made public, the Communist Chinese were reported to have completed the pullout of all of their 40,000 (noncombatant) engineering troops that had been stationed along the transport and communication lines between southern China and North Vietnam, where their function had been to construct and repair those lines.[65]

Like the Vietnam settlement, the neutralization of Laos has not been fool-proof for three main reasons: difficulties surrounding the maintenance of a stable coalition government by the three feuding Laotian factions, the weak power of the International Control

Commission to oversee compliance, and opposing interventions by a number of guaranteeing powers.[66] By and large, however, the CPR has maintained a relatively prudent course with regard to Laos as to Vietnam. Senate Majority Leader Mike Mansfield, in his 1968 report on the 1954 and the 1962 Geneva agreements, observed that "the Chinese have not been in direct or unilateral violation of these agreements." [67] Other reports in 1969 indicated that Peking's influence in Laos was noticeable but restrained,[68] while at the same time there was growing anxiety in the United States Senate over the extent of United States military involvement in Laos.[69]

The actual breakdown of the Indochina settlements, including the neutralization of Laos, is a regional manifestation of the much larger conflict between the opposing powers concerned. It is not any worse or better than the larger conflict. Yet, so long as Peking maintains "defensive" (rather than "expansive") goals with regard to this area, the solutions of neutralization and mutual disengagement are not necessarily foredoomed to failure if all parties concerned are willing to take cognizance of these "defensive" goals. From Peking's point of view, the catastrophe in Indochina was caused by the very "intrusion" of foreign powers that it had sought to liquidate, something as alarming as if Peking had intruded into the Carribbean in defiance of United States interests or into East Europe against the will of the Soviet Union. It is not without reason that Peking has seen a revival of the "ghost of Dulles" in the much-talked-about Soviet proposal for a "system of collective security in Asia" to contain Communist China.[70] In view of this latest development, it may not be total conjecture that the CPR had accepted the 1962 neutralization of Laos to pressure the Soviet Union to disengage from the area as well.

Self-Restraint and Armed Peace

It is immaterial whether Communist China's participation in the Korean War was, as Mao was to reveal in 1962, motivated by a strategic necessity to prove Peking's ally-worthiness to Stalin, who allegedly had deep suspicions that Mao would become another Tito and come to terms with the United States.[71] What matters is that since the Korean conflict the CPR has deliberately pursued a cautious policy of not getting involved in another direct confrontation with the United States. A clear example is the tenor of the Treaty of Friendship, Cooperation and Mutual Assistance, signed between the CPR and North Korea, on July 11, 1961. It is clear that the treaty has mutual defense obligations within its purview, which can be seen in the following provisions:

> Article I. The Contracting Parties will continue to make every effort *to safeguard the peace of Asia and the world* and the security of all peoples.
>
> Article II. The Contracting Parties undertake jointly to adopt all measures to *prevent aggression* against either of the Contracting Parties by any State. In the event of one of the Contracting Parties being subjected to the *armed attack* by any state, or several states jointly, and thus being involved in a state of war, the other Contracting Party shall immediately render military and other assistance by all means at its disposal.[72] (Emphasis added.)

However, it is also clear that the CPR would not want to be embroiled in a recurrent Korean War. To preclude that eventuality, a carefully worded article in the treaty—obviously inserted at Chinese behest—provides:

> The Contracting Parties hold that the unification of Korea must be realized along *peaceful* and democratic lines and that such a solution accords exactly with the national interest of the Korean people and *the aim of preserving peace in the Far East*.[73]

The language remotely resembles the joint statement by President Chiang Kai-shek of the Republic of China and United States Secretary of State John Foster Dulles, signed in Taipei on October 23, 1958, by which the Nationalist Chinese leader agreed to renounce the use of force as a means to regain the lost mainland.[74]

The same posture of self-restraint seemed to guide Peking's policy toward the Vietnam conflict. Amidst speculation as to whether the Communist Chinese would intervene directly in behalf of North Vietnam, it was reported in the Western press in 1967 that the CPR had, through the French foreign ministry, laid down three conditions for remaining out of the Vietnam War. The reported conditions were: (a) that the United States not invade the China mainland, (b) that it not bomb the dikes of the Red River in North Vietnam, and (c) that it not invade North Vietnam.[75] Although these were later officially denied, the actual CPR conduct throughout the Vietnam War seemed to conform to a policy of restraint which took these conditions in view. Empirical evidence seemed to bear out the speculation that an all-out CPR intervention in the Vietnam War was not likely unless her own security was threatened and, furthermore, unless North Vietnam should appear like concluding a "sell-out" peace with the United States.[76]

Cynics may conclude that Peking's practical restraint was due to the superior American military prowess in Vietnam. This is undoubtedly true. But the presence of equally superior American might in the Korean War did not deter the Communist Chinese when other overriding considerations dictated their forceful entry into the war. When one considers Peking's "self-reliance" exhortation to foreign "national liberation movements," the deliberate effort to exempt China from embroilment in a recurrent Korean War, and its general practice of self-restraint in regard to adjacent nations (considering Tibet and Taiwan as questions of a different category), one gains a sustained impression that self-restraint is a crucial constituent of the CPR's foreign policy, its ideological flamboyance regardless.

Self-restraint is far from pacifism. In fact, Communist China has persistently demonstrated a resolve to improve its unfavorable position in the existing strategic balance. Its attitudes have, not surprisingly, followed the changing patterns of power balance consequent upon the progressive development of its own nuclear capabilities. In 1958, reacting to the United States deployment of missiles with atomic warheads in Taiwan, South Korea, and Japan, the CPR government proposed "the establishment throughout Asia of an *area of peace free from atomic weapons* and the conclusion of collective peace . . . of all Asian countries." [77] In 1960, it proposed that "the countries in Asia and around the Pacific, including the United States, conclude a peace pact of mutual non-aggression, and make this a nuclear-free area." [78] The idea of a nuclear-free zone in Asia and the Pacific region was repeated on July 31, 1963, in a disarmament proposal that specifically named the United States, the Soviet Union, the CPR, and Japan as the parties concerned.[79] This is the first elaborate disarmament proposal ever put forward by Peking, offered as a comment on the Test Ban Treaty newly concluded in Moscow. If previous CPR pronouncements on disarmament were limited to an Asian nuclear-free zone and to complete nuclear disarmament, the 1963 proposal extended the nuclear-free zone idea to Central Europe, Africa, and Latin America. Besides, it demanded the dismantling of foreign military bases, and called for the nondissemination of nuclear weapons and an end to all nuclear tests, including those conducted underground. These first steps" were laid down as a basis for discussion by a world summit conference, with an aim to bringing about eventually "the complete, thorough, total, and resolute prohibition and destruction of nuclear weapons." [80]

After its first successful atomic explosion on October 16, 1964, Peking again called for a world-wide summit conference to discuss complete prohibition and destruction of nuclear weapons. In a departure from its 1963 proposal, it now suggested as a "first step" that the nuclear powers reach an agreement to ban the use of nuclear weapons.[81] The unilateral insistence by Peking in subsequent months on a "no-first-use" agreement or understanding with the existing nuclear powers betrayed an apprehension—recalling a similar fear by the Soviet Union during the early stages of its nuclear development—that the other nuclear powers might launch a preventive attack against its nascent nuclear facilities.[82] There is probably more than propaganda or self-justification in Chou En-lai's statement that China was forced to develop an atomic arsenal because the United States refused to accept a "no-first-use" agreement.[83]

In examining the evolving Chinese attitudes regarding nuclear armaments, one is struck by a close similarity with those of the Soviet Union in the past as it grew from a nonnuclear power threatened by the massive destructive power exclusively held by the United States to a nuclear equal of the latter. But beneath the seeming similarity is a deeper Chinese apprehension not experienced by the Soviets before, in the sense that a pre-emptive attack could not only come from the United States but also from the Soviet Union, as some reports indicated.[84] In this respect, as elsewhere, the Communist Chinese have been prudent in action, lest either of the two jealous nuclear adversaries should find a pretext for striking first. Peking has insisted since 1964 that its own nuclear development is defensive in nature ("to break your nuclear monopoly"), that it will not be the first to use nuclear power, and that it hopes that all nuclear armaments will be eliminated eventually.[85] Presumably, the last statement suggests that Peking wants to gain a nuclear respectability—not necessarily a strict parity with the two superpowers—so that it can negotiate a more thorough nuclear disarmament with the United States and the Soviet Union. In a typical paradoxical fashion, the *Jen-min jih-pao* in 1964 revealed this complex line of reasoning in a comment on a remark by President Lyndon B. Johnson: [86]

> Johnson had the impudence to say that China wanted to "trade away its small accumulation of nuclear power against the mighty arsenal" of the United States. Mr. President, you have completely miscalculated. China is developing nuclear weapons not in order to use them to bargain a deal with you. No, China is developing nuclear weapons to break your nuclear monopoly [in order] to eliminate them so that the danger of nuclear war threatening mankind can be removed once and for all.[87]

Not totally unmindful of world public opinion and implications under international law, the CPR has defended its own nuclear program in the name of a country's right of self-defense, being threatened by the superior destructive power wielded in hostile hands. More than that, Peking has pictured itself in a role of maintaining a nuclear balance of power by its avowed effort to break the existing imbalance. Typical of these arguments is the following statement issued by the CPR government, on October 16, 1964, shortly after its first successful atomic detonation:

> To defend oneself is the inalienable right of every sovereign state. To safeguard world peace is the common task of all peace-loving countries. China cannot remain idle in the face of the ever-increasing nuclear

threats from the United States. China is conducting nuclear tests and developing nuclear weapons under compulsion.[88]

Under existing international law, strictly speaking, a state which has not signed away its right by treaty is not prohibited from developing its own atomic and nuclear arsenals. The CPR has consciously refrained from becoming a party to the partial test ban treaty of 1963 and the treaty banning the dissemination of nuclear arms, open for signature in 1968.[89] In spirit, the Chinese negative decisions paralleled the United States Senate refusal to give its advice and consent to the ratification of the 1925 Geneva Protocol prohibiting the use in war of asphyxiating, poisonous, or other gases, and the bacteriological methods of warfare.[90] But, whereas the norms prohibiting the use of gases and chemical and bacteriological warfare have, in the view of the Nuremberg Tribunal, become part of general international law, a state's right to develop its own nuclear capability is not as yet similarly restricted unless by treaty obligations.

If the Soviet experience is to be borrowed as a guide for judging the future development of Peking's attitudes, a suggestion may be ventured that when it has acquired a nuclear capability sufficient to dispel its current fear of vulnerability and, more especially, when it is anxious to protect its *status quo status* as a nuclear super power and to deny India, or any other aspirant next in line, to bid for membership in the coveted Nuclear Club, the CPR can then be safely expected to affix its signature to the treaties banning nuclear tests and the dissemination of nuclear arms. Given the present circumstances, however, Peking is expected to maintain its intransigency, and act very much like the Soviet Union did before 1960, with regard to nuclear disarmament.

The nuclear race, of course, is not a cause but a product of the existing atmosphere of tension and distrust. The ultimate conflict enwrapping the CPR, the United States, and the Soviet Union is focused on the Taiwan question. Elsewhere I have dealt with this uneasy triangular tangle in greater detail.[91] Suffice it to suggest that, between the CPR and the United States, the Taiwan question has held the key to fundamental issues outstanding between the two countries, including the "normalization" of relations and the representation question in the United Nations. The impasse over two decades of time has, among other things, brought the United States Seventh Fleet in direct confrontation with mainland China in the Taiwan Strait. Peking's feelings about the confrontation were best summed up in Ch'en Yi's remarks made at a Peking reception for a visiting Algerian delegation in 1958:

> The Chinese people will hate the United States imperialists as long as they continue their territorial aggression [in Taiwan] and hostility; but will be friendly toward the American people, because the latter must be separated from the government.[92]

The deterioration of Sino-Soviet relations can also be linked to the Taiwan question, dated from the Soviet reluctance to give Peking backing in an attempted showdown over Taiwan in 1954 and again in 1958.

The CPR has alternately tried force and negotiation (CPR-United States Ambassadorial Talks) in its attempts to resolve the Taiwan dilemma. From the Communist Chinese viewpoint, settlement of the Taiwan question is an "internal" affair well within the CPR's sovereignty. But, for the United States, the question involves not only a mutual defense treaty commitment to the Republic of China on Taiwan but also a pledge, as President Nixon repeatedly stressed while endeavoring to scale down the existing tension with Peking, not to abandon the Nationalists ("an old friend") both in bilateral relations and in the United Nations. The wide gulfs are not likely to be bridged as long as Washington subscribes to a "two Chinas" or "one China, one Taiwan" policy, which Peking has condemned as absolutely unacceptable, although for practical reasons both sides would want to maintain wider contacts and keep the door open for more rounds of the Ping-pong Diplomacy. The Taiwan question will continue to trouble Peking-Washington relations. The Ambassadorial Talks, begun in 1955, have been fruitless on this score. Peking has consistently attacked the United States for its alleged intransigency and refusal to reach an understanding on the basis of "peaceful coexistence." [93] It has made much propaganda capital of American commitment to Nationalist China and its presence in Taiwan as a symbol of aggression.[94] At one time, Peking even proposed to negotiate a peaceful settlement with the "authorities in

Taiwan." In a policy announcement in 1956, Premier Chou purposely displayed flexibility and suggested that direct talks with the Nationalist Chinese leaders could take place "either in Peking or another appropriate site." [95] It is not unlikely that, if the current thaw with Washington continues, Peking would offer once again to "negotiate" a settlement directly with the Nationalist Chinese.

On the other hand, in the absence of a peaceful settlement thus far, Peking has reserved for itself the "right" to "liberate" the island by military means when necessary and feasible. It has been noted in Chapter V above that the CPR delegation at the Ambassadorial Talks refused to accept fully the United States proposal for a joint renunciation of the use of force generally and in the Taiwan Strait except in self-defense. While it was ready to renounce the use of force generally, the CPR took issue with its application to the Taiwan Strait, contending that its sovereign right to use force for "internal" purposes was not to be compromised.[96] Besides, CPR jurists have challenged United States claims that its mutual defense treaty with Nationalist China was justified by the "inherent right" of self-defense recognized by general international law and in Article 51 of the United Nations Charter. Citing works by Hershey (*The Essentials of International Public Law*) and the Inter-American Juridical Committee (a report in 1945), Ch'en T'i-ch'iang [97] notes that a state's right of self-defense applies solely to its own "territory" by virtue of its territorial inviolability. "Is there," he asks, "any national territory in the Taiwan area which the United States has [a right] to defend?" The presence of the United States in Taiwan, he contends, constitutes an "aggression" against a piece of Chinese territory, which gives the CPR—the "victim of aggression"—cause to use force if necessary in the exercise of its right of self-defense.[98]

To sum up, while it pursues limited goals of a defensive nature including self-preservation, the CPR reserves for itself the "right" to develop nuclear capabilities and to "liberate" Taiwan by force if necessary. If the stalemate continues, a prolonged period of a *status mixus* of neither peace nor war is likely to prevail in East Asia. The CPR can be expected to pursue a policy of armed peace, professing "peaceful coexistence" and espousing the right in behalf of the "oppressed" of armed struggle against "imperialism" at the same time, which is likely to continue even when relations with Washington are improving.

Pacific Settlement of Disputes

A wide range of methods are available under international law for the pacific settlement of disputes between states, although the choice of certain particular methods over others depends on the states concerned and the prevailing circumstances. Article 33 of the United Nations Charter gives an enumeration of the usual means available for such purposes:

> The parties to any dispute, the continuance of which is likely to endanger the maintenance of international peace and security, shall, first of all, seek a solution by negotiation, enquiry, mediation, conciliation, arbitration, judicial settlement, resort to regional agencies or arrangements, or other peaceful means of their own choice.

Of these possible methods, enquiry would entail investigation by a third party which, under the present conditions of sensitivity and distrust, would give the impression of prying into one's "national secrets," and its inacceptability to Peking can reasonably be expected. In traditional China, mediation and conciliation were the most favored procedures for settling disputes between individuals and families. But the mediator called upon to hear the grievances and help bring the disputants to a settlement was usually either a family elder or a community leader greatly venerated by both parties. His personal prestige and respectability not only lent weight to his findings and recommended solutions but also served to channel the partisan dispute to a level of benign patronage and blessings such as his exalted social status could confer.[99] Although CPR practice accepts mediation and conciliation, the difficulty of finding an acceptable mediator can be readily seen, not merely because of the existing atmosphere of distrust but also because of Peking's own overblown sense of pride.[100]

Judicial settlement is even more difficult in the existing circumstances. The lack of representation among the judges of the International Court of Justice makes that tribunal unacceptable. The CPR has, in fact, criticized the I.C.J. for having lent itself to serving the interests of the "imperialists," as in the *Corfu Channel* and *Anglo-Iranian Oil Co.* cases.[101] There is no other international tribunal which the CPR can be expected to trust and to which it would agree to submit a dispute for adjudication. The question is more complicated than mere trust. In traditional China, Confucian *li* presupposed the ability of each respectable member of the community to keep his own conduct within the limits defined by the pervading but largely internalized moral code. Only "moral midgets" (*hsiao-jen*) and "pettifoggers" (*sung-shih*) would take to litigation before a magistrate. Despite their official adherence to the Marxist-Leninist ideology, with the professed aim to eradicate China's Confucian past, officials of the CPR do not seem to have gotten over the traditional attitude toward judicial settlement, both in domestic and international disputes.[102]

By its exclusion from international organizations except those of Communist origin (even in these its membership was in question in the 1960s), the CPR cannot turn to any regional agency or arrangement even if it wished to. By the same reasons given above, it is unlikely that the CPR will accept the good offices or mediatory role of any such machinery in the event it does become a member.

This natural process of elimination leaves negotiation and arbitration, plus *bilateral* conciliation, as the more practicable means for the pacific settlement of disputes, although mediation and conciliation under third-party auspices are also possible if an agreement on the proper third party can be reached. (For our purposes here, bilateral conciliation worked out between the contending parties themselves without going through third-party auspices is still a form of negotiation.) By and large, bilateral negotiation is the most acceptable form of settlement, since it gives the CPR the greatest possible control over the situation and entails the least possible danger of incurring obligations incompatible with its interests. Thus, during the Sino-Indian border dispute in 1962, Peking repeatedly offered to negotiate a settlement, and rejected Prime Minister Nehru's suggestions of referring the issue to an international tribunal.[103] At the 1954 Geneva Conference on Indochina, Chou En-lai lauded the agreements reached by the sponsoring powers and by the belligerents as an example that "international disputes can be resolved through *negotiation* and *consultation*." [104] Chou reaffirmed this view in his report on the Geneva settlement to the Central People's Government Council.[105]

In the two decades since its founding, the CPR has, very much like other countries, negotiated for a number of purposes. It has negotiated for the normalization of relations with other states (e.g., diplomatic recognition; Korean Armistice, etc.), for the innovation of new relationships (e.g., trade; boundary delineation; economic cooperation; technical assistance and loans to Afro-Asian nations, etc.), and for the extension of existing patterns of relations (e.g., renewal of friendship treaties; cultural agreements, etc.). Furthermore, it has employed negotiation for the revision of the *status quo* and a redistribution of values, rights, and political influence. The Ambassadorial Talks with the United States are a typical example by which the CPR has attempted to change the existing status of Taiwan. While this attempt has been fruitless, the negotiation has been continued because of its side effects, including the desires to maintain the only contacts between the two governments, to minimize the possibility of violence, and to generate tension in United States relations with Nationalist China.[106]

While negotiation has brought about concrete results in the areas of normalization, innovation, and extension, it has not reached similar achievements in issues primarily of a redistribution character. The Sino-Soviet talks that were initiated in 1964 to negotiate a settlement of boundary problems in the face of CPR attacks on "unequal treaties" inherited from the past have not produced much result,[107] any more than the CPR-United States Ambassadorial Talks, although the side effects from these talks should not be completely overlooked. The Sino-Indian border dispute is not even susceptible to a negotiated settlement in view of Indian reluctance. Ironically, the three most acute areas of international conflict which Peking has confronted—Taiwan, Sino-Soviet border, and Sino-Indian boundary—have been the least susceptible of pacific settlement by direct bilateral negotiation. International negotiations for the purpose of a redistribution are characterized by a demand by an offensive side for a change in its favor, at the expense of the defensive side.[108] In the first two cases, the CPR has been the offensive side, pressing its demands for revision on the United States and the Soviet Union, respectively. As typical of all redistribution negotiations, the reluctance of the defensive side to yield to the Chinese Communist demands has resulted in a fruitless stalemate, which is unlikely to be resolved in the face of Peking's inability to carry out meaningful coercion. In the case of the Sino-Indian boundary dispute, negotiation seemed to have been equally a waste of effort, and India, the party seeking a redistribution of territory, knew in advance that Peking would stubbornly stand by its position and that she herself did not have the capability to coerce the Chinese into a favorable agreement.

We have noted that some treaties signed between the CPR with other states contain a negotiation clause in case of a dispute arising from the interpretation of the provisions.[109] In others, like the Sino-Afghan Treaty of Friendship and Non-Aggression (August 26, 1960), it is stipulated that all disputes between the parties are to be settled by means of "peaceful negotiation without resorting to force."[110] In the politically less sensitive areas, such as foreign trade, disputes may be settled by other channels, such as reviewing boards,[111] mixed commissions,[112] and arbitration.[113] These do not replace negotiation but follow in the wake of its failure as an alternative means for settling a dispute. These procedures are standard in the CPR's trade agreements with socialist states, and are also found in a number of cases where nonsocialist states are Peking's trading partners. The first two Sino-Japanese trade agreements provided for arbitral settlement of disputes and named China as the place for such settlement, with an arbitration commission to be composed of members from both countries. The third and fourth Sino-Japanese trade agreements named the state of the defendant as the place for arbitration and provided for one national arbitrator designated by each side and a mutually acceptable third-party arbitrator to serve on the commission.[114] Similar arbitral procedures are available in the CPR's trade relations with other nonsocialist countries, such as Finland and France.[115]

Very little information is available on how actually the arbitral procedures have worked in practice. According to one of the few published Western sources, the Italian experience is that the Communist Chinese are tough negotiators but, once contracts have been signed, they quite scrupulously carry out the contract terms. As a result, very few disputes regarding contract fulfillment have arisen, and in the few cases where they did occur an amicable settlement was speedily found. The Chinese, according to the report, often do not even make a claim, and usually they do not seek to recover more than the actual damage.[116] The Chinese are also known to prefer "adjustment" or bilateral conciliation, rather than going through the length of the arbitral procedure. This is substantiated in an independent study of sixty-one disputes between CPR foreign trade companies and Western firms brought before the CPR Foreign Trade Arbitration Commission. Not one of them reached the stage of the final arbitral award, and all were settled in the meantime.[117]

For maritime disputes, arbitral procedures are provided by the CPR Maritime Arbitration Commission, established in 1958 under the China Council for the Promotion of International Trade.[118] In one known case, in which a Norwegian vessel M/S *Varild* went aground near Shanghai, on April 4, 1961, and was salvaged by the Shanghai Salvage Bureau, disputes arose over the amount of fees to be paid to the salvager. In accordance with contract terms, the salvager filed an application for arbitration with the Maritime Arbitration Commission. The arbitral tribunal, with the consent of the disputants, proceeded with conciliation, in pursuance of Article 19 of the Rules of Procedure of the commission. The dispute was resolved in the end with both sides making some concessions.[119]

Needless to say, in all these cases of settlement by arbitral or other third-party procedures, the subject matter is nonpolitical and almost invariably related to trade. In other words, the CPR's acceptance of these procedures is facilitated by the lack of political sensitivity (such as sovereign rights) and the presence of an immediate practical interest in a speedy settlement in order that the same relations (trade, for example) can be resumed. Furthermore, in the cases of the mixed arbitration commissions, the CPR has complete control over the designation of the national arbitrator and a measure of control over the choice of the third-party arbitrator. In other cases, the arbitral tribunal is totally made up of Chinese arbitrators under Chinese laws. Whether similar procedures can be extended to political issues will naturally depend on the presence of similar conditions in an overall relaxation of the international political atmosphere. Again, the ineffectualness of these means of pacific settlement is a product, not a cause, of the existing international tension.

Conclusions

THE PRECEDING chapters embody an attempt to increase our understanding of the CPR's foreign policy and world view from an empirical study of her attitude and practice with respect to international law, focusing on the interrelations between law and policy. We have observed a more than cursory concern on her part for regularity, stability, and continuity in foreign relations.

The use of international law has been made necessary either to facilitate Peking's foreign relations, to support its claims to certain international rights, to protect Chinese interests and nationals abroad, to defend certain official conduct, or to help the carrying out of trade or other similar relations. A measure of deference to and reliance on international law is noticeable in the CPR's domestic legislation, treaties, formulation of foreign policy, and even in domestic court proceedings. The Chinese Communist attitude toward international law does not blindly follow the "clean slate" theory, which would repudiate all obligations as well as rights assumed by pre-1949 China.

Both in theory and practice, the CPR has been quite selective and more pragmatic than is usually assumed, accepting certain norms of the established code of international conduct but rejecting others. Policy needs, though often ideologically defined, guide this selective process. As her policy needs never remain the same, her attitudes toward international law have also been evolutionary (e.g., the changing implications of peaceful coexistence); so has been her practice (e.g., her changing patterns of diplomatic recognition). While she has made claims to historical rights on the basis of state continuity, the CPR has also reserved the right to denounce past obligations under the assumption that she is in part also a successor to the old Chinese state (the continuity being interrupted by the revolution). When compared with previous Chinese governments, Peking has introduced some modifications—but not complete departures—to traditional views, as regards suzerainty, *jus sanguinis,* etc. But, as a whole, it has not deviated very widely, especially on issues affecting the vital interests of China (e.g., the status of Tibet, boundary questions, etc.).

While there is no agreement on whether there is a general international law universally applicable to states of different ideologies, most CPR commentators hold out the view that there is one in the making, though they tend to overstate the contribution of the socialist states. For lack of representation the CPR cannot fully attribute modern norms which she accepts or advocates (e.g., the Five Principles of Peaceful Coexistence) to the United Nations Charter or other international conventions of a legislative character. There have been attempts to find the basis for the universality of these norms in *ordre public* or a comprehensive body of *jus congens,* bypassing the question of explicit "agreement." For the same reason, the CPR has not followed the Soviet position that treaties are "*the* major source" of international law, but has maintained a parity between treaties and custom.

Either because of her Marxist ideology or recent Chinese experience with "imperialist" dominance or both, the CPR adheres to the doctrine of absolute sovereignty and "equal treatment" (as distinct from "international standards") of aliens. She has invoked "self-determination" not only to argue that diplomatic recognition is merely declaratory but also to sanctify "people's liberation wars" she supports.

Like many other states the CPR has sought maximum protection from international law while she does not necessarily apply as fully the same standards to others. During the Sino-Indian boundary disputes, she accused India of violating the "human rights and fundamental freedoms" of the Chinese residents and of maltreatment of Chinese consular personnel. This does not mean that her own treatment of foreign nationals and diplomatic-consular representatives measures up to the same standards. As a whole, however, her behavior has been much more restrained than is generally depicted. Besides, her compliance with treaty law is far better. As we have seen, it is rather difficult to pinpoint direct and unilateral violations by Peking of treaties it has voluntarily entered into. The regime's credit standing in foreign trade (e.g., with Japan and Canada) has been rated quite good.

In CPR treaty practice, we have noted a narrow margin of differentiation between trade with the socialist countries and those outside the bloc. The ideological factor, though important, has not played as predominant a role as might be expected. A large measure of realism has characterized CPR trade agreements with "bourgeois" and nonaligned countries. The ideological bond even approaches the vanishing point when the CPR's national interests, however subjectively conceived, clash with those of another socialist country (such as in the Sino-Soviet conflicts).

Since 1954, "peaceful coexistence" has received much play-up and, during the Sino-Soviet polemic exchanges, CPR doctrine has insisted that peaceful coexistence does not mean surrender to the "imperialists." In practice, however, the CPR has gone on record that questions like Taiwan, Hong Kong, and Macao will await a negotiated settlement. Verbal threats notwithstanding, realism has compelled Peking to forego an outright armed "liberation" of Taiwan but to resort to the Ambassadorial Talks with the United States in search of a solution.

Although she does not always follow the rules which she has invoked against other countries, the CPR has quite consciously attempted to maintain at least a semblance of consistency on a given issue. She has shown an awareness of the "game" in customary international law of preventing or inducing expectation and reliance. If one abandons the "either or" attitude in evaluating the CPR's record of compliance, it becomes clearer that international law does seem to have exercised a *restraining* effect on the Chinese Communist decision-makers in foreign policy. Although she charged invasions of her sovereignty by Indian reconnaissance planes which flew well into Chinese airspace, the CPR is not known to have sent reconnaissance planes over the territory of any other country, not even during her disputes with India. Again, during the same disputes, CPR troops generally refrained from crossing the McMahon Line though she did not recognize that line as the boundary. If President Syngman Rhee of South Korea claimed a belt of territorial waters extending to an average of sixty miles (the "Rhee Line"), the Communist Chinese have not made any similar claims. They have shown a degree of respect for the freedom of the high seas in general, though they have quite jealously guarded the security and inviolability of what they claim to be China's territorial sea, which extends twelve miles seaward measured from straight baselines.

It is generally true that the extent to which the CPR subscribes to the primacy of international law is in inverse proportion to the political nature of an issue at stake. To varying degrees, this is true even of countries most directly involved in the formulation of much of the content of existing international law. The important thing is that ideological predilection is not the sole factor determining CPR international conduct. Even in political issues, as over Taiwan and Southeast Asia, the CPR has not abandoned the counsels of realism (*Realpolitik*). CPR practice lacks the automaticity or immutable character which one expects from a pure ideological commitment. Among the various factors which have a more or less claim on the attention of CPR leadership is the restrictive effect, as well as the utility, of international law itself.

The CPR displays a "contextual" outlook in this connection, which is characterized by calculations of the maximal advantages accruing from the application of international law, weighed in view of a whole range of desiderata including ideological soundness, national interests, the expectation and reliance to be created or denied, *Realpolitik,* and the merits of the norms being applied. Since the facts vary from situation to situation, the precedence given to certain desiderata over others is determined on a pragmatic basis. Precedence, of course, does not mean the exclusion of the others. If any projection can be made of the future, the CPR's science of international law can be expected to reject both the naturalist-moralist outlook, whose obsession with the law *de lege ferenda* denies any sense of reality to the true legal order, and the positivist approach, whose subservience to legal absolutes would require complete abandoning of the ideological posture. It may even reject any pure sociological approach since this would challenge the validity of the Marxist ideology of class struggle at the doctrinal plane. (Of course, Marxism itself claims to be sociologically based.) The "contextual" outlook is broader than any of these.

The CPR's initial application of norms of international law may be heavily weighed toward the optimal advantage to be gained over and above the restrictive effect attendant to it. Yet, by the workings of reciprocity and the cumulative and correlative impact of such application, the CPR finds herself subject to more or less the same restrictions that she has sought to impose on others. The reciprocal obligations in foreign trade and those assumed from the neutralization of Laos are among the many examples that can be cited. The desire to encourage others to be bound by certain restrictions under law requires a prior condition that the CPR maintains a minimum level of credibility in her own conduct. Credibility means the least possible breach of voluntarily contracted international commitments, reasonable compliance with generally accepted standards and norms, a degree of consistency and continuity sufficient to induce reliance. Credibility may also be enhanced by rhetoric, denouncing the "imperialists" and others for their violations of international law.

For the CPR, it appears, psychological complications also arise when compliance with the existing patterns of public order is too conspicuously compelled by the overwhelming power wielded by the "imperialists." This does not mean the the CPR's international conduct will be more credible when that challenge is removed, nor that an intensification of the pressure will make for greater credibility. Not unlike the Soviet Union in the early years, the CPR is caught in a very uncomfortable position between a militant ideology and a physical milieu compelling practical sobriety. The result is a strange combination of verbal militancy and prudence in real action. The level of verbal militancy may increase in direct proportion to the degree of compulsion which dictates pragmatic prudence. At the same time, verbal militancy in turn generates greater hostility from the "imperialists."

As long as this vicious cycle continues, the role that international law can play in the circumstances is twofold. First, and most immediately, the law will continue to be useful for maintaining a minimum framework within which certain basic needs of international life can be satisfied. Secondly, and more important, the utilization of international law to fulfill the basic needs may hopefully contribute to the maintenance of a *modus vivendi* conducive to an abatement in both the CPR's ideological fervor and the real or imagined "imperialist" threat. One should not delude oneself that legal considerations will, in the short run at least, replace ideological stance or other considerations in the CPR's foreign policy. But it is not impossible that, by virtue of reciprocity, international law may play an expanded role under the self-momentum generated by its initial application. Reciprocity, needless to say, is still the effective obligatory basis of international law, and the limitations found in the present case are found in international relations in general.

Although the second stage cannot be expected to emerge shortly, every step in that direction may in and of itself have a cumulative effect. In the meantime, international law will continue to be used by the CPR as she has done. The hope for the future is, to reiterate, that use of international law entails a minimal measure of commitment sufficient to sustain the law's utility. Given this transitional nature of the situation, there can be no clear-cut answer to either of the two opposite questions: Is the CPR completely "lawless?" Or, is she a faithful supporter of international law? Available evidence certainly casts doubt on charges made by certain commentators that "international law does not even receive [the] lip service" of Communist China. On the other hand, there is still a great deal to be desired of her international conduct. The more pertinent questions to ask, it seems, are: How much more can we expect from the CPR beyond her lip service to that law? What are the conditions which will help enhance the CPR's sense of participation in a world order which the law can serve to sustain?

From available evidence, the CPR actually goes beyond just

paying lip service to international law. Despite her verbal dissent, she has shown desire for a modicum of international stability and security, such as the safety of her nationals abroad, border tranquility, and the dependable shipments of goods in and out of China. Her commitment to norms aimed at greater uniformity and conformity has generally been on the increase as her contacts with the outside world widen. These contacts and the CPR's efforts to protect Chinese nationals in India and Indonesia have both instilled a keener sense of reciprocity and provided *quid pro quo* for the observance of certain common norms and standards. Reciprocal considerations have led the CPR to accept modifications of her doctrine of absolute sovereignty, as is indicated by her endorsement of cojurisdiction by foreign courts over Chinese nationals abroad. For similar reasons, since she maintains an increasing number of representatives abroad, the CPR has come to appreciate the importance of the norms governing diplomatic and consular immunities and privileges.

While the Sino-Soviet feud may tend to reinforce Peking's ideological rigidity, it has also paved the way for an expansion of contacts (trade, especially) with countries outside the Communist bloc. Consequently, a new discrepancy has emerged from her increasing dependency upon the outside world in contrast to her ideological bonds with the Communist bloc. Ironically, as her contacts widen with the "bourgeois" and nonaligned nations, the CPR has been concentrating her doctrinal fire on the United States—so long as the stalemate continues—if only because her freedom of attacking the other Western powers has been greatly curtailed.

The widening gaps between the CPR's doctrinal bellicosity and pragmatic cautiousness, and between her ideological identification with the Communist bloc and her expanding ties with countries outside the bloc, signify an *evolutionary* (as opposed to dogmatically immutable) character of her foreign policy. However, it may be years before the CPR can be expected to attain a level of maturity and flexibility that we would like to see. The relative isolation she has long experienced has not only hardened the hostile mentality of her leadership but, presumably, has also prevented a greater detachment from her dogmatic stand. The diplomatic isolation has apparently kept her leaders and international lawyers relatively poorly informed of current international law and the conditions which underscore its evolution and functioning. Their very heavy reliance on L. Oppenheim's *International Law*[1] (in Chinese translation) may be a good indication of the paucity of information. Ch'en T'i-ch'iang, an Oxford-trained scholar, was purged in 1958 after he had counseled greater understanding of international law, the lack of which, he asserted, was the source of China's problems in the past century. This view, though not without validity, was rejected by the Chinese Communist party, since it would put the blame of China's prostration on her own ignorance rather than on "imperialist" exploitation.

It is not to be denied that the CPR has matured considerably since the early years. But her attitude toward international law is still very much dominated by a strong belief in the rule of "legitimacy," the feeling that certain absolute values should take precedence over the established legal order when realistic conditions permit it. The belief leads to a self-righteousness, at times gravely out of proportion to the justifiability of the issues. This axiomatically oriented perspective is less disposed to accepting compromise and conformity. Sometimes the lack of justifiability has to be compensated for by projecting the blame for the instability of the existing public order onto someone else—for example, the "imperialists" and their "stooges." The phenomenon is common among revolutionary nations, both in and outside the Communist bloc. While all national actors on the international scene are to varying degrees legitimacy-motivated, it remains true that the Chinese Communist leaders are yet to gain a better appreciation for the vital importance of justifiability in the interest of world public order. They as well as other decision-makers in revolutionary nations will have to learn the virtue of refraining from indulgence in maximum discretion ("that which is not restricted is permitted") and to guard against unnecessary encroachments upon international stability, security, and justice.[2]

Thus far, international law has played a role in defining the boundaries between what is permissible and what is not. Any significant expansion of its role would have to await the re-emergence of a true sense of world community beyond the current ideological division. Moreover, changes in the structure of international society also call for corresponding changes in international law. For instance, the extensive use of civilian agents in the Vietnam War (Vietcong political agents and American "pacification" workers) has rendered meaningless the traditional distinction between combatants and noncombatants in warfare.[3]

By and large, traditional international law has become somewhat inadequate in the face of the differences in the internal structures of states embracing different ideologies (such as the impact of state ownership upon traditional norms on expropriation). In part, the inadequacy is also a result of disparate perspectives of decision-makers in the opposing camps. It is not the intent of the present volume to indulge in historical speculation. But, for illustrative purposes, it may be suggested that in the history of the West, decision-makers were generally concerned with three major forces at clash at various times: those seeking imperial or hegemonial power, those supporting the multistate system, and those asserting the aspirations of popular sovereignty and irredentism. Throughout the past two centuries, forces defending the existing multistate system (e.g., Concert of Europe; the Allied and Associate Powers, etc.) have time and again rallied together to crush expansionist designs (from Napoleon to Nazi Germany), whittle down residual imperial predominance (from the Ottoman Empire to Austria-Hungary), and to intervene either to help nationalist movements (e.g., the independence of Greece) or to suppress undesired revolutions (from Metternichism to Russian interventions in Poland).

When unable to agree on whether an independence should or should not be supported, the major European powers at times found themselves at war with one another (e.g., the Balkan wars). At other times, they fought or clashed over the division of spoils either on the Continent or overseas. Religious differences also led to wars (e.g., the Crimean War), somewhat anticipating the current ideological conflicts. When the United States inherited the mantle of the Concert of Europe, it also inherited these perspectives. If the American intervention in World War II to check Hitler expansionism was conceived in the same perspective as the European Allies in their habitual resistance to contenders for hegemonial power, the policy thinking behind the Truman Doctrine and the Eisenhower Doctrine could find antecedents in the traditional European patterns of intervention abroad. Even the Soviet Union by its 1969 intervention in Czechoslovakia has not shown any significant departure from tsarist reflexes to similar East European insurrections.

This rapid sketch of modern Western history—with all its loopholes characteristic of generalizations—provides a stark contrast to the historical experience inherited by decision-makers in East Asia. Although conflicts between political units resembling modern nation-states had existed in ancient China (before the third century B.C.), the East Asian continent since then saw prolonged periods of relative placid peace. The stability was assured by the preponderance of power anchored in China, whose agrarian economy and attendant sedentary culture had made the nation habitually look within rather than outside for material and spiritual well-being. (For one thing, there was no need for overseas markets or raw materials.) Whereas in the European system balance of power was indispensable to the maintenance of equilibrium among the several states of more or less the same size and strength, the situation was different in East Asian history. Only among the contending units in ancient China, during the Warring States period (403–221 B.C.), was balance of power consciously practiced. In the long history since then, the disparate power held by the colossal Chinese empire in its relations with neighboring peoples allowed no room for the concept of "balance" to operate. Chinese decision-makers held the belief that peace in East Asia hinged on the preponderance of power and the cultural model which their country could provide. Cultural exemplification and absorption—an intangible—was held as no less important than brute power itself.[4] The system broke down only after the penetration by the West with gunboats and technological power.

Contemporary Chinese decision-makers do not seem to have abandoned completely the traditional perspectives. Their concern with China's role as stabilizer is only matched by a concomitant concern for the "impermeability" of the East Asian system, being equally jealous of continuing Western dominance as of possible challenge from Japan or India.[5] East Asian leaders like Norodom Sihanouk, Ho Chi Minh, and Kim Il Sung have shown an awareness of the strategic role which China could play as stabilizer and counterweight to Western (and Russian) influence.[6]

The clash between the disparate perspectives of decision-makers is nowhere borne out so distinctly as in the Vietnam tragedy. The war is only part of a larger conflict which has underscored a number of conflicting perspectives: (a) disparities between the "balance" and the "preponderance" concepts of power, (b) between the Europe-derived tradition of forceful intervention and the East Asian tradition of cultural-ideological absorption and exemplification, (c) between an overworked strategy based on superior military penetrative power and a strategy which transmutes direct vulnerability into gradual attrition in a guerrilla war, and (d) between calculations primarily based on tangibles (such as physical presence in the form of foreign bases and the landing of troops abroad; the number of guns and ammunitions available; the stage of nuclear development, etc.) and policy considerations that emphasize equally the intangibles (such as ideological leadership; model offering; psychological exhaustion of the foe; long-range gains, etc.).[7]

These vast gulfs in perspectives have blinded each to the true intentions of the other side and the real issues at hand. As demonstrated in the Vietnam tragedy, policy solutions derived from such enormous anomalies can only be anachronistic, in that massive American military response has replaced proper solutions to what is originally a socio-political problem and, conversely, what is probably an equivalent of the traditional European mode of intervention has been interpreted by the other side in the light of "imperialist" oppression. With all their grave consequences, these discrepancies in perspectives are not as readily recognizable as the power struggle or the ideological differences. While the latter had their counterparts in Western history, differences in perspectives of such magnitude did not arise until the contemporary age, when decision-makers from totally different cultural and historical backgrounds have come to read and misread each other's "inscrutable" minds and blunder through grotesque misreadings.

Ideological and perspective gulfs have deprived the world community of a consensus on values, an agreed concept of order, and common standards of legitimacy. In their absence, the awesome available power has been unrestrained and guided only by one's sense of self-righteousness. Until such time as a true meeting of minds has made significant headways, world order will remain precarious in our culturally and ideologically divided world. The problem of Communist China is but a part, admittedly a crucial part, of this larger colossus of anomalies.

Abbreviations

AJIL *American Journal of International Law*
CB Current Background (United States Consulate-General, Hong Kong)
CCP Communist Party of China (word order in Chinese: Chinese Communist Party)
CN treaty Treaty of commerce and navigation
Ch. Chancery *Reports,* Court of Chancery (Britain)
CDSP Current Digest of Soviet Press (Columbia University)
CFYC *Chen-fa yen-chiu* [Studies of Politics and Law]
Cmd. *Command Papers* (London)
COMECON [Communist] Council on Mutual Economic Aid
CPR People's Republic of China (word order in Chinese: Chinese Communist Republic)
CPSU Communist Party of the Soviet Union
DRV Democratic Republic of Vietnam
ECMM *Extracts from China Mainland Magazines* (United States Consulate-General, Hong Kong)
FCN treaty Treaty of friendship, commerce, and navigation
FKHP *Chung-hua jen-min kung-ho-kuo fa-kuei hui-pien* [Compendium of Laws and Regulations of the People's Republic of China]
FLP Foreign Language Press, Peking
GAC Government Administrative Council
GPRA The Revolutionary Provisional Government of Algeria
Hackworth, Digest Green H. Hackworth, *Digest of International Law,* 8 vols. (1940–1944)
Hague, Recueil *Recueil des Cours de l'Académie de Droit international de la Haye*
HC *Hung-ch'i* [Red Flag]
HFTT *Chung-hua jen-min kung-ho-kuo hsing-fa tsung-tse chiang-yi* [Lectures on the Fundamentals of the Criminal Law of the People's Republic of China] (Peking: Legal Publications, 1958)

Hudson, International Legislation Manley O. Hudson, ed., *International Legislation: A Collection of Texts of Multipartite International Instruments of General Interest,* 9 vols.

ICAO International Civil Aviation Organization

ICJ International Court of Justice

IGY International Geophysical Year

ILC International Law Commission, United Nations

IMCO Intergovernmental Maritime Consultative Organization

JMJP *Jen-min jih-pao* [People's Daily]

JPRS Joint Publications Research Service (Washington, D. C.)

JPWT *Jih-pen wen-t'i wen-chien hui-pien* [Collection of Documents Relating to Problems Concerning Japan]

KCWT *Kuo-chi wen-t'i yen-chiu* [Study of International Problems]

LNTS *League of Nations Treaty Series*

MFCPWT *Chung-hua jen-min kung-ho-kuo min-fa chi-pen wen-t'i* [Basic Issues in the Civil Law of the People's Republic of China]

Moore, Digest John Bassett Moore, *A Digest of International Law,* etc., 8 vols. (1906)

NCNA New China News Agency

NPC National People's Congress

PCIJ Permanent Court of International Justice

PCX Peaceful coexistence

PI Proletarian internationalism

PLO Palestine Liberation Organization

POWs Prisoners of war

PR *Peking Review* (English edition)

SCMP *Survey of China Mainland Press* (United States Consulate-General, Hong Kong)

Stat. *United States Statutes-at-Large*

TIAS *United States Treaties and Other International Acts Series*

TKWC *Kuo-chi kung-fa ts'an-k'ao wen-chien hsuan-chi* [Selected Reference Materials on Public International Law]

TWKH *Chung-hua jen-min kung-ho-kuo tui-wai kuang-hsi wen-chien chi* [Collection of Documents Relating to the Foreign Relations of the People's Republic of China]

TYC *Chung-hua jen-min kung-ho-kuo t'iao-yüeh chi* [Treaty Series of the People's Republic of China]

UN United Nations

UNTS *United Nations Treaty Series*

YHTY *Chung-hua jen-min kung-ho-kuo yu-hao t'iao-yüeh hui-pien* [Collection of the Friendship Treaties of the People's Republic of China] (Peking, 1965)

YTCN *Yin-tu chih-na wen-t'i wen-chien hui-pien* [Collection of Documents on the Indochina Question]

Notes

PREFACE

1. "Communist China's Conception of World Public Order: An Attitudinal and Pragmatic Analysis of Some Basic Issues of International Law," Columbia University, Department of Public Law and Government, 1967. Available on microfilm, University Microfilms, Ann Arbor, Michigan.
2. Letter to the author, dated August 16, 1971. I have further discussion of the question of expropriation in Chapter VII below, text at reference for nn. 35–50.

INTRODUCTION

1. A. Doak Barnett, *Communist China and Asia: A Challenge to American Policy* (New York: Vintage Books, 1961), p. 1.
2. H. A. Smith, *The Crisis in the Law of Nations* (London: Stevens, 1947), pp. 17–32, and *passim;* K. Wilk, "International Law and Global Ideological Conflict," *American Journal of International Law* (A.J.I.L.), Vol. XLV, No. 4 (October, 1951), p. 648. For the Department of State's views on the Soviet Union's outlook of world revolution, see Department of State, *Soviet World Outlook: A Handbook of Communist Statements* (Department Publication No. 6838, 1959), esp. 65 *et seq*.
3. Julius Stone, *Quest for Survival: The Role of Law and Foreign Policy* (Cambridge, Mass.: Harvard University Press, 1961), p. 88.
4. Richard L. Walker, *China Under Communism: The First Five Years* (New Haven: Yale University Press, 1955); H. Arthur Steiner, "The

Mainsprings of Chinese Communist Foreign Policy," *A.J.I.L.*, Vol. XLIV, No. 1 (January, 1950). India in 1963 accused the CPR of being "the first state which has defied all rules of international law and international behavior after the second World War." Embassy of India in China, "Chinese Aggression and International Law," *India Calling* (official Embassy publication in Peking), April, 1963, cited in a CPR note of protest to the Indian Embassy, dated June 3, 1963, reproduced in Indian Ministry of External Affairs, *White Paper: No. IX* (1963), p. 165.

5. Walker, *China Under Communism,* p. 237. Also his *The Continuing Struggle: Communist China and the Free World* (New York: Athene, 1958), *passim,* and esp. p. 92.
6. Steiner, *supra,* n. 4, p. 89.
7. Steiner, "Communist China in the World Community," *International Conciliation,* No. 533 (May, 1961) (New York: Carnegie Endowment for International Peace), p. 394.
8. Wolfgang Friedmann, *The Changing Structure of International Law* (New York: Columbia University Press, 1964), pp. 297–340; Oliver J. Lissitzyn, *International Law Today and Tomorrow* (Dobbs Ferry, N.Y.: Oceana, 1965), pp. 68–71, 94–101.
9. Friedmann, *The Changing Structure,* p. 55.
10. Lissitzyn, *International Law, supra,* n. 8, p. 94.
11. R. Randle Edwards, "The Attitude of the People's Republic of China Towards International Law and the United Nations," *Papers on China,* Vol. XVII (Cambridge, Mass.: East Asian Research Center, Harvard University, 1963), p. 235. The treatise was based mainly on CPR scholarly writings.
12. Lissitzyn, *supra,* n. 8, pp. 3–4.
13. Cf. R. S. Peters, *The Concept of Motivation* (New York: Humanities Press, 1958), pp. 1–26; Gustav Bergmann, *Philosophy of Science* (Madison: University of Wisconsin Press, 1957), esp. pp. 75–84; William Dray, *Laws and Explanation in History* (London: Oxford University Press, 1957), esp. pp. 122–25; Vernon van Dyke, *Political Science: A Philosophical Analysis* (Stanford: Stanford University Press, 1960), pp. 23 *et seq.*
14. During its heyday of development in the European state system around the turn of the century, international was defined as "the body of customary and conventional rules which are considered legally binding by civilized States in their intercourse with each other." L. Oppenheim, *International Law: A Treatise,* 2d ed. (London: Longmans Green, 1912), Vol. I, p. 3.
15. Morton Kaplan and N. deB. Katzenbach, *The Political Foundations of International Law* (New York and London: John Wiley & Sons, 1961), p. 231. The theory of decision-making process as applied to international law is most effectively expounded and developed by Myres S.

McDougal. See, generally, McDougal and Associates, *Studies in World Public Order* (New Haven: Yale University Press, 1960).

16. The idea and the term of a "hard core" of widely applied norms is proposed by Richard A. Falk, "The Adequacy of Contemporary Theories of International Law—Gaps in Legal Thinking," *Virginia Law Review,* Vol. L, No. 2 (March, 1964), pp. 240–42.
17. Lissitzyn, *International Law, supra,* n. 8, p. 36. Resting the ultimate basis of general international law upon "general consensus and expectations of states" is clearly an improvement upon the traditional precept of *opinio juris sive necessitatis.* The difficulties of ascertaining the existence of *opinio juris,* that is, a conviction that a conduct is required or permitted by international law, are patent. Furthermore, this new precept, as advanced by Professor Lissitzyn, is much broader than the old and it considers "custom" or "general practice" as but one form of evidence of "consensus and expectations." Whereas the traditional view considers that customary international law is created by uniformities in the *actual conduct* of many states which is accompanied by *opinio juris,* the new thesis makes it possible to accept norms created by other forms of communication. These include even the verbal form of communication among others, so long as they create expectations and, hence, reliance by other states. I believe Professor Lissitzyn's view is more explanatory than the attempt by Mr. Bing Cheng to associate *opinio juris* with an "instant" international customary law so as to make room for rapid changes in the law in the space age. Cf. B. Cheng, "United Nations Resolutions on Outer Space: 'Instant' International Customary Law?" *Indian Journal of International Law,* Vol. V (1965), p. 23.
18. *New York Times,* July 1, 1966, p. 6. See, generally, Rosalyn Higgins, *Conflict of Interests: International Law in a Divided World* (London: Bodley Head, 1965), esp. pp. 77–78, 95; Lissitzyn, *supra,* n. 8, pp. 36–37, 72–101. For an exposition of the dissenting views of the underdeveloped nations regarding norms which were formed before they gained independence, see J. Castaneda, "The Underdeveloped Nations and the Development of International Law," *International Organization,* Vol. XV, No. 1 (Winter, 1961); also *Howard Law Review,* Vol. VIII, No. 2 (Spring, 1962). See also G. Abi-Saab, *Carnegie Endowment Conference on the Newly Independent States and International Law* (Geneva: Carnegie Endowment for International Peace, 1964), pp. 29–46, for an extensive bibliography.
19. James C. Hsiung, *Ideology and Practice: The Evolution of Chinese Communism* (New York: Praeger, 1970).
20. Zbigniev K. Brzezinski, *Ideology and Power in Soviet Politics* (New York: Praeger, 1962).
21. Vidya Prakash Dutt, *China and the World: An Analysis of Communist China's Foreign Policy* (New York: Praeger, 1966), p. 27.

22. The term "philosophy of organism" was first used by Joseph Needham, *Science and Civilization in China,* 2 vols. (Cambridge University Press, England, 1954 and 1956). The concept of *ta-t'ung* first appeared in "Li Yün" (The Evolution of Propriety), *Li Chi* (Book of Rites [i.e., Propriety]). It was adopted and developed in modern times by K'ang Yu-wei, *Ta-t'ung Shu* (The Book of Great Harmony) (Shanghai: Chung-hua, 1935).
23. See *Yi-ching* (Book of Changes) for a most extensive exposition of the *yin-yang* antinomy; also discussions in Fung Yu-lan, *A History of Chinese Philosophy,* translated by Derk Bodde (Princeton, N.J.: Princeton University Press, 1952), Vol. I, pp. 32, 159, 382–84.
24. Liu Shao-ch'i, *Internationalism and Nationalism* (Peking: Foreign Language Press, 1949), p. 32, stated: "The world today has been divided into two mutually hostile camps . . . , the world imperialist camp . . . [and] the world anti-imperialist camp."
25. Li Ta, *Mao-tun-lun chieh-shuo* (Annotations on "On Contradiction" [by Mao Tse-tung]) (Peking: San-lien, 1953), p. 69, cited as containing precursory elements of dialectics, in addition to the *ying-yang* theory of the *Book of Changes:* (a) *Tao-te ching* by Laotze; (b) the *ho-t'ung-yi* thesis (combining similarities and differences) of the School of Hui Shih (a Chinese dialectician); (c) the *li-chien-pai* theory of the School of Kung-sun lung-tzu (another dialectician); and (d) Book of Motze.
26. The "cyclical" notion of historical development in traditional Chinese thinking was adduced from studies of the *Book of Changes* by Wu Nien-chung, "The Time-Space Notions in Chinese Philosophy," *Tung-fa tsa-chih* (Eastern Miscellany) (Peiping), Vol. XXXII, No. 7 (1933), pp. 101–19.
27. C. P. Fitzgerald, *The Birth of Communist China* (New York: Praeger, 1965). Cf. James P. Harrison's book review in the *New York Times Book Review*, April 24, 1966, p. 6.
28. Barnett, *Communist China and Asia, supra,* n. 1, p. 79. Also Dennis Doolin, *Territorial Claims in the Sino-Soviet Conflict: Documents and Analysis* (The Hoover Institution on War, Revolution, and Peace, Stanford University, 1965), esp. p. 43.
29. Robert S. Elegant, *Center of the World: Communism and the Mind of China* (Garden City, N.Y.: Doubleday, 1964), esp. Chapters 9 and 10.
30. Andrew L. March, "Letter to the Editor: China's Role," *New York Times,* December 30, 1965. He was commenting on the remarks made earlier by Senator George D. Aiken, calling Vietnam "an ancient enemy of China's," which had been cited by the *Times* editorial "The Irony of Vietnam," of December 23, 1965. Such allusions, March stressed, "seem to have as little immediate relevance to the present situation as the Norman Conquest has to the relations between de Gaulle and Wilson." *Id.*

31. John K. Fairbank, "Why Peking Casts Us as the Villain," *New York Times Magazine,* May 22, 1966, p. 106 *et seq.*
32. *Id.,* p. 106.

CHAPTER I

1. Cf. Percy E. Corbett, *Law in Diplomacy* (Princeton, N.J.: Princeton University Press, 1959), Chapter VIII and *passim.*
2. Bernard Ramundo, *Peaceful Coexistence: International Law in the Building of Communism* (Baltimore: Johns Hopkins Press, 1967), p. 1.
3. Charles de Visscher, *Theory and Reality in Public International Law,* translated by Percy E. Corbett (Princeton, N.J.: Princeton University Press, 1968), rev. ed., p. 89.
4. *Id.,* p. 47.
5. In the international system of ancient China, the prevailing code of conduct was *li,* which, although it subsumed the more positivist version of law known as *fa,* was essentially a broadly conceived morality code. See W. A. P. Martin, *The Lore of Cathay* (New York, 1912), p. 431; Liu Tchoan Pao, "Le Droit des gens et la Chine antique," *Les Idées* (Paris: Librairie de Jurisprudence Ancienne et Moderne, 1926), Vol. I, Part 1; Te-hsu Cheng, "International Law in Early China," *Chinese Social and Political Science Review* (Peking), Vol. XI, Nos. 1 and 2 (January and April, 1927); Chün-p'ei Hung, *Ch'un-ch'iu kuo-chi kung-fa* (Shanghai: Chung-hua shu-chü, 1939); and also Shao-chuan Leng, "Sovereignty Within the Law in the Chinese Legal System," in Harold Larson, ed., *Sovereignty Within the Law* (Duke World Rule of Law Center, 1964). For the Islamic view, see Majid Khadduri, *War and Peace in the Law of Islam* (1955); and "The Islamic System" (1959) *Proceedings* of the American Society of International Law; and Habachy's comment, *id.* Useful materials on the Indian tradition can be found in the symposium on *Indian Traditions and the Role of Law Among Nations,* held in March, 1960, at New Delhi (published by the University of Delhi); and Chacko, "India's Contribution to the Field of International Law Concepts," Hague *Recueil* (1958), p. 122 ff.
6. Oliver J. Lissitzyn, *International Law Today and Tomorrow* (Dobbs Ferry, N.Y.: Oceana, 1965), p. 3.
7. Cf. B. V. A. Röling, *International Law in an Expanded World* (Amsterdam, the Netherlands: Djambatan, 1960), pp. *xi,* 17–44.
8. In addition to the works by Lissitzyn, Röling, and Ramundo, already cited, the following are also important: Wolfgang Friedmann, *The Changing Structure of International Law* (New York: Columbia University Press, 1964); Rosalyn Higgins, *Conflict of Interests: Interna-*

tional Law in a Divided World (London: Bodley Head, 1965); Edward McWhinney, *Peaceful Coexistence and Soviet-Western International Law* (Leyden: A. W. Sythoff, 1964); "The 'New' Countries and the 'New' International Law: The United Nations' Special Conference on Friendly Relations and Cooperation Among States," 60 *AJIL* 1–33 (1966); and John N. Hazard, "Codifying Peaceful Coexistence," 55 *AJIL* 109–120 (1961); and "Coexistence Codification Reconsidered," 57 *id.* 88–97 (1963).

9. Ying T'ao, "Understanding the True Face of the Bourgeois International Law from a Few Fundamental Concepts," *KCWT,* No. 1 (January, 1960), pp. 42–51, at 43. Emphasis added.
10. *Id.*
11. See, for example, Chou Fu-lun, "An Inquiry into the Nature of Modern International Law," *Chiao-hsüeh yü yen-chiu* [Teaching and Research] (Peking), No. 3 (1958), p. 52.
12. Chu Li-ju, "Refuting the Absurdities Raised by Ch'en T'i-ch'iang Concerning International Law," *JMJP* (September 18, 1958), p. 3. Also Ho Hsi-shuang and Ma Chün, "A Criticism of the Reactionary Views of Ch'en T'i-ch'iang with Respect to International Law," *CFYC,* No. 6 (1957), pp. 35–38.
13. According to the anonymous but authoritative "Thesis on International Law" published in 1938 in the journal *Sovetskoe gosudarstvo,* edited by Andrei Vyshinsky, the Soviet Union employs those institutions of bourgeois international law which it finds acceptable (e.g., consular and diplomatic law, treaty law, etc.). Triska and Slusser, *Theory, Law and Policy of Soviet Treaties* (Stanford: Stanford University Press, 1962), pp. 16–17.
14. See, for example, Myres S. McDougal, "International Law, Power, and Policy: A Contemporary Conception," Hague *Recueil* (1953), p. 137 *et seq.;* and McDougal and Feliciano, *Law and Minimum World Public Order* (New Haven: Yale University Press, 1961), *passim.*
15. For an apt commentary on the controversy between traditional (pure legalistic) approach and McDougal's policy-science approach, especially on the point of what constitutes the values of human dignity, see Richard A. Falk, "International Legal Order: Alwyn V. Freeman vs. Myres S. McDougal," 59 *AJIL* 66–71 (1965). Cf. the views of Dean Acheson, former Secretary of State, expressed over the propriety of the Cuban quarantine, that the "survival of States is not a matter of law." (1963) *Proceedings* of the American Society of International Law, p. 13.
16. G. I. Tunkin, "The 22nd Congress of the CPSU and the Tasks of the Soviet Science of International Law," *Soviet Law and Government* Vol. I, No. 2 (White Plains, N.Y.: International Arts and Science Press, Winter, 1962/1963), pp. 19 and 21.

17. A comprehensive report on the "extensive organizational work [in legal science] carried out after 1958 under the leadership of the Chinese Communist Party" was given by Chou Hsin-min, former dean of the Shanghai College of Law and Political Science, in a Moscow address in May, 1961. English translation by JPRS: No. 4649 (1961), p. 1 *et seq.* Also, "Present State of International Law in Communist China," *China News Analysis* (Hong King), No. 203, November 1, 1957, p. 6. Two other accounts in English on the development of interest in international law studies in Communist China are available, based on a study of the establishment of research institutions, compilation of source materials, publication of monographs and periodicals, translation of foreign language writings on international law, etc.: R. Randle Edwards, "The Attitude of the People's Republic of China Toward International Law and the United Nations," *Papers on China,* Vol. 17 (December, 1963), published and distributed by the East Asian Research Center, Harvard University; and Hungdah Ch'iu, "Communist China's Attitude Toward International Law," 60 *AJIL* 245–67 (1966).
18. These writings usually appear in periodicals and journals like: *Cheng-fa yen-chiu* [Studies of Political Science and Law], published by the Chinese Society of Political and Legal Sciences, Peking; *Kuo-chi wen-t'i yen-chiu* [Studies of International Problems], published by the Institute of International Relations, Chinese Academy of Sciences, Peking; *Chiao-hsüeh yü yen-chiu* [Teaching and Research] (Peking); *Fa-hsüeh* [Jurisprudence], published by the Shangai Society of Law; *Hsueh-shu yüeh-k'an* [Academic Monthly]; *Jen-min jih-pao* [People's Daily], official organ of the Central Committee of the Chinese Communist Party; *Peking Review* (in English and other foreign languages), etc. Some are published in monograph form.
19. Lin Hsin, "A Discussion of the Post-World War II Systems of International Law," *Chiao-hsüeh yü yen-chiu* [Teaching and Research] (Peking), No. 1 (1958), pp. 34–38. Cf. discussion in Ch'iu, "Communist China's Attitude," *supra* n. 17.
20. Chou Fu-lun, "An Inquiry," *supra* n. 11.
21. Chu Ch'i-wu, "Looking at the Class Character and the Successive Nature of Law from the Viewpoint of International Law," *Kuang-ming jih-pao* [Bright Daily] (May 13, 1957); and Chou Tzu-ya, "The Nature and Character of Modern International Law," *Hsüeh-shu yüeh-k'an* [Academic Monthly], No. 7 (1957), pp. 71–72.
22. K'ung Meng, "A Critique of the Bourgeois International Law Regarding 'Subjects of International Law' and Theories of Recognition of States," *KCWT,* No. 2 (1960), at 52.
23. Ying T'ao, "A Critique of Bourgeois International Law Concerning State Sovereignty," *KCWT,* No. 3 (1960), at 47.

24. Yi Hsin, "What Is Implied in the Bourgeois International Law Concerning Intervention?" *KCWT,* No. 4 (1960), at 47; Ch'ien Szu, "A Critique of the Bourgeois International Law Concerning Individuals," *id.,* No. 5 (1960), at 49; and Hsin Wu, "A Critique of Territory in Bourgeois International Law," *id.,* No. 7 (1960), *passim.*
25. Chou Keng-sheng, *Hsien-tai ying-mei kuo-chi-fa te szu-hsiang tung-hsiang* [Trends in Contemporary Anglo-American Thinking on International Law] (Peking: World Knowledge, 1962), p. 1 and *passim.*
26. The symposium was jointly sponsored by the Shanghai Society of Law and the East China Institute of Political Science and Law. Most of the papers were later published in *Fa-hsüeh* [Jurisprudence] (Shanghai), No. 3 (1958), under the heading: "A Symposium on the Systems of Contemporary International Law." Only one participant, Keng Fu-ch'eng, supported the views of Lin Hsin that the bourgeois and the socialist systems exist at the same time necessitating two systems of law (*supra* n. 19). Keng, "Talks on Current Systems of International Law," *id.,* pp. 52–54. For the Soviet debates, see Ramundo, *Peaceful Coexistence, supra* n. 2, pp. 17–24.
27. Ying T'ao, *supra* n. 9, pp. 42–51; K'ung Meng, *supra* n. 22, p. 44; and Ch'ien Szu, *supra* n. 24, pp. 40, 41, 44, 48, and 49.
28. A. Y. Vyshinsky, *International Politics and the Problems of International Law* (n.d.), p. 480. Chou may be quoting from its Chinese translation.
29. Chou Tzu-ya, *supra* n. 21. 30. *Id.,* p. 63.
31. Ying T'ao, *supra* n. 9, p. 47.
32. Wei Liang, "Notes on International Treaties Concluded Since World War II," *Kuo-chi t'iao-yüeh chi* [International Treaty Series] (Peking), volume for 1953–1955, p. 685. Ying T'ao also spoke of the "conspiracy" by capitalist states to foist their class interests into sources of international law, *supra* n. 9, pp. 46–47.
33. Wang Yao-t'ien, *Kuo-chi mao-yi t'iao-yüeh ho hsieh-ting* [International Trade Treaties and Agreements] (Peking: Finance and Economic Publications, 1958), pp. 47–49.
34. Institute of Diplomacy, Department of International Law, *Kuo-chi kung-fa ts'an-k'ao wen'chien hsüan-chi* [A Selection of Reference Materials on Public International Law] (Peking: World Knowledge, 1958), pp. 11–12 (hereinafter cited as *Reference Materials*).
35. I have not been able to locate Chou Tzu-ya's textbook. Chou's article, *supra* n. 21, may reflect the position and views in the book.
36. Li Hao-p'ei, "Nationalization and International Law," *CFYC,* No. 2 (1958), p. 10.
37. See the section on "Sovereign Equality and National Determination," in the *Reference Materials, supra* n. 34, p. 21.

38. 60 *AJIL* 259 (1966). 39. Chou Keng-sheng, *supra* n. 25, p. 67.
40. 56 *AJIL* 490 (1962).
41. *Reference Materials, supra* n. 34, pp. 418–92.
42. Chou Tzu-ya, *supra* n. 21, p. 69. The *Reference Materials* (*supra* n. 34) lists the Soviet office of commercial attachés as the state organ for executing the Soviet Union's foreign trade. It reproduces the Soviet organic rules on commercial attachés' offices abroad, dated September 3, 1933, and the Soviet-French agreement of September 3, 1951, on reciprocal trade and the status of Soviet commercial attachés in France, pp. 351–55.
43. Triska and Slusser, *supra* n. 13, p. 29.
44. Appendix to the Sino-Mongolian Treaty of Commerce (April 26, 1961): "The legal status of the commercial attaché's office of the People's Republic of China in the Mongolian People's Republic and the legal status of the commercial attaché's office of the Mongolian People's Republic in the People's Republic of China," 13 *FKHP,* pp. 80–81.
45. Kuo Chi, "Major Measures for Preserving the Nation's Sovereignty," *CFYC,* No. 5 (1958), p. 10.
46. Fu Chu, *Kuan-yü wo-kuo ling-hai te wen-t'i* [Problems Concerning China's Territorial Sea] (Peking, 1959).
47. Ni Cheng-ao, *Kuo-chi-fa chung te szu-fa kuan-hsia wen-t'i* [Judicial Jurisdiction in International Law] (Peking: World Knowledge, 1964), e.g., pp. 30; 38, n. 4; 39, n. 2; 41, n. 4, etc.
48. *Id.,* pp. 90–91. For CPR laws concerning maritime criminal jurisdiction, see 10 *FKHP,* pp. 331–36.
49. The *stare decisis* approach in Anglo-American law is criticized in the CPR as a dangerous practice of legislation by the judiciary. Cf. Wang Yü, "A Critique of American Legal Realism: 'Court Rulings Are Law'," *CFYC,* No. 2 (1964), pp. 47–52.
50. Ni, *Kuo-chi-fa, supra* n. 47, *Preface.*
51. 10 *FKHP,* pp. 331–36. See further discussion in Chapter VI.
52. C. Wilfred Jenks, *International Law and Activities in Space* (The Hague, 1956); also 5 *International and Comparative Law Quarterly* 99–114 (1956).
53. Myres S. McDougal and Leon Lipson, "Perspectives for a Law of Outer Space," 52 *AJIL* 407–31 (1958).
54. Liu Tse-jung, "The Legal Status of Cosmic Space," *KCWT,* No. 8 (1958), pp. 44–49.
55. Mei Ju-ao, "Strip Off the Legal Garb of the Aggressor," *CFYC,* No. 2 (1955), p. 48.
56. Ch'en T'i-ch'iang, "Taiwan—A Chinese Territory," *Review of Contemporary Law* (Brussels), No. 5 (1956), pp. 38–44.
57. Wei Liang, *supra* n. 32, p. 660.

58. *TYC, passim.* Cf. Douglas M. Johnston and Hungdah Chiu, eds., *Agreements of the People's Republic of China, 1949–1967: A Calendar* (Harvard, 1968).
59. 1963 International Law Commission *Yearbook* (II), pp. 154–56.
60. Sir Gerald Fitzmaurice, "Third Report on the Law of Treaties, 1958," ILC *Yearbook* (II), p. 40; and Sir Humphrey Walkock, "Second Report on the Law of Treaties, 1963," *id.* (II), p. 52.
61. Egon Schwelb, "Some Aspects of International *Jus Cogens* as Formulated by the International Law Commission," 61 *AJIL* 946–75 (1967).
62. Chou Keng-sheng, "Peaceful Coexistence in International Law," *CFYC,* No. 6 (1955). See discussion for n. 38 in Chapter II below.
63. On Soviet "conscious deprecation" of custom, see Edward McWhinney, *Peaceful Coexistence, supra* n. 8, p. 62.
64. Quoted in Ramundo, *Peaceful Coexistence, supra* n. 2, p. 62.
65. When a CPR consul was placed under house arrest by the Indonesian Government in May, 1960, for example, the Chinese Embassy protested that Jarkarta was violating the "universally acknowledged international norms." *PR,* May 20, 1960, p. 35. In 1964 certain CPR personnel were "persecuted" by the new military junta that had come to power by *coup d'etat.* The official *People's Daily* carried an article, written by the authoritative Chou Keng-sheng, condemning the act as a violation of "international custom." *JMJP,* April 24, 1964. Similar invocation of international custom and practice was made in CPR protests against Indonesia invasions of the rights of Chinese consular and embassy premises. *PR,* November 12, 1965, p. 24; *id.,* October 29, 1965, p. 13. See further discussion in Chapter IX below.
66. Article 2; text in *TYC,* p. 7. English translation in PR, June 16, 1961, p. 11. Emphasis added.

CHAPTER II

1. See Chapter I above, text at reference for nn. 9, 11, 20–25, and 59–66.
2. *Infra* n. 38. In the Soviet view current international law is composed of three types of principles and norms: (a) reactionary, bourgeois principles which have resisted the progressive forces unleashed by the Great October Revolution; (b) bourgeois democratic principles which have become more progressive under the influence of these forces; and (c) new progressive principles introduced by the forces of socialism. G. I. Tunkin, "The Twenty-Second Congress of the CPSU and the Tasks of the Soviet Science of International Law," *Soviet Law and Government* Vol. I, No. 2 (White Plains, N.Y.: International Arts and Science Press, Winter,

1962/63), pp. 23 and 24. See also Bernard Ramundo, *Peaceful Co-existence* (Baltimore: Johns Hopkins Press, 1967), p. 23.

3. *Infra* nn. 39–42; and Ying T'ao, "Understanding the True Face of the Bourgeois International Law from a Few Fundamental Concepts," *KCWT*, No. 1 (January, 1960), at 43.
4. Chou Keng-sheng, *Hsien-tai ying-mei kuo-chi-fa te szu-hsiang tung-hsiang* [Trends in Contemporary Anglo-American Thinking on International Law] (Peking: World Knowledge, 1962), pp. 23–43; also cf. Chapter IV below.
5. Leon Lipson, "Peaceful Coexistence," in Hans W. Baade, ed., *The Soviet Impact on International Law* (Dobbs Ferry N.Y.: Oceana, 1965), at 28.
6. The Five Principles were laid out in the preamble of the agreement. See 299 *UNTS* 70.
7. Text included in *Kuo-chi kung-fa ts'an-k'ao wen-chien hsüan-chi* [Selection of Reference Materials on Public International Law], pp. 2–3; English text in G. V. Ambekar and V. D. Divekar, eds., *Documents on China's Relations with South and Southeast Asia (1949–1962)* (Bombay, India: Allied Publishers, 1964), pp. 7–9.
8. 1 *TWKH* 4 (1949–1950).
9. English text in Theodore Ch'en, ed., *The Chinese Communist Regime* (New York: Praeger, 1967), at 45.
10. Preamble of the CPR Constitution, adopted in 1954, English text in *id.*, at 76.
11. A. Doak Barnett, *Communist China and Asia* (New York: Harper, 1960), pp. 97–103; and Kenneth Young, *Negotiating with the Chinese Communists* (New York: MacGraw-Hill, 1968), pp. 23–44.
12. Cf. Fang Ch'ao, "Great Victories in China's Diplomacy over the Past Decade," 6 KCWT 1–12, esp. 4 (1959).
13. 3 *TWKH* at 138 and 158 (1954–1955).
14. *Id.*, p. 142. See also *JMJP*, July 2, 1954; and *Chung-hua jen-min kung-huo-kuo hsien-fa hsüeh-hsi ts'an-k'ao tzu-liao* [Reference Materials for the Study of the CPR Constitution] (Peking, 1957), Vol. I, pp. 143–48.
15. Harold C. Hinton, *Communist China in World Politics* (Boston: Houghton Mifflin, 1966), pp. 258–64.
16. Cf. Tang Tsou and Morton Halperin, "Mao Tse-tung's Revolutionary Strategy and Peking's International Behavior," *American Political Science Review*, Vol. LIX, No. 1 (March, 1965), pp. 80–99.
17. *People's China* (Peking), No. 10 (May 16, 1955), Supplement; and *New York Times*, April 24, 1955.
18. Kenneth Young, *supra* n. 10, p. 44 ff.
19. Chacko, "Peaceful Coexistence as a Doctrine of International Affairs," 4 *Indian Yearbook of International Affairs* (1955), at 35. See also

George Kahin, *The Asian-African Conference* (Cornell, 1956), pp. 18 ff.

20. Chou En-lai's address to the Political Committee of the Bandung Conference, April 23, 1955; English text in Ambekar and Divekar, *Documents, supra* n. 7, pp. 19–21. Cf. George Kahin, *id.*
21. Text in Ambekar and Divekar, *Documents, supra* n. 7, at 29.
22. For a typical Chinese Communist condemnation of the SEATO, see Peking's statement of March 10, 1958, 5 *TWKH* 76 (1958), in which Peking urged that Afro-Asian states "should abide by commitments made at the Afro-Asian Conference at Bandung not to capitulate to the U.S. interference in the internal affairs of Afro-Asian countries."
23. Sino-Pakistan Boundary Agreement (March 2, 1963), Chinese text in 12 *TYC* 64; English translation in *PR,* March 15, 1963, p. 67. Emphasis added.
24. 3 *TWKH* 332–333 (1954–1955). 25. 4 *id.* 48–49 (1955–1956).
26. Li P'ing, "A Further Development of the Five Principles of Peaceful Coexistence," *CFYC,* No. 1 (1960), pp. 35–36.
27. J. J. G. Syatauw, *Some Newly Established Asian States and the Development of International Law* (The Hague: Martinus Nijhoff, 1961), at 216.
28. *New York Times,* June 2, 1956. 29. Hinton, *supra* n. 15, p. 264.
30. 4 *TWKH* 446 and 447 (1955–1956). Chou was reporting to the Second Session of the Second National Committee of the Chinese People's Political Consultative Conference.
31. *Id.* 32. *Id.*, pp. 186–91.
33. Liu's full report appears in English translation in *Eighth National Congress of the Communist Party of China* (Peking: FLP, 1956), Vol. I, pp. 13–111. The particular section (Sec. 5) dealing with foreign affairs is included in 4 *TWKH* 474–480 (1956–1957).
34. 4 *TWKH* 490. 35. *JMJP,* November 7, 1957.
36. Mao, *On People's Democratic Dictatorship* (1949).
37. Relevant parts of Mao's speech are included in 4 *TWKH* 303. Full text appears in *JMJP,* June 19, 1957.
38. Chou Keng-sheng, "Peaceful Coexistence in International Law," *CFYC,* No. 6 (1955), pp. 37–41. Emphasis added.
39. Mao To, "The Important Achievements of the Conference of Afro-Asian Jurists," *CFYC,* No. 2 (1958), pp. 3–9. (The said conference met in Damascus, January 7–11, 1957.) See also Fang Ch'ao, *supra* n. 12, p. 4; and Ying T'ao, in *KCWT,* No. 3 (1960), at 47, in which he claimed that the Five Principles, the essence of "modern international law," represented the "aspirations of the great majority of the peoples of the world."
40 Mao To, *id.*, at 8. 41. *Id.*, at 5. 42. *Id.*
43. For CPR belief that "modern" international law is on the side of the so-

cialist states and that "bourgeois" international law is on its way out, see, among others, K'ung Meng, "A Critique of the Bourgeois International Law Regarding the 'Subjects of International Law' and Theories of Recognition of States," *KCWT,* No. 2 (1960), *passim.*

44. Ramundo, *Peaceful Coexistence, supra* n. 2, p. 13. Emphasis added.
45. "Peaceful Coexistence—Two Diametrically Opposed Policies: Comment on the Open Letter of the Central Committee of the Communist Party of the Soviet Union (VI)," by the editorial departments of the *JMJP* and *HC,* December 12, 1963. Text in English published by the FLP; original Chinese text in *JMJP,* November 19, 1963, and *HC,* No. 22 (1963), pp. 1–18.
46. *Id.,* pp. 15–16. Emphasis added.
47. *Id.* at 16.
48. "Chinese Association of Political Science and Law Held Its Fourth General Meeting," *CFYC,* No. 4 (1964), at 28. Emphasis added.
49. Ying T'ao, "A Critique of the Bourgeois International Law on State Sovereignty," *KCWT,* No. 3 (1960), at 47.
50. See this point elaborated in Chapter IV below.
51. Mao's statement to Japanese visitors, January 27, 1964, published in both Chinese and English in Mao Tse-tung, *Ch'uan shih-chieh jen-min t'uan-chieh ch'i-lai ta-pai mei-kuo ch'in-lüeh-che chi ch'i yi-ch'ieh tsou-kou* [The World's People Unite to Defeat the American Aggressor and His Lackeys] (Peking: *Shang-wu,* 1965), at 32.
52. In his talks with a French delegation in 1964, Mao stated: "France, Germany, Italy, Britain and—if she can cease to be America's agent—Japan and ourselves [China]—that is the *third force.*" *L'Humanité* (Paris), February 21, 1964. See James C. Hsiung, "China's Foreign Policy: The Interplay of Ideology, Practice Interests, and Polemics," in William Richardson, ed., *China Today (Maryknoll, N. Y.: Maryknoll Publications, 1969), at 22.*
53. Cf. Lipson, "Peaceful Coexistence", *supra* n. 5, pp. 30–32.

CHAPTER III

1. See Chapter II above, text for nn. 38 and 39; and also Chapter I above, text for n. 62.
2. G. I. Tunkin, "The 22nd Congress of the CPSU and the Tasks of the Soviet Science of International law," *Soviet Law and Government* Vol. 1, No. 2 (White Plains, N. Y.: International Arts and Science Press, Winter, 1962/63), at 19. See also Bernard Ramundo, *The Socialist Theory of International Law* (Washington, D.C.: George Washington University, Institute for Sino-Soviet Studies, 1964), p. 25.
3. G. I. Tunkin, "Sorok Let Sosushchestvovania i Mezhdunarodnoe Pravo"

[Forty Years of Coexistence and International Law], in *Sovetskii Ezhegodnik Mezhdunarodnovo Pravo, 1958* The Soviet Yearbook of International Law, 1958], at 44; cited in Ramundo, *id.*, p. 19.

4. Tunkin, *id.*, at 47; cited in Ramundo, *id.* 5. *Id.*, p. 20.
6. Oliver J. Lissitzyn, *International Law Today and Tomorrow* (Dobbs Ferry, N.Y.: Oceana, 1966), p. 49.
7. G. I. Tunkin, *Voprosy Teorii Mezhdunarodnovo Prave* [Problems of the Theory of International Law] (Moscow: State Publishing House of Legal Literature, 1962); and F. I. Kozhevnikov, ed., *Mezhdunarodnoe Pravo* [International Law] (Moscow: Publishing House "International Relations," 1964), cited in Bernard A. Ramundo, *Peaceful Coexistence* (Baltimore: Johns Hopkins Press, 1964), p. 33, n. 102.
8. V. M. Shurshalov, "Mezhdunarodno, pravovye Printsipy Sotrudnichestva Sotsialisticheskikh Cosudarstv" [International Legal Principles of the Collaboration of Socialist States], *SGIP,* No. 7 (1962), cited in Ramundo, *Peaceful Coexistence, ibid.*, p. 35, n. 112.
9. The "capitalist" states used here include the "imperialists." See Tunkin, *Voprosy Teorii, supra* n. 7, at 316; Ramundo, *id.*, p. 31.
10. John N. Hazard, "Legal Research on 'Peaceful Coexistence,' " 51 *AJIL* 63–71 (1957); "Codifying Peaceful Coexistence," 55 *AJIL* 109–120 (1961); and "Coexistence Codification Reconsidered," 57 *AJIL* 88–97 (1963). See also Edward McWhinney, *Peaceful Coexistence and Soviet-Western International Law* (Leyden: A. W. Sythoff, 1964). For the Chinese view regarding *jus cogens,* see Chapter I above, n. 62; and Chapter II above, nn. 38 and 39.
11. D. B. Levin and G. P. Kaliuzhnaia, eds., *Mezhdunarodnoe Pravo* [International Law] (Moscow: Publishing House "Legal Literature," 1964), pp. 76 and 77, cited in Ramundo, *Peaceful Coexistence, supra* n. 7, p. 35, n. 111.
12. Tunkin, *Voprosy Teorii, supra* n. 7, at 64; and Shurshalov, "Mezhdunarodno," *supra* n. 8, at 98 and 100; Ramundo, *id., supra* n. 7, p. 34, n. 105, and p. 35, n. 113.
13. Shurshalov, "Mezhdunarodno," *supra* n. 8, at 96 and 103.
14. See *New York Times,* June 19, 1969, p. 6.
15. This was an important part of the polemic exchanges between the CCP and the CPSU, in 1963. See the discussion in Chapter II above, nn. 4–50; and also *infra* nn. 64–65.
16. James C. Hsiung, "Communist China's Foreign Policy: The Interplay of Ideology, Practical Interests, and Polemics," in William J. Richardson, ed., *China Today* (Maryknoll, N. Y.: Maryknoll Publications, 1969), pp. 20–55.
17. Mao's *in-camera* speech made to the Tenth Plenum of the Eighth Central Committee of the CCP, at Chungnanhai in Peking, on September 28, 1962, a summary of which was published in *Mainichi shimbun*

(Tokyo), on the evening of March 9, 1967. The *Mainichi* dispatch was sent from Peking by its correspondent Takada, who obtained the information from a wall poster (tatzupao) which appeared in Peking the previous day. The dispatch was reproduced in *Chinese Law and Government* Vol. I, No. 1 (White Plains, N. Y.: International Arts and Science Press, Spring, 1968), pp. 4–6. For a discussion of the striking parallels between the CPR and the Yugoslavia, see Zbiniew Brzezinski, *The Soviet Bloc,* rev. ed. (Harvard, 1967), pp. 130 and 133.

18. Hsiung, "Communist China's Foreign Policy," *supra* n. 16; also Allen S. Whiting, *China Crosses the Yalu* (New York: Macmillan, 1960), pp. 46, 159, and *passim.*
19. Following the Sino-Soviet talks in February, 1950, for instance, the former "Sinkiang Nationality Army" was reorganized under Saifudin as part of the CPR's People's Liberation Army (PLA). *JMJP,* February 27, 1950.
20. *JMJP,* May 7, 1950.
21. *Id.,* February 28, 1954.
22. Mao's demand, however, remained unreported until 1964. See *Seikai Shuho* (Tokyo), August 11, 1964; *Pravda,* September 2, 1964; *Current Digest of Soviet Press* (CDSP), No. 34 (1964), pp. 6–7; and also George Ginsburgs and Carl Pinkele, *The Genesis of the Territorial Issue in the Sino-Soviet Dialogue* (American Society of International Law, 1968), mimeo., p. 7.
23. Liu Pei-hua, *Chung-kuo chin-tai shih* [China's Modern History] (Peking, 1954). One such map was reproduced in Dennis Doolin, *Territorial Claims in Sino-Soviet Conflict: Documents and Analysis* (Stanford: Stanford University, Hoover Institution, 1965), at 16.
24. Texts of the Mao-Khrushchev agreements in 3 *TWKH* 174–182 (1954).
25. 3 *TYC* 55.
26. *TWKH* 177.
27. *Id.,* at 176. In Contrast to the Mao-Khrushchev communiqué, Chou En-lai, speaking at an official reception at the Soviet Embassy, praised the agreements as monuments to the concerns and spirit of "internationalism." It is not clear what "internationalism" rather than "proletarian internationalism" really meant. *Id.,* at 184.
28. "Proletarian internationalism" was codified in Soviet bilateral agreements with the East European "people's democracies" in the wake of the 1956 unrest. In these cases, the CPR even lent its support. But, CPR support of Soviet primacy under PI applied only to Soviet relations with East European "people's democracies," but not to Sino-Soviet relations. See *infra* n. 46.
29. The Treaty of Warsaw, concluded in 1955, is still conceived in the "traditional" framework of bloc solidarity and Soviet primacy. In its preamble, the treaty refers to a desire further to promote and develop "friendship, cooperation, and mutual assistance, in accordance with the principles of respect for the independence and sovereignty of states and

of non-interference in their internal affairs." This recalls the language used in Soviet bilateral treaties with East European Communist states concluded during the Stalinist era. See Brzezinski, *supra* n. 17, p. 109. However, a contrary view alleging that the Warsaw Treaty is an instrument of the principles of peaceful coexistence is held by Kazimierz Grzybowski, *The Socialist Commonwealth of Nations: Organizations and Institutions* (New Haven, Conn.: Yale University Press, 1964), pp. 198–99.

30. Wei Liang, "Notes on International Treaties Concluded Since World War II," *Kuo-chi t'iao-yüeh chi* [International Treaties Series] (Peking), Volume for 1953–1955, at 685.
31. *CDSP,* VIII, 4 (1956).
32. *Pravda,* October 31, 1956; *New York Times,* same date.
33. *Id.*
34. 4 *TWKH* 149 (1956–1957). An English translation by the American Consulate-General in Hong Kong is in *SCMP,* No. 1405 (November 6, 1956).
35. *Id.,* at 150.
36. Mao Tse-tung, "In Memory of Dr. Sun Yat-sen," cited in Fang Ch'ao, "Great Victories in China's Diplomacy over the Past Decade," *KCWT,* No. 6 (1959), at 6. Mao again picked up the danger of "big-nation chauvinism" in his "More on the Historical Experience of the Dictatorship of the Proletariat," *JMJP,* December 29, 1956.
37. Brzezinski, *supra* n. 17, pp. 279 and 282–83.
38. CPR-Polish-Soviet agreement of January 11, 1957, in 4 *TWKH* 218–19; CPR-Polish agreement of January 16, 1957, *id.,* pp. 223–26; CPR-Soviet agreement of January 18, 1957, *id.,* pp. 245–50; and CPR-East German news bulletin of January 8, 1957, *id.,* pp. 217–18.
39. See, for example, the CPR-Polish agreement of January 16, 1957, 4 *TWKH* 223–26. The same was repeated in the CPR-Bulgarian agreement of October 11, 1957, *id.,* at 390. In a report to the Third Plenary Session of the Second National Committee of the Chinese People's Political Consultative Conference, on March 5, 1957, Premier Chou En-lai reaffirmed the same principles, *id.,* at 276–78.
40. *Id.,* at 250.
41. Letter of CPSU CC to CCP CC, June 15, 1964; *JMJP,* February 4, 1964.
42. *Le Monde,* December 19, 1957; John Gittings, *Survey of the Sino-Soviet Dispute, 1963–1967* (New York: Oxford University Press, 1968), p. 74.
43. The Chinese claimed in 1963 that the Soviet Union in 1957 had promised to supply such samples but never fulfilled its promise. Moscow never denied it. See Suslov's report to the CPSU CC, in February 1964, *Pravda,* April 3, 1964, quoted in Vernon V. Aspaturian, "The Soviet Union and International Communism," in Roy C. Macridis, ed., *For-*

eign Policy in World Politics (Englewood Cliffs, N. J.: Prentice-Hall, 1967), at 232.

44. Gittings, *Survey, supra* n. 42, pp. 103 ff.
45. Editorial departments of *People's Daily* and *Red Flag,* "The Origin and Development Between the Leadership of the CPSU and Ourselves—Comment on the Open Letter of the CC of the CPSU," *JMJP,* September 6, 1963.
46. 5 *TWKH* 146 (1958). Emphasis added.
47. "Declaration of the Meeting of Communist and Workers' Parties of Socialist Countries, Moscow, November 16, 1957," reproduced in Gittings, *Survey, supra* n. 42, pp. 310 ff.
48. This was confirmed in 1963, *PR,* September 13, 1963, pp. 6–23. The Soviet Union later charged that the Chinese in 1958 deliberately provoked the Taiwan crisis in an attempt to force a Soviet-United States confrontation. See Harrison E. Salisbury, "The Urgent Question That Dominates the Asian Heartland Today Is: Will There Be War Between Russia and China?," *New York Times Magazine,* July 27, 1969, at 56.
49. *PR,* September 13, 1963.
50. *Current Background* (Hong Kong: American Consulate-General), No. 851; David A. Charles, "The Dismissal of Marshall P'eng Te-huai," *China Quarterly,* No. 8 (October-December, 1961), at 67; William Dorrill, *Power, Policy and Ideology in the Making of China's 'Cultural Revolution'* (Santa Monica, Calif., RAND Corp., 1968); and John Gittings, *The Role of the Chinese Army* (New York: Oxford University Press, 1967), p. 226.
51. Aspaturian, "The Soviet Union," *supra* n. 43, p. 235.
52. Cf. Donald S. Zagoria, *The Sino-Soviet Conflict: 1956–61* (Princeton, N. J.: Princeton University Press, 1962), p. 366.
53. *Kommunist,* No. 1 (January, 1961), p. 34.
54. Cf. the comment by the Italian Communist leader, Luigi Longo, in *L'Unita,* December 23, 1961.
55. "Dangerous Seat of Tension in Asia," *Pravda,* September 19, 1965.
56. *JMJP,* September 1, 1963; *PR,* September 6, 1963.
57. *Whence the Differences? A Reply to Commrade Thorez and Other Comrades* (Peking, FLP, 1963), pp. 11–12.
58. *JMJP,* November 2, 1963.
59. *PR,* September 13, 1963.
60. *Pravda,* September 21, 1963.
61. Gittings, *Survey, supra* n. 42, pp. 158 ff.
62. "Statement by the Spokesman of the Chinese Government—A Comment on the Soviet Government Statement of August 3" (August 15, 1963), *PR,* August 16, 1963.
63. "Statement of the CPR Government," in *JMJP,* July 31, 1963; and *PR,* August 2, 1963.
64. "CCP CC Comment on the Letter of March 30, 1963, from the CPSU

CC" (June 14, 1963), reproduced in *kuan-yü kuo-chi kung-ch'an chu-yi yün-tung tsung-lu-hsien te chien-yi ho yu-kuan wen-chien* [Comments on the General Line of the International Communist Movement and Related Documents] (Peking: People's Publishing House, 1963), at 33.

65. Editorial departments of *Red Flag* and *People's Daily,* "Peaceful Coexistence—Two Diametrically Opposed Policies: Comment on the Open Letter of the Central Committee of the CPSU (VI)" (December 12, 1963), English text by FLP, 1963. Original Chinese text in *JMJP,* November 19, 1963, and *HC,* No. 22 (1963), pp. 1–18. See also discussion in the last section of Chapter II above.
66. *Id.*
67. "A Great Victory of Leninism," *HC,* No. 4 (1965); *PR,* May 7, 1965.
68. "What Shastri's Soviet Trip Reveals," *JMJP,* May 27, 1965; *PR,* June 4, 1965. CPR accusations of Soviet-Indian complicity were repeated during the Indo-Pakistan war of August-September, 1965. *JMJP,* September 18, 1965; *PR,* September 24, 1965.
69. "Unity of Action Is an Imperative Requirement of the Anti-Imperialist Struggle," *Pravda,* June 20, 1965.
70. "Refutation of the New Leaders of the CPSU on 'United Action'," *JMJP,* November 11, 1965; *PR,* November 12, 1965.
71. *Id.*
72. Cf. N. A. Ushakov and E. P. Meleshko, "Novyi Uchebnyi Kurs Mezhdunarodnovo Prava" [The New Text on International Law], *SGIP,* No. 10 (1964), pp. 153–55; Ramundo, *Peaceful Coexistence, supra* n. 7, p. 15, n. 37.
73. Cf. G. Starushenko, "Fiction and Truth About Wars of Liberation," tr. from *Kommunist* (August, 1968), in *CDSP,* XVII, 34, p. 5 ff.
74. Aspaturian, "The Soviet Union," *supra* n. 43, p. 242.
75. Red Guard publications in 1966–1967 accused P'eng Te-huai of "secret dealings" with Khrushchev before his removal from office in 1959. Translations of some of the Red Guard charges can be found in *Current Background* No. 851. A *Red Flag* editorial claimed that P'eng Te-huai had opposed Mao's policies at the Lushan Plenum in 1959 "with the support and shelter of the bourgeois headquarters headed by China's Khrushchev [Liu Shao-ch'i]." *PR,* August 18, 1967. In a remark attributed to Liu Shao-ch'i in 1961—but not made known until 1967—Liu allegedly said in reference to the disgraced "rightists," including P'eng, who had been Minister of Defense and a ranking member of the CCP Poliburo until removed in 1959, that "those who held similar views as P'eng Te-huai should be rehabilitated, so long as no implications with any foreign country were involved." Liu's remark at an "expanded work conference" in 1961 was quoted in *Chingkang Mountain,* a Red Guard bulletin, February 8, 1967; reprinted in *Liu chu-hsi yü-lu* [Quo-

tations from Chairman Liu], compiled and published by the Tzu-lien Publishers, Hong Kong, 1967, at 110. Thus, the possible link between P'eng's permanent disgrace and his "dealings" with Soviet leaders may be substantiated.

76. *JMJP,* August 23, 1968; *New York Times,* August 23, 1968, p. 1.
77. *PR,* May 30, 1969, p. 13; and *HC,* No. 5 (1969). For reports on Peking's preparation for a Soviet invasion, see *New York Times,* July 6, 1969, p. 2; and Salisbury, "The Urgent Question," *supra* n. 48.
78. Communiqué of the 12th Plenum of the Eighth Central Committee of the CCP (October 31, 1968), *HC,* No. 5 (1968), at 32.
79. *PR,* April 30, 1968, at 33. 80. *Id.,* at 34. 81. *Id.*
82. *Id.,* at 32. 83. *Pr,* July 4, 1969, p. 24.
84. *New York Times,* November 27, 1968, p. 1.
85. Document adopted by the World Conference of Communist Parties, *New York Times,* June 19, 1969, p. 6.

CHAPTER IV

1. On this issue the CPR's position resembles the Soviet doctrine of the illimitability of sovereignty held in the initial years of the Soviet Union. Taracouzio, *The Soviet Union and International Law* (New York: Macmillan, 1935), pp. 26–27. For comparisons with the Soviet views on international law, see: B. A. Ramundo, *The Socialist Theory of International Law* (Washington: George Washington University, Institute for Sino-Soviet Studies, Series No. 1, January, 1964); Tunkin, "Legal Principles of Coexistence," 3 Hague *Recueil* (1958); Academy of Sciences of the USSR, Institute of State and Law, *International Law* (Moscow: Foreign Languages Publishing House [1961]; and Oliver J. Lissitzyn, *International Law Today and Tomorrow* (Dobbs Ferry, N. Y.: Oceana, 1965).
2. Yang Hsin and Ch'en Chien, "Expose and Criticize the Absurd Theories of the Imperialists Concerning the Question of State Sovereignty," *CFYC,* No. 4 (1964), at 6.
3. Ying T'ao, "A Critique of the Bourgeois International Law on the Question of State Sovereignty," *KCWT,* No. 3 (1960), at 48.
4. *Id.,* p. 52; Shao Chin-fu, "The Absurdity of the 'Two Chinas [Idea]' and International Law," *id.,* No. 2 (1959), pp. 7–17.
5. Yi Hsin, "What Is Implied in the Bourgeoise International Law Concerning Intervention," *KCWT,* No. 4 (1960), at 49. Peking attacked the United States landing of marines in the Dominican Republic "for the protection of American nationals" in 1965 as an inexcusable act of

intervention. See "The Johnson Administration Is the Murderer of the Independence and Sovereignty of Other Countries," *JMJP,* May 3, 1965.

6. Yi Hsin, *id.,* at 50.
7. *Id.,* p. 51; Ch'ien Szu, "A Critique of Bourgeois International Law Concerning Individuals," *id.,* No. 5 (1960), pp. 42, 43; and Chou Keng-sheng, "The United Nations Intervention over the 'Tibet Question' Is Illegal," *CFYC,* No. 6 (1959), in which Chou cites Article 2 (7) of the United Nations Charter and a CPR government statement on the issue. In point of fact, the "Tibet Question" was never brought to the General Assembly by the United States, but by El Salvador in 1950 (A/1534, November 18, 1950) and by Ireland and Malaya in 1959 (A/4234, September 29, 1959). But, representatives of Hungary and the Soviet Union alleged that Ireland and Malaya were acting merely as puppets of the United States. Sidney D. Baily, *The General Assembly of the United Nations* (New York: Praeger, 1960), p. 240.
8. Yang and Ch'en, "Expose and Criticize the Absurd Theories," *supra* n. 2, p. 6.
9. *Id.,* pp. 7–8.
10. Mao's interview was published in *Sekai Shuho* (Tokyo), August 11, 1964; excerpts reproduced in Dennis J. Doolin, *Territorial Claims in the Sino-Soviet Conflict* (Stanford University, Hoover Institution, 1965), p. 43. Because of these and other similar remarks by Mao and the reported Sino-Soviet talks (Doolin, *id.,* p. 34; Pravda editorial, September 2, 1967), I tend to believe that the CPR reserves to herself the right to denounce the 1936 treaty signed between the Soviet Union and Outer Mongolia, which was then a dependency of China under the Nationalist government. Pending future developments in the relative power configuration in the area, the Chinese attitude concerning the legal validity of the treaty may be characterized as holding its denunciation in abeyance, rather than outright denunciation.
11. See Chapter III above, text for n. 74. The CPR also expressed its empathy for the Vietnamese in their struggle against U.S. "imperialists," *JMJP,* March 29, 1965.
12. Academy of Sciences of the USSR, *International Law, supra.* n. 1, p. 97.
13. "Theory of International Dictatorship Is a Gangster Theory of Social-Imperialism," *HC,* No. 5 (1969); *PR,* May 16, 1969, pp. 4–5.
14. *New York Times,* June 10, 1969. The CPR was reported to expect war with the Soviet Union, *id.,* July 6, 1969, p. 2.
15. Yang and Ch'en, "Expose and Criticize the Absurd Theories," *supra* n. 2, at 9.
16. The European Coal and Steel Community's court system and the Euro-

pean Court of Human Rights have already initiated innovations in this direction.

17. Yang and Ch'en, *id.;* also Chou Keng-sheng, *Hsien-tai ying-mei kuo-chi-fa te szu-hsiang* [Trends in Contemporary Anglo-American Thinking on International Law] (Peking: World Knowledge, 1962), pp. 34 and 68. For a critique of the American "universalism" see Chiang Yang, "The Reactionary Thought of 'Universalism' in American Jurisprudence," *JMJP,* December 17, 1963.
18. 260 *UNTS* 442 (1957).
19. In Chu Hsi, *T'ung-chien kang-mu* [Outline of the T'ung-chien Annals], *chüan* 8, p. 17B, a commentary was entered for the passage: "The Red Brow routed Lien-tan and 'chu' [slew] him." "The word 'chu,' " said the commentary, "is used here because anyone under the sun is entitled to execute a *luan-ch'en tse-tzu* [i.e., a rebel or offender of the prevailing public order]." The dictum is known in Chinese as *luan-ch'en tse-tzu jen-jen te erh chu chih.* The Harvard Research "Draft Convention on Jurisdiction with Respect to Crime" (1935) gives the Western view on *delicta juris gentium.*
20. "Letter of Acting Legal Adviser, Jack B. Tate, to Department of Justice, May 19, 1952," Department of State, *Bulletin,* Vol. XXVI (1952), p. 984. In advising the change from previous U.S. position which accepted the doctrine of absolute sovereign immunity, the Tate letter stated: ". . . it will hereafter be the Department's policy to follow the restrictive theory of sovereign immunity in the consideration of requests of foreign governments for a grant of sovereign immunity." For comment on the Tate letter, see William Bishop, "New United States Policy Limiting Sovereign Immunity," 47 *AJIL* 93 (1953).
21. Chou Keng-sheng, *supra* n. 17, pp. 54–64.
22. In his "proposed speech" (but not delivered) to the Political Committee of the U.N. General Assembly, scheduled for November 28, 1950, Wu Hsiu-ch'üan, the CPR delegate, stated: "The Charter of the United Nations clearly stipulates that no justification whatsoever may be used as an excuse for aggression." *China Accuses* (Peking: FLP, 1951), p. 77. On CPR views about the "imperialist" domination of the United Nations, see Wan Chia-chün, *Lien-ho-kuo shih shen-mo* [What Is the United Nations?], Chapter 2; and "The Crimes of the American Imperialists in Manipulating the United Nations," *JMJP,* January 9, 1965. In a cablegram dated December 17, 1954, sent to the secretary-general, the CPR government stated: "The Ninth Session of the United Nations General Assembly [was] under the domination of the United States and its allies. . . ." U.N. Doc. A/2889.
23. Chou Keng-sheng, *Hsien-tai ying-mei, supra* n. 17, p. 44. For a critique of the "imperialist abuses" of the United Nations, see "The United Na-

tions Must be Reorganized," *JMJP,* June 26, 1966; and "Justice Cannot Be Upheld in the U.N.," *PR,* No. 4 (January 22, 1965), p. 13, and "The U.N. Cannot Solve Questions, An Example," *PR, id.,* p. 14. In his reply to a letter from Bertrand Russell, Premier Chou En-lai accused the United States of "aggression" in the Congo. By that Chou meant that the entire UNOC operations were American "aggression" carried out in the name of the U.N., *id.*

24. Yang and Ch'en, "Expose and Criticize the Absurd Theories," *supra* n. 2, at 10.
25. Chou Keng-sheng, *Hsien-tai ying-mei, supra* n. 17, p. 19. For a systematic study of the development of the theory concerning the "international personality" possessed by the United Nations since the *Reparations* case, see Guenter Weissberg, *The International Status of the United Nations* (Dobbs Ferry, N.Y.: Oceana, 1961).
26. *Shih-chieh chih-shih shou-ts'e* [World Knowledge Handbook] (Peking), 1954 edition, p. 815; and 1958 edition, p. 837. Also Chou Keng-sheng, *id.,* p. 53.
27. Wolfgang Friedmann, *The Changing Structure of International Law* (New York: Columbia University Press, 1964), p. 35.
28. Cf. generally Fred R. von der Mehden, *Politics of the Developing Nations* (Englewood Cliffs, N.J.: Prentice-Hall, 1964) and Paul Sigmund, ed., *Ideologies of the Developing Nations* (New York: Praeger, 1963).
29. See Chapters II and III above for a discussion of the CPR's views on PCX; also Yang and Ch'en, *supra* n. 2, p. 6.
30. In the textbook *Kuo-chi kung-fa ts'an-k'ao wen-chien* [Reference Materials on International Law], various documents issued by the Soviet Union in the initial years of its existence on self-determination are reproduced verbatim, including the declarations of November 2 and November 20, 1917, and Soviet statement of September 24, 1941, at the Allied meeting in London. In the same section on "Sovereign Equality and the Right of National Self-Determination," the Chinese textbook also reproduces the General Assembly resolution of December 16, 1952, on national self-determination, and the G. A. resolution of December 21, 1952, on the right to the exploitation of natural wealth and resources of each sovereign state.
31. We shall deal with the question of diplomatic recognition in CPR doctrine and practice in Chapter XI below.
32. Chou En-lai's speech at the May 12, 1954, meeting of the Geneva Conference on Indochina, in *Jih-nei-wa hui-yi wen-chien hui-pien* [Collection of Documents from the Geneva Conference] (Peking: World Knowledge, 1954), pp. 163–69, at 168.
33. Yang and Ch'en, "Expose and Criticize the Absurd Theories," *supra* n. 2, p. 6.
34. 4 *TWKH* 446 ff.

35. Chou Tzu-ya, "The Nature and Character of Modern International Law," *Hsüeh-hsi yüeh-k'an* [Academic Monthly], No. 7 (1957), p. 69.
36. Harold C. Hinton, *Communist China in World Politics* (Boston: Houghton Mifflin, 1966), p. 148.
37. CPR Government Statement of December 19, 1961 (NCNA); reproduced in Ambekar and Divekar, *Documents on China's Relations with South and Southeast Asia: 1949–1962* (Bombay: Allied, 1964), at 71.
38. *SCMP,* No. 3660, p. 28; and No. 3876, p. 32; and NCNA (Peking), December 1, 1967 and December 4, 1967.
39. Mao To, "The Great Achievements of Afro-Asian Jurists' Conference," *CFYC,* No. 2 (1958), at 6. D. W. Bowett made a most meaningful evaluation of the dangers posed by such trends toward intervention in the service of "self-determination," American Society of International Law, 1966 *Proceedings* 129–35. An incisive criticism of the political hollowness of the nebulous "self-determination" is given by Rupert Emerson, "Self-Determination Revisited in the Era of Decolonization," *Occasional Papers on International Affairs* (Cambridge, Mass.: Harvard Center of International Affairs), No. 9 (1964).
40. At its Mexico City Conference in 1964, the U.N. Special Committee on Principles of International Law Concerning Friendly Relations and Cooperation among States heard exuberant pronouncements in support of intervention on behalf of "self-determination." Cf. Edward McWhinney, "The 'New' Countries and the 'New' International Law," 60 *AJIL* 1-33 (1966).
41. For CPR government pronouncements on the right to self-determination enjoyed by the "oppressed" and colonial peoples, see Mao-Khrushchev joint communiqué of August 3, 1958, in 5 *TWKH* 146 (1958); statements concerning Algerian independence movement, 5 *id.* 187 (1958), and 9 *id.* 309, and 359 (1962); message on the independence of Guinea, 5 *id.* 196 (1958); and message on the independence of the Republic of South Yemen sent by Chou En-lai, November 30, 1967, *SCMP,* No. 4072, p. 46.
42. Shih Tsu-chih, "The Basic Road of the National Liberation Movements by Colonial and Semi-Colonial Peoples," *KCWT,* No. 5 (1960).
43. Cf. Rupert Emerson, *From Empire to Nation* (Cambridge, Mass.: Harvard University Press, 1960), p. 25.
44. Donald S. Zagoria, "Russia, China, and the New States," in Donald W. Treadgold, ed., *Soviet and Chinese Communism: Similarities and Differences* (Seattle, Wash.: University of Washington Press, 1967), at 409; Richard Lowenthal, "On National Democracy," *Survey,* No. 47 (April, 1963).
45. Shih Tsu-chih, *supra* n. 42, at 7.
46. The "unequal" status which China experienced under restrictions imposed by treaty consisted in: (1) China's loss of tariff autonomy (Treaty

of Nanking, 1842); (2) possession by foreign power of the right to navigate in China's internal rivers and to transport freely goods inland without imposts (Treaty of Peking, 1860); (3) China's loss of frontier regions (Treaty of Aigun, 1858); (4) loss of Annam to France (Treaty of Peking, 1885); (5) loss of Chinese control over Burma (Treaty of Peking, with Britain, 1886); (6) loss of Korea and Taiwan and concession of rights to Japan to manufacture and market goods in China (Treaty of Shimonoseki, 1896)—the same rights were extended automatically to other powers by the "most-favored-nation" clause; (7) stationing of foreign troops in Legation Quarters in Peking (Treaty of Peking, 1901); and (8) "economic sanction" which prohibited import to China of foreign armaments (same).

47. Ch'ien Szu, "A Critique of Law," *supra* n. 7, at 46; also K'ung Meng, "A Critique of the Theories Concerning the 'subjects of International Law' and Recognition of States Under the Bourgeois International Law," *KCWT,* No. 2 (1960), at 44; and Ying T'ao, "Understand the True Face of the Bourgeois International Law from a Few Basic Precepts," *id.,* No. 1 (1960), at 43. The Treaty of Nanking of 1842 granted to Britain the right of consular jurisdiction only in criminal cases. However, it was extended to civil cases under the Sino-American Treaty of 1844. By the "most-favored-nation" clause, Britain and other powers also benefited from the extension. The texts of these and other treaties are found in China Maritime Customs, *Treaties, Conventions, etc., Between China and Foreign States,* 2nd ed. (Shanghai, 1917), 2 vols.
48. E.g., U.S.-Mexico General Claims Commission, *Chattin Claim* case (1927), in Herbert Briggs, *The Law of Nations,* 2d ed. (New York: Appleton-Century-Croft, 1952), 660 ff.
49. Ch'ien Szu, *supra* n. 7, at 48.
50. *Id.*
51. Chou En-lai's report on his African trip to the Standing Committee of the National People's Congress, excerpts released by the NCNA, April 25, 1964; also "Eight Principles Governing China's Economic and Technical Aid To Other Countries," *PR,* August 21, 1964, p. 16.
52. Robert Slusser and Jan Triska, *The Theory, Law, and Policy of Soviet Treaties* (Stanford: Stanford University Press, 1962), p. 347.
53. Gene Hsiao, "Communist China's Trade Treaties and Agreements (1949–1964)," 21 *Vanderbilt Law Review,* No. 5, p. 644 ff (October, 1968).
54. Chou's statement at the April 19, 1955, meeting, quoted in Yang and Ch'en, *supra* n. 2, p. 6.
55. Chou's speech at a Peking reception for Prince Sihanouk, August 16, 1958, in 5 *TWKH* 148–49 (1958).
56. Article 2, Sino-Burmese Boundary Treaty, October 1, 1960, 9 *TYC* 68. Emphasis added.

57. *ID.* 58. Art. 4, *id.* 59. Cf. *supra* n. 47.
60. Ch'ien Szu, *supra* n. 47.
61. See discussion in Chapter XII below; text at reference for nn. 139–57.
62. Article 59 of the CPR's Common Program provided: "The People's Government . . . protects law-abiding foreign nationals in China." Aliens and stateless persons are required to follow, for example, the same procedure and requirements of household registration as Chinese nationals, under the "Articles of the Law Concerning Household Registration of the CPR," passed by the Standing Committee, National People's Congress and promulgated by the CPR Chairman on January 9, 1958, text in 8 *FKHP* 204–209. For a discussion of the treatment of aliens in mainland China, see Chapter VII below.
63. Chou Tzu-ya, *Chung-kuo wai-chiao chih lu* [The Diplomatic Future of China] (Chungking: Kuo-min, 1943), pp. 34–35. See also Tung Lin, *China and Some Phases of International Law* (London: Oxford University Press, 1940), p. 34. The Manifesto of the National People's Convention of China in 1931 declared: "(1) The Chinese people will not recognize all the past unequal treaties imposed by the Powers on China. (2) The National Government shall, in conformity with Dr. Sun Yat-sen's testamentary injunction, achieve with the least possible delay China's equality and independence in the Family of Nations." *Id.*
64. 21 *AJIL* 289 (1927).
65. Yü Neng-mo, *Fei-ch'u pu-p'ing-teng t'iao-yüeh chih ching-kuo* [The Abolition of Unequal Treaties] (Taipei: Commercial Press, 1951).
66. Liang Ching-ch'un, *Tsai-hua ling-shih ts'ai-p'an-ch'üan lun* [On the Right of Consular Jurisdiction in China] (Shanghai: Commercial Press, 1930), p. 2.
67. *Id.*, 42 ff. Liang quoted Hall (*International Law,* p. 351) to press his view.
68. *Id.*, p. 169 ff.
69. Chou Keng-sheng, "The Treaty Basis of the Western Powers' Spheres of Influence in China," *Hsien-tai ko-chi-fa wen-t'i* [Problems of Modern International Law] (Shanghai: Commercial Press, 1930), p. 252.
70. Chang Chung-fu, *Chung-hua min-kuo wai-chiao shih* [The Diplomatic History of the Republic of China], pp. 28–29, quoted in T'ang Wu, *Chung-kuo yü kuo-chi-fa* [China and International Law] (Taipei, 1957), Vol. I, p. 24.
71. Tse-tsung Chow, *The May Fourth Movement* (Cambridge, Mass.: Harvard University Press, 1960), p. 84 ff; also Maurice Meisner, *Li Ta-chao and the Origins of Chinese Marxism* (Harvard University Press, 1967); Benjamin Schwartz, *Chinese Communism and the Rise of Mao* (Harvard University Press, 1951).
72. Chou Tzu-ya, *supra* n. 63.

73. See text in Chapter XI at reference for n. 88.
74. See Paul Varg's comments in Ho Ping-Ti and Tsou Tang, *China in Crisis* (University of Chicago Press, 1968), II, at 106.
75. *JMJP* editorial, March 8, 1963, and Mao's statement to the Japanese Socialist party delegation, in *Seikai Shuho,* August 11, 1964; both excerpted in Dennis J. Doolin, ed., *Territorial Claims in the Sino-Soviet Conflict* (Stanford University, Hoover Institution, 1965), pp. 29–31, 43.
76. Sino-Indonesian Dual Nationality Treaty, 13 *TYC* 12; Donald E. Willmott, *The National Status of the Chinese in Indonesia,* rev. ed. (Cornell University Press, 1961); and Hsia Tao-t'ai, "Settlement of Dual Nationality Between Communist China and Other Countries," *Osteuropa Recht* (Stuttgart, West Germany), XI (March, 1965), pp. 27–38. A discussion of the traditional Chinese nationality laws based on *jus sanguinis* is found in Tung, *supra* n. 63, p. 86.
77. See *supra* n. 10. The CPR has accused India of committing cartographic "great-power chauvinism" because of alleged omissions of Sikkim and Bhutan on certain Indian maps. "CPR Foreign Ministry note to the Indian Embassy, May 31, 1962," reproduced in India, Ministry of External Affairs, *Sino-Pakistan Agreement of March 2, 1963: Some Facts* (New Delhi, 1963), Appendix II. In fact, the CPR today lays claims to Tibet on grounds other than suzerainty and considers that British description of China's relations with Tibet as one of suzerainty was an "imperialist" attempt to weaken China's lawful sovereignty over a "locality," an integral part of China, though enjoying autonomous rights. Yu Fan, "Speaking About the Relationship between China and the Tibetan Region from the Viewpoint of Sovereignty and Suzerainty," *JMJP,* June 5, 1969.

CHAPTER V

1. *Sino-Soviet Treaty and Agreements: Signed in Moscow on February 14, 1950* (Peking: FLP, 1952), p. 5.
2. CPR Foreign Ministry, *Chung-hua jen-min kung-ho-kuo yu-hao t'iao-yüeh hui-pien* [Collection of CPR Friendship Treaties] (Peking: World Knowledge, 1965), pp. 87–92, 98–99. Unless otherwise indicated or when the context suggests otherwise, all translations are the author's own.
3. Treaty of Friendship and Mutual Non-Aggression Between the People's Republic of China and the Kingdom of Afghanistan, *id.,* pp. 18–19 (Article 1).
4. Report by Chang Ting-ch'eng, Chief Procurator of the Supreme Peo-

ple's Procuratorate, to the Third Session of the First National People's Congress, June 22, 1956, reproduced in 2 *JPWT* 139–41.

5. Report by Chang Ting-ch'eng to the Fourth Session of the First National People's Congress, July 1, 1957, *id.*, 158–59.
6. 3 *FKHP* 176–77; 2 *JPWT* 124–25. The "Decision" was promulgated by the CPR chairman after passage by the Standing Committee of the National People's Congress, *id.*
7. Department of State, Publication No. 2613, Far Eastern Series No. 12, *Trial of Japanese War Criminals.*
8. Mei was declared a "rightist" in 1958 (*CFYC*, No. 5 (1958), p. 19), but apparently was cleared of that charge in 1964 (see his article in the *JMJP*, April 25, 1964).
9. Cf. Joseph B. Keenan and Brendan F. Brown, *Crimes Against International Law* (Washington, D. C.: Public Affairs Press, 1950), p. 188, n. 5; also Mei Ju-ao's comments concerning Taiwan, in *CFYC*, No. 2 (1955), at 48.
10. The trial of Suzuki Hirohisa, in 2 *JPWT* 127. In the trial of Takebe Rokuzo and twenty-seven others, former Emperor Pu Yi was summoned to appear as witness, *id.*, p. 148.
11. 2 *JPWT* 126. Emphasis added. 12. *Id.*, p. 127.
13. The codefendants were: Fujita Shigeru, Kamisaka Masaru, Sasa Shinnosuke, Nagashima Tsutomu, and Funaki Kenjiro.
14. *Id.*, p. 127.
15. Sakakibara Hideo was commanding officer of the 162nd Contingent of the 731st Troop Unit of the Japanese Kwantung Army, according to the Prosecution, *id.*
16. *Id.* Japan was, in fact, not a party to the 1925 Geneva Protocol Prohibiting the Use in War of Asphyxiating, Poisonous, or Other Gases, and of Bacteriological Methods of Warfare. See *infra* n. 23. The CPR announced her acceptance of the protocol on July 13, 1952, 6 *TYC* 319.
17. *Id.*, pp. 145, 147. 18. *Id.*, pp. 151–54; 155–58.
19. 36 U.S. *Statutes at Large* 2277; also in William W. Bishop, *International Law*, 2d ed. (Boston: Little, Brown, 1962), pp. 802–17. Relevant articles are 46 (protection of private property and lives of person) and 47 (forbidding pillage).
20. Judgment of the Nuremberg Trial, September 30, 1946, quoted in Bishop, *id.*, at 851. By Article 6 of the charter annexed to the London Agreement of August 8, 1945, war crimes were defined as "violations of laws or customs of war." "Such violations shall include, but not be limited to, murder, ill-treatment or deportation to slave labor or for any other purpose of civilian population of or in occupied territory, murder or ill-treatment of prisoners of war . . . , killing of hostages, plunder of public or private property, wanton destruction of cities, towns or villages, or devastation not justified by military necessity." International

Military Tribunal, Nuremberg, *Official Documents* I, p. 173; also "Principles of International Law Recognized in the Charter and Judgment of the Nuremberg Tribunal," *Report of the International Law Commission,* 2nd Session, U. N. General Assembly, *Official Records,* 5th Session (1950), Supp. No. 12 (A/1316), p. 11.

21. By her reservations regarding Article 85 attached to her ratifications of the Geneva Conventions of 1949, it is clear that the CPR, following the example of other Communist states, maintains the position—similar to that held by the Nuremberg Tribunal—that the conventions are only declaratory in nature. "Regarding Article 85," the CPR reservations stated, "the People's Republic of China is not bound by Article 85 in regard to the treatment of POWs convicted under the laws of the Detaining Power in accordance with the principles laid down in the trials of war crimes or crimes against humanity by the Nuremberg and the Tokyo International Military Tribunals." 260 *UNTS,* No. 442 (1957).
22. 118 League of Nations *Treaty Series* 343.
23. Text in Manley O. Hudson 3 *International Legislation* 1671.
24. Text of the Charter of the International Military Tribunal for the Far East, in *Occupation of Japan, Policy and Progress,* Department of State Publication No. 2671, Far Eastern Series No. 17, Appendix 32, at 149; cf. also *Ch'ien jih-pen lu-chün chün-jen yin chun-pei ho shih-yung hsi-chün wu-ch'i pei k'ung an: shen-p'an ts'ai-liao* [The Trial of Former Japanese Army Personnel for the Making and Employment of Bacteriological Weapons: Materials from the Trial] (Moscow: Foreign Language Publishing House, 1950).
25. The defendants who stood trial at Tokyo in 1946 were, on the other hand, top Japanese leaders, i.e., statesmen, politicians, propagandists, financiers, military leaders, diplomats, economists, and jurists. These men had seized the power of the Japanese state and used it to breach the international law of humanity, but they did not personally commit the crimes against humanity and were responsible insofar as they ordered, permitted, or agreed to such acts, or made no effort to prevent or stop them.
26. 2 *JPWT* 128.
27. Cf. N. Doman, "Political Consequences of Nuremberg Trial," American Academy of Political and Social Sciences, *Annals,* Vol. CCXLVI (July, 1946), at 82.
28. Article 7 of the Tokyo Charter, *supra* n. 24.
29. CPR Government Statement Regarding the Suez Canal Issue, August 15, 1956, text in *Chung-tung wen-t'i wen-chien hui-pien* [Collection of Documents Relating to the Middle East Question], compiled by the Institute of International Relations (Peking), pp. 224–26, at 225. A similar statement is in the CPR government's reply, September 17, 1956, to a letter from the Egyptian government, *id.,* p. 251.

30. The term "nationality" is used here in the traditional sense under international law, to mean immigration status, naturalization, choice of citizenship, repatriation, etc. It has nothing to do with minority nationality groups within China. See Chapter XII, text for nn. 125–29 for further discussion.
31. 7 *FKHP* 30–35.
32. Exchange of notes between Chou En-lai and U Nu of Burma, October 1, 1961, concerning the Sino-Burmese Boundary Treaty, signed the same day; 7 *FKHP* 46–48. Inhabitants of areas to be transferred by one side to the other in pursuance of the treaty (Articles 1, 2, and 3) "shall, after the handing over of the areas, be definitely considered citizens of the side to which the areas belong." But any inhabitant who wishes to retain his original citizenship despite the territorial transfer "may, within two years, move into the territory of the original side."
33. Exchange of Notes between the CPR and Nepal concerning the Option for Nationality and Trans-Frontier Cultivation and Herds-Grazing by Border Inhabitants, 13 *id.* 82–88.
34. For Soviet practice see Robert Slusser and Jan Triska, *Theory, Law and Policy of Soviet Treaties* (Stanford: Stanford University Press, 1962), p. 106 ff; and George Ginsburgs, "Validity of Treaties in the Municipal Law of the 'Socialist' States," 59 *AJIL* 545–69 (1965).
35. 12 *FKHP* 35–36. The Regulations were formulated in pursuance of Article 9 (2) of the "Measures for the Implementation of the Sino-Indonesian Dual Nationality Treaty (1955)," agreed upon by both governments on December 15, 1960, *id.* at 34.
36. 1 *id.* 208–209.
37. "It is certain," said the Permanent Court of International Justice in the *Free Zones* case (France v. Switzerland), "that France cannot rely on her own legislation to limit the scope of her international obligations." PCIJ, Ser. A, No. 24 (1930), p. 12, and Ser. A/B, No. 46 (1932), p. 167. Cf. also *Case Concerning Germany Interests in Polish Upper Silesia* (Merits), *id.,* No. 17 (1928), pp. 33–34. In the *Shufeldt Arbitration* case (1930), U.S. v. Guatemala, the Arbiter held that "it is a settled principle of international law that a sovereign cannot be permitted to set up one of his own municipal laws as a bar to a claim by a foreign sovereign for a wrong done to the latter's subject." Department of State, *Arbitrations,* Ser. 3, pp. 851, 876–77 (1932).
38. Cf. Byron Weng, "Communist China's Changing Attitudes Toward the United Nations," *International Organization,* Vol. XX, No. 4 (Autumn, 1966), at 683.
39. Security Council *Official Records,* 5th Year (1950), No. 48, pp. 3–5.
40. For general discussion, see Sheldon Appleton, *The Eternal Triangle?* (East Lansing, Mich.: Michigan State University Press, 1961); and "Red China and the United Nations," *Current History,* September, 1961, p.

144. In 1950 and 1955, the CPR brought complaints to the United Nations, presumably under Article 35 (2) of the Charter of the United Nations, which reads: "A state which is not a Member of the United Nations may bring to the attention of the Security Council or of the General Assembly any dispute to which it is a party if it accepts in advance, for the purposes of the dispute, the obligations of pacific settlement provided in the present Charter." The Charter basis for the Security Council's invitation to the CPR is apparently Article 32: ". . . any state which is not a Member of the United Nations, if it is a party to a dispute under consideration by the Security Council, shall be invited to participate, without vote, in the discussion relating to the dispute."

41. Mei Hao-shih, "The Great Victories of the Chinese People in Combating American Imperialism over the Past Decade," *KCWT,* No. 6 (1959), p. 20. Text of the CPR complaint in *People's China* (Peking), November 1, 1954, supplement; also U.N. Doc. S/1715 (August 24, 1950). For Peking's rejection of a 1955 invitation by the Security Council and its reasons, see U.N. Doc. S/3358 (1955).
42. U.N. Doc. S/1921; and A/c.1/661.
43. Department of State, *Renunciation of Force* (Press Release No. 37, January 21, 1956, reprinted as Publication 6280, General Foreign Policy Series 107, February 1956). Annex B: "U.S. Statement and Proposal on Renunciation of Force, October 8, 1955." See CPR statements concerning the talks, 1959 *Jen-min shou-ts'e* [People's Handbook], pp. 356–59; 5 *TWKH* 88–92 (1958).
44. *Id.,* Annex C: "Chinese Communist Draft Declaration on Renunciation of Force, October 27, 1955."
45. *Id.,* pp. 3–4; and Annexes D, E, and F.
46. Mei Hao-shih, *supra* n. 41, p. 20; also State Department, *supra* n. 43, p. 5; *Jen-min shou-ts'e, supra* n. 43.

CHAPTER VI

1. U.S. Supreme Court, *The Schooner Exchange v. McFaddon* (1812), 7 *Cranch* 116.
2. Cf. *Chung-hua jen-min kung-ho-kuo min-fa chi-pen wen-t'i* [Basic Problems of the CPR's Civil Law] (Peking: Legal Publications, 1958), p. 36; and *Chung-hua jen-min kung-ho-kuo hsing-fa tsung-tse chiang-yi* [Lectures on the Fundamentals of CPR Criminal Law] (Peking: Legal Publications, 1958), p. 36. Hereinafter referred to as *MFCPWT* and *HFTT,* respectively.
3. The Sino-Soviet Agreement on the Chinese Ch'ang-ch'un Railway, Port

Arthur and Dairen, February 16, 1950, in *Sino-Soviet Treaty and Agreements* (Peking: FLP, 1952).

4. The first lease was that of Kiaochow to Germany, under a convention signed on March 6, 1898. Cf. Tung Lin, *China and Some Phases of International Law* (New York: Oxford University Press, 1940), p. 19.
5. Treaty-based concessions were first granted by China to England under the Treaty of Nanking in 1842, which authorized British subjects "to reside for the purpose of carrying on their mercantile pursuits, without molestation or restraint at the cities and towns of Canton, Amoy, Foochowfoo, Ningpo, and Shanghai," *Id.*, p. 24.
6. *Id.*, pp. 12 ff. 7. *Id.* pp. 27 ff.
8. Hong Kong and Macao, however, remain ceded territories in accordance with the Treaty of Nanking (1842) with Britain and the Protocol of Lisbon (1887) with Portugal, respectively. The "new territory" in Hong Kong was leased to Britain in 1898. The retrocession of Taiwan to China is considered by the CPR to have been legally consummated. See Chapter IX below, text at reference for nn. 23–37.
9. *HFTT*, p. 36, n. 1. 10. *Id.* 11. *Id.*, p. 37.
12. The National Government of the Republic of (Nationalist) China recognized Outer Mongolia's independence in 1945. The CPR, in an exchange of notes with the Soviet Union, on February 14, 1950, also formally recognized the same. Cf. State Department, Division of External Research and Publications, *Reported Agreements Between the USSR and Communist China* (Washington, D.C., n.d.). For Mao's attack on the Soviet role in alienating Outer Mongolia from China, see Chapter IV, n. 10, above.
13. The CPR's claim to the right of representation in the United Nations and sovereignty over Taiwan on the basis of state continuity is discussed in Chapter IX, at reference for nn. 1–41, below. At other times, the CPR also claims legitimacy by dint of self-determination, Chapter XI, n. 88, below. The fact that she does not feel bound by treaty obligations inherited from the past but insists on a right of choice indicates that the CPR also in part considers herself a successor state to the erstwhile China. The spirit in which Article 55 of the Common Program was conceived is also indicative of the CPR's attitude that her legitimacy is derived from both state succession and state continuity. Under the said article the CPR reserves to herself the right to recognize, abrogate, or revise or renegotiate treaties concluded by pre-1949 Chinese governments. The CPR does not seem to adhere strictly to the Soviet theory that states which undergo fundamental social revolutions are not the same legal persons as those which they replace. The difference may be due to the CPR's desire to inherit China's seat in the Security Council of the United Nations and sovereign rights over Taiwan, etc.

14. The CPR has insisted that there is a "traditional" boundary line and that in some of the areas previous Chinese governments exercised effective control as late as 1927. She has left no misunderstanding of the fact that the same Chinese sovereignty over these territories still continues under the Communist government in Peking. Chapter X, nn. 35–49, below.
15. *JMJP* editorial, March 8, 1963. Dennis J. Doolin, *Territorial Claims in the Sino-Soviet Conflict* (Stanford: Stanford University, Hoover Institution, 1965), pp. 29–31 and *passim.*
16. *Id.*
17. Under the Sino-Burmese Boundary Treaty of 1960, the CPR renounced China's mining right in Burma. Article 4 of the treaty stated that the act was "in line with [the CPR's] consistent policy of opposing foreign prerogatives and respecting the sovereignty of other countries." Chapter IV, nn. 56–58, above.
18. Article 1 of the Sino-Pakistani Agreement, text in 12 *TYC* 64.
19. See further discussion in Chapter XI, at reference for nn. 65–71, below.
20. *HFTT,* p. 36, n. 1. Since the book was put together before the CPR Government in September, 1958, announced its adoption of the twelve-mile territorial-sea doctrine, its authors left the question open, stating merely that some states followed the three-mile rule and others the twelve-mile rule.
21. CPR Declaration Regarding Territorial Waters, September 4, 1958, in 8 *FKHP* 112–13.
22. Article 4 of the convention. Kuo Chi, *infra* n. 32, explicitly alluded to the 1958 Geneva Conference on the Law of the Seas. Only twenty-one of the eighty-six states attending the conference accepted the three-mile limit; see the table prepared by the secretariat of the conference, in Max Sorensen, "The Law of the Sea," *International Conciliation,* No. 520 (1958), at 244. On the decline of the three-mile rule and the increasing popularity of the six- or twelve-mile rule, see D. W. Bowett, *The Law of the Sea* (Dobbs Ferry, N.Y.: Oceana, 1967), at 13.
23. William Butler, *The Law of Soviet Territorial Waters* (New York: Praeger, 1967), p. 6.
24. Ch'eng T'ao, "Communist China and the Law of the Sea," 63 *AJIL* 47–73 (1969), at 47–53.
25. Department of State, *Bulletin,* XXXIX, 1004 (1958), pp. 445–46.
26. Chou's statement is reproduced in *CFYC,* No. 5 (1958), at 2; also *PR,* September 9, 1958, pp. 15–16.
27. Fu Chu, *Kuan-yü wo-kuo ling-hai wen-t'i* [On the Territorial Sea of Our Country] (Peking, 1959), pp. 2–3.
28. See remarks by a spokesman of the U.S. Department of State, on September 4, 1958, *New York Times,* September 5, 1958, p. 1, col. 6, and statement by the Assistant Legal Adviser for Far Eastern Affairs, on

November 20, 1958, Department of State, *American Foreign Policy: Current Documents* (1958), p. 1198; and *SCMP,* No. 1871, p. 89, for a British note to Peking taking exception to the Chinese announced twelve-mile limit of its territorial sea.

29. For Soviet support and that by other Communist states, see *SCMP* No. 1853, p. 41; No. 1855, p. 50; No. 1868. On the Indonesian support, see Syatauw, *Some Newly Established Asian States and the Development of International Law* (The Hague: Martinus Nijhoff, 1961), p. 173 ff.
30. *New York Times,* September 8, 1958, p. 1; Fu Chu, *Kuan-yü wo-kuo, supra* n. 27, p. 4.
31. Fu Chu, *id.,* pp. 4–5; Ch'eng T'ao, *supra* n. 24, pp. 54–55.
32. Kuo Chi, "A Great Measure for the Protection of State Sovereignty," *CFYC,* No. 5 (1958), at 9–10. He pointed out that on October 16, 1864, U.S. Secretary of State Seward had proposed to Britain the extension of territorial waters to five miles. At the 1958 conference at Geneva, he further noted, Arthur H. Dean, the U.S. delegate, even suggested a six-mile solution. See also Liu Tse-yung (Liu Tse-jung), "A Major Step to Protect China's Sovereign Rights," *PR,* September 16, 1958, pp. 11–13.
33. Wei Wen-han, "On the Question of the Width of the Territorial Sea," *Fa-hsüeh pan-yüeh-k'an* [Jurisprudence Fortnightly], June 1, 1957; tr. into English by Union Research Service, VII, 29 (September 6, 1957), quoted in Ch'eng T'ao, *supra* n. 24, at 56.
34. Kuo Chi, *supra* n. 32, at 10.
35. Liu Tse-yung, *supra* n. 32, at 12; and Kuo Chi, *id.,* at 10; also Fu Chu, *supra* n. 27, at 13.
36. Liu, *id.,* at 11 and 13.
37. Fu Chu, *supra* n. 27, at 17.
38. Cf. William Butler, *supra* n. 23, p. 13.
39. Fu Chu, *supra* n. 27, at 17.
40. *Id.,* at 18. Answering a reader's question, the *JMJP* pointed out that the Po-hai Bay did not exceed twenty-four miles. In support of China's historic claims (prescription), it cited the famous episode of 1864 in which the Prussian minister to Imperial China was obliged to release three Danish merchant ships seized in Po-hai Bay, after the Chinese government had protested that the place of seizure was in China's internal waters. *Hsin-hua pan-yüeh-k'an* CXL, p. 59; Ch'eng T'ao, *supra* n. 24, p. 60. For an account of the historic incident, see Imannuel Hsü, *China's Entry into the Family of Nations: 1858–1880* (Harvard, 1960), pp. 132–33.
41. The International Court of Justice, in the *Corfu Channel* case (Merits) (1949), ruled: "It is, in the opinion of the Court, generally recognized and in accordance with international custom that States in time of peace have a right to send their warships through straits used for international navigation between two parts of the high seas without the pre-

vious authorization of the coastal State, provided that the passage is innocent." *ICJ Reports* (1949), p. 26. The principle of innocent passage was codified in the 1958 Convention on the Territorial Sea. According to Article 14 of the convention, "ships of all States, whether coastal or not, shall enjoy the right of innocent passage through the territorial sea." Article 15 stipulates: "The coastal State must not hamper innocent passage through the territorial sea." Under Article 16 (4), it is further provided: "There shall be no suspension of the innocent passage of foreign ships through straits which are used for international navigation between one part of the high seas and another part of the high seas or the territorial sea of a foreign State." (The last part is an allusion to the Gulf of Aqaba.) Cf. *infra* n. 47.

42. Liu Tse-yung, *supra* n. 32, p. 13. Emphasis added.
43. International Law Commission, 1956 *Yearbook,* II, p. 276, A/CN.4/SER. A/1956/Add. 1 (1957).
44. See G. I. Tunkin's objections, 3 *U.N. Conference on the Law of the Sea,* p. 32 (1958); also Butler, *supra* n. 23, p. 45. The Soviet Union entered its reservation regarding Article 23, which would permit foreign warships to have the right of innocent passage without prior authorization by the coastal state. Butler, *id.,* at 140.
45. Fu Chu, *supra* n. 27, pp. 23–24. Cf. Soviet views, Butler, *id.,* p. 37.
46. *Id.,* pp. 24–25.
47. U.N. Doc. A/CONF. 13/L.52, reproduced in Ian Brownlie, *Basic Documents of International Law* (Oxford, 1967), at 76.
48. Fu Chu, *supra* n. 27, p. 22.
49. Quoted in Ch'eng T'ao, *supra* n. 24, at 67.
50. Levin and Kalinzhnaia, *Mezhdunarodnoe pravo* [International Law] (1960), p. 171. Koretskii contended that the establishment of special zones was a circuitous means to extend sovereign rights. 3 *U.N. Conference on the Law of the Sea* 67 (1958).
51. 2 *Hua-tung-ch'ü ts'ai-cheng ching-chi fa-ling hui-pien* [Collection of Laws and Regulations Concerning Financial and Economic Matters for the East China Region], pp. 1333–37.
52. *JMJP,* August 18, 1957, p. 4.
53. Sea areas west of the following lines were designated as off-limits to trawler fishing: 37°20'N and 123°03'E; 35°11'N and 120°38'E; 29°N and 122°45'E; 27°N and 121°10'E; 36°48'10"N and 122°44'30"E; 30°44'N and 123°25'E; and 27°30'N and 121°30'E. U.S. consulate-general in Hong Kong, *Current Background* (CB), No. 1724, p. 6; Ch'eng T'ao, *supra* n. 24, p. 65, n. 94.
54. Letter from the Delegation of the Japanese Fishery Council to the Delegation of the China Fishery Association, November 9, 1963, *CB,* No. 724, pp. 5–6.
55. Wei, *supra* n. 33, p. 360.

56. 10 *Federal Register* 12304 (1945); 59 *Stat.* 885.
57. Arts. 3 and 4, U.N. Doc. A/CONF. 13/L. 55. 58. *Supra* n. 54
59. U.S. Department of State, "Statement on the Proposed 12-Mile Fishery Zone," (May 18, 1966), 5 *International Legal Materials,* at 616 (1966).
60. Para. (4) of the 1958 CPR Declaration on the Territorial Sea.
61. Fu Chu, *supra* n. 27, p. 20. 62. Article II (2), CB, No. 724, p. 1.
63. Ch'eng T'ao, *supra* n. 24, p. 64.
64. Id., p. 64, n. 91. 65. Letter, *supra* n. 54.
66. Fu Chu, *supra* n. 27, p. 25. 67. Text in *TKWC,* pp. 263–264.
68. Chang Yuan-kuang, "New China's Sea Transportation," tr. in *ECMM,* No. 133, p. 28.
69. *Id.,* pp. 22–27; also Ch'eng T'ao, *supra* n. 24, p. 51, nn. 23–26.
70. Arts. 14 and 1, Foreign Vessels Measures, in *TKWC,* 263–64.
71. Art. 2.
72. Art. 3. In the original phrase "the state to which the ship belongs" is used; but we have used "the state of registry" for convenience.
73. Art. 4. 74. Art. 5. 75. Art. 6.
76. Art. 7. 77. Art. 8. 78. Art. 9.
79. Art. 10. 80. Art. 11. 81. Art. 12. 82. Art. 13.
83. Text in 1964 *Jen-min shou-ts'e* [People's Handbook], p. 342.
84. Arts. 2, 3 and 4. 85. Art. 5. 86. Art. 6.
87. Arts. 7 and 8. 88. Art. 9. 89. Arts. 10 and 11. 90. Art. 12.
91. English translation in *JPRS,* No. 36202, pp. 98–101, at 99; see also Ch'eng T'ao, *supra* n. 24, p. 69, n. 119.
92. Cf. Douglas Johnston and Hungdah Ch'iu, *Agreements of the People's Republic of China, 1949–1967: A Calendar* (Cambridge, Mass.: Harvard University Press, 1968), *passim.*
93. Sino-Korean Agreement Concerning Navigation and Transport Cooperation on Border Rivers, May 23, 1960, 10 *FKHP* 335. In August, 1969, the Soviet Union and the CPR signed a protocol on border river navigation following talks at the Soviet Far Eastern city of Khabarovsk, which began on June 18, 1969. *New York Times,* August 9, 1969, p. 1, col. 1. However, the CPR on August 18, 1969, protested to the Soviet government on alleged Soviet obstruction of navigation by Chinese ships on the Heilungkiang and the Ussuri rivers. *PR,* August 22, 1969, at 5.
94. Art. 4, Sino-Soviet Agreement on Merchant Marine Navigation on Rivers and Lakes Along Their Borders, signed on December 21, 1957; text in 6 *TYC* 278.
95. Art. 4, Sino-Korean agreement of May 23, 1960, *supra* n. 93.
96. Britain, Court of Criminal Appeals (1868), 11 *Cox Criminal Cases* 198.
97. U.S. Supreme Court (1933), 289 *U.S.* 137. 98. Art. 20 (1).
99. Regulations Governing the Investigation of Maritime Accidents and Damages, October 10, 1959, 10 *FKHP* 331–37.

100. Art. 2, *id.* 101. Art. 3. 102. Art. 13.
103. *Harvard Research Convention on Jurisdiction with Respect to Crime* (Cambridge, Mass.: Harvard Law School, 1935), p. 445.
104. The 1952 Brussels Convention Relating to Penal Jurisdiction in Matters of Collision or Other Incidents of Navigation (text in 53 *AJIL* 536 [1959]) recognizes jurisdiction by the state of habitual residence of the defendant, the state within whose territory the offence has occurred, and the state which has arrested the ship. Article 11 of the 1958 Geneva Convention on the High Seas recognizes jurisdiction by reference to the nationality of the ship or the nationality of the defendant.
105. The last paragraph of Art. 19 concerns jurisdiction over illicit traffic in narcotics. But there is no counterpart in the CPR Maritime Accidents Regulations.
106. This point was made by Ni Cheng-ao, *Kuo-chi-fa chung te szu-fa kuan-hsia wen-t'i* [Judicial Jurisdiction in International Law] (Peking: World Knowledge, 1964), pp. 91–92.
107. Art. 8 (6), Maritime Accidents Regulations. 108. Art. 9.
109. Art. 13, *supra* n. 94.
110. Art. 4, Appendix III of the agreement specifies the conditions under which assistance is to be given to the fishing vessels of the other party in distress, including (a) severe injuries or sickness (excluding epidemics) suffered by members of the crew; (b) severe stoppages or damages to the engine or the hull of the vessel; (c) severe leakage of the vessel likely to lead to its sinking; and (d) attacks by typhoons. Sino-Japanese Fishery Agreement, April 15, 1955, 4 *TYC* 265 ff.
111. Appendix III, Article 6, *id.*
112. Keilin, *Sovetsko morskoe pravo* [Soviet Maritime Law] (1954), p. 64, cited in William Butler, *supra* n. 23, p. 45.
113. Peking has accused the United States of interfering with the "peaceable" fishery operations on the high seas by Chinese fishing vessels. Flaunting the freedom of the high seas, the CPR has alleged that U.S. planes consistently bomb and strafe Chinese fishing vessels on the high seas and has branded such attacks as "acts of piracy." *Peking Review,* June 3, 1966, p. 11.
114. See *supra* n. 21.
115. Article 1, Convention on International Civil Aviation (open for signature at Chicago, December 7, 1944), *TIAS* 1591. The 1919 Convention Relating to the Regulation of Aerial Navigation purported to "accord freedom of innocent passage" to the aircraft of parties to the convention. 11 League of Nations *Treaty Series* 173. Only thirty-seven states—not including the United States—were sometime parties to this convention, which was superseded by the 1944 Chicago Convention. In light of the statements made at the 1958 Geneva Conference on the Law of the Sea, foreign aircraft are not entitled to innocent passage

through the airspace over a state's territorial sea or territory under existing international law.

116. See Chapter X, text for nn. 31–34 below.
117. *New York Times,* February 15, 1968. Trespassing in airspace is a common cause of international tension; see David Johnson, *Rights in Air Space* (Dobbs Ferry, N.Y.: Oceana, 1965), pp. 70–74.
118. Article 1 (B), English text in 306 *UNTS* 36.
119. *Id.* p. 42 (Article 10). 120. *Id.*
121. Oliver J. Lissitzyn, *International Air Transport and National Policy* (New York: Council on Foreign Relations, 1942), pp. 365–66.
122. Cf. ICAO, *Handbook on Administrative Clauses* (Circular 63-AT/6). In addition to Burma, the CPR has bilateral air transport agreements with the Soviet Union (December 30, 1954), 3 *TYC* 192; North Vietnam (April 5, 1956), 5 *id.* 194; Outer Mongolia (January 17, 1958), 8 *id.* 173; Ceylon (March 26, 1959), *id.* 175; Indonesia (November 6, 1964), 13 *TYC* 368; Cambodia (November 25, 1963), 12 *TYC* 242; Pakistan (August 29 and August 30, 1963), *JMJP,* August 31, 1963, *PR,* September 6, 1963, and *Asian Recorder* (New Delhi) 5444; etc.
123. Article 5, *supra* n. 115.
124. The CPR in 1958 adhered to the 1929 Warsaw Convention for the Unification of Certain Rules Relating to International Carriage by Air. Text of CPR accession appears in 7 *TYC* 182. Text of the 1929 Warsaw Convention can be found in 137 *League of Nations Treaty Series* 876.
125. Liu Tse-jung, "The Legal Status of Cosmic Space," *KCWT,* No. 8 (1959), at 45.
126. *Id.,* at 46. 127. *Id.,* at 45. 128. *Id.,* at 47. 129. *Id.,* at 48.
130. "The Dilemma of American Jurists," *JMJP,* October 19, 1967.
131. "Another Fraud in U.S.-Soviet Conspiracy," *JMJP,* January 28, 1967.
132. Natural boundaries usually consist of mountains, rivers, forests, deserts, the open sea, marshes, territorial waters, etc. Artificial boundaries are generally marked by various landmarks, such as stones, posts, walls, trenches, canals, and the like.
133. The CPR has signed boundary treaties or agreements with Burma (October 1, 1960), Nepal (October 5, 1961), Pakistan (March 2, 1963), Outer Mongolia (December 26, 1962), and Afghanistan (November 22, 1963).
134. Article 5, Sino-Burmese Boundary Treaty, 9 *TYC* 68.
135. Article 8, *id.* Article 8 of the Sino-Mongolian Boundary Treaty (December 26, 1962) contains a similar provision, 11 *TYC* 19.
136. U.S. v. Mexico, *The Chamizal Arbitration,* 5 *AJIL* 785 (1911).
137. Article 2, *supra* n. 135.
138. Article 2 (3), Sino-Pakistan Boundary Agreement (March 2, 1963), 12 *TYC* 64.

139. 10 *TYC* 45.
140. Cf. Peking's boundary treaties with Burma (Art. 10); Nepal (Art. 3); Pakistan (Art. 4); Outer Mongolia (Art. 3); and with Afghanistan (Art. 3).
141. See text in Chapter X at reference for n. 43 below.

CHAPTER VII

1. *MFCPWT,* p. 40. 2. 3 *TYC* 12.
3. E.g., Foreign Minister Ch'en Yi's letter to Foreign Minister Subandrio, dated December 24, 1959; text in G. V. Ambekar and V. D. Divekar, *Documents on China's Relations with South and Southeast Asia: 1949–1962* (Bombay: Allied, 1964), p. 253.
4. *Infra* n. 22. 5. *HFTT,* pp. 38–40.
6. Although the two categories are not defined or differentiated, it seems that they are used interchangeably in practice.
7. English tr. of the Electoral Law (March 1, 1953) is included in Theodore Ch'en, *The Chinese Communist Regime: Documents and Commentary* (New York: Praeger, 1967), pp. 65–74.
8. Art. 98. For a discussion of the CPR's practice in protecting nationals abroad, see Chapter IX, nn. 58–69.
9. Cf. *The Mavrommatis* (Jurisdiction), PCIJ, Ser. A, No. 1(1934).
10. *Blackmer v. United States,* 284 *U.S.* 421 (1932).
11. See *supra* Chapter IV, text for n. 51.
12. See *infra* Chapter X, text for n. 51.
13. Tung Lin, *China and Some Phases of International Law* (London: Oxford University Press, 1940), 85 ff.
14. Under the 1955 Sino-Indonesia Dual Nationality Treaty, the Exchange of Notes concerning the Sino-Nepalese Option for Nationality and Trans-Frontier Cultivation and Herds-Grazing by Border Inhabitants, the individuals who possessed dual nationality were given the freedom of choice within a given period. See *supra* Chapter IV, n. 76.
15. See *supra* n. 2.
16. Text was published in *JMJP,* April 20, 1964, and in 1964 *Jen-min shou-ts'e* [People's Handbook], pp. 341–42. The "Alien Law" replaces the following regulations previously in force: (1) Provisional Regulations Governing the Entry, Exit, and Stay of Alien Nationals (promulgated on November 28, 1951); (2) Provisional Measures Governing Alien Residence Registration and Issuance of Residence Certificate (August 10, 1954); (3) Provisional Measures Governing the Departure of Alien Nationals (same date); (4) Provisional Measures Governing Travels by

Aliens (same date). All these older regulations were reproduced in *TKWC* 180–83.

17. Aliens who stay in China must report their residence within specified periods and are subject to the household registration regulations of the CPR (Article 10). Alien household registration follows the same "Articles of the Law Concerning Household Registration" (January 9, 1958) that applies to nationals; text in 7 *FKHP* 204–209.
18. *MFCPWT*, p. 41; and *HFTT*, pp. 41–42.
19. *HFTT*, p. 42. 20. *Id.*, pp. 38–40.
21. Under the "equal treatment" principle it may be assumed that the following categories of criminal offenses punishable for Chinese citizens are equally applicable to aliens in China: (1) crimes of a counterrevolutionary character; (2) acts detrimental to China's (socialist) public order; (3) infringement on public property; (4) invasion upon the person and interests of Chinese citizens; (5) violations of economic order; (6) interference with the maintenance of the social order; (7) interference with marriage and family relations of others; (8) infringement on the properties of Chinese citizens, etc. *HFTT*, pp. 79–80.
22. Cf. 2 *Min-fa tzu-liao hui-pien* [Collection of Materials on Criminal Law] (Peking: Chinese People's University, 1954) pp. 397–401; English translation in M. H. van der Valk, "Documents Concerning Conflict of Laws in Matters of Marriage in Communist China," 8 *Nederlands Tifdschrift International Recht,* 328–31 (1961).
23. Britain, House of Commons, *Parliamentary Debates,* Ser. 5, CDLXXXVII (1950–1951), p. 177.
24. Department of State, *The Conduct of Communist China* (Washington, D.C.: Goverment Printing House, 1963), p. 10.
25. Klaus Mehnert, *Peking and Moscow* (New York: Putnam & Sons, 1963), pp. 231 ff.; and Mihail A. Klochko, *Soviet Scientist in Red China* (New York: Praeger, 1964).
26. *New York Times,* August 13, 1967.
27. CPR-Denmark Exchange of Notes, September 7 and 23, 1961, 446 *UNTS* 6397.
28. E.g., Sino-Swedish Exchange of Notes, April 6 and 8, 1957, 428 *UNTS* 6179.
29. E.g., Sino-Finish Exchange of Notes, March 31, 1956, and April 1, 1956, 5 *TYC* 61.
30. Department of State, *Bulletin,* XXII, 551 (January 23, 1950); see further discussion in *infra* Chapter VIII text at reference for n. 42; and Chapter IX, nn. 43–44.
31. *New York Times,* December 17, 1950, p. 1, col. 2.
32. *New York Times,* December 30, 1950, p.3.
33. Decree of the Government Administrative Council on the Control of

U.S. Property and Freezing of U.S. Bank Deposits in China (December 28, 1950), 1 *Chung-yang jen-min cheng-fu fa-ling hui-pien* [Collection of Decrees of the Central People's Government], at 204.

34. *Id.* Emphasis added.
35. See Article 46, Hague Convention Respecting the Laws and Customs of War on Land (1907), prohibiting the confiscation of private property, 4 *Encyclopedia of Social Science 183–187* (1931); Schneeberger, "Property and War," 34 *Georgia Law Journal* 265, 267 (1946); *Brown v. U.S.* (1814), 8 *Cranch* 122; and Edward D. Re, *Foreign Confiscation* (Dobbs Ferry, N.Y.: Oceana, 1951), pp. 10–11.
36. 2 C. C. Hyde, *International Law Chiefly as Interpreted and Applied by the United States* (1922) 239.
37. *Expropriation of American-Owned Property by Foreign Governments in the 20th Century,* report prepared by the Legislative Reference Service, Library of Congress, for the House Committee on Foreign Affairs, 88th Cong. 1st Sess. (Washington, D.C.: U.S. Government Printing Office, 1963), p. 16.
38. *Id.*
39. *Hearing Before the Subcommittee on the Far East and the Pacific of the Committee on Foreign Affairs,* House of Reprs., 89th Cong. 2nd Sess., on S. 3675 (Washington, D.C.: Government Printing House, 1966), p. 15.
40. *New York Times,* December 30, 1950, p. 3.
41. Public Law 89–780 (November 6, 1966), 80 *Stat.* 1365.
42. *Federal Register,* XXXIII, 4.
43. Letters to the author, dated October 4, 1968, and August 16, 1971.
44. Cf. Report by Edward Re, chairman of the Foreign Claims Settlement Commission, in *Hearing, supra* n. 39, p. 4.
45. Britain, House of Commons, *Parliamentary Debates,* Ser. 5, DV, p. 194. The information was provided by Anthony Eden, then secretary of state for foreign affairs, to oral interpellations in the Commons, October 15, 1952.
46. Decree of the Government Administrative Council Concerning the Requisition of the Properties of the Asiatic Petroleum Company within China (April 30, 1951), in 2 *Chung-yang* . . . , supra n. 33.
47. See *supra* n. 45, pp. 1007–1008. The figure was given by Anthony Nutting, joint under-secretary of state for foreign affairs, before the Commons, October 22, 1952.
48. See Soviet decrees in R. David and John N. Hazard, 2 *Le droit sovietique* (Paris, 1954) 9; 153–85; 187–221; also Koustantin Katzarov, *The Theory of Nationalization* (The Hague: Martinus Nijhoff, 1964), pp. 34 ff.
49. Audrey Donnithorne, *China's Economic System* (New York: Praeger, 1967), p. 146.

50. Li Hao-p'ei, "Nationalization and International Law," *CFYC*, No. 2 (1958) at 10. Li subsumes expropriation and other forms of "taking" of alien property under the general rubric "nationalization."
51. Hackworth, *International Law* 662–63; U.S. Department of State, 19 *Press Releases* 50, 136, 139, 165 (1938).
52. 47 *AJIL* 325 (1953).
53. 1 Lauterpacht-Oppenheim, *International Law*, 8th ed. (1955), p. 352.
54. A. de La Pradelle, "Les Effets internationaux des Nationalisations," *Annuaire de l'Institut de Droit international* (1950), 42 ff.
55. Sir John Fischer Williams, "International Law and the Property of Aliens," 1928 *British Yearbook of International Law* 1–30.
56. S. Friedman, *Expropriation in International Law* (London: Stevens, 1953).
57. League of Nations, *Documents*, C.46, M.23 (1926).
58. *Id.*, C.74, M. 53 (1928), II (Ann.), p. 29.
59. Minutes of the Conference, in League of Nations, *Documents*, C. 97, M.23 (1930), II, p. 274.
60. Cf. James Hyde, "Permanent Sovereignty over National Wealth and Resources," 50 *AJIL* 854 (1956).
61. Li, "Nationalization and International Law," *supra* n. 50, p. 14.
62. U.N. G.A. Res. 1803 (XVII), December 14, 1962. Other resolutions preceding it include: Res. 523 (VI), January 12, 1952, Res. 626 (VII), December 21, 1952, Res. 1314 (XIII), December 12, 1958, and Res. 1515 (XV), December 15, 1960. For a discussion of the issues, see Karol N. Gess, "Permanent Sovereignty over Natural Resources," 13 *International and Comparative Law Quarterly* 398–447 (April, 1964).
63. Richard I. Miller, *Dag Hammarskjold and Crisis Diplomacy* (Dobbs Ferry, N.Y.: Oceana, 1961), pp. 24–58.
64. *New York Times*, November 27, 1968, p. 11, and October 5, 1969, p. 24; *Wall Street Journal*, February 20, 1969. For an insightful discussion see Jerome A. Cohen, "Will Jack Make His 25th Reunion?" Op-Ed Page, *New York Times*, July 7, 1971, p. 37.
65. *New York Times*, May 3, 1968.
66. *New York Times*, July 11, 1970. 67. *Id.*
68. I heard the bishop talk at a meeting of the China Panel, Division of Overseas Ministries, the National Council of the Churches of Christ, in New York, on May 17, 1971. After the meeting I asked Bishop Walsh whether his imprisonment could have been avoided if he had taken advantage of the Chinese permission to leave in 1958. The answer was: "Probably." The arrest came two weeks after he refused to leave mainland China voluntarily.
69. "British Spy Case Broken in Lanchow," *PR*, March 22, 1968, p. 14.
70. *Id.* 71. *JMJP*, July 5, 1968; *PR*, July 12, 1968, p. 4.
72. *New York Times*, April 24, 1968.

73. *New York Times,* December 5, 1968.
74. *New York Times,* October 5, 1969, p. 24.
75. *New York Times,* February 16, 1969.
76. *New York Times,* December 7, 1969, pp. 1 and 5.
77. *Japan Times Weekly,* September 14, 1968. 78. *Id.,* March 9, 1968.
79. *New York Times,* November 13, 1963; November 15, 1963; November 16, 1963; and November 17, 1963.
80. *Id.,* June 4, 1968.
81. Lisa Hobbs, *I Saw Red China* (New York: Avon, 1966), p. 190.
82. Majorie Whiteman, *Damages in International Law* (Washington, D.C.: Government Printing Office, 1937–43); S. Friedman, *Expropriation in International Law* (London: Stevens, 1953); B. A. Wortley, *Expropriation in Public International Law* (Cambridge University Press, 1959); and Gillain White, *Nationalization of Foreign Property* (London: Stevens; New York: Praeger, 1961).
83. Lissitzyn, *International Law Today and Tomorrow* (Dobbs Ferry, N.Y.: Oceana, 1965), pp. 75–85.
84. G. H. Hackworth, "Responsibility of States for Damages Caused in Their Territory to the Person or Property of Foreigners," 24 *AJIL* 500 (1930).
85. Tung, *China, supra* n. 13, pp. 61–70.
86. B. H. Williams, "The Politics of Missionary Work in China," *Current History,* XXIII, 1 (1925–1926), p. 73.
87. In his new book, *International Law in an Organizing World* (1968), William Tung (Tung Lin) cited the mob violence against the Chinese at Rock Springs, Wyoming, in 1885, and U.S. refusal of responsibility (p. 139).
88. E. M. Borchard, *The Diplomatic Protection of Citizens Abroad,* p. 222, cited in Tung, *supra* n. 13, p. 63.
89. These ties can be seen from the sizable amounts of remittances sent in to relatives in mainland China by overseas Chinese. According to one report, from 1949 and the beginning of the Great Leap Forward, total overseas Chinese remittances averaged $30 million per year. Edward F. Szczepanik, ed. *Symposium on Economic and Social Problems in the Far East* (Hong Kong University Press, 1962), pp. 117 and 129.
90. The Soviet Union is opposed to the U.S. measure, see Academy of Sciences of the USSR, Institute of Law, *International Law* (Moscow: Foreign Language Publishing House [1961]), p. 161. The Chinese, like the Soviets, do not have any similar regulations.

CHAPTER VIII

1. *New York Times,* November 3, 1966. Tung Pi-wu seemed to have been acting as the chief of state ever since. For example, he received the credentials of the new ambassador of the Arab Republic of Yemen on July 4, 1968, *JMJP,* July 5, 1968. The practice goes back to 1950. When Chairman Mao (chief of state) was in Moscow, Liu Shao-ch'i, then the vice-chairman of the CPR, received the credentials of the ambassador of Czechoslovakia on January 14, 1950. *Shih-chieh chih-shih shou-ts'e* [World Knowledge Handbook] (Peking: World Knowledge, 1954), p. 1172.
2. National People's Congress, Standing Committee, *Kung-pao* [Bulletin], No. 3 (1965), p. 15.
3. 1 *TWKH* 33–72.
4. *JMJP,* September 12 and 14, 1959; also *Hsin-hua pan-yüeh k'an* [New China Fortnightly], No. 18 (1959), p. 12 ff.
5. Resolution of the NPC Standing Committee, passed on December 20, 1955, text in 1 *Chung-hua jen-min kunk-ho-kuo hsien-fa hsüeh-hsi ts'an-k'ao tzu-liao* [Reference Materials for Studies of the Constitution of the People's Republic of China] (Peking, 1957), p. 387. The Constitutional basis for the passage of the resolution seems to be Article 31 (19), under which the NPC Standing Committee is "to exercise such other functions and powers as are vested in it by the National People's Congress." The NPC itself may vest such law-making power in its Standing Committee in accordance with Article 27 (14), which empowers the NPC "to exercise such other functions and powers as the National People's Congress considers it should exercise."
6. See *infra* Chapter XII, n. 70.
7. See Harold C. Hinton, *Communist China in World Politics* (Boston: Houghton Mifflin, 1966), p. 106 and its footnotes.
8. Cf. U.S. Department of State, Research Memorandum RFE23, January 13, 1968; figures revised here in accordance with my personal files. See also the list in *Jen-min shou-ts'e* [People's Handbook] (Peking), 1965 ed., pp. 225 f.
9. See the yearly editions of the *Jen-min shou-ts'e*. The NPC Standing Committee *Kung-pao* [Bulletin] publishes all appointments of the CPR's diplomatic representatives.
10. *TKWC,* p. 63.
11. 1 *TWKH* 1–32 (1949–1950).
12. *Supra* n. 2.
13. *Id.*
14. Department of State, Division of Intelligence and Research, *Directory of Chinese Communist Officials,* A66–8 (March, 1966), pp. 380, 359–81.

15. Cited in *MFCPWT,* p. 40. I have not been able to locate the original document, despite a painstaking search.
16. *Id.,* p. 41. 17. *Id.* 18. *HFTT,* p. 42.
19. *Id.* 20. *Id.* 21. *Id.,* p. 41, and n. 1 on p. 41.
22. *Chung-hua jen-min kung-ho-kuo yu-kuan kung-an kung-tso fa-kuei hui-pien* [Collection of Documents Concerning Laws and Regulations Relating to the CPR's Security Work] (Peking, 1952), pp. 128, 132, 136.
23. Articles 7,6, and 5 of the three sets of "Provisional Rules," respectively, *id.* Presumably, the separate "regulations to be laid down by the Ministry of Foreign Affairs" provided for exemption or preferential treatment. See discussion below and n. 27.
24. *JMJP,* April 20, 1964; see *supra* Chapter VII, text at reference for n. 16.
25. *Id.*
26. Article 17, Chapter 15, of the *Chung-hua jen-min kung-ho-kuo chan-hsing hai-kuan fa* [CPR Provisional Customs Regulations] (in effect as from May 1, 1951) (Peking: People's Publications, 1951).
27. *CB,* No. 53 (November 3, 1958).
28. Customs Measures Concerning the Release [Exemption from Inspection] of Gift Items Imported into or Exported from China (in effect as from July 1, 1958); text in 8 *FKHP* 183–86 (1958).
29. Sino-Czech Consular Treaty (1960), English text in 402 *UNTS* 224.
30. See *infra* Chapter IX, text accompanying nn. 66–72.
31. The CPR has consular treaties with: the Soviet Union (June 23, 1959), text in 8 *TYC* 20; East Germany (January 27, 1959), *id.* 26; Czechoslovakia (May 7, 1960), 9 *id.* 52; and Laos (October 7, 1961), *JMJP* October 8, 1961.
32. *HFTT,* p. 41 and n. 1 on the same page; and *MFCPWT,* p. 41.
33. The status of Chinese technical assistance personnel abroad is usually determined by the terms of the agreement under which they are sent. Article 5 of the Sino-Yemen Scientific, Technical and Cultural Cooperation Agreement (January 12, 1958), for example, provided that the Chinese personnel would be given protection of their person and property and guaranteed "appropriate living conditions" in their host country. The same article also required the Chinese personnel to respect the laws, religious code, customs, and tradition of Yemen, and not to interfere in the latter's domestic politics. 7 *TYC* 1.
34. See "The Legal Status of the Commercial Representative's Office of the CPR in the Mongolian People's Republic and That of the Commercial Attaché's Office of the Mongolian People's Republic in the CPR," Appendix to the Sino-Mongolian Treaty of Commerce (April 26, 1961), 13 *FKHP* 80–81 (1963).
35. Cf. the documents relating to the diplomatic practices of other states included in *TKWC,* pp. 356–82.

36. The CPR is not a party to either convention. For general discussions of the two Vienna conventions, see Philippe Cahier and Luke Lee, "Vienna Conventions on Diplomatic and Consular Relations," *International Conciliation,* No. 571 (January, 1969); Michael Hardy, *Modern Diplomatic Law* (Dobbs Ferry, N.Y.: Oceana, 1968); Luke T. Lee, *The Vienna Convention on Consular Relations* (Leyden: Sijhoff, 1966); and Clifton E. Wilson, *Diplomatic Privileges and Immunities* (Tucson, Ariz.: University of Arizona, 1967).
37. 4 *TYC* 258. 38. *New York Times,* January 30, 1950, p. 1, col. 6.
39. *Id.,* November 9, 1949, p. 31, col. 1.
40. *Id.,* February 1, 1950, p. 2, col. 3 (Mackiernan left China for India); and *id.,* January 4, 1950 (Ward arrived in San Francisco).
41. Cf. Art. 26 of the Vienna Convention on Consular Relations (1963): "The receiving state shall, *even in case of armed conflict,* grant to members of the consular post and members of the private staff, other than nationals of the receiving state, and to members of their families forming part of their households irrespective of nationality, the necessary time and facilities to enable them to prepare their departure and to leave at the earliest possible moment after the termination of the functions of the members concerned. . . ." Article 41: "Consular officers shall not be liable to arrest or detention pending trial, except in the case of a grave crime and pursuant to a decision by the competent judicial authority . . . consular officers shall not be committed to prison or liable to any other form of restriction on their personal freedom save in execution of a judicial decision of final effect."
42. Even before the Korean War broke out, the CPR was not so nice to the Americans in Shanghai. United States efforts to repatriate her nationals were defeated and delayed until April, 1950, when the CPR finally permitted the S.S. *General Gordon* to dock at Shanghai and take American nationals away. *New York Times,* April 27, 1950, p. 12, col. 6. The Chinese Communists in January, 1950, seized U.S. consular properties in Peking. Chapter VII, n. 30, above. After the United States in December, 1950, froze the CPR's assets in this country (*New York Times,* December 17, 1950, p. 1, col. 2), the Chinese Communists retaliated by seizing U.S. property and freezing American assets, both public and private, that were located in mainland China. Total U.S. investments in China were put at $100–200 million. *New York Times,* December 30, 1950, p. 3. See *supra* Chapter VII, n. 34 and accompanying text.
43. *New York Times,* February 8, 1950, p. 9, col. 4.
44. NCNA (Mukden), November 4, 1950; *SCMP,* No. 3, 1950, p. 7.
45. Cf. Chapter IX *infra,* text for nn. 58–64.
46. "Protests to the Ghanaian Authorities," *PR,* March 11, 1966, pp. 7–8. The CPR signed two agreements on economic and technical cooperation

with Ghana, one in 1961 and the other on July 15, 1964, which was supplementary to the 1961 agreement.

47. NCNA (Peking), September 20, 1967; *SCMP,* No. 4026; *New York Times,* October 2, 1967. Indonesia and the CPR severed diplomatic relations in 1967, *infra* n. 60.
48. *PR,* January 17, 1967, p. 3. In the spring of 1969, it was reported that two showcases of photographs outside the CPR Embassy in Warsaw, Poland, were smashed and a picture of Chairman Mao was slashed. *New York Times,* April 2, 1969.
49. Reports in *New York Times,* July 19, 1966, p. 6, col. 2; July 23, 1966, p. 2, col. 4; and August 20, 1966, p. 4, col. 3.
50. Ko Swan Sik, *Reflections on the Attitude of the People's Republic of China Toward International Law as Manifested in Its Relations with the Netherlands, 1950–1966,* mimeo. (American Society of International Law, 1968), p. 10 ff.
51. *Id.,* pp. 13–14. 52. *Id.,* pp. 18–19. 53. *Id.*
54. Such practices were recorded in *Yi-li,* cited in Hung Chün-p'ei, *Ch'un-ch'iu kuo-chi-fa* [The International Law of Ancient China During the Autumn and Spring Period] (Shanghai: Chung-hua, 1939), p. 211–12.
55. *Id.,* pp. 236–37.
56. Cf. Article 39 of the 1961 Vienna Convention; also *Satow's Guide to Diplomatic Practice,* 4th ed. by Sir Nevile Bland (New York: David McKay, 1957), Paragraph 478, p. 276.
57. Lauterpacht-Oppenheim, 2 *International Law,* 6th ed., Sec. 33–43.
58. *Nieuwe Rotterdamse Courant,* January 2, 1967, quoted in Ko Swan Sik, *Reflections, supra* n. 50, p. 22 (n. 86).
59. *Id.*
60. Justus M. van der Kroef, "The Sino-Indonesia Rupture," *China Quarterly,* No. 33 (January-March, 1968), at 44.
61. *New York Times,* August 23, 1967, p. 4, col. 5.
62. *Id.,* August 16, 1967. 63. *Id.,* February 15, 1967, p. 8, col. 2.
64. *JMJP,* June 30, 1963; *PR,* July 5, 1963; and William Griffith, *The Sino-Soviet Rift* (MIT Press, 1964), p. 151.
65. *New York Times,* February 8, 1967, p. 1, col. 2; November 27, 1966.
66. *Id.,* February 4, 1967, p. 6, col. 6. 67. See *supra* n. 63.
68. *New York Times,* February 15, 1967, p. 8. When thousands of demonstrators paraded on August 29, 1966, near the Soviet Embassy in Peking in a rally against "revisionism," about two hundred Chinese troops and policemen, in two rows, immediately guarded the embassy. The young Chinese marchers were described by Western correspondents as "well disciplined," apparently under official injunctions to remain so. *Id.,* August 30, 1966, p. 1.
69. *Peking Municipal People's Procuracy v. Raghunath,* Peking Municipal

People's Court, June 13, 1967, digested in 62 *AJIL* 205 (1968); also *New York Times,* June 15, 1967.

70. The Indian government retaliated by expelling two CPR diplomats in New Delhi, *New York Times,* June 15, 1967.
71. *New York Times,* August 23, 1967, and August 24, 1967.
72. *Id.,* August 23, 1967, p. 1, col. 8.
73. Arts. 22 and 29.
74. B. Sen, *A Diplomat's Handbook* (The Hague: Martinus Nijhoff, 1965), p. 92.
75. Paul Louis-Lucas, "L'affaire de la legation de Roumanie a Berne," 1955 *Annuaire français de droit international,* 175–82.
76. Moore, 6 *Digest* 62.
77. See P. Cahier, "Vienna Convention on Diplomatic Relations," in *International Conciliation,* No. 571 (January, 1969), at 24.
78. Article 6, the "Sixteen Articles" (Decision of the Central Committee, Chinese Communist Party, on the Great Proletarian Cultural Revolution, August 8, 1966), *JMJP,* August 9, 1966.
79. The Eight-Point Directive of the Military Affairs Commission CCP Central Committee, issued on January 28, 1967, under Mao's personal signature; text in *Chung-kung wen-hua ta ko-ming tzu-liao hui-pien* [Collection of Materials Relating to the Chinese Communist Great Cultural Revolution], comp. by Ting Wang, Editorial Board, Ming Pao Monthly (Hong Kong: *Ming Pao* Monthly, 1967), 37–38.
80. The incident took place on August 7, 1967; cf. Michael B. Yahuda, "Chinese Foreign Policy After 1963: The Maoist Phases," *China Quarterly,* No. 36 (October-December, 1968), at 107.
81. *New York Times,* April 19, 1968. The attack on the Burmese Embassy came in the wake of the murder of a Chinese technical adviser in Burma sent under Sino-Burmese technical assistance agreements. *SCMP,* No. 4013.
82. See report by Seymour Topping from Peking, in *New York Times,* June 21, 1971, p. 1, col. 4.
83. See generally Peter Fleming, *The Siege in Peking* (New York: Harper and Row, 1959); Victor Purcell, *The Boxer Uprising* (Cambridge: Cambridge University Press, 1963); and Chester Tan, *The Boxer Catastrophe* (New York: Columbia University Press, 1955).
84. Kenneth Latourette, *A Short History of the Far East,* 3d ed. (Macmillan, 1951), p. 436.
85. *New York Times,* May 8, 1960.
86. *Id.,* April 27, 1965.
87. *Id.,* June 14, 1967.
88. *Id.,* September 28, 1968, p. 3. Gunmen in Brazil even kidnapped U.S. Ambassador C. Burke Elbrick on September 4, 1969, and held him as hostage until the Brazilian government released fifteen political prisoners. *New York Times,* September 5, 1969.

89. 1968 *Annual Report of the Secretary-General on the Work of the Organization,* General Assembly *Official Records* (23rd Sess.), Supp. No. 1 (A/7201), 207–208.
90. *Id.,* p. 209. U.N. Res. 2328 (XXII).
91. *TIAS* 1676; 43 *AJIL,* Supp. (1949).
92. Arts. 48–53, Vienna Convention on Diplomatic Relations (1961); and Arts. 74–79, Vienna Convention of Consular Relations (1963).
93. See discussion on this point in Luke T. Lee, *Vienna Convention on Consular Relations* (Leyden: A. W. Sijthoff, 1966), p. 205.

CHAPTER IX

1. For a discussion of the CPR's attitude on the practical utility of international law, see *supra* Chapter I, nn. 10–15.
2. Oliver J. Lissitzyn, *International Law Today and Tomorrow* (Dobbs Ferry, N.Y.: Oceana, 1965), p. 35.
3. Cf. Georg Schwarzenberger, *The Inductive Approach to International Law* (London: Stevens, 1965), p. 20.
4. Immanuel Hsü, *China's Entrance into the Family of Nations* (Cambridge, Mass.: Harvard University Press, 1960), esp. Chapter I and II.
5. For Nationalist China's relations with international law, see Tung Lin (William Tung), *China and Some Phases of International Law* (Shanghai: Kelly and Walsh; London: Oxford University Press, 1940); and T'ang Wu, *Chung-kuo yü kuo-chi-fa* [China and International Law] (Taipei, 1957).
6. Hungdah Ch'iu, "Communist China's Attitude Toward the United Nations: A Legal Analysis," (assisted by R. R. Edwards), 62 *AJIL* 20–50 (1968); Byron S. Weng, "Communist China's Changing Attitudes Toward the United Nations," 20 *International Organization,* 4 (Autumn, 1966), pp. 677–704; Myres S. McDougal and Richard M. Goodman, "Chinese Participation in the United Nations: The Legal Imperatives of a Negotiated Solution," 60 *AJIL* 671–727 (1966). Also, Sheldon Appleton, *The Eternal Triangle* (Michigan State University, 1961); Boyer and Akra, "The U.S. and the Admission of Communist China," *Political Science Quarterly,* LXXVI (1961), pp. 352 ff; Herbert W. Briggs, "Chinese Representation in the U.N.," 6 *International Organization,* January, 1952, pp. 192–209; David Brook, "The Problem of China's Representation in the U.N.," 5 *Journal of East Asiatic Studies* (Manila), January, 1956, pp. 43–68; *The U.N. and the China Dilemma* (Vantage Books, 1956); G. G. Fitzmaurice, "Chinese Representation in the U.N.," 1952 *Yearbook of World Affairs* (London), pp. 36–55; Stanley K. Hornbeck, "Which China?" 34 *Foreign Affairs* (1955), pp. 24–39;

"The Representation of China in the U.N.," *External Affairs Review* (New Zealand), XII (1962), pp. 3–12 (contains a chronology of events, 1949–1961); F. B. Schick, "The Question of China in the U.N.," 12 *International and Comparative Law Quarterly* (1963), pp. 1232–50; Shigejiro Tabata, "Admission to the U.N. and Recognition of States: In Connection with the Matter of Chinese Representative," 5 *Japanese Annual of International Law* (1961), pp. 1–4; Richard Harvey, "The United States and the Legal Status of Formosa," 30 *World Affairs Quarterly* (London) 134–53 (1959–1960); J. P. Jain, "Legal Status of Formosa, A Study of British, Chinese and Indian Views," 57 *AJIL* 25–45 (1963); D. P. O'Connell, "The Status of Formosa and the Chinese Recognition Problem," 50 *id.* 405–16 (1956); and Mervyn Adams, "Communist China and the United Nations: A Study of China's Developing Attitude Towards the United Nations Role in International Peace and Security," M.A. thesis (New York: Columbia University, 1964).

7. U.N. Doc. A/1123 (November 18, 1949), p. 2.
8. U.N. Security Council *Official Records,* 5th yr., 459th mtg. (January 10, 1950), No. 1, p. 2.
9. Cf. Weng, "Communist China's Changing Attitudes," *supra* n. 6.
10. E.g., *JMJP* editorial, October 12, 1962; and T'ang Ming-chao, "Oppose United States Schemes to Obstruct China's Rights in the United Nations," 10 *China Reconstructs* (Peking), 12 (December, 1961), pp. 7–9. The General Assembly resolution, Res. 1668 (XVI), December 15, 1961, which defeated an attempt to seat Peking and expel the Nationalist Chinese, was denounced by Peking as "completely illegal and null and void." *PR,* December 29, 1961, pp. 8–9.
11. This point is suggested in Byron S. Weng, "Some Conditions for Peking's Participation in International Organizations," unpublished paper, first delivered at a regional meeting of the American Society of International Law, February 8, 1969.
12. On September 17, it was reported that both the Canadian Foreign Minister, Mitchell W. Sharp, and Secretary-General U Thant believed that the CPR now wanted to enter the United Nations. *New York Times,* September 18, 1969. In view of the CPR's negotiation then with Canada on the establishment of diplomatic relations, it was not unlikely that Peking had expressed the interest to the Canadian side in the course of the talks. Furthermore, Chou En-lai also indirectly conveyed Peking's renewed interest. At a banquet in Peking in honor of Premier Alfred Raoul of the Congo (Brazzaville), Chou thanked Raoul for the Congo's advocacy of the "restoration of China's legitimate rights in the United Nations and the expulsion of the Chiang Kai-shek clique." *New York Times,* October 6, 1969.
13. *PR,* December 29, 1961, pp. 8–9.

14. *Id.* See also Seymour Topping's report from Peking, *New York Times,* June 23, 1971, p. 1.
15. *JMJP,* November 25, 1966; *New York Times,* November 26, 1966.
16. *PR,* October 8, 1965, pp. 7–14.
17. *New York Times,* July 29, 1971, p. 6.
18. *New York Times,* August 3, 1971, p. 1.
19. James Reston's report from Peking, *New York Times,* August 6, 1971, p. 1.
20. 9 Department of State *Bulletin* 393 (1943).
21. 13 *id.* 153 (1945). 22. 22 *id.* 79 (1950).
23. *Id.,* 80–81. 24. 23 *id.* 5 (1950).
25. Text reproduced in Chinese People's Institute of Foreign Affairs, ed., *Oppose U. S. Occupation of Taiwan and the "Two Chinas" Plot* (Peking, FLP, 1950), pp. 5–6.
26. U. N. Doc. S/1715.
27. Chou En-lai, "Statement Regarding the 'Mutual Defense Treaty' Between the Chiang Kai-shek Clique and the United States Imperialism (December 8, 1954)," NCNA, December 9, 1954; excerpts in English in Ambekar and Divekar, *Documents on China's Relations with South and Southeast Asia 1949–1962* (Bombay: Allied, 1964), pp. 362–64.
28. "There Is Only One China, Not Two," *JMJP,* July 14, 1961; Shao Chin-fu, "The Absurdity of the 'Two Chinas' [Idea]," *KCWT,* No. 2 (1959), pp. 7–17; tr. in *JPRS,* 1102D (January 12, 1960), pp. 12–30. The CPR has protested to many governments allegedly engaged in a "two Chinas plot." E.g., the protests sent by CPR Ambassador Liu Ch'un to the government of Laos, October 19, 1963, and November 12, 1963, 5 *YTCN* 371–73 (1965).
29. Text of the Peace Treaty with Japan (1951) in *TIAS,* No. 2490, and *UNTS,* No. 136, p. 45.
30. The Nationalist government's awareness of the legal limbo can be seen in Foreign Minister George Yeh's testimony before the Legislative Yuan on July 16, 1952, when he warned: "The delicate international situation makes it that they [Taiwan and Penghu] do not [legally] belong to us." Quoted in Allen Whiting, "The United States and Taiwan," in American Assembly, *The United States and the Far East* (New York: Columbia University, 1956), p. 176. The CPR's awareness of the fact that the lack of Chinese representation at the San Francisco peace settlement presents a challenge to China's legal claims to Taiwan may be seen in *JMJP,* May 12, 1964.
31. Statement by Premier Chou En-lai Concerning the 'Peace Treaty' with Japan (December 4, 1950), attached to the text of the peace treaty in 1950–1952 *Kuo-chi t'iao-yüeh chi* [International Treaty Series] (Peking), p. 356.
32. Shao Chin-fu, *supra* n. 28. 33. *Supra* n. 26.

34. Cf. Ch'iu Hungdah, "The Theory and Practice of Communist China with Respect to the Conclusion of Treaties," 5 *Columbia Journal of Transnational Law,* No. 1 (1966), esp. pp. 7–8.
35. "China's Sovereignty over Taiwan Brooks No Intervention," *JMJP,* May 12, 1964; *PR,* May 15, 1964, p. 7. The *JMJP* omitted the part of the Truman statement which had said that Taiwan had been "surrendered to Generalissimo Chiang Kai-shek."
36. The statement was attributed to a spokesman of the British Foreign Office, *JMJP,* May 15, 1964. Sir Anthony Eden, then British Foreign Secretary, claimed on February 4, 1955, that the Cairo Declaration was "a statement of intention that Formosa should be retroceded to China after the war." This description clearly was meant to play down the legal binding force of the Cairo Declaration. House of Commons *Debates,* DXXXVI (5th yr.) (1955) (Written Answers to Questions), p. 159.
37. Ch'en T'i-ch'iang, "Taiwan—A Chinese Territory," *Review of Contemporary Law* (Brussels), No. 5 (1956), p. 42. In a statement on August 15, 1951, Chou En-lai also recalled the "no separate peace treaty" obligation assumed by the wartime Allies with respect to Japan. He denounced the 1951 San Francisco Peace Treaty without the signature of China as a violation of the earlier agreement, hence "null and void," 2 *TWKH* 30–36.
38. *Id.,* p. 43. See also Mei Ju-ao, "Take Off the Legal Garb of the Aggressor," *CFYC,* No. 2 (1955), p. 48; reproduced in *JMJP,* January 31, 1955.
39. Ch'en, *id.* 40. *Id.* 41. *Id.,* p. 42; Mei, *supra* n. 38.
42. Cf. Chapter I above, nn. 1–2.
43. Department of State *Bulletin,* XXII, 551 (January 23, 1950). Also Herbert Briggs, "American Consular Rights in Communist China," 44 *AJIL* 243–58 (1950).
44. "Statement by the CPR Foreign Ministry Spokesman Regarding the Withdrawal of Former United States Diplomatic Personnel from China (February 5, 1950) (Excerpts)," 1 *TWKH* 97 (1949–1950). The Military Control Commission had the responsibility of maintaining order and security and other administrative functions pending the establishment of a civilian government. Cf. also Luke T. Lee, "Consular Status under Unrecognized Regimes—with Particular Reference to Recent United States Practice," 32 *British Yearbook of International Law* 295–300 (1955–1956).
45. *Id.*
46. *Id.* The statement, ironically, resembles a similar accusation made by India of CPR diplomats' activities in that country some thirteen years later, in 1963. Indian Ministry of External Affairs, *White Paper,* No. IX (1963), p. 103.
47. U.N. Doc. S/1902 (November 15, 1960), Security Council *Official*

Records, Supp., 5th yr. (1950). The statement was contained in a letter from Chou En-lai, dated November 11, 1950.

48. *Id.* 49. *White Paper, supra* n. 46, pp. 90–92, at 90.
50. In the *Caroline* case (1841), U.S. Secretary of State Webster, in a note to Lord Ashburton of Britain, made the definition which came to be widely accepted: "*Necessity of* . . . self-defense is instant, overwhelming, and leaving no choice of means, and no moment for deliberation." Moore, 2 *International Law* 409–14 (1906). Emphasis added. Also Jennings, "The Caroline-MacLeod Cases," 32 *AJIL* 82 (1938).
51. *PR,* July 11, 1969, p. 6.
52. Peking's note to the Indian Embassy, May 18, 1963, text in *White Paper, supra* n. 46, p. 160.
53. Among the comments on the 1949 Geneva conventions, and especially the POWs, see Gutteridge, "The Geneva Conventions of 1949," 1949 *British Yearbook of International Law* 294 ff; and Yingling and Ginnane, "The Geneva Conventions of 1949," 46 *AJIL* (1952). Texts of the conventions in *TIAS*, No. 3364.
54. "Statement by the Government of the People's Republic of China (October 16, 1964)," English text in *Break the Nuclear Monopoly, Eliminate Nuclear Weapons* (Peking, FLP, 1965). Peking's policy and views concerning disarmament in general are contained in *Ts' ai-chün wen-t'i wen-chien hsüan-chi* [Selected Documents on the Disarmament Problem] (Peking: World Knowledge, 1958); "Partial Nuclear Test Ban—What the Chinese Press Says," *PR,* August 2, 1963, p. 3; "Mass Organizations Oppose the [1963 Moscow] Tripartite Treaty [on Nuclear Test Ban]," *PR,* August 23, 1963, p. 4; and "The Test Ban Talks," *id.,* July 26, 1963, p. 61. A general discussion is in Morton Halperin and Dwight H. Perkins, *Communist China and Arms Control* (New York: Praeger, 1965); also Shao-chuan Leng, "Communist China's Position on Nuclear Arms Control," *Virginia Journal of International Law,* December, 1966, pp. 101–16. See further discussion, *infra* Chapter XIV, nn. 77–90.
55. That is, no treaty is binding upon a third state not a party to an agreement, except when it has expressly indicated a willingness to be bound.
56. *JMJP,* April 3, 1962; *PR,* No. 17 (1962). Ch'iu Hungdah, "Communist China's Attitude Towards Nuclear Tests," *China Quarterly,* No. 21 (January-March, 1965), p. 101.
57. *JMJP,* November 22, 1964. Leng, *supra* n. 54, pp. 101–16.
58. The Chinese Communists, for instance, arrested American Consul-General Angus Ward in Mukden, in November, 1949, and expelled the former British consul in Mukden, L. Steventon, the next year. *New York Times,* November 9, 1949, p. 31, col. 6; and NCNA, Mukden, November 4, 1950, English text in *SCMP,* No. 3 (1950), p. 7. See further *supra* Chapter VIII, nn. 38–44.

59. E.g., CPR Embassy (Djkarta) protests of November 4, 1965, and November 19, 1965, *PR*, November 26, 1965, pp. 20–23.
60. *Id.*, p. 21.
61. *Id.* Also, "China Protests Against Outrages by Indonesian Right-Wing Forces," *PR*, March 18, 1966, pp. 5–6; "Campaign Against Chinese Nationals in Indonesia Condemned," *id.*, April 15, 1966, pp. 9–10. In these cases, Peking made it plain that protecting its nationals abroad was "a right." This claim would find support under international law. Cf. the *Mavrommatis* (Jurisdiction), in which the Permanent Court of International Justice ruled: "It is an elementary principle of international law that a state is entitled to protect its subjects, when injured by acts contrary to international law committed by another state, from whom they have been unable to obtain satisfaction through ordinary channels." PCIJ, Ser. A, No. 1 (1934).
62. *PR*, November 26, 1965, p. 21; also *id.*, December 3, 1965, pp. 8–10. International law holds a state's nonsuppression of crime sufficient cause to establish an international delinquency. *Janes Claims* (U.S. v. Mexico), cited in William Bishop, *International Law: Cases and Materials*, 2d ed. (1962), p. 657.
63. *PR*, November 26, 1965, p. 22.
64. *Id.*, December 3, 1965. In mid-December, 1966, riots broke out in Macao. A few Chinese were shot at and killed by Portuguese police. Peking charged the Portuguese authorities with direct "criminal responsibility." *New York Times*, December 13, 1966.
65. CPR Foreign Ministry note to the Indian Embassy in Peking, February 23, 1963, *White Paper*, *supra* n. 46, pp. 99–100. In another note, Peking declared: "Recently, the Maharashtra State government openly ordered requisition of the property of Chinese nationals. If the Indian government sincerely means what it stated, it should immediately stop such practice which is completely *in violation of international law*. In contrast to the Indian government's persecution of Chinese nationals, the Indian nationals in China always enjoy equal treatment with nationals of other countries in China. Their proper rights and interests and their property have always been protected, and they have always enjoyed, and now still enjoy, facilities to take away their property on leaving China." *Id.*, p. 92.
66. E.g., CPR expropriation of the (British) Asia Petroleum Co.'s assets, by a "decree" of the Government Administrative Council, dated April 30, 1951, text in 2 *Chung-yang cheng-fu fa-ling hui- pien* [Collection of the Laws and Decrees of the Central Government] (Peking, 1953).
67. This point was developed by George Ginsburgs, "The Validity of Treaties in the Municipal Law of the 'Socialist' States," 59 *AJIL* 541 (1965).
68. CPR Foreign Ministry note to the Indian Embassy, April 27, 1963,

White Paper, supra n. 46, p. 123. Peking by this note demanded in detail the type of treatment to be accorded by India to Chinese nationals in conformity with the Geneva Conventions of 1949. Also its note of March 26, 1963, *id.*, p. 111.

69. CPR Foreign Ministry note to the Indian Embassy, April 25, 1963, *id.*, p. 121. A similar demand was made by the CPR Embassy in New Delhi, "in exercise of its right of protecting Chinese nationals," note to the Indian government, May 6, 1963, *id.*, p. 132. For a documented charge against India's alleged violations of international law in mistreating Chinese nationals, see Chou Keng-sheng, "The Persecution of Chinese Nationals and Infringement upon Their Rights and Interests by the Indian Government Are Serious Violations of International Law," *JMJP*, January 22, 1963. Over the years, the CPR government has made numerous similar protests to other countries over the treatment and status of Chinese nationals. See, for example, "China's Protest Against Hongkong Restrictions on the Chinese," *China Monthly Review* (Shanghai), LXIX, 2, Supp. (October, 1959), p. 9, reprod. in Ambekar and Divekar, eds., *Documents on China's Relations, supra* n. 27, pp. 275–76; and "Chinese Foreign Ministry's Statement on the 'Report on Kowloon Riots' Made by British Authorities in Hongkong (January 22, 1957)," *China Today*, I, 3 (1957), reprod. in *id.*, pp. 276–79.
70. *Supra* n. 58.
71. Protest by the CPR Embassy, May 13, 1960, *PR*, No. 20 (1960), pp. 34–35.
72. *PR*, November 12, 1965, p. 24. Emphasis added.
73. *PR*, October 29, 1965, p. 13. The Indonesian troops were said to have invaded the premises of the living quarters of the Chinese technical assistance personnel sent to Indonesia under government contracts.
74. Memorandum from the CPR Embassy to the Indian government, March 7, 1963, text in *White Paper, supra* n. 46, p. 101.
75. *Supra* n. 67. Also notes from the CPR Embassy to the Indian government, November 7, 1962, and January 10, 1963, *White Paper, supra* n. 46, p. 80.
76. See *supra* Chapter VIII, n. 21. Also Montell Ogden, *Juridical Basis of Diplomatic Immunity* (Washington, D.C.: John Byrne & Co., 1936).

CHAPTER X

1. Department of State, *The Conduct of Communist China* (Washington, D.C.: Government Printing Office, 1963), printed for the use of the House Committee on Foreign Affairs, 88th Cong., 1st Sess. See also "Chinese Aggression and International Law," *India Calling* (Official In-

dian Embassy publication in Peking), April, 1963, cited in a CPR note of protest to the Indian Embassy, dated June 3, 1963, reprod. in *White Paper,* No. IX (1963), p. 165, published by the Indian Ministry of External Affairs.

2. Address by Chou En-lai, May 3, 1954, before the 1954 Geneva Conference, text in *Jih-nei-wa hui-yi wen-chien hui-pien* [Collection of Documents of the Geneva Conference] (1954), p. 35.
3. Wen Yao-chin, "Gas Warfare—Johnson Administration's Heinous War Crime," *PR,* April 2, 1965, p. 23. In 1969 domestic opinion in the United States was divided on whether this country should continue to maintain its stockpile of bacteriological and chemical weapons. *New York Times,* July 31, 1969, p. 8 and September 24, 1969; and Seymour M. Hersh, "Dare We Develop Biological Weapons," *New York Times Magazine,* September 28, 1969, p. 28 ff.
4. *Id.,* at 24. The U.S. Law of Land Warfare, Army FM 27–10 (1956), states: "38 Gases, Chemicals, and Bacteriological Warfare. The United States is not a party to any treaty, now in force, that prohibits or restricts the use in warfare of toxic or nontoxic gases, or smoke or incendiary materials, or of bacteriological warfare." Cited in Bishop, *International Law: Cases and Materials,* 2d ed. (1962), pp. 807–808. A CPR writer, Fu Chu, considers that the 1925 Geneva Protocal is only declaratory of customary law and hence binding upon the United States. "American Imperialists' Use of Poisonous Gases in South Vietnam Is a War Crime in Flagrant Violation of International Law," *JMJP,* April 3, 1965.
5. *JMJP,* March 29, 1965.
6. The Laws and Customs of War laid down in the Hague Regulations of 1907 provided: "The attack or bombardment, by whatever means, of towns, villages, dwellings or buildings which are undefended is prohibited." See Lawyers Committee on American Policy Towards Vietnam, *Vietnam and International Law* (Flanders, N.J.: O'Hare Books, 1967); William L. Standard (chairman) and Joseph H. Crown (secretary), Lawyers Committee on American Policy Towards Vietnam, "Letter to the Editor," *New York Times,* July 6, 1966. Also, William Standard, "United States Intervention in Vietnam Is Not Legal," 52 American Bar Association *Journal* (1966); and "Memorandum of the Lawyers Committee on American Policy Towards Vietnam," *Congressional Record,* CXII (daily ed., February 9, 1966), p. 2552 ff. The U.S. government has sought to defend its bombing of North Vietnam on grounds of the latter's "armed attack" on South Vietnam. "Legitimate Defense," said Leonard C. Meeker, the State Department legal adviser, "includes military action against the aggressor wherever such action is needed to halt the attack." *New York Times,* December 14, 1966. Another defense of U.S. actions in Vietnam is in John Norton Moore, "The Law-

fulness of Military Assistance to the Republic of Vietnam," 61 *AJIL* 1–34 (1967). See also "The Legality of U.S. Participation in the Defense of Vietnam," Memorandum from the Department of State, Office of the Legal Adviser, March 4, 1966, *Congressional Record,* CXII, 43 (March 10, 1966), pp. 5274–79. For comparative views, see Richard Falk, ed., *The Vietnam War and International Law* (Princeton: Princeton University Press, 1968).

7. E.g., "The Johnson Administration's Piratical Talks," *JMJP,* February 10, 1965.
8. *Mei-kuo tui yüeh-nan nan-fang kan-she ho ch'in-lüeh cheng-ts'e* (U.S. Policy of Intervention and Aggression in the South of Vietnam) (Peking: World Knowledge, 1963), p. 68. Text of the Final Declaration and the Agreement of the 1954 Geneva Conference can be found in "Further Documents Relating to the Discussion of Indochina at the Geneva Conference," *Cmd.* 9239, Misc. No. 20 (1954). Her Majesty's Stationery Office, London, pp. 5–11, 27–38.
9. Para. 13 states: "The members of the Conference agree to consult one another on any question which may be referred to them by the International Supervisory Commission in order to study such measures as may prove necessary to ensure that the agreements on the cessation of hostilities in Cambodia, Laos, and Vietnam are respected."
10. *Mei-kuo . . . , supra* n. 8, p. 69; also *New York Times,* July 20, 1954. See further *infra* Chapter XII, n. 34.
11. Chapter XII, nn. 34–36.
12. "How the U.S. Imperialists Have Torn up the Geneva Agreements," *PR,* April 2, 1965, p. 24. For North Vietnam's views on the implementation of the 1954 Geneva Agreements, see Democratic Republic of Vietnam, Ministry of Foreign Affairs, *Documents Related to the Implementation of the Geneva Agreements Concerning Vietnam* (Hanoi, 1956).
13. *Id.;* also *supra* n. 8. 14. *PR,* April 2, 1965, p. 24.
15. D. W. Bowett, "Estoppel Before International Tribunals and Its Relation to Acquiescence," 1957 *British Yearbook of International Law* 195. The principle of weighing evidence with a view to detecting inconsistency, as Arnold McNair put it, "is not estoppel *eo nomine,* but it shows that international jurisdiction has a place for some recognition of the principle that a State cannot blow hot and cold—*allegans contraria non audiendus est.*" "Legality of the Ruhr," *id.* (1924), pp. 34–37. McNair, in *Law of Treaties* (London: Clarendon Press, 1938), p. 407, cited a similar example in the dispatch from the British Secretary of State for Foreign Affairs (Sir Edward Grey) to the British Ambassador at Tokyo (Sir F. MacDonald), July 14, 1916, which took the view that France, by her attitude on the effect of annexation on existing commer-

cial rights in Madagascar [that is, the island's existing treaties with other states] after the French annexation [i.e., declaring Madagascar a French colony], was debarred from appealing to Great Britain to join in protest to Japan over the latter's annexation of Korea.

16. Chou En-lai's statement on the U.S. declaration concerning the coming into force of the peace treaty with Japan, May 5, 1952, text in 1950–1952 *Kuo-chi t'iao-yueh chi* [International Treaty Series], p. 389.
17. Note of March 11, 1963 to the Indian government, *White Paper, supra* n. 1, p. 172.
18. Chou En-lai's message, July 6, 1950, U.N. Doc. S/1583; and his cablegram, dated August 20, 1950, U.N. Doc. S/1703.
19. Mei Ju-ao, "Aggressor and the Law," *People's China* (Peking) March 1, 1955, pp. 10–14.
20. Chou En-lai's statement, December 8, 1954, NCNA (Dec. 9, 1954), reprod. in Ambekarand Kivekar, *Documents on China's Relations with South and Southeast Asia* (Bombay: Allied, 1964), p. 362.
21. "CPR Government Statement on the Anglo-French Armed Aggression Against Egypt (November 1, 1956)," in *Chung-tung wen-t'i wen-chien hui-pien* [Collection of Documents on the Middle East Problem] (Peking: World Knowledge, 1958), p. 265.
22. "CPR Government Statement Concerning Support to Egypt in Her Fight Against Anglo-French Aggression (Nov. 7, 1956)," *id.*, p. 277.
23. "Protest of the CPR Government to the Governments of Britain and France (Nov. 3, 1956)," *id.*, p. 268. A discussion of the legal issues involved in the Suez crisis is found in Chao Li-hai, "The Suez Canal Problems and International Law," *CFYC,* No. 1 (1957), p. 12.
24. "CPR Government Statement in Opposition to U.S. Armed Intervention in Lebanon (July 16, 1958)," in *Chung-tung . . . , supra* n. 21, p. 515.
25. "A Grave Protest of the CPR Government to the British Government Regarding the Dispatch of British Forces to Jordan and the Threat They Pose to the Republic of Iraq (July 18, 1958)," *id.*, p. 531.
26. "A Symposium on the Criminal Acts by Britain and the United States Committed Against International Law and the United Nations Charter," *CFYC,* No. 4 (1958), pp. 3–8. Among the international lawyers present were Chou Keng-sheng, Li Hao-p'ei, Shao T'ien-jen, and Jen Chi-sheng.
27. Kou Chi-chou and Wu Hsiu, "What the Congo Situation Reveals," *HC,* March 1, 1962; and Wang Lin, "Colonialists Get Out of Congo," *PR,* January 25, 1963, pp. 15–16.
28. T'ien Pao-shan, "Is the Dispatch of Soviet Army to Hungary an Intervention in the Internal Affairs of Another State?" *Shih-shih shou-ts'e* [Current Affairs Handbook], No. 2 (January 21, 1957); tr. in ECMM, No. 76 (April 1, 1957), pp. 1–3.

29. *JMJP,* October 25, 1962, p. 1.
30. Chou En-lai's speech at a Rumanian Embassy reception marking Rumania's National Day, August 23, 1968, *PR,* supp., August 23, 1968.
31. NCNA, Peking, December 15, 1966; *New York Times,* same date.
32. *New York Times,* September 20, 1966; February 22 and February 10, 1967.
33. *JMJP,* May 27, 1960.
34. *Id.* See further *supra* Chapter VI for Peking's position on the law of territorial waters.
35. Government of India, *Report of the Officials of the Governments of India and the People's Republic of China on the Boundary Question* (New Delhi, 1961), p. CR-53 ("CR" precedes all pages in the section which contains the report of the CPR officials).
36. *Id.,* p. CR157–CR186. 37. *Id.,* pp. CR7–CR33.
38. *Id.,* pp. CR75–CR154.
39. *Id.,* p. CR8 and *passim.* Also see Yang Yün, "China Restates Her Position on the Settlement of the Sino-Indian Border Dispute Through Negotiation," *KCWT,* No. 2 (1960), pp. 55–56.
40. *Id.* 41. *Id.,* pp. CR75–CR110.
42. *Id.,* p. CR101 ff. General international law accepts effective control as the most superior basis of territorial claims. Cf. the *Palmas Island* case: ". . . the actual continuous and peaceful display of State functions is in case of dispute the sound and natural criterion of territorial sovereignty." 2 *Reports of International Arbitral Awards* 829; 22 *AJIL* 867 (1928).
43. Wei Liang, "Viewing the 'McMahon Line' from the Standpoint of International Law," *KCWT,* No. 6 (1959), p. 52.
44. The *watershed* principle was accepted in the Treaty of Nerchinsk of 1689 (with Czarist Russia), the Convention of 1896 relating to Sikkim and Tibet (with Britain), and the Convention of 1895 relating to Tonkin China border (with France); and these were enumerated in K. Krishna Rao, "The Sino-Indian Boundary Question and International Law," 11 *International and Comparative Law Quarterly* (London), Part II (April, 1962), pp. 406–407.
45. For the same reason, various governments of China in the nineteenth century refused to accept the British proposal to make the Irrawaddy-Salween *watershed* as the boundary between China and Burma. To accept it China would have to give up certain areas west of that watershed which were strategic to China. After the British attempt to buy out China's right met with Chinese refusal, Britain proceeded to occupy the areas in 1913. J. J. G. Syatauw, *Some Newly Established Asian States and the Development of International Law* (The Hague: Martinus Nijhoff, 1961), pp. 126–27.
46. Wei Liang, *supra* n. 43, p. 52.

47. 2 *Reports of International Arbitral Awards* 829; 22 *AJIL* 867 (1928).
48. *PR*, March 21, 1969, at 9.
49. *Id.;* In August, 1969, Peking charged that the Soviet Russians in the preceding two months had instigated 429 border incidents, ranging from intrusions by Soviet aircraft to ground attacks by troops and the building of military emplacements. *New York Times,* August 20, 1969, p. 1, col. 8.
50. D. W. Bowett, *supra* n. 15, p. 198. In the Costa Rica-Nicaragua *Boundary* case, the arbiter rejected Nicaragua's argument that a treaty of 1858 defining the boundary was not binding since a third state, San Salvador, had not ratified in its capacity as guarantor. "These views," he ruled, "are strengthened by a consideration of the evidence adduced on the part of Costa Rica to prove *acquiescence* by Nicaragua for ten or twelve years in the validity of the treaty . . . . But the Government of Nicaragua *was silent when it ought to have spoken,* and so waived the objection now made. It saw fit to proceed to exchange of ratifications without waiting for San Salvador . . . . Neither may now be heard to allege, as reasons for rescinding this completed treaty, any facts which existed and were known at the time of its consummation." (Emphasis added.) Moore, 2 *International Arbitrations,* pp. 1945, 1961.
51. Note of January 19, 1963, text in *White Paper, supra* n. 1, p. 91.
52. *Id.*, p. 84. 53. *Id.*
54. *Id.; Report of Official, supra* n. 35, p. CR161. Emphasis added.
55. *Report of Officials, id.*, emphasis added.
56. *Id.*, p. CR6. 57. See *supra* n. 15.
58. U.N. Doc. A/2954 (September 9, 1955), p. 2.
59. General Assembly Res. 906 (IX), December 10, 1954, which accused the CPR of "detention and imprisonment of United Nations military personnel in violation of the Korean Armistice Agreement."
60. Letter of Nehru, March 5, 1963, in *White Paper,* supra n. 1, p. 6. The tactful wording in Nehru's letter runs: "As you [Premier Chou] are already aware, I stated in Parliament on 10th December 1962 that 'I am prepared, when the time comes, provided there is approval of Parliament, even to refer the basic dispute of the claims on the frontier to an international body like the International Court of Justice at the Hague.' There could be no fairer and more reasonable approach than this proposal for peaceful resolving of our differences, once the appropriate climate is created."
61. *Id.*, p. 12; also *Sino-Indian Boundary Question II* (Peking: FLP, 1965), 17.
62. *Id.*
63. In the *Certain Germany Interests* case, the Permanent Court of International Justice said that: "A treaty only creates law as between the States which are parties to it; in case of doubt no rights can be deduced from

it in favor of third states." PCIJ (1926), Ser. A, No. 7, p. 29. Cf. Art. 30 and 31, 1966 Draft Articles of the Law of Treaties, adopted by the International Law Commission on July 18, 1966, 61 *AJIL* at 365 (1967).

64. "China Will Never Recognize the 'ROK-Japan Basic Treaty,' " *PR,* July 2, 1965, p. 7. Peking even made a formal protest to Japan. "China Protests Sato Government's Forcible Adoption of the 'Japan-ROK Treaty,' " *id.,* November 19, 1965, p. 5.
65. An English text of the ROK-Japan Treaty on Basic Relations appears in 4 *International Legal Materials* 924 ff (1965). See also Shigeru Oda, "The Normalization of Relations Between Japan and the Republic of Korea," 61 *AJIL* 35–56 (1967), esp. 41.
66. CPR Foreign Ministry note to the Indian Embassy, March 25, 1963, in *White Paper, supra* n. 1, pp. 8–9.
67. Text of the Sino-Pakistan Agreement, March 2, 1963, appears in English in Ambekar and Divekar, *supra* n. 20, pp. 218–21.
68. *PR,* Oct. 16, 1964, pp. ii–iv. Peking gives its reasons for conducting this and successive detonation tests as chiefly attempting to break "the nuclear monopoly and nuclear blackmail by the United States and the Soviet Union acting in collusion"; but it pledged not to use nuclear weapons. *New York Times,* October 28, 1966, p. 18. See further *infra* Chapter XIV, text for nn. 77–90.
69. Peking's cautiousness over the possible restrictive effect which its own words or actions may have upon its future conduct (if other states should invoke them against it) can be seen in the following rebuttal to India: "When did the Chinese Government accept without any reservation [as was alleged by India] the position that Kashmir is under Indian sovereignty? The Indian Government could not cite any official Chinese document to prove this arbitrary contention . . . [which] is not only unilateral misrepresentation but a conclusion imposed on [the Chinese Government], which the Chinese Government categorically rejects." Text of the Chinese note is included in Indian Ministry of External Affairs, *Sino-Pakistan "Agrement" of March 2, 1963: Some Facts* (New Delhi, 1963), App. II: "Note Given by the Ministry of Foreign Affairs, Peking, to the Embassy of India in China, 31 May 1962," p. 10. See also *supra* Chapter V for a discussion of the possible influence of international law in the making of the CPR's foreign policy.

CHAPTER XI

1. Robert Newman, *Recognition of Communist China* (New York: Macmillan, 1961); G. Fitzmaurice, "Chinese Representation in the U.N.," 1952 *Yearbook of World Affairs* (London) 36–55; Quincy Wright, "The Status of Communist China," 11 *Journal of International Affairs* (New York, Columbia University, School of International Affairs) 171–89 (1957); Herbert Briggs, "Chinese Recognition in the U.N.," 6 *International Organization* (1952); Charles G. Fenwick, "The Recognition of Communist China," 47 *AJIL* (1953); L. C. Green, "The Recognition of Communist China," 3 *International Reporter* (1952); D. P. O'Connell, "The Status of Formosa and the Chinese Recognition Problem," 50 *AJIL* (1956); Pitman B. Potter, "Communist China," 50 *AJIL* (1956), etc.
2. This chapter is drawn from my essay "Communist China's Recognition Practice and Its Implications in International Law," to be published in a volume on Communist China and international law edited by Professor Jerome A. Cohen of Harvard University Law School; an excerpted version was delivered at a regional meeting of the American Society of International Law in New York City, February 8, 1969.
3. E.g., possessing a people and a defined territory, and being effectively controlled by an independent authority.
4. Sir Hirsch Lauterpacht, *Recognition in International Law* (Cambridge: Cambridge University Press, 1947).
5. Mao's proclamation, in 1 *TWKH* 3; and Chou's letter of transmittal, *id.* 5.
6. After its formation, the Democratic Republic of Vietnam on January 15, 1950, sent a note to the CPR, expressly extending "recognition" and requesting that diplomatic relations be established between the two countries. *Infra* n. 33.
7. *USSR Foreign Policy,* 1949 (Gospolitizdat, 1953), p. 171, quoted in Academy of Sciences of the USSR, Institute of Law, *International Law* (Moscow, Foreign Language Publishing House [1961]), p. 119. Chinese translation of the Soviet response in 1 *TWKH* 6 (1949–1950).
8. Chou's reply to Gromyko, the Soviet foreign minister, in 1 *TWKH* 5–6.
9. Moore, *Digest* 73.
10. U.S. Secretary of State Colby to the U.S. Chargé d'Affaires in Mexico (Summerlin), May 25, 1920, 3 *Foreign Relations* 167 (1920), cited in H. Briggs, *Law of Nations,* 2d ed. (1952), at 126.
11. 1 Hackworth, *Digest* 166.

12. The term is borrowed from Lucian Pye, *The Spirit of Chinese Politics* (Cambridge, Mass.: MIT Press, 1968), pp. 3, 166.
13. K'ung Meng, "A Critique of the Bourgeois International Law Regarding 'Subjects of International Law' and Theories of Recognition of States," *KCWT*, No. 2 (1960).
14. *Supra* n. 5.
15. Academy of Sciences of the USSR, *International Law, supra* n. 7, p. 117.
16. 1 *TWKH* 22–24. Emphasis added.
17. Chou's note to Burma, *id.*, at 17. The same condition was insisted upon by the CPR to Norway (p. 20), Sweden (p. 25) and Switzerland (p. 29), among others.
18. See Pakistan's note to the CPR, which recognized the CPR and declared that its recognition of Nationalist China was "duly withdrawn." 1 *TWKH* 28. Also, Peking's note to the Netherlands, recalling the latter's earlier promise to sever diplomatic ties with Nationalist China, *id.* 30.
19. Cf. Ko Swan Sik, *Reflections on the Attitude of the People's Republic of China Toward International Law, as Manifested in Its Relations with the Netherlands, 1950–1966,* mimeo. (American Society of International Law, 1968), at 4.
20. In the case of Britain, Norway, Switzerland, and the Netherlands, for example, when each had notified Peking that a Chargé d'Affaires had been appointed, the CPR did not accept him as such but received him as an *ad hoc* negotiator for the specific purpose of negotiating in Peking the terms for the establishment of diplomatic relations. The same applied to the cases of Norway and Pakistan after they had respectively appointed a minister and a special envoy. The appointees were in most cases already in Nanking, where they had been accredited to the National Chinese government. 1 *TWKH* 19, 29, 30, 22, 26–27.
21. Remarks by the Netherlands foreign Minister, quoted in Ko Swan Sik, *supra* n. 19, at 6.
22. As in the cases of Israel and Afghanistan, see 1 *TWKH* 22–24.
23. Although I presume this to be true, very few cases can be cited in this category. Most probably Indonesia, with which the CPR on March 28, 1950, decided to establish diplomatic relations, is one example in point. In a notification of that date, the CPR informed the new Indonesian government of its decision, presumably following prior negotiations. No separate joint communiqué regarding the establishment of diplomatic relations is known to exist. 1 *TWKH* 31–32.
24. For example, after recognizing (expressly) the Republic of Mali, on October 17, 1960, the CPR entered into negotiations with its government on the establishment of diplomatic relations. On October 27, a joint communiqué issued simultaneously in both capitals announced that the

two governments had decided to exchange ambassadors. In fact, the same procedure of *ad hoc* negotiations was followed in the establishment of diplomatic relations between the CPR and Cuba in 1960 (joint communiqué on September 28, 1960). 7 *TWKH* 294, 306, and 253.

25. *New York Times,* August 3, 1969, p. 15.
26. K'ung Meng, *supra* n. 13, at 51. For a study of U.S. policy of not recognizing the CPR, see Dorothy Rae Dodge, "Recognition of the Central People's Government of the People's Republic of China: Legal and Political Aspects" (Ph. D. dissertation, Ann Arbor, Mich.: University Microfilms, 1955); and A. Doak Barnett, *Communist China and Asia* (New York: Harper, 1960), pp. 430–1458.
27. For an interesting (and the only available) account, see Kenneth Young, *Negotiating with the Chinese Communists* (New York: McGraw-Hill, 1968).
28. In the 1960s, after its policy had changed, the CPR used U.S. nonrecognition as an excuse for not participating in international undertakings, such as the disarmament talks, which would result in undesirable restrictions on its own freedom of action. *JMJP,* April 3, 1962; *PR,* No. 17 (1963); also O. Edmund Clubb, *The International Position of Communist China* (Association of the Bar of the City of New York, 1965), p. 31. In retrospect, the CPR-U.S. Ambassadorial Talks could have first given the CPR the idea that the recognition impasse could be bypassed. At least since 1955, when the talks began, CPR attitudes toward the issue have undergone some changes, as we shall see later.
29. The CPR was recognized, during 1949–1955, by twenty-four pre-existing states: the Soviet Union, October 3, 1949; Bulgaria, October 3, 1949; Rumania, October 3, 1949; Hungary, October 4, 1949; North Korea, October 4, 1949; Czechoslovakia, October 5, 1949; Poland, October 5, 1949; Yugoslavia, October 5, 1949; Outer Mongolia, October 6, 1949; Albania, November 21, 1949; Burma, December 16, 1949; India, December 30, 1949; Pakistan, January 5, 1950; Britain, January 6, 1950; Ceylon, January 7, 1950; Denmark, January 9, 1950; Israel, January 9, 1950; Norway, January 10, 1950; Afghanistan, January 12, 1950; Finland, January 13, 1950; Sweden, January 14, 1950; Switzerland, January 17, 1950; the Netherlands, March 27, 1950; and Nepal, August 1, 1955. On the other hand, the CPR recognized (without using the word "recognize" explicitly) three newly independent states: the Democratic Republic of Germany, October 25, 1949; the Democratic Republic of Vietnam, January 18, 1950; and Indonesia, March 28, 1950. *TWKH,* Vols. 1, 2, and 3, *passim.*
30. 1 *TWKH* 14–15.
31. Message from Chou En-lai on behalf of the CPR government, January 18, 1950, 1 *TWKH* 24–25.
32. *Id.* 33. *Id.,* pp. 31–32; also *supra* n. 22.

34. 4 *TWKH* 1 (1956–1957). 35. *Id.* 55–56. 36. *Id.* at 363.
37. Sino-Tunisian joint communiqué of January 11, 1964, English text in *SCMP,* No. 3139, at 43.
38. Richard Lowenthal, "China," in Z. Brzezinski, ed., *Africa and the Communist World* (Stanford: Stanford University Press, 1963), at 164–65.
39. *Id.;* cf. U.S. Department of State, *Research Memorandum,* REA 23, June 13, 1968, p. 4.
40. Joint CPR-Moroccan communiqué, in 5 *TWKH* 197 (1958).
41. 4 *id.* 304 (1957); also discussion below accompanying n. 60.
42. *Id.* at 364 and 365. To this day Malaya has no diplomatic relations with Peking; on the other hand, it maintains a consular office in Taiwan.
43. 5 *id.,* at 71. 44. *Id.* at 131. 45. *Id.* at 185, 187, 188.
46. See discussion on this below. 47. 5 *TWKH* 195–97 (1958).
48. Alexander Eckstein, *Communist China's Economic Growth and Foreign Trade* (New York: McGraw-Hill, 1966), p. 202 ff.
49. Egypt is a good example, see Lowenthal, *supra* n. 38, p. 153; Eckstein, *id.,* pp. 192, 194, 234. More significant, CPR writers openly admit that trade is useful as a first step toward diplomatic recognition. Wang Yao-t'ien, *Kuo-chi mao-yi t'iao-yüeh ho hsieh-ting* [International Trade Treaties and Agreements] (Peking, 1958), p. 116. Further discussion in Chapter XIII, nn. 24–26.
50. Text in 4 *TWKH* 348–54, at 353 (1956–1957).
51. *Id.,* pp. 59–60; and n. 1 on p. 60.
52. *Id.* 93. 53. *Id.,* 101. 54. 5 *id.* 142.
55. See, for example, *SCMP,* No. 2249, p. 54, in regard to Togo (April 27, 1960); No. 2284, p. 32, Mali Federation (June 19, 1960): No. 2288, p. 49, Malagassy (June 25, 1960); *id.,* p. 50, Somaliland (June 25, 1960), etc. In most recognition cases after 1960, there is hardly any exception to this formula.
56. See Chou's message on the independence of the People's Republic of South Yemen, NCNA, Peking, November 30, 1967; *SCMP,* No. 4072, p. 46.
57. *Id.*
58. As on the independence of the Congo (L), June 26, 1960, *SCMP,* No. 2288, p. 50; the establishment of the Republic of Ghana, July 1, 1956, SCMP, No. 2292, p. 27; and the independence of Zambia (former Northern Rhodesia), *PR,* October 30, 1964, p. 4.
59. *SCMP,* No. 2292, pp. 26, 27. 60. *Supra* n. 41.
61. See statement by Secretary of State Stimson, February 6, 1931, Department of State, Latin American Series, No. 4, p. 6.
62. Peking greeted Kuwait's independence, June 29, 1961, but did not expressly extend recognition. 8 *TWKH* 202 (1961); also *SCMP,* No. 2531, p. 41. Other exceptions are Singapore and Senegal.

63. 21 F. 2d, 396, reproduced in Briggs, *Law of Nations, supra* n. 10, at 194.
64. Cf. Stimson, *supra* n. 61.
65. On CPR claims to being a continuation of the same Chinese state, see Premier Chou's communications to the United Nations, U.N. Doc. A/1123 (November 18, 1949, and U.N. Sec. Council, *Official Records,* 5th yr., 459th meeting (January 10, 1950), No. 1, p. 2; also JMJP editorial, October 12, 1962; and comments by Jerome A. Cohen, in 1968 *Proceedings* of the American Society of International Law, at 211. See also Chapter VI, nn. 13–14, and Chapter IX, n. 13, *supra.*
66. For the 1956 CPR recognition of Yemen, see 4 *TWKH* 101 (1956–1957); its recognition on October 6, 1962, of Yemen under the republican form of government, 9 *id.* 367 (1962). The diplomatic mission maintained in each other's capital was later elevated from legation to embassy level. The first Yemeni ambassador presented his credentials on February 6, 1967, *SCMP,* No. 3879, p. 38.
67. 9 *TWKH* 309 (1962). 68. *Id.,* p. 158.
69. 4 *TWKH* 93 (1956–1957). 70. 10 *id.* 183 (1963).
71. *SCMP,* No. 3143, p. 51.
72. Sir Hirsch Lauterpacht, *supra* n. 4, p. 329.
73. Academy of Sciences of the USSR, *supra* n. 7, p. 118.
74. Oliver J. Lissitzyn, *International Law Today and Tomorrow* (Dobbs Ferry, N. Y.: Oceana, 1965), pp. 12–13.
75. Briggs, *supra* n. 10, at 161.
76. In 1948, while extending recognition to Israel, the president of the United States stated: "The United States recognizes the provisional government as the *de facto* authority of the new State of Israel." Although recognition of a *de facto* government as such does not necessarily qualify the act of recognition itself, the U.S. delegate in the Security Council, Philip Jessup, said in the council that "the United States did extend *de facto* recognition to the Provisional Government of Israel." "*De facto* recognition" used here does not, strictly speaking, do justice to what was conveyed in the president's statement above (which gave U.S. recognition of a *de facto* government). Deys P. Meyers, "Contemporary Practice of the United States Relating to International Law," 55 *AJIL* at 697 (1961).
77. Arnold D. McNair, *Legal Effects of War* (1948), p. 353.
78. *The Arantzazu Mendi,* Great Britain, House of Commons, 1939 [1939] *A.C.* 256, cited in Briggs, *supra* n. 10, 142 ff; *Bank of Ethiopia v. National Bank of Egypt and Liquori,* 1 *Ch.* 513.
79. Misra, *India's Policy of Recognition of States and Governments* (Bombay: Allied, 1966), p. 192 and *passim.*
80. Premier Chou and Emperor Haile Selassie even issued a joint commu-

niqué, touching on issues of extreme political importance (e.g., Ethiopian support for the CPR's right of representation in the U.N.), February 1, 1964; text in *PR,* February 7, 1964, pp. 31–32.

81. For example, when the CPR protested on January 28, 1964, to France on its continued relations with Nationalist China, after France had recognized the CPR, *SCMP,* No. 3151, p. 23. See also Peking's protest to Kenya following a visit in Taiwan by an official of Kenya, NCNA, Peking, November 23, 1967; *SCMP,* No. 4067, p. 33.
82. 8 *TWKH* 141–42 (1961). 83. See *supra* n. 81.
84. Academy of Sciences of the USSR, *supra* n. 7, at 120. 85. *Id.*
86. *JMJP,* January 2, 1957. 87. K'ung Meng, *supra* n. 13.
88. *Id.* My paraphrase.
89. See Ch'en Yi's speech at a Peking reception honoring the visiting South Yemen foreign minister, September 18, 1968, *PR,* September 27, 1968, p. 29; also his denunciation of Israel for the "June War" of 1967, NCNA (Peking), June 12, 1967; *SCMP,* No. 3960, pp. 28–31.
90. W. E. Hall, *International Law,* 8th ed. (1924), Sec. 94.
91. *New York Times,* September 20, 1958, p. 1.
92. *SCMP,* No. 1911, p. 41.
93. Joint communiqué issued by Chou En-lai and Abbas Ferhat, October 5, 1960, *SCMP,* No. 2356, pp. 28–30.
94. Premier Chou's letter to Premier Ben Hatta of the GPRA, 9 *TWKH* 309 (1962).
95. For further discussion of the question, as viewed from the clash between traditional international law (given to the preservation of the *status quo*) and the aspirations for self-determination and revolutionary change of peoples having little or no interest maintaining the *status quo,* see my essay referred to in *supra* n. 2.
96. *SCMP,* No. 3660, p. 28; No. 3657, pp. 17–19; and No. 3705, p. 31.
97. *SCMP,* No. 3876, p. 32.
98. NCNA (Peking), December 1, 1967, and December 4, 1967. My attention was called to this by Donald Klein of the East Asian Institute, Columbia University.
99. I. William Zartman, "Tiger in the Jungle," in Francis Harper, ed., *This is China* (Hong Kong: Dragonfly, 1965), p. 322; also Harold Hinton, *Communist China in World Politics* (Boston: Houghton-Mifflin, 1966), pp. 194 ff.
100. John Cooley, *East Wind in Africa* (New York: Walker, 1965), p. 112.
101. Justus M. van der Kroef, "The Sino-Indonesia Rupture," *China Quarterly,* No. 33 (January-March 1968), pp. 17–46.
102. See further my essay, *supra* n. 2.
103. *PR,* October 16, 1970, p. 12. Emphasis added. 104. *Id.*
105. See *supra* n. 5.

106. For CPR-Italian agreement, see *PR,* November 13, 1970, p. 6; and for the CPR-Chilean agreement, *PR,* January 8, 1971, p. 3.
107. *PR,* June 4, 1971, p. 11.
108. See *PR,* October 23, 1970, p. 10; *id.,* December 11, 1970, p. 6; *id.,* February 19, 1971, p. 5; *id.,* April 2, 1971, p. 16; *id.,* April 9, 1971, p. 7; *id.,* May 14, 1971, p. 11; and *id.,* August 6, 1971, p. 22.
109. The wording seems to confirm our earlier speculation that recognition had been exchanged *de facto* during Premier Chou's state visit in Ethiopia in 1964.
110. "Welcome the Establishment of Diplomatic Relations Between China and Canada," *JMJP,* October 15, 1970; English translation in *PR,* October 16, 1970, p. 19.
111. "Greeting the Establishment of Diplomatic Relations Between China and Kuwait," *JMJP,* March 31, 1971; English translation in *PR,* April 2, 1971, p. 16.

CHAPTER XII

1. Wei Liang, 'On International Treaties Since World War II," 1953–1955 *Kuo-chi t'aio-yüeh chi* [International Treaty Series] (Peking, World Knowledge, 1961), pp. 660–90, at 660. Emphasis added.
2. *Supra* Chapter I, text at reference for nn. 57–66.
3. Academy of Sciences of the USSR, Institute of Law, *International Law* (Moscow: Foreign Language Publishing House [1961]), p. 247. Emphasis added.
4. *Supra* Chapter II, text at reference for nn. 37–38.
5. Wang Yao-t'ien, *Kuo-chi mao-yi t'iao-yüeh ho hsieh-ting* [International Trade Treaties and Agreements] (Peking: Finance and Economic Publications, 1958), p. 9.
6. See *supra* Chapter IV, nn. 22–25 and accompanying text; also Chapter I, n. 39.
7. The Soviet Union now accepts the capacity of international organizations, such as the United Nations, to conclude treaties. See *supra* n. 3, p. 247.
8. Sir Arnold McNair, *Law of Treaties,* 2d ed. (London: Clarendon Press, 1961), p. 42.
9. *The Sino-Indian Boundary Question,* enlarged ed. (Peking: FLP, 1962), pp. 57–58. In responding to an accusation by Secretary of State Dulles of CPR "armed occupation of Tibet," Chang Han-fu, CPR vice-foreign minister, declared on July 15, 1957 that everybody knew that Tibet was part of China. In an agreement signed between the CPR and

India in 1954, he noted, India had formally recognized the fact. Even the United States itself, in a memorandum to Britain in 1942, had also recognized Chinese sovereignty over Tibet as unquestionable. See Chang's report to the fourth session of the First National People's Congress, in 4 *TWKH* 348–54, at 351.

10. Cf. Ch'u Yuan, *Meng-ku jen-min kung-ho-kuo* [The Mongolian People's Republic] (Peking, 1961). Outer Mongolia became independent in 1945 under the shadow of Soviet influence.
11. See *International Affairs* (Moscow), No. 10 (1964), at 83.
12. See Chapter XI, nn. 92–95 and accompanying text, *supra.*
13. Wang, *supra* n. 5, p. 9; Wei Liang, *supra* n. 1; Chapter I, nn. 27–33 *supra.*
14. *Id.,* p. 10.
15. *Id.,* p. 11. The author cited the Chou-Nehru statement of 1954 on the "Five Principles of Peaceful Coexistence" as an "important contribution to modern international law."
16. *Supra* Chapter II, text at reference for nn. 38–39.
17. Academy of Sciences of the USSR, *supra* n. 3, p. 12. By comparison the CPR view seems relatively closer to the Western view, cf. Oliver J. Lissitzyn, *International Law Today and Tomorrow* (Dobbs Ferry, N. Y.: Oceana, 1965), p. 27.
18. Luke T. Lee, *China and International Agreements* (Leyden: Sijthoff, 1969). See discussion below.
19. Ch'en Yi's remarks in *PR,* No. 37 (1962), p. 11; and Wei Liang, *supra* n. 1, at 685.
20. E.g., the Sino-Korean Treaty of Friendship, Cooperation, and Mutual Assistance, July 11, 1961. The preamble of the treaty reads, in part: "The Chairman of the People's Republic of China and the Presidium of the Supreme People's Assembly of the Democratic People's Republic of Korea, determined in accordance with *Marxism-Leninism* and the principle of *proletarian internationalism* . . . to make every effort to further strengthen and develop the fraternal relations of friendship . . . between [the two countries]. . . , have concluded the present treaty. . . ." 10 *TYC* 25.
21. See *infra* Chapter XIII, nn. 40–47 and accompanying text.
22. The term "treaties" here is used broadly to include less formal agreements, except when otherwise restricted in context.
23. 11 *TYC* 226–84 (index for 1949–1962).
24. Douglas Johnston and Hungdah Ch'iu, *Agreements of the People's Republic of China, 1949–1967: A Calendar* (Cambridge, Mass.: Harvard University Press, 1968), pp. 218–24. It goes without saying that many other agreements are unreported and unknown to the outside; cf. Lee, *supra* n. 18, p. 17, n. 6.
25. 4 *TYC* 1; *New York Times,* September 11, 1955.

26. Kenneth Young, "American Dealings with Peking," *Foreign Affairs,* XLV, 1 (October, 1966), p. 79; also his *Negotiating with the Chinese Communists* (New York: McGraw-Hill, 1968).
27. English text in 1953 *Yearbook of the United Nations* 136–46; and *TIAS,* No. 2782; Chinese text in 2 *TYC* 382.
28. All the seventeen treaties of friendship are published in a single volume, *Chung-hua jen-min jung-ho-kuo yu-hao t'iao-yüeh hui-pien* [Collection of the CPR's Friendship Treaties] (Peking: World Knowledge, 1965).
29. Calculated with the semiofficial treaties included.
30. See the table in Ch'iu's review of the *TYC* in 61 *AJIL* at 1097 (1967).
31. Johnston and Ch'iu, *supra* n. 24.
32. The four criteria employed by Johnston and Ch'iu are: (a) official listing by the governments concerned; (b) status and function of those who signed or issued the document and of the institutions they represent; (c) government approval or acceptance of some responsibility before or after signing; and (d) predominant national governmental interest in the subject matter. *Id.,* ix.
33. The Soviets reject the Western distinction between "law-making" and "contract" treaties. Whether an agreement is "legislative," or creates binding norms, depends on the intent of the parties, they argue. G. I. Tunkin, *Voprosy Teorii Mezhdunarodnovo Prave* [Problems of the Theory of International Law] (Moscow: State Publishing House of Legal Literature, 1962), pp. 66–72; cited in Bernard Ramundo, *Peaceful Coexistence* (Baltimore: Johns Hopkins, 1967), p. 50, n. 26.
34. *New York Times,* July 20, 1954; also *supra* Chapter X, text for n. 10.
35. ". . . [The] Chinese side resolutely maintains that all agreements between the two sides [the CPR and the U.S.] must take the form of *joint* announcements of both sides, and *no longer* take that of statements issued by them separately." *PR,* No. 37 (1960), p. 30.
36. *PR.,* No. 1 (1965), p. 20; Morton H. Halperin and Dwight H. Perkins, *Communist China and Arms Control* (New York: Praeger, 1965), pp. 127–28.
37. See *supra* n. 23.
38. Texts in Chinese in 4 *TYC* 258; and also 2 *JPWT* 160–69; and 225–33.
39. Wang, *supra* n. 5, p. 12.
40. Established in June, 1955; see Grzybowski, *The Socialist Commonwealth of Nations* (New Haven, Conn.: Yale University Press, 1964), 130–35; 6 *TYC* 318 (1957).
41. Established in 1957, *id.,* p. 147; 6 *TYC* 271.
42. Established in 1956 by the CPR, the Soviet Union, Outer Mongolia, North Korea, and North Vietnam, 5 *TYC* 169 (1956); also *SCMP,* No. 1310, pp. 20–21.
43. Grzybowski, *supra* n. 40, pp. 27–73, 212.
44. *Id.,* p. 147.

45. UPI dispatch (London), July 13, 1966.
46. The CPR was a party to the Agreement for the Establishment of the Joint Institute for Nuclear Research. 10 *TYC* 408 (1961).
47. I am using the word "accede" in a broad sense to incorporate "adherence" and "acceptance."
48. 6 *TYC* 319. 49. 260 *UNTS* 438–444.
50. 7 *TYC* 182. 51. 6 *TYC* 282.
52. 6 *TYC* 294. In addition to these eight accessions to international conventions, the *TYC* between 1949 and 1961 listed twelve other items under "multilateral treaties," including five agreements regarding railway passenger and cargo transport, two on scientific cooperation, two communiqués of international conferences (the 1954 Geneva Conference Declaration, and the Bandung Conference Communiqué), one agreement with the Soviet Union and North Korea concerning rescue on the high seas, and two on postal and telecommunications cooperation (including one document which contains "verbal proceedings" of a conference attended by the directors of the weather and oceanographic bureaus of the CPR, North Korea, Mongolia, and Soviet Union). Some of these have already been discussed above.
53. Ch'iu's views in 61 *AJIL* 1097 (1967).
54. Britain, *Treaty Series,* No. 39 (1957), *Cmd.* 727.
55. 1964 U.S. *Treaties in Force* 258.
56. *JMJP,* July 16, 1962. I am indebted to Dr. Hungdah Ch'iu of Harvard University Law School for this information.
57. E.g., Article 16, Sino-North Vietnamese Treaty of Commerce and Navigation provided that the exchange of ratifications was to take place in Hanoi. The treaty was signed in Peking in 1962. 13 *FKHP* 93–97. Cf. Hungdah Ch'iu, "The Theory and Practice of Communist China with Respect to the Conclusion of Treaties," 5 *The Columbia Journal of Transnational Law,* No. 1 (1966), 1–13.
58. K. Young, *Negotiating, supra* n. 26; Arthur Lall, *How Communist China Negotiates* (New York: Columbia University Press, 1968).
59. For a discussion of Peking's insistence that states recognizing it and seeking to establish diplomatic ties with it must sever their relations with Nationalist China, etc., see Chapter XI, nn. 19–24, 103–115 *supra.*
60. Lee, *supra* n. 18, p. 57. Cf. also C. Turner Joy, *How Communists Negotiate* (New York: Macmillan, 1955); William Vatcher, Jr., *Panmunjom* (New York: Praeger, 1948).
61. E.g., the Sino-Mali Treaty of Friendship, November 3, 1964, was signed by Liu Shao-ch'i. Text in NPC Standing Committee, *Kung-pao* [Bulletin], No. 3 (1965), pp. 3–4.
62. The CPR's Boundary Treaty with Outer Mongolia, December 26, 1962,

was signed by Premier Chou, who no longer held the concurrent position of foreign minister as before. *Id.* No. 2 (1963), pp. 3–19.

63. Foreign Minister Ch'en Yi signed the Sino-Pakistan Boundary Agreement on March 2, 1963. *Id.*, No. 1 (1963), pp. 7–10.
64. The Treaty of Commerce and Navigation with North Vietnam of 1962 was signed by CPR Minister of Foreign Trade Yeh Chi-chuang, *supra* n. 57.
65. E.g., the NPC Standing Committee by a resolution on September 19, 1964, "decided" that "Chairman Liu Shao-ch'i of the People's Republic of China be the Plenipotentiary for the Signing of the Treaty of Friendship Between the People's Republic of China and the Republic of the Congo (Brazzaville)." NPC Standing Committee, *Kung-pao,* No. 1 (1965), p. 3.
66. E.g., Sino-Cambodia Treaty of Friendship and Mutual Non-Aggression, December 19, 1960, 9 *TYC* 25.
67. Treaty of Friendship between the CPR and the Congo (B), October 2, 1964, *supra* n. 65.
68. Wei Liang, "The So-called McMahon Line from the Standpoint of International Law," *KCWT,* No. 6 (1959), at 48.
69. *Id.* Emphasis added.
70. "Resolution Concerning the Procedure of Ratification in the Conclusion of Treaties with Foreign Countries," passed on October 16, 1954, by the NPC Standing Committee. Text in *TKWC,* p. 413.
71. The treaty was then signed by Chairman Liu (chief of state) with his Nepalese counterpart on the same day and it came into force immediately. 12 *FKHP* 65. Other treaties which came into force on the day of signing without going through the normal procedure of ratification because of "prior authorization" by the NPC Standing Committee include: Boundary Treaty with Afghanistan, November 22, 1963, and Treaty of Friendship with Yemen, June 9, 1964.
72. *SCMP,* No. 3907, p. 38.
73. 260 *UNTS* 438–44. CPR accessions to these conventions were technically called "ratifications."
74. CPR foreign ministry, *Yi-chiu ssu-chiu nien pa-yüeh shih-erh jih jih-nei-wa kung-yüeh* [The Geneva Conventions of August 12, 1949] (Peking, 1958), pp. 178–82.
75. 1947–1948 *Documents on International Affairs* (London) 664.
76. Article 55 of the Common Program is included among the documents relating to state succession in *TKWC* 80.
77. Before the 1960 treaty was signed, Premier Chou pledged that treaties concluded with Burma by former Chinese governments would be respected "according to general international practice." See Chou's "Report on the Question of the Boundary Line between China and Burma

to the Fourth Session of the First National People's Congress, July 9, 1957," 4 *TWKH* 343.

78. "Unequal treaties" will be discussed in a separate section below.
79. Until February 14, 1950, the CPR at least twice reaffirmed the validity of the said treaty and agreements, once in a North Shensi broadcast, on March 18, 1949, and once in a speech by Kuo Mo-jo, on August 13, 1949. Department of State, Division of External Research and Publications, *Reported Agreements Between the USSR and Communist China* (Washington, D. C., n.d. [1958?]), p. 38, n. 2. The CPR and the Soviet Union signed the Treaty of Friendship, Alliance and Mutual Assistance, and the Agreement on the Chinese Ch'ang-ch'un Railway, Port Arthur and Dairen, both in February 14, 1950.
80. Wang, *supra* n. 5, p. 9. See Chapter X for a discussion of Peking's accusations of other states violating international obligations assumed by treaty.
81. Art. 4, 8 *TYC* 1.
82. Liu Tse-jung, "The Legal Status of Cosmic Space," *KCWT,* No. 8 (1958), pp. 44–49. See also *supra* Chapter VI, nn. 129–31.
83. 100 *British and Foreign State Papers* 555 (1906–1907).
84. Yu Fan, "Speaking About the Relationship Between China and the Tibetan Region from the Viewpoint of Sovereignty and Suzerainty," *JMJP,* June 5, 1959.
85. See Chapter XI, n. 28, *supra; PR,* No. 20 (1964).
86. Chou En-lai's statement concerning the Mutual Defense Treaty between the United States and the Republic of (Nationalist) China, issued on December 8, 1954, NCNA (Peking), December 9, 1954; reprod. in Ambekar and Divekar, *Documents on China's Relations with South and Southeast Asia* (Bombay, 1964), p. 362.
87. 1956–1957 *Kou-chi t'iao-yüeh chi* [International Treaty Series] 716. Text of the Hague Convention of 1954 in 249 *UNTS* 240.
88. James Brierly, *Law of Nations,* 6th ed. (New York: Oxford University Press, 1963), p. 326 ff.
89. Article 2 (6) of the U.N. Charter reads: "The Organization shall ensure that states which are not Members of the United Nations act in accordance with these Principles so far as may be necessary for the maintenance of international peace and security."
90. "Reparation for Injuries Suffered in the Service of the United Nations," Advisory Opinion, International Court of Justice (1949), ICJ *Report* (1949): "Fifty States, representing the vast majority of the members of the international community, had the power, in conformity with international law, to bring into being an entity possessing *objective international personality,* and not merely personality recognized by them alone . . ."
91. "Speech by Wu Hsiu-ch'üan," *CB,* No. 36 (1950); cited also in R. Ran-

dle Edwards, "The Attitude of the People's Republic of China Toward International Law and the United Nations," *Papers on China* (Cambridge: Harvard University, East Asian Research Center, 1963), No. 17, p. 261. Wu's remarks, being directed to a particular issue, do not necessarily mean at a higher level of analysis that the CPR rejects all United Nations decisions as possibly possessing a legislative character. Cf. supra Chapter I, text at reference for nn. 40–41.

92. 12 *TYC* 64.
93. Art. 5, Sino-Nepalese Treaty of Peace and Friendship of 1960, provides: "The present treaty is subject to ratification . . . [and] will come into force immediately on the exchange of the instruments of ratification." *PR,* No. 8, (1960), pp. 6–7, 10 *TYC* 13.
94. E.g., the Sino-Pakistan Boundary Agreement of 1963, *supra* n. 92. In contrast, the Sino-North Korean Economic and Cultural Cooperation Agreement of November 23, 1953, despite its title "Agreement," was subject to the procedure of ratification (Art. 3), 2 *TYC* 6.
95. Art. 11, 10 *TYC* 390.
96. 10 *TYC* 25.
97. Art. 11, *supra* n. 95.
98. Wang, *supra* n. 5, pp. 9–10. The author cited statements from the *Selected Works of Lenin,* 4th ed. (Russian ed.), XXVI, pp. 223, 302. Wei Liang, *supra* n. 1.
99. *Id.*
100. *JMJP* editorial, March 8, 1963. Emphasis added. During the 1969 Sino-Soviet border conflict on the Ussuri River, the CPR even invoked the 1860 Treaty of Peking to show that the boundary between the two countries was defined in that treaty to be along the Missuri River (i.e., the middle channel of navigation [thalweg]). CPR foreign ministry protest, March 15, 1969, to the Soviet Union, *PR,* March 21, 1969, at 9.
101. Chinese text in *Ti-san-tz'u ya-fei t'uan-chieh hui-yi wen-chien hui-pien* [Collection of Documents from the Third Afro-Asian Solidarity Conference] (Peking, 1963), p. 23. For Soviet views on "unequal treaties," see Lissitzyn, *supra* n. 17, p. 53.
102. Still another resolution, in language very similar to that used by the Chinese Communists in their pronouncements on the subject, condemned the United Nations for serving the interests of the United States "imperialists" and demanded its reorganization. *Id.,* p. 23.
103. A 1964 Chinese textbook is said to contain a map showing China's frontiers as including parts of the Soviet Far East—the Maritime Krai, Vladivostok, and Sakhalin, etc. Stuart Fraser, *Chinese Communist Education* (Nashville, Tenn.: Vanderbilt University, 1965), p. 138. But what legal effect this has with respect to the territories in question is at best obscure.
104. Chou En-lai has declared that the 1951 San Francisco Peace Treaty with Japan signed without China's cosignature is null and void because

it violates the United Nations Declaration of 1942, in which the wartime Allies pledged not to sign a separate peace treaty with the enemy. 2 *TWKH* 30–36 (1951).

105. A CPR writer asserted that the Mutual Defense Treaty between Nationalist China and the United States (1964) was a U.S. attempt to "split China, provoke war, and interfere in China's internal affairs." Invoking Art. 103 of the U.N. Charter, which stipulates that no treaty obligations could override those already assumed under the charter, the writer concluded that the treaty had no validity. Shao Chin-fu, "The Absurdity of the 'Two Chinas' [Idea] and International Law," *KCWT,* No. 2 (1959), at 14.
106. See *infra* Chapter XIV, n. 64.
107. E.g., the CPR's agreement with Sweden on mutual registration of trade marks, 428 *UNTS* 267; Sino-Burmese Air Transport Agreement, 306 *UNTS* 36; and Sino-Czechoslovak Consular Treaty, 402 *UNTS* 222.
108. 260 *UNTS* 438–44.
109. Art. 7, *PR,* No. 24 (1961), pp. 11.
110. 5 *TYC* 199.
111. *JMJP,* August 5, 1967.
112. 10 *TYC* 25.
113. One CPR commentator explicitly stated the Sino-Japanese War of 1937–1945 *ipso facto* terminated all treaties existing between the two countries. Shao Chin-fu, *supra* n. 105.
114. Text in *Chung-hua . . . , supra* n. 28, pp. 25–26.
115. *Id.,* p. 51.
116. See commentary for Article 59 of the 1966 Draft Articles on the Law of Treaties, formulated by the International Law Commission, text in 61 *AJIL* at 428 (1967). This article finally became Article 62 of the Vienna Convention on the Law of Treaties, adopted on May 23, 1969; text in 63 *AJIL* at 894 (1969).
117. The agreement stated that the two countries:

"note that since 1945 the following radical changes have taken place in the Far East: Imperialist Japan has suffered defeat; the reactionary Kuomintang Government has been overthrown; China has become a People's Democratic Republic; and there has been established in China a new People's Government which has united all China, followed a policy of friendship and cooperation with the Soviet Union, and proved capable of upholding the national independence and territorial integrity of China and the national honor and dignity of the Chinese people. . . . In accordance with these *new circumstances* the Presidium of the Supreme Soviet of the Union of Soviet Socialist Republics and the Central People's Government of the People's Republic of China *have decided to conclude this Agreement* concerning the Chinese Ch'ang-ch'un Railway, Port Arthur and Dairen." 1 *TYC* 3 (1949–1950).

118. 4 *TWKH* 341, 346–47.
119. Chou Tzu-ya, "Talks on the Question of the Suez Canal," *Hua-tung*

cheng-fa k'an [East China Journal on Politics and Law], No. 3 (1956), at 38.

120. Art. 61 of the 1969 Vienna Convention, *supra* n. 116, 63 *AJIL* at 894 (1969).
121. Art. 66 of Draft Articles, Commentary (4), *supra* n. 116, 61 *AJIL* at 447 (1967).
122. 18 *CDSP*, No. 40 (October 26, 1966), at 14.
123. NCNA, November 6, 1966; *SCMP*, No. 3818 (November 9, 1966).
124. "Statement by the Spokesman of the CPR Government—A Comment on the Soviet Government Statement of August 3" (August 15, 1963), *PR*, August 16, 1963.
125. *FKHP*, vols. III, X, and XII. 126. 12 *id*. 30–35.
127. CPR Bureau of Ship Inspection, *Hai-ch'uan tsai-chung-hsien kwei-fan* [Manual for Load Lines of Ocean-Going Ships] (Peking: People's Transport, 1959).
128 135 *UNTS* 301.
129. The best account of the CPR's Foreign Trade Arbitration Tribunal is probably the article by Harry Fellhauer, in *Recht im Aussenhandel* (Beilage zur Zeitschrift "Der Aussenhandel," No. 12 (1960) [Foreign Trade Law (Supplement to the magazine "Foreign Trade," No. 12 (1960)] (Berlin), No. 6 (1960), pp. 7–8; tr. in *JPRS*, No. 8612 (July 28, 1961). See *infra* Chapter XIV, n. 117.
130. 4 *TYC* 17. 131. 12 *TYC* 64.
132. Lin Hsin, who held the view that international law was bifurcated into "bourgeois" and "socialist" versions, believed that interpretation of treaties between states hailing from different ideological backgrounds would be all but impossible. "On the System of International Law After World War II," *Chiao-hsüeh yü yen-chiu*, No. 1 (1958), at 34–38. He was refuted by others who believed that one "correct" interpretation is possible. Chou Fu-lun, "On the Nature of Modern International Law—A Discussion with Comrade Lin Hsin," *id.*, No. 3 (1958), at 52–56.
133. See *infra* Chapter XIV, text at reference for nn. 110–19.
134. The Sino-Burmese Treaty of Friendship, 9 *TYC* 44 (Article 5).
135. Art. 6, *id*.
136. In 1926, for instance, the then warlord Peking Government renounced the Sino-Belgian Treaty of 1865; 21 *AJIL* 289 (1927). As a result Western jurists became aroused to the topic of unequal treaties. At the 1927 annual meeting of the American Society of International Law a session was specifically devoted to China's unequal treaties.
137. See generally Ch'ien T'ai, *Chung-kuo pu-p'ing-teng t'iao-yüeh chih yuan-ch'i chi fei-ch'u ching-kuo* [The Origins of China's Unequal Treaties and Their Abolition] (Taipei, 1961). Also Hungdah Ch'iu,

"Comparison of the Nationalist and Communist Chinese Position on the Problem of Unequal Treaties," unpublished paper; an excerpted version was delivered at a regional meeting of the American Society of International Law in New York, February 8, 1969.

138. Cf. the Declaration of the Nationalist government on June 16, 1928, cited in *Chinese Social and Political Science Review, Public Documents* (Peking, 1928), XII, pp. 47–48.

139. See *supra* n. 15 and 98.

140. Arts. 51 and 52 of the 1969 Vienna Convention, *supra* n. 116, 63 *AJIL* at 891 (1969).

141. Wang, *supra* n. 5, p. 51. Art. 21 of the treaty reads: "Between the territories of the High Contracting Parties there shall be freedom of commerce and navigation." Art. 27 reads: "Subject to any limitation or exception provided in this Treaty or hereafter agreed upon between the Governments of the High Contracting Parties, the territories of the High Contracting Parties to which the provisions of this Treaty extend shall be understood to comprise all areas of land and water under the sovereignty or authority of either High Contracting Party, *except* the Panama Canal Zone." 25 *UNTS* 128, 138.

142. *JMJP,* December 31, 1956.

143. *JMJP,* November 29, 1956.

144. *JMJP,* September 13, 1965; February 14, 1966; and February 19, 1966.

145. C. K. Cheng, "The Philippines: America's Show Window of Democracy in Asia?" *PR,* February 5, 1965, p. 21.

146. 1950–1952 *Kuo-chi t'iao-yüeh chi* [International Treaty Series] (Peking), at 395.

147. When the Sino-British Treaty for the Relinquishment of Extraterritorial Rights in China and the Regulation of Related Matters was signed in 1943 (205 League of Nations *Treaty Series* 69), the Nationalist Chinese leaders only raised the question of the retrocession of the leased territory of Kowloon. Hong Kong was not mentioned. Cf. Wang Tieh-yeh, "A General Analysis of the Contents of the New Treaties," *Shih-chieh cheng-chih* [World Politics], special issue (Chunking, Chinese Association for the League of Nations, April 30, 1943), reprinted in Pao Tsun-p'eng, et al., eds., *Chung-kuo chin-tai shih lun ts'ung* [Essays on Modern Chinese History], 2d Series, I (Taipei, 1958), p. 311. Cf. also Ch'iu, *supra* n. 137, p. 13 ff.

148. See *supra* n. 100.

149. *JMJP,* March 8, 1963.

150. See *supra* n. 11.

151. *JMJP,* August 10, 1963.

152. Kuo Ch'un, *Lien-ho kuo* [The United Nations] (Peking, 1956), pp. 101–107.

153. Ch'iu, *supra* n. 137, p. 30–31.

154. See *supra* Chapter IV above, text at reference for nn. 56–58; also Premier Chou's report to the NPC, July 9, 1957, in NPC Standing Com-

mittee, *Kung-pao* [Bulletin], No. 30 (1957), pp. 635–39; and Luke T. Lee, *supra* n. 18, pp. 31–36.

155. Franco-Chinese agreement of February 28, 1946, 14 *UNTS* 137. This agreement was signed as Nationalist Chinese forces were being withdrawn from Indochina, where they had entered at the end of World War II to effect the Japanese surrender and maintain order and security.
156. Text of the agreement is summarized in NCNA news release, April 12, 1957; *SCMP,* no. 1512, at 58.
157. Luke T. Lee, *supra* n. 18, at 121–22.

CHAPTER XIII

1. *Chung-hua jen-min kung-ho-kuo yu-hao t'iao-yüeh hui-pien* [Collection of the CPR's Friendship Treaties] (Peking: World Knowledge, 1965) contains all the seventeen treaties.
2. Cf. Zbniew Brzezinski, *The Soviet Bloc,* rev. and enlarged ed. (Cambridge Mass.: Harvard University Press, 1967), pp. 109 and 108–112.
3. *Id.*, p. 112 ff.
4. For a discussion of the Albanian issue in the Sino-Soviet dispute, see William Griffith, *Albania and the Sino-Soviet Dispute* (Cambridge, Mass: M.I.T. Press, 1963).
5. Brzezinski, *supra* n. 2, p. 131.
6. Whether the treaty is still considered by both parties to be in force is immaterial here.
7. The first CPR cultural agreement was signed with Poland, April 3, 1951, followed by Hungary, July 12, 1951, East Germany, November 9, 1951, Czechoslovakia, May 6, 1952, and Albania, October 14, 1954. 1 *TYC* 102, 100, 107, and 105; and 2 *TYC* 190, 185, and 160.
8. 4 *TYC* 7. 9. 6 *TYC* 40. 10. 8 *TYC* 1.
11. See Chapter III, nn. 16–25, *supra.* 12. Brzezinski, *supra* n. 2, p. 466.
13. *Id.*, p. 467.
14. E.g., Sino-Cambodia Treaty of Friendship and Mutual Non-Aggression of 1960 (Art. 1), and Sino-Burmese Treaty of Friendship and Mutual Non-Aggression of 1960 (Art. 2). 9 *TYC* 44 and 25.
15. *Id.*
16. E.g., Sino-Nepalese Treaty of Peace and Friendship of 1960 (Art. 2), 10 *TYC* 13.
17. E.g., The CPR's treaties of friendship with Indonesia (Art. 4), Nepal (Art. 3), and Burma (Art. 4).
18. E.g., the CPR's treaties of friendship with Indonesia (Art. 1), Cambodia (Art. 2), Nepal (Art. 1), and Burma (Art. 1).

19. The fourth friendship treaty signed in 1960 was with Guinea (September 13, 1960).
20. 9 *TYC* 65 and 68.
21. 9 *TYC* 63; 10 *id.* 51. Afghanistan only has a narrow strip bordering on China; hence, no need for a boundary treaty.
22. The figures do not include other "economic" treaties, such as concern with economic and technical aid, registration of trademarks, etc.
23. Wang, *infra* n. 44, pp. 114–18.
24. Gene Hsiao, "Communist China's Trade Treaties and Agreements (1949–1964)," 21 *Vanderbilt Law Review,* No. 5 (October, 1968), p. 624.
25. Wang, *infra* n. 44, p. 116.
26. Yeh Chi-chuang, "A New State in the Development of Economic Relations Between China and Egypt." 2 *Tui-wai kuan-hsi lun-wen hsuan* [Selection of Essays on Foreign Trade] (Peking: Ministry of Foreign Trade, 1957), p. 99.
27. Cf. Gene Hsiao, "Communist China's Trade Organizations," 20 *Vanderbilt Law Review* 313–18 (1967).
28. 2 *TYC* 372 (1953). 29. *Id.* 285, 260 (1955).
30. 7 *TYC* 197 (1958).
31. In this incident a CPR national flag on display at a fair in Nagasaki was insulted by Japanese who were later punished by imposition of a 500-yen fine. 2 *JPWT* 214.
32. Named after Liao Ch'eng-chih and Takasaki, trade liaison officers in each other's country. The trade agreements were signed in the form of an exchange of memoranda. 13 *TYC* 386.
33. A. Eckstein, *Communist China's Economic Growth and Foreign Trade* (McGraw-Hill, 1966), p. 281 ff; Lee, *China and International Agreements* (Leyden: Sijthoff, 1969), pp. 77 and 78.
34. *New York Times,* April 12, 1969; *Japan Times Weekly,* April 19, 1969, p. 1.
35. Chou En-lai, "The Three Principles of Sino-Japanese Trade," 1961 *Jen-min shou-ts'e* [People's Handbook], pp. 167 f.
36. Eckstein, *Communist China, supra* n. 33; and Pauline Lewin, *The Foreign Trade of Communist China* (New York: Praeger, 1964), esp. Chapter 4.
37. Wang, *infra* n. 44, pp. 7 and 114. All these treaties and agreements can be found in different volumes of the *TYC*.
38. Lewin, *supra* n. 36, Chapters 4, 5, and 6.
39. Texts in 7 *TYC* 42; 9 *id.* 134; 10 *id* 290; *id.* 361; 11 *id.* 92; and 11 *id.* 100. Strictly speaking, the treaty with Mongolia is only a treaty of commerce, the omission of navigation is due to the fact that Mongolia is a landlocked country.

40. The Sino-Polish Trade Agreement, April 7, 1958, was for the period of 1959–1962.
41. Art. 8, 2 *TYC* 33.
42. Art. 10; English text in 308 *UNTS* 148; Chinese text in 6 *TYC* 207.
43. Art. 11, 10 *TYC* 372.
44. Wang Yao-t'iao, *Kuo-chi mao-yi t'iao-yueh ho hsieh-ting* [International Trade Treaties and Agreements] (Peking: Finance and Economic Publications, 1958), pp. 125–132.
45. E.g., Art. 13, Sino-Soviet Treaty of Commerce and Navigation, April 23, 1958, in 7 *TYC* 42.
46. E.g., Art. 2 of the Appendix to the Sino-Soviet Treaty of Commerce and Navigation, *id.*
47. E.g., Art. 3, *id.* The Sino-Mongolian CN Treaty, April 26, 1961, contains a similar appendix, 10 *id.* 361.
48. See 4 *TYC* 118 and 159, respectively.
49. Exchange of notes with India, April 29, 1954, in 3 TYC 5. The freedom from arrest and other privileges granted to trade representatives were also extended to their family members.
50. 5 *TYC* 7; and 4 *TWKH* 93 (1956–1957).
51. Syria did not recognize the CPR until July 3, 1956, 4 *TWKH* 93 (1956–1957). Lebanon still recognizes the Republic of China on Taiwan.
52. Wang, *supra* n. 44, p. 116.
53. Gene Hsiao, *supra* n. 24.
54. Wang Yi-wang, "What Is the Difference Between a Commercial Treaty and a Trade Agreement," *Kwang-ming jih-pao* [Bright Daily], May 12, 1950.
55. Art. 2, text in 7 *TYC* 42. Italics added.
56. *Supra* n. 39.
57. 10 *TYC* 238.
58. See, respectively, 7 *TYC* 94; *id,* 96; *id.* 57; 8 *TYC* 53 and 13 *TYC* 277; 9 *TYC* 82; 10 *TYC* 327; *id.* 252 and 12 *TYC* 324; 11 *TYC* 56; 12 *TYC* 178; 13 *TYC* 281 and 366; *id.* 262; *id.* 269.
59. Gene Hsiao, *supra* n. 24, at 649, n. 127.
60. Art. 7, *supra* n. 55.
61. Article 15.
62. 6 *TYC* 203.
63. 5 *TYC* 61.
64. Aside from the Sino-Finish exchange of notes, the following are also included in the same category as the CN treaties: (a) exchange of notes with Denmark, January 12, 1958, on the most-favored-nation treatment regarding taxation and navigation, 6 *TYC* 45; (b) exchange of notes with Pakistan, December 24, 1957, April 9, 1958, and October 4, 1958, on the granting of most-favored-nation treatment to each other's commodities, 7 *TYC* 35; (c) exchange of notes with Cambodia, on the most-favored-nation question, September 17, and October 14, 1958; October 20, November 14, and November 21, 1959, 8 *TYC* 95.

65. Cf. John N. Hazard, "Commercial Discrimination and International Law," 52 *AJIL* 495 (1958); Hazard and Domke, "State Trading and the Most-Favored-Nation Clause," *id.*, p. 55 (1958); Stanley D. Metzger, *International Law, Trade, and Finance* (Dobbs Ferry, N. Y.: Oceana, 1964).
66. Art. 7, in 6 *TYC* 74.
67. Note by Wilmot Perera, ambassador of Ceylon in Peking, September 19, 1957, in Ambekar and Divekar, eds., *Documents on China's Relations with South and Southeast Asia* (Bombay: Allied, 1964), pp. 321–22.
68. Wang, *supra* n. 44, pp. 28, 134.
69. E.g., Art. 15, CPR Treaty of Commerce and Navigation with North Korea, November 5, 1962; and Art. 15, Sino-North Vietnamese CN Treaty, December 5, 1962.
70. Art. 8, in 7 *TYC* 197.
71. E.g., Art 10, Sino-Burmese Trade Agreement of 1961, provides that "matters arising from the implementation of the Agreement" shall be settled by "consultation." 10 *TYC* 372.
72. See, for example, Art. 3 of the Sino-Indonesian agreement of November 30, 1953; Art. 2 of the Sino-Burmese agreement of January 9, 1961; and Sino-Ceylonese agreement of September 19, 1957.
73. The first Sino-Japanese agreement, June 1, 1952, set the total value each way at 30 million pounds sterling. The Sino-Indonesian agreement of September 1, 1954, had an appended list which, among other things, specified that the total value of export from each party would be 3,000,000 pounds sterling.
74. 3 *TYC* 37.
75. E.g., Art. 2, Sino-Danish Trade and Payment Agreement of December 1, 1957, 6 *TYC* 44.
76. E.g., Art. 2 of the Sino-Egyptian Trade Agreement of August 22, 1955, 4 *TYC* 123.
77. Art. 9 of the Sino-Lebanese Trade Agreement of December 31, 1955, 4 *TYC* 159.
78. E.g., Art. 5 of the Sino-Egyptian Trade Agreement of 1955.
79. "Eight Principles Governing China's Economic and Technical Aid to Other Countries Set Forth by Premier Chou En-lai during his Visit to Africa: December, 1963–February, 1964," *PR*, No. 34 (1964), p. 16. See further Chapter IV, n. 51; and Chapter VII, n. 11, *supra*.
80. Wang, *supra* n. 44, pp. 23–24. See further discussion in Chapter IV, text at reference for nn. 52–53; and *infra* nn. 83–84.
81. Art. 9, in 7 *TYC* 42.
82. Wang, *supra* n. 44, p. 51.
83. Wang, *id.*, p. 52.
84. *Id.*, p. 112 ff.
85. Department of State, *The Conduct of Communist China* (Washington,

D.C.: Government Printing Office, 1963), prepared for the House Committee on Foreign Affairs, 88th Cong., 1st Sess., pp. 8–9.

86. U.S.-CPR agreement on the exchange of civilians, English text in Appendix B, Kenneth Young, *Negotiating with the Chinese Communists* (McGraw-Hill, 1968), pp. 412–13.
87. Young, *id.*, pp. 51; 63–75.
88. Ambassador Johnson's statement, in Dept. of State, *Bulletin,* XXXIII, 848 (September 26, 1955), p. 489. The United States also insisted that the CPR agree to a joint renunciation of the use of force in the Taiwan area before any progress toward the substantive issues could be expected. *Id.* See also *supra* Chapter V, nn. 42–45.
89. *JMJP,* October 13, 1955.
90. Ambassador Johnson's interview with Luke Lee; see Lee, *supra* n. 33, p. 44.
91. *New York Times,* January 7, 1956.
92. *People's China,* No. 7, (April 1, 1956), p. 19.
93. Lee, *supra* n. 33, p. 43; Young, *supra* n. 86, p. 84.
94. *New York Times,* January 30, 1957; Young, *id.*, pp. 87–88.
95. *New York Times,* January 7, 1956.
96. *JMJP,* October 3, 1955; October 12, 1955; and October 13, 1955. CPR foreign ministry statement, March 11, 1956, in 4 *TWKH* 52-54 (1956–1957).
97. Among the numerous works that have appeared on the Sino-Indian border dispute, the most detailed and objective account of the historical and legal aspects of the issue is Alfred P. Rubin, "The Sino-Indian Border Disputes," 9 *International and Comparative Law Quarterly* (January, 1960), p. 96 ff.
98. *New York Times,* December 13, 1954.
99. U.N. Doc. A/2889 (December 17, 1954); italics added. See also Dag Hammarskjold, "The Secretary-General's Mission to Peking," *United Nations Review,* February 1955, pp. 2–8.
100. *Id.*
101. For apt comments on the role of legal advisers as "promoter," rather than "judge," of government policy aims, see Gerald Fitzgerald, 59 *AJIL* 72–86 (1965).
102. Luke T. Lee, "Treaty Relations of the People's Republic of China: a Study of Compliance," 116 *University of Pennsylvania Law Review,* No. 2 (December, 1967), at 263–72.
103. *Id.*, at 266. 104. *Id.*, at 267.
105. Letter from the Neutral Nations Supervisory Commission to the Military Armistice Commission in Seoul, South Korea, September 17, 1953; Lee, *id.*, p. 267, n. 73.
106. Record of the forty-first meeting of the Military Armistice Commis-

sion, April 20, 1954; fourty-fifth meeting, August 3, 1954; Lee, *id.*, n. 74.

107. Report of the Neutral Nations Inspection Teams of August 20, 1955, discussed at the sixty-ninth meeting of the Military Armistice Commission, February 25, 1966; Lee, *id.*, n. 75.
108. Lee, *id.*, p. 268.
109. Arthur Lall, *How Communist China Negotiates* (New York: Columbia University Press, 1968), p. 187; Lee, *id.*, pp. 34–35.
110. Lee, *id.*, pp. 34–35, and n. 13 on p. 35.
111. *Japan Times Weekly,* November 12, 1966, p. 7, col. 2; *Toronto Globe and Mail,* March 1, 1962. For CPR wheat transactions, see annual reports of the Canadian Wheat Board. Also cf. Lee, *supra* n. 33, 82–85.
112. 2 *JPWT* 214; 3 *id.* 43; and Ch'en Yi's statement of May 9, 1958, 5 *TWKH* 104–106.
113. 2 *id.* 184.
114. Ts'ao Chung-shu, "Perspectives of Sino-Japanese Trade," 3 *Tui-wai* . . . , *supra* n. 26, pp. 94–98; Hsiao, *supra* n. 24, p. 631.
115. Lei Jen-min, "For an Early Normalization of Sino-Japanese Economic and Trade Relations," *id.*, pp. 87–93.
116. *Japan Times,* January 29, 1967, p. 10, col.1.
117. See a sample of the L-T contract in Lee, *supra* n. 33, Appendix 8, at 212. Emphasis added.
118. A sample of such private contracts has been translated and distributed by Gene Hsiao as an appendix to his essay "Communist China's Trade Treaties and Agreements" (originally published in *Vanderbilt Law Review,* see *supra* n. 24) at a regional meeting of the American Society of International Law, New York City, February 7–8, 1969. The *force majeure* reads: "If due to incidents of *force majeure,* Seller is unable to make the delivery according to schedule, he may postpone the delivery, wholly or in part; or he may cancel this contract as a whole. However, [in either case,] Seller must present to Buyer documents of proof issued by the China Council for the Promotion of International Trade, showing the cause of the incident."
119. Soviet Foreign Ministry Statement, July 5, 1963, *CDSP,* XV, 27 (July 31, 1963), p. 10; also *supra* Chapter VIII, nn. 63–64.
120. Speech by Premier Fidel Castro, June 2, 1966, cited in Lee, *supra* n. 33, p. 88.
121. The CPR has a cultural agreement with the Soviet Union, signed on July 5, 1956, 5 *TYC* 158, and with Cuba, July 23, 1960, 10 *TYC* 388.
122. See CPR reply dated July 4, 1963, to the Soviet protest of June 27, 1963, in *JMJP,* July 5, 1963.
123. *New York Times,* November 1, 1967; August 6, 1967; September 15, 1967; and October 3, 1967; also *supra* Chapter VIII, n. 81.

124. Sino-Burmese treaty (May 6, 1959), 8 *TYC* 1; and Sino-Indonesian treaty (April 1, 1961), 10 *TYC* 7.
125. See related discussions of this question in my book, *Ideology and Practice: The Evolution of Chinese Communism* (New York: Praeger, 1970), pp. 158–65; and Peter Van Ness, *Revolution and Chinese Foreign Policy* (Berkeley, Calif.: University of California Press, 1970). More discussion on the export of "correct" ideology in Chapter XIV, at reference for nn. 24–29, *infra*.

CHAPTER XIV

1. Dept. of State, *The Conduct of Communist China* (Washington, D. C.: Government Printing Office, 1963), p. 3.
2. Mao Tse-tung, *Hsüan-chi* [Selected Works] (1966 ed.), II, p. 511; English tr. in *Selected Works* (1965 ed.), II, p. 223.
3. To Lafayette, November 15, 1781, quoted in John Bartlett, *Familiar Quotations,* 13th ed. (Boston: Little, Brown, 1955), p. 366b.
4. First Annual Address to both Houses of Congress, January 8, 1790, *id.,* p. 367.
5. *HC,* April 16, 1960. 6. No source is given for the quotation.
7. CCP letter to the CPSU, June 14, 1963.
8. *Id.* 9. *HC,* April 16, 1960.
10. Cf. Maurice Meisner, *Li Ta-chao and the Origins of Chinese Marxism* (Cambridge, Mass.: Harvard University Press, 1967); Benjamin I. Schwartz, *Chinese Communism and the Rise of Mao* (Cambridge, Mass.: Harvard University Press, 1951).
11. Cf. *Civil Disobedience* (Santa Barbara, Calif.: Center for the Study of Democratic Institutions, 1966); *Rights in Conflict* (The "Walker Report" to the National Commission on the Causes and Prevention of Violence) (New York: Bantam, 1968); "Report from Black America," *Newsweek,* June 30, 1969, p. 17 ff.
12. This can be seen from Peking's sustained interest in promoting a nuclear free zone in Asia ever since 1958, when the United States deployed missiles with atomic warheads in Taiwan, South Korea, and Japan. See *infra* n. 77.
13. *New York Times,* August 13, 1969, p. 1, col. 5.
14. Khrushchev's speech at an evening meeting of the Supreme Soviet, December 12, 1962, Moscow Domestic Service broadcast, December 12, 1962. A partial text was printed in *New York Times,* December 13, 1962, p. 2.
15. "The Cuban Crisis and the Struggle for World Peace," *The Worker*

(New York), January 13, 1963; reprint of CPUSA statement of January 9, 1963. See excerpts in Dennis J. Doolin, *Territorial Claims in the Sino-Soviet Conflict* (Stanford, Calif.: Hoover Institution, 1965), pp. 28–29.

16. "A Comment on the Statement of the Communist Party of the United States of America," *JMJP* editorial, March 8, 1963.
17. Sometimes the Chinese Communists also use the term "people's democratic revolutionary movement," CCP letter to the CPSU, June 14, 1963. The "people's liberation war" is the main theme of a resolution passed by the NPC Standing Committee on April 20, 1965, in support of the cause of North Vietnam in its war with the United States; *New York Times,* April 21, 1965, p. 2.
18. Shih Tsu-chih, "The Basic Road of National Liberation Movement of Colonial and Semi-Colonial Peoples," *KCWT,* No. 5 (1965), at 3 and 7.
19. G.A. Res. 1514 (XV), Dec. 14, 1960.
20. CCP letter to the CPSU, June 14, 1963, Point #16.
21. Richard A. Falk, "Revolutionary Nations and the Quality of International Legal Order," in Morton Kaplan, ed., *The Revolution in World Politics* (New York: John Wiley, 1962), at 323.
22. Shih, *supra* n. 18; cf. also George Ginsburgs, " 'Wars of Liberation' and the Modern Law of Nations," in Hans W. Baade, ed., *The Soviet Impact on International Law* (Dobbs Ferry, N.Y.: Oceana, 1965), 66–98.
23. See Chapter XI, text at reference for nn. 99–101, *supra;* and generally Peter Van Ness, *Revolution and Chinese Foreign Policy* (Berkeley: University of California Press, 1970).
24. Lin Piao, "Report to the Ninth Congress of the Communist Party of China" (April 1, 1969), *HC,* No. 5 (1969), p. 27.
25. Richard J. Barnet, *Intervention and Revolution* (New York and Cleveland: World Publishing Co., 1968), p. 262.
26. Cf. Ernest Halperin, "Peking and Latin American Countries," *China Quarterly,* January-March, 1967.
27. Cf. Benjamin Schwartz, "The Reign of Virtue: Some Broad Perspectives on Leader and Party in the Cultural Revolution," *China Quarterly,* No. 35 (July-September 1968), pp. 1–17.
28. The "self-reliance" doctrine was expounded in Lin Piao, *Long Live the People's War* (Peking, 1965). Although Dean Rusk, secretary of state, saw in this a Chinese Mein Kampf (*New York Times,* April 17, 1966), a more correct interpretation was provided by Professors A. Doak Barnett and Donald Zagoria, *U.S. Policy With Respect to Mainland China: Hearings Before the Committee on Foreign Relations, U.S. Senate,* (March, 1966), pp. 26, 371.
29. John K. Fairbank, ed., *The Chinese World Order* (Cambridge, Mass.: Harvard University Press, 1968); also my book, *Ideology and Practice* (New York: Praeger, 1970), pp. 158–65.

30. Chou's assurances to Premier Ayub Khan of Pakistan, in 1966, *Le Monde,* July 1, 1966; and Chang's remarks to A. Lall, in Lall, *How Communist China Negotiates* (New York: Columbia University Press, 1968), at 31.
31. Chou En-lai's comment on Soviet occupation of Czechoslovakia, given in a speech at the Rumanian Embassy in Peking on the Rumanian National Day, August 23, 1968, in *PR,* Supplement, August 23, 1968.
32. Mao, "Tactics of Fighting Japanese Imperialism," *Selected Works,* English ed. (New York: International Publishers, 1954), I, pp. 173–74. Emphasis added.
33. E.g., quotations of Mao's doctrine in *JMJP,* October 6–7, 1960; *Nanfang jih-pao* [*South China Daily*], November 3, 1960; and *HC,* October 1, 1960.
34. Chou's message to the Presidium of the Indochina People's Conference, dated February 23, 1965, in 5 *YTCN* 612.
35. Cf. Arthur Nussbaum, *A Concise History of the Law of Nations,* 3rd ed. (New York: Macmillan, 1954), pp. 10, 35–37, 49, 80–82, 92.
36. See *supra* Chapter II, text at reference for nn. 38–43.
37. See *supra* Chapter IX, n. 49.
38. See *supra* Chapter IX, n. 51; *PR,* August 15, 1969, p. 3.
39. Chou En-lai's reply to Secretary of State Dulles's statement of September 4, 1958, on the Taiwan situation, dated September 6, 1958, in *PR,* September 9, 1958, pp. 15–16.
40. Chou En-lai's cablegram to the U. N. secretary-general, November 14, 1950. U.N.Doc. S/1902, November 15, 1950, in U. N. Security Council, *Official Records,* Supp., 5th yr. (1950), p. 115.
41. After the "June War" of 1967, commando raids were often staged by the Palestine Liberation Organization and others against the Israeli-held west bank of the Jordan River. *New York Times,* November 5, 1968, p. 1.
42. See article by Victor Louis, believed to be an international agent from Moscow, in *London Evening News,* September 17, 1969; *New York Times,* September 18, 1969, p. 5.
43. *New York Times,* September 13, 1969, p. 5.
44. Harold C. Hinton, "China and Vietnam," in William Richardson, ed., *China Today* (Maryknoll, N.Y.: Maryknoll Publications, 1969), 117 ff; also Donal Zagoria, "The Strategic Debate in Peking," in Tang Tsou, ed., *China in Crisis,* II (Chicago: Chicago University Press, 1968), pp. 237–68.
45. *JMJP,* March 25, 1956; 5 *YTCN* 321.
46. CPR memoranda to the Swedish and Swiss diplomatic missions, 3 *TWKH* 236 (1954–1955); Luke Lee, *China and International Agreements* (Leyden: Sijthoff, 1969), p. 56.
47. Ch'en Yi's report to the Eighth Party Congress of the CCP, September 25, 1956, 4 *TWKH* 486 (1956–1957).

48. Chou-Sihanouk joint communiqué, August 24, 1958, 5 *TWKH* 154 (1958).
49. Chou En-lai's address on April 28, 1954, text in Chinese in *Jih-nei-wa hui-yi wen-chien hui-pien* [Collection of Documents from the Geneva Conference] (Peking, 1954), pp. 10–17. Also A. Doak Barnett, *Communist China and Asia* (New York: Harper and Row, 1960), p. 66; and "Red China's Impact on Asia," *The Atlantic Monthly,* December, 1959.
50. *Jih-nei-wa . . . , id.,* p. 167.
51. All agreements were reproduced in *id.* For the CPR's comment on the agreements, see "Peaceful Negotiations Score Another Victory," *JMJP,* July 22, 1954.
52. *JMJP,* August 19, 1960.
53. *PR,* September 14, 1960, p. 41.
54. 3 *YTCN* 109–10, 123–24.
55. A. Lall, *How Communist China Negotiates* (Columbia, 1968), 2, 45–46; Chae-jin Lee, "Communist China and the Geneva Conference on Laos: A Reappraisal," *Asian Survey,* IX, 7 (July, 1969), at 525.
56. *Chieh-chüeh lao-wo wen-t'i k'uo-ta te jih-nei-wa hui-yi wen-chien hui-pien* [Collection of Documents of the Expanded Geneva Conference for the Solution of the Laotian Question] (Peking, 1962), p. 52 ff.
57. See views expressed in *JMJP,* May 20, 1961.
58. Text in *Chieh-chüeh . . . , supra* n. 56, pp. 2–5. Also Department of State, *Bulletin,* XLVII, 1207 (August 13, 1962), pp. 259–61.
59. *Id.,* p. 119.
60. Cf. Robert F. Kennedy, *Thirteen Days* (New York: W. W. Norton, 1969). However, the United States eventually pulled out its "obsolete" missiles from Turkey, toward the end of 1962.
61. Gromyko's speech at the U.N. General Assembly, full text in *New York Times,* September 20, 1969, p. 10. Emphasis added.
62. Cf. Richard A. Falk, ed., *The Vietnam War and International Law,* sponsored by the American Society of International Law (Princeton: Princeton University Press, 1968).
63. The Declaration on Indochina of the 1954 Geneva Conference, July 21, 1954 (Art. 12), text in *supra* n. 49, p. 258; English text in *Cmd.* 9329, Miscellaneous No. 20 (1954) (Her Majesty's Stationery Office, London).
64. To my knowledge, the CPR only has a Treaty of Commerce and Navigation with North Vietnam, signed on December 5, 1962, and a few other agreements of a technical nature.
65. *New York Times,* September 3, 1969, p. 1, col. 8.
66. Eric Pace, "Laos: Continuing Crisis," *Foreign Affairs,* XLIII, 1 (October, 1964), pp. 67–74.
67. Mike Mansfield, "Retrospect and Prospect," *War/Peace Report,* May, 1968, p. 10.
68. *New York Times,* September 14, 1969, p. 8.

69. Senator Stuart Symington, who headed the inquiry by the Foreign Relations Committees' subcommittee on foreign commitment and was also on the Armed Services Committee, flatly declared: "We have been at war in Laos for years, and it is time the American people knew more of the facts." *New York Times,* September 20, 1969, p. 1, col. 5; September 22, 1969. North Vietnam, meanwhile, was reported to have 50,000 ground troops in Laos.
70. *PR,* July 4, 1969, p. 22 ff.
71. Mao's talk at the tenth plenum of the eighth Central Committee of the CCP, September 28, 1962; a summary was published in *Mainichi shumbun* (Tokyo), on the evening of March 9, 1967, in a dispatch sent from Peking by its correspondent Takada, who copied the information from a wall poster which appeared in Peking the previous day; reprinted in *Chinese Law and Government,* Vol. 1 No. 1. (Spring, 1968), (White Plains, N.Y.: IASP), pp. 4–6. For a fascinating study of Peking's decision to enter the Korean war, see Allen S. Whiting, *China Crosses the Yalu* (Stanford, Calif.: Stanford University Press, 1960).
72. 10 *TYC* 25.
73. Art. 6, *id.*
74. The Chiang-Dulles statement declared: "The Government of the Republic of China considers that the restoration of freedom to its people on the mainland as its sacred mission. It believes that the foundation of this mission resides in the minds and the hearts of the Chinese people and that the principal means of successfully achieving its mission is the implementation of Dr. Sun Yat-sen's three people's principles (nationalism, democracy, and social well-being) and *not the use of force.*" Dept. of State, *Bulletin,* XXXIX, 1011 (November 10, 1958), pp. 721–22.
75. According to René Dabernat, foreign editor of the magazine *Paris-Match,* the message was transmitted by France to the United States, and it was "verified in Washington." *New York Times,* January 16, 1967, p. 1, col. 2.
76. Premier Chou reportedly made remarks to this effect in an interview with Simon Malley, in March 1967, *New York Herald Tribune,* May 16, 1967, cited in Dennis Duncanson, *Government and Revolution in Vietnam* (New York: Oxford University Press, 1968), at 275, n. a.
77. CPR government statement regarding the SEATO meeting, dated March 10, 1963, *PR,* March 18, 1958, pp. 22–23.
78. Chou En-lai's speech at the Swiss National Day celebration in Peking, NCNA, August 1, 1960.
79. Morton H. Halperin and Dwight H. Perkins, *Communist China and Arms Control* (New York: Praeger, 1965), p. 101.
80. CPR Government Statement on the Complete, Thorough, Total, and Resolute Prohibition and Destruction of Nuclear Weapons, July 31,

1967; see discussion in Shao-chuan Leng, "Communist China's Position on Nuclear Arms Control," *Virginia Journal of International Law,* December 1966, pp. 101–16, at 112.

81. *JMJP,* November 22, 1964.
82. Hallperin and Perkins, *supra* n. 79, pp. 123–28.
83. NCNA, Peking, May 10, 1966.
84. See *supra* n. 42.
85. *Break the Nuclear Monopoly, and Eliminate Nuclear Weapons* (Peking, FLP, 1965).
86. President Johnson's comment on Peking's proposal for the complete destruction of nuclear weapons, in 2 Dept. of State, *Bulletin,* No. 1323 (1964), p. 612.
87. *JMJP,* October 22, 1964; Leng, *supra* n. 80, p. 115.
88. *Supra* n. 85, p. 1. On September 30, 1969, Chou En-Lai once again reiterated that China was developing nuclear arms "only for defensive purposes in order to smash the nuclear monopoly" held by the United States and the Soviet Union. *New York Times,* October 1, 1969, carrying a dispatch by Agence-France-Presse.
89. The treaty was open for signature in Moscow, London, and Washington, on July 1, 1968, and came into effect on March 5, 1970, after the required fortieth state had desposited its instrument of ratification. For text of the treaty (known as the Treaty on the Non-Proliferation of Nuclear Weapons, or NPT), see General Assembly Resolution 2373 (XXII), June 12, 1968, Annex.
90. U.S. Law of Land Warfare, Army FM 27–10 (1956); see William Bishop, *International Law: Cases and Materials,* 2d ed. (1962), p. 807.
91. James C. Hsiung, "China's Foreign Policy: The Interplay of Ideology, Practical Interests, and Polemics," in William Richardson, ed., *China Today* (Maryknoll, N.Y.: Maryknoll Publications, 1969), pp. 20–55.
92. Ch'en Yi's remarks, December 7, 1958, 5 *TWKH* 210–14 (1958).
93. During the 1958 Taiwan Strait crisis, Premier Chou declared: "In pursuance of its foreign policy of peace, the Chinese Government has always stood for *peaceful coexistence* of countries with different social systems in accordance with the Five Principles and for the settlement of all international disputes by peaceful means of negotiation. Despite the fact that the *United States* has invaded and occupied China's territory of Taiwan and the Penghu Islands by armed force and crudely violated the minimum codes of international relations, the Chinese Government proposed to sit down *to negotiate* with the United States Government to seek relaxation and elimination of the tension in the Taiwan area." *PR,* September 9, 1958.
94. *Id. JMJP* in an editorial on May 27, 1960, wrote: "China and the United States *are not at war*. China is consistently devoted to the attainment of peaceful coexistence among nations of different social systems, relaxation of international tension, and prevention of a world war. But

whether peaceful coexistence is to be attained does not depend upon our side only, but also upon the side of American imperialism." In a report to the Standing Committee of the National People's Congress, in April, 1964, Chou En-lai laid down the CPR's "General Line of Foreign Policy," as follows: "We shall continue to strive, on the basis of the Five Principles, to establish peaceful coexistence with countries of different social systems . . . *including the United States.* . . . [The] United States Government has time and again refused to reach an agreement with the Chinese Government on the Five Principles of Peaceful Coexistence. . . ." NPC Standing Committee, *Kung-pao* [Bulletin], No. 1, (1964), pp. 14–15.

95. In the CPR "peace offensive," individual Nationalist government and military personnel were offered amnesty, jobs on the mainland, the right to revisit their original homes, and even the right to return to Taiwan. Chou En-lai, "Questions Concerning the Current International Situation, China's Foreign Policy, and the Liberation of Taiwan," a report at the June 28, 1956, meeting of the Third Session of the First National People's Congress, text in 4 *TWKH* 73–82 (1956–1957).
96. See *supra* Chapter V, n. 46.
97. Although Ch'en was condemned in 1957 as a "rightist," the views he advanced in this article (1956) are representative of other more "orthodox" CPR jurists. See, for example, Shao Chin-fu, "The Absurdity of the 'Two Chinas' [Idea] and International Law," *KCWT,* No. 2 (1959), pp. 7–17.
98. Ch'en T'i-ch'iang, "United States distortion of International Law Refuted," *Kuang-ming jih-pao* [Bright Daily], January 28, 1956.
99. Cf. Ch'ü T'ung-tsu, *Law and Society in Traditional China* (Paris and the Hague: Mouton & Co., 1961); Escarra, *Le Droit Chinois* (1936), English tr. by Gertrude R. Browne, reprod. by Harvard Law School, 1961; Joseph Needham, *Science and Civilization in China,* II (Cambridge: Cambridge University Press, 1962), pp. 338–39; and 529–32; and Derk Bodde and Clarence Morris, *Law in Imperial China* (Cambridge, Mass.: Harvard University Press, 1967).
100. The Chinese urge to be independent again, after a century of foreign domination, can be seen in the tenor of an article by Tsai Cheng, "Our Country Is Now a Socialist Country Without Internal or External Debts," *PR,* May 23, 1969, 15–17. According to the author, the country in 1949 was "in an utter mess," but, quoting Lin Piao's report to the Ninth CCP Congress, the CPR by the end of 1968 had redeemed all the national bonds as well as cleared all foreign debts. This urge for regained independence, political and economic, has often been misinterpreted as a drive toward a return to the ancient *pax sinica* if that ever existed.
101. See *supra* Chapter IV, n. 26.

102. Gene Hsiao's interview with an official of the CPR-controlled Chinese General Chamer of Commerce in Hong Kong, "Communist China's Foreign Trade Contracts and Means of Settling Disputes," unpublished paper distributed for discussion at a regional meeting of the American Society of International Law, February 7–8, 1969, in New York City.
103. See *supra* Chapter X, n. 61.
104. Chou's address, July 21, 1954, at the Geneva Conference (1954), text in *Jih-nei-wa hui-yi., supra* n. 49, pp. 272–74. Emphasis added.
105. *Id.*, pp. 287–96, at 291.
106. See Fred Charles Ikle, *How Nations Negotiate* (New York: Praeger, 1964), for a discussion of the five major purposes of international negotiation, pp. 26–58.
107. Following Chinese complaints, a Soviet delegation was reported to have arrived in Peking on February 23, 1964, to discuss frontier questions; but negotiations appeared to have broken down by autumn of the same year, though later resumed. See John Gittings, *Survey of the Sino-Soviet Dispute* (New York: Oxford University Press, 1967), p. 158.
108. Iklę, *supra* n. 106, p. 27.
109. E.g., Art. 4 of the Sino-Nepalese Treaty of Peace and Friendship, April 28, 1960, in 10 *TYC* 13; see also *supra* Chapter XII, nn. 133–34.
110. Art. 2 of the Sino-Afghan Treaty, in 9 *TYC* 12.
111. E.g., Art. 22, Protocol on the General Conditions of Delivery between the CPR and Poland, for 1959 (December 31, 1959), in 8 *TYC* 56, 66–67 (1959).
112. Art. 12, Sino-Central African Republic Agreement on the Exchange of Goods and Payment, in 13 *TYC* 262.
113. An arbitration clause is included in all "general conditions of delivery" protocols with socialist countries.
114. For a discussion see Luke Lee, *China and International Agreements* (Leyden: Sijthoff, 1969), p. 71.
115. Sino-Finish protocol of June 5, 1953, in 2 *TYC* 35; and Sino-French protocol, June 5, 1953, *id.* 377.
116. Reghizzi, "Legal Aspects of Trade with China: the Italian Experience," 9 *Harvard International Law Journal* at 3 (1968).
117. Fellhauser, *JPRS* 8612 (1961); see *supra* Chapter XII, n. 129.
118. See State Council Decision adopted on November 21, 1958, and Provisional Rules of Procedure of the Maritime Arbitration Commission, adopted on January 8, 1959; both texts in English translation reproduced in Lee, *supra* n. 114, Appendix 9.
119. The M/S *Varild* case. Maritime Arbitration Commission, China Council for the Promotion of International Trade, Peking. Conciliatory Conclusion: (63) Tiao Tzu No. 011. See Lee, *id.*, pp. 90–91.

CONCLUSIONS

1. In a survey of the documented sources used in a series of articles criticizing the "bourgeois" international law, I had the following findings:
   (a) Oppenheim was cited three times, in comparison to one citation each from Verdross and Kelson, in Yin T'ao, "A Critique of the Bourgeois International Law from Several Basic Precepts," *KCWT*, No. 1 (1960), pp. 42–51;
   (b) Oppenheim was cited three times in K'ung Meng, "A Critique of the Bourgeois International Law Concerning 'Subjects of International Law' and Theories of Recognition of States," *id.*, No. 2 (1960), pp. 44–53. The author also cited once each from Liszt (Russian ed.), Jessup, Hyde (Russian ed.), and a Japanese source;
   (c) In Ying T'ao, "A Critique of the Bourgeois International Law Concerning State Sovereignty," *id.*, No. 3 (1960), pp. 47–52, there were three citations from Oppenheim, as compared to two from the *Hsien-tai kuo-chi-fa chi-pen yuan-tse ho wen-t'i* [Fundamental Principles and Problems of Modern International Law] (Peking, 1957), a collection of translations from Russian writings;
   (d) In Yi Hsin, "What Is Implied in the Bourgeois International Law Concerning Intervention?" *id.*, No. 4 (1960), pp. 47–54. Oppenheim was cited four times, while it contained one citation each from Pitman Potter, Stalin's report to the CPSU's Eighteenth Congress, and Resolution 5213 of the Eighty-second Congress of the United States; and
   (e) Oppenheim was cited as many as eight times in Ch'ien Ssu, "A Critique of Bourgeois International Law Concerning Individuals," *id.*, No. 5 (1960), pp. 40–49, which also had two citations from Brierly and one from Lenin and a Leftist publication in Argentina. (All the above citations from Oppenheim were based on the Chinese edition.)
2. For a stimulating treatise on "minimum encroachment" versus "maximum discretion," see Richard A. Falk, *Law, Morality, and War in the Contemporary World* (New York: Praeger, 1963).
3. In a thirteen-month-old intelligence-gathering operation named Phoenix, between December, 1967, and January, 1969, more than 15,000 of the 80,000 Viet-cong political agents thought to be in South Vietnam were said to have been captured or killed. U.S. specialists in guerrilla warfare were reported to say that it was as important to eliminate enemy political agents (civilian noncombatants) as enemy soldiers. *New York Times*, January 6, 1969.

4. John K. Fairbank, ed., *The Chinese World Order* (Cambridge, Mass.: Harvard University Press, 1968).
5. Cf. C. P. Fitzgerald, *The Chinese View of Their Place in the World* (New York: Oxford University Press, 1964).
6. This may be indirectly seen from the fact that Southeast Asian nations' interest in the SEATO falls short of the United States expectations. The dilemma of these countries is that, on the one hand, they need some protection against the possible threat from Communist China and, on the other, they have an inherited fear from the past century that continued Western dominance in the area would impair their independence and sovereignty. Cf. Henry A. Kissinger, *American Foreign Policy* (New York: Norton, 1969), p. 66.
7. Cf. generally Kissinger, *id.*, pp. 101–108; also my discussion in *supra* Chapter XIV, and in "China's Foreign Policy: The Interplay of Ideology, Practical Interests, and Polemics," in William Richardson, ed., *China Today* (Maryknoll, N.Y.: Maryknoll Publications, 1969), pp. 20–55. For a discussion of China's problem of communication with the outside world as a whole, see John M. H. Lindbeck, "China and the World: The Dilemmas of Communication," in *China Today, id.*, pp. 105–16.

Selected Bibliography

PART I. SOURCE MATERIALS IN CHINESE

A. Primary Sources

1. CPR Official Document Collections

Ch'ao-hsien wen-t'i wen-chien hui-pien [Collection of Documents Relating to Korea]. 5 vols Peking, People's Publications, 1954.

Chieh-chüeh lao-wo wen-t'i k'uo-ta jih-nei-wa hui-yi wen-chien hui-pien [Collection of Documents of the Expanded Geneva Conference for Settling the Laotian Question]. Peking, World Knowledge, 1962.

Chung-hua jen-min kung-ho-kuo. Ch'uan-kuo jen-min tai-piao ta-hui. Ch'ang-wu wei-yuan-hui [CPR National People's Congress, Standing Committee]. *Kung-pao* [Bulletin]. Peking, 1955–1965.

Chung-hua jen-min kung-ho-kuo. Fa-kuei hui-pien [CPR Compendium of Laws and Regulations]. 13 vols. Peking, Legal Publications, 1954–1962.

———. *Tiao-yüeh chi* [CPR Treaty Series]. 13 vols. Peking, Legal Publications, 1950–1964.

———. *Tui-wai kuan-hsi wen-chien chi* [Collection of Documents Relating to the Foreign Relations of the CPR]. 10 vols. Peking, World Knowledge, 1957–1965.

———. *Yu-hao t'iao-yüeh hui-pien* [Collection of the Friendship Treaties of the CPR]. Peking, World Knowledge, 1965.

Chung-tung wen-t'i wen-chien hui-pien [Collection of Documents Concerning Problems in the Near East]. Peking, World Knowledge, 1958.

Jih-nei-wa hui-yi wen-chien hui-pien [Collection of Documents of the Geneva Conference]. Peking, World Knowledge, 1954.

Jih-pen wen-t'i wen-chien hui-pien [Collection of Documents on Questions Relating to Japan]. 4 vols. Peking, World Knowledge, 1958–1964.

Kuo-chi t'iao-yüeh chi [International Treaty Series]. Peking, World Knowledge. (Series began with 1917).

Mao Tse-tung. *Hsüan-chi* [Selected Works]. 4 vols. Peking, People's Publications.

Ti-san-tz'u ya-fei t'uan-chieh hui-yi wen-chien hui-pien [Collection of Documents of the Third Afro-Asian Solidarity Conference]. Peking, World Knowledge, 1963.

Ts'ai-chün wen-t'i wen-chien hsüan-chi [Selected Documents on the Disarmament Problem]. Peking, World Knowledge, 1958.

Wai-chiao hsüeh-yüan. Kuo-chi-fa chiao-yen-shih. [Institute of Diplomacy. Department of International Law] *Kuo-chi kung-fa ts'an-k'ao wen-chien hsüan-chi* [A Selection of Reference Materials on Public International Law]. Peking, World Knowledge, 1958.

Ya-fei jen-min t'uan-chieh ta-hui wen-chien hui-pien [Collection of Documents of the Afro-Asian Solidarity Conference] (1957–1958). Peking, World Knowledge, 1958.

Yin-tu-chih-na wen-t'i wen-chien hui-pien [Collection of Documents on the Indo-China Question]. 5 vols. Peking, World Knowledge, 1965.

2. Relevant Legal Enactments

Chung-hua jen-min kung-ho-kuo. Chan-hsing hai-kuan fa [CPR Provisional Customs Regulations]. Peking, People's Publications, 1951.

———. *Hsien-fa* [CPR Constitution]. Peking, People's Publications, 1954.

———. *Kuan-yü ling-hai te sheng-ming* [CPR Declaration Regarding Territorial Waters], September 4, 1958. In *FKHP,* Vol. VIII, pp. 112–13.

———. *Tui ko-kuo wai-chiao-kuan chi ling-shih-kuan huo-mien shui-fei chan-hsing pan-fa* [CPR Provisional Measures Governing the Exemption from Taxation of Foreign Diplomatic and Consular Personnel]. Reported in *Chukajin-minkyowakoku horei sakuin* [Index to the Laws and Decrees of the People's Republic of China]. October, 1949–December, 1959. Tokyo, *Kokuritsu kokkai Toshokan* [Library of the National Diet].

———. *Tui ko-kuo wai-chiao-kuan chi ling-shih-kuan hsing-li wu-p'in chin-ch'u kuo-ching cheng-mien yen-fang yu-tai chan-hsing pan-fa* [Provisional Measures Relating to the Exemption from Inspection of the Luggage of Foreign Diplomatic and Consular Personnel upon Entry into and Departure from China]. *Id.*

———. *Tui-ko-kuo wai-chiao-kuan chi ling-shih-kuan yu-yü chan-hsing*

pan-fa [Provisional Measures Relating to the Preferential Treatment of Foreign Diplomatic and Consular Personnel]. *Id.*
———. *Tui wai-kuo-chi ch'uang-p'o chin-ch'u kang-k'ou kuan-li pan-fa* [Measures Governing Foreign Vessels Entering and Departing from CPR Ports and Harbors], in *FKHP*. Vol. V.
Wai-kuo-chi fei-chün-yung ch'uan-p'o t'ung-kuo ch'iung-chou hai-hsia kuan-li kuei-tse [Rules Governing Passage Through the Ch'iung-chou Strait by Foreign Nonmilitary Vessels], in *Jen-min shou-ts'e* [People's Handbook]. Volume for 1964, p. 342.
Wai-kuo-jen ju-ching ch'u-ching chü-liu lü-hsing kuan-li t'iao-li [Articles Governing the Entry, Exit, Transit, Stay and Travel of Aliens], in *id.*, p. 341.

B. Secondary Sources

1. Monographs

Chou, Keng-sheng. *Hsien-tai ying-mei kuo-chi-fa te szu-hsiang tung-hsiang* [Trends in Contemporary Anglo-American Thinking on International Law]. Peking, World Knowledge, 1962.
Chung-yang cheng-fa kan-pu hsüeh-hsiao [Central Political and Legal Cadres Institute]. *Chung-hua jen-min kung-ho-kuo hsing-fa tsung-tse chiang-yi* [Lectures on the Fundamentals of the Criminal Law of the People's Republic of China]. Peking, Legal Publications, 1958.
———. *Chung-hua jen-min kung-ho-kuo min-fa chi-pen wen-t'i* [Basic Issues in the Civil Law of the People's Republic of China]. Peking, Legal Publications, 1958.
———. *Chung-hua jen-min kung-ho-kuo min-fa tzu-liao* [Source Materials on the Civil Law of the People's Republic of China]. Peking, Legal Publications, 1954.
Fu, Chu. *Wo-kuo te ling-hai wen-t'i* [The question of China's Territorial Sea]. Peking, Legal Publications, 1959.
Lien-ho-kuo na-li ch'ü [Whither the United Nations]. Hong Kong, San-lien, 1965.
Ni, Cheng-ao. *Kuo-chi-fa chung-te szu-fa kuan-hsia wen-t'i* [Judicial Jurisdiction in International Law]. Peking, World Knowledge, 1964.
Wan, Chia-chün. *Shen-mo shih lien-ho-kuo* [What is the United Nations]. Peking, Popular Publications, 1957.
Wang, Yao-t'ien. *Kuo-chi mao-yi t'iao-yüeh ho hsieh-ting* [International Trade Treaties and Agreements]. Peking, Finance and Economic Publications, 1958.

2. Articles

Chou, Keng-sheng. "Ts'ung kuo-chi-fa lun ho-p'ing kung-ch'u te yüan-tse [Peaceful Coexistence in International Law]," *Cheng-fa yen-chiu* [Studies of Politics and Law], No. 6 (1955), pp. 37–41.

Chou, Tzu-ya. "Hsien-tai kuo-chi-fa te hsing-chih wen-t'i [The Nature and Character of Modern International Law]," *Hsüeh-shu yüeh-k'an* [Academic Monthly], No. 7 (1957), pp. 67–72.

"Fan-tui ying-mei ch'in-lüeh-cheh p'o-huai kuo-chi-fa: tso-t'an [A Symposium on the Criminal Acts by Britain and the United States Against International Law and the United Nations Charter]," *Chen-fa yen-chiu* [Studies of Politics and Law], No. 4 (1958), pp. 3–8.

Wei, Liang. "Lüeh-lun erh-tz'u shih-chieh ta-chan hou-te kuo-chi t'iao-yüeh [Notes on International Treaties Concluded Since World War II]," *Kuo-chi t'iao-yüeh chi* [International Treaty Series], Volume for 1953–1955, pp. 660–90.

Yang, Hsin, and Ch'en Chien. "Chieh-lu ho p'i-p'an ti-kuo-chu-yi-cheh kuan-yü kuo-chia chu-ch'üan wen-t'i te miu-lun [Expose and Refute the Absurd Views of Imperialists on Sovereignty of States]," *Cheng-fa yen-chiu* [Studies of Politics and Law], No. 4 (1964), pp. 6–11.

Yao, Yüeh. "Tui-yü tzu-ch'ang chieh-chi kuo-chi-fa te ch'u-pu p'i-p'an [A Preliminary Critique of the Bourgeois International Law]," *KCWT*, No. 3 (1959). Also see other articles in the *KCWT* series, 1959–1960.

PART II. SOURCE MATERIALS IN WESTERN LANGUAGES

A. Primary Sources

1. Public Documents in General

League of Nations. *Treaty Series* (LNTS). 205 vols. Geneva.

United Nations. *Treaty Series* (UNTS). New York.

United States. Department of State. *Bulletin*. Washington, D. C.

———. *Treaties and Other International Acts Series* (TIAS). Washington, D. C.

———. *Treaties in Force*. Washington, D. C.

2. United Nations Documents

A/1123 Premier Chou En-lai's cablegrams to the Secretary-General and to the President of the General Assembly, United Nations, November 18, 1949.

A/2469 CPR cablegram to the Secretary-General, September 13, 1953.

A/2888 CPR cablegram to the Secretary-General, December 17, 1954.

A/2889 CPR cablegram to the Secretary-General, December 17, 1954.

S/1703 Premier Chou En-lai's cablegram to the Secretary-General, August 20, 1950.

S/1715 Premier Chou En-lai's cablegram to the President of the Security Council, August 24, 1950.

S/1921 CPR statement on the Taiwan question, November 29, 1950.

3. Collections of CPR and Other Documents

Ambekar, G. V. and V. D. Divekar, eds. *Documents on China's Relations with South and Southeast Asia: 1949–1962*. Bombay, Allied Publishers, 1964.

Break the Nuclear Monopoly, Eliminate Nuclear Weapons. Peking, FLP, 1965.

China and the Asian-African Conference. Peking, FLP, 1955.

Doolin, Dennis. *Territorial Claims in the Sino-Soviet Conflict: Documents and Analysis*. Stanford, The Hoover Institution on War, Revolution, and Peace, Stanford University, 1965.

Important Documents Concerning the Question of Taiwan. Peking FLP, 1955.

India. Ministry of External Affairs. *Report of the Officials of the Governments of India and the People's Republic of China on the Boundary Question*. New Delhi, 1960.

———. *White Paper: Notes, Memoranda and Letters Exchanged Between the Governments of India and China*. Nos. 1 through 9. New Delhi, up to 1963.

United States. *Department of State. Renunciation of Force: United States and Chinese Communist Positions*. Press Release 37, January 21, 1956. Reprinted in Department of State Publication 6280, General Foreign Policy Series No. 107, February, 1956.

Wu, Hsiu-ch'üan. *China Accuses: Speeches of the Special Representative of the Central People's Government of the People's Republic of China at the United Nations*. Peking, FLP, 1951.

4. Translated and Bibliographical Sources

Chinese Communist Views on International Affairs (SBTS No. 475), translated by the United States Joint Publications Research Service (JPRS). Purchasable through Research and Microfilm Publications, P.O. Box 267, Annapolis, Md.

International Arts and Sciences Press (IASP). *Chinese Law and Government,* Vol. III, No. 1 (Spring, 1970), special issue on international law, guest-edited by James C. Hsiung. White Plains, N. Y.

Johnston, Douglas, and Hungdah Ch'iu. *Agreements of the People's Republic of China, 1947–1967: A Calendar*. Cambridge, Mass.: Harvard University Press, 1968.

Lin, Fu-shun. *Chinese Law Past and Present: A Bibliography of Enactments and Commentaries in English Text*. New York, Columbia University, East Asian Institute, 1966. Part III: Section L. "International Law, Treaties and Foreign Relations," pp. 126–34.

Mao, Tse-tung. Speech at the Tenth Plenary Session of the Eighth Central Committee (September 24, 1962) [on Sino-Soviet dispute], translated in IASP, *Chinese Law and Government,* Vol. I, No. 2 (Winter, 1968–1969), pp. 85–93.

Yuan, T'ung-li. *China in Western Literature*. New Haven, Conn., Far Eastern Publications, 1958.

B. Secondary Sources

1. Books and Monographs

Academy of Sciences of the U. S. S. R. Institute of State and Law. *International Law*. Moscow, Foreign Language Publishing House [1961].

Appleton, Sheldon. *The Eternal Triangle? Communist China, the United States, and the United Nations*. East Lansing, Mich., Michigan State University Press, 1961.

Barnett, A. Doak. *Communist China and Asia: Challenge to American Policy*. New York, Harper and Row, 1960.

———, ed., *Communist Strategies in Asia: A Comparative Analysis of Governments and Parties*. New York, Praeger, 1963.

Beaute, Jean. *La Republique populaire de Chine et le droit international*. Paris, Pedone, 1964.

Boyd, R. C. *Communist China's Foreign Policy*. New York, Praeger, 1962.

Brandt, Conrad, Benjamin I. Schwartz, and John K. Fairbank. *A Documentary History of Chinese Communism*. Cambridge, Mass., Harvard University Press, 1952.

Buchan, Alsstair, ed. *China and the Peace of Asia.* New York, Praeger, 1965.

Ch'iu, Hungdah, and Shao-chuan Leng, eds. *Law in Chinese Foreign Policy: Communist China and Selected Problems of International Law.* Dobbs Ferry, N. Y., Oceana, 1972.

Clubb, O. Edmund, and Eustace Seligman. *The International Position of Communist China.* Dobbs Ferry, N. Y., Oceana, 1965.

Cohen, Jerome A. *The Criminal Process in the People's Republic of China, 1949–1963.* Cambridge, Mass., Harvard University Press, 1968.

Eckstein, Alexander. *Communist China's Economic Growth and Foreign Trade: Implications for U. S. Policy.* New York, McGraw-Hill, 1966.

———, ed. *China Trade Prospects and U. S. Policy.* New York, Praeger, 1971.

Fairbank, John K., ed. *The Chinese World Order.* Cambridge, Mass., Harvard University Press, 1968.

Falk, Richard A. *Legal Order in a Violent World.* Princeton, N. J., Princeton University Press, 1968.

———, ed. *The Vietnam War and International Law.* Princeton, N. J., Princeton University Press, 1968.

Friedmann, Wolfgang, Oliver J. Lissitzyn, and Richard C. Pugh. *International Law: Cases and Materials.* St. Paul, Minn., West Publishing Co., 1969.

Gittings, John. *Survey of the Sino-Soviet Dispute: A Commentary and Extracts from the Recent Polemics, 1963–1967.* London, New York, and Toronto, Oxford University Press, 1967.

Henkin, Louis. *How Nations Behave.* New York, Praeger, 1968.

Hinton, Harold C. *China's Turbulent Quest: An Analysis of China's Foreign Relations since 1945.* New York, Macmillan, 1970.

Hsiung, James C. *Ideology and Practice: The Evolution of Chinese Communism.* New York, Praeger, 1970.

Iriye, Akira, ed. *U. S. Policy Toward China.* Boston, Little, Brown, 1968.

Lall, Arthur. *How Communist China Negotiates.* New York, Columbia University Press, 1968.

Lee, Luke T. *China and International Agreements: A Study of Compliance.* Leyden, the Netherlands, A. W. Sijthoff, 1969.

Lissitzyn, Oliver J. *International Law Today and Tomorrow.* Dobbs Ferry, N. Y., Oceana, 1965.

Halperin, Morton H., ed. *Sino-Soviet Relations and Arms Control.* Cambridge, Mass., M.I.T. Press, 1967.

Halperin, Morton H., and Dwight H. Perkins. *Communist China and Arms Control.* New York, Praeger, 1965.

Halpern, A. M., ed. *Policies Toward China: Views from Six Continents.* New York, McGraw-Hill, 1965.

McDougal, Myres S., and Associates. *Studies in World Public Order*. New Haven, Conn., Yale University Press, 1960.

North, Robert. *The Foreign Policy of China*. Belmont, Calif., Dickenson, 1969.

Northrop, Filmer S. *The Meeting of East and West: An Inquiry Concerning World Understanding*. New York, Macmillan, 1946.

Passin, Herbert. *China's Cultural Diplomacy*. New York, Praeger, 1962.

Ramundo, B. A. *The Socialist Theory of International Law*. Institute of Sino-Soviet Studies, Series No. 1. Washington, D. C., George Washington University, 1964.

———. *Peaceful Coexistence: International Law in the Building of Communism*. Baltimore, Md., Johns Hopkins University Press, 1967.

Röling, B. V. A. *International Law in an Expanded World*. Amsterdam, the Netherlands, Djambatan, 1960.

Scalapino, Robert A. *The Communist Revolution in Asia*. 2d ed. Englewood Cliffs, N. J., Prentice-Hall, 1969.

Schwartzenberger, Georg. *The Frontiers of International Law*. London, Stevens, 1962.

Slusser, Robert, and Jan Triska. *The Theory, Law, and Policy of Soviet Treaties*. Stanford, Stanford University Press, 1962.

Tsou, Tang, ed. *China in Crisis*. Vol. 2 ("China's Policies in Asia and America's Alternatives"). Chicago, University of Chicago Press, 1968.

Tung, William L. *China and the Foreign Powers*. Dobbs Ferry, N. Y., Oceana, 1970.

United States Department of State. *The Conduct of Communist China*. Printed for the Committee on Foreign Affairs, House of Representatives, 88th Congress, 1st sess. Washington, D. C., United States Government Printing Press, 1963.

———. Division of External Research and Publications. *Reported Agreements between the U.S.S.R. and Communist China*. Based on information available up to June 21, 1956. n. p., n. d.

Van Ness, Peter. *Revolution and Chinese Foreign Policy*. Berkeley, University of California Press, 1970.

Whiting, Allen S. *China Crosses the Yalu: The Decision to Enter the Korean War*. Stanford, Stanford University Press, 1960.

Young, Kenneth T. *The Southeast Crisis*. Dobbs Ferry, N. Y., Oceana, 1966.

———. *Negotiating with the Chinese Communists*. New York, McGraw-Hill, 1968.

Zagoria, Donald S. *The Sino-Soviet Conflict, 1956–1961*. Princeton, N. J., Princeton University Press, 1962.

———. *Vietnam Triangle: Moscow, Peking, Hanoi*. New York, Pegasus, 1967.

2. Articles

Ch'eng, Tao. "Communist China and the Law of the Sea," *American Journal of International Law,* (AJIL), Vol. 63, No. 1 (January, 1969), pp. 47–73.

Ch'iu, Hungdah. "Communist China's Attitude Toward International Law," *AJIL,* Vol. 60, No. 2 (April, 1966), pp. 245–67.

———. "The Theory and Practice of Communist China with Respect to the Conclusion of Treaties," *Columbia Journal of Transnational Law,* Vol. 5, No. 1 (1966), pp. 1–13.

———, and R. R. Edwards. "Communist China's Attitude Toward the United Nations: A Legal Analysis," *AJIL,* Vol. 62, No. 1 (January, 1968), pp. 20–50.

Cohen, Jerome A. "Chinese Attitudes Toward International Law—and Our Own," paper given for the Panel on the People's Republic of China and International Law, *Proceedings* of the American Society of International Law, Washington, D. C., April 27–29, 1967, pp. 108–17. See also the other two papers on Communist China's treaty practice by Hungdah Ch'iu and Douglas M. Johnston, pp. 117–26; 126–35.

Edwards, R. Randle. "The Attitude of the People's Republic of China Toward International Law and the United Nations," *Papers on China,* Vol. 17 (December, 1963). Published and distributed in Boston, Harvard University, East Asian Research Center.

Ginsburgs, George. "Validity of Treaties in the Municipal Law of the 'Socialist' States," *AJIL,* Vol. 59, No. 3 (July, 1965), pp. 523–44.

Gniffke, Frank L. "German Writings on Chinese Law," *Osteuropa Recht,* Vol. 15, No. 3 (September, 1969). Reprinted in Studies in Chinese Law series, No. 12, Harvard Law School.

Hazard, John N. "Renewed Emphasis upon a Socialist International Law," *AJIL,* Vol. 65, No. 1 (January, 1971), pp. 142–48.

Houn, Franklin W. "The Principles and Operational Code of Communist China's International Conduct," *Journal of Asian Studies,* Vol. 27, No. 1 (January, 1968), pp. 21–40.

Hsiao, Gene T. "Communist China's Trade Treaties and Agreements (1949–1964)," *Vanderbilt Law Review,* Vol. 21, No. 5 (October, 1968), pp. 623–58.

Hsiung, James C. "China's Foreign in Policy: The Interplay of Ideology, Practical Interests, and Polemics," in William Richardson, ed., *China Today*. Maryknoll, N. Y., Maryknoll Publications, 1969, pp. 22–55.

Leng, Shao-chuan. "Communist China's Position on Nuclear Arms Control," *Virginia Journal of International Law,* Vol. 7 (December, 1966), pp. 101–16.

McDougal, Myres S., and Richard M. Goodman. "Chinese Participation in the United Nations," *AJIL,* Vol. 60, No. 4 (October, 1966), pp. 671–727.

Stahnke, Arthur A. "The Place of International Law in Chinese Strategy and Tactics: The Case of the Sino-Indian Boundary Dispute," *Journal of Asian Studies,* Vol. 30, No. 1 (November, 1970), pp. 95–120.

Weng, Byron S. "Communist China's Changing Attitudes Toward the United Nations," *International Organization,* Vol. 20, No. 4 (Autumn, 1966), pp. 677–704.

N.B.: Those who are interested in a more detailed bibliography are advised to scan the extensive notes used for the various chapters. The present selected bibliography is literally a trickle in the wealth of materials actually used for the study.

Index

DATE DUE

11 17 '83